Weep, Grey Bird, Weep

The Paraguayan War 1864-1870

by

Roger Kohn

authorHOUSE®

AuthorHouse™ UK Ltd.
500 Avebury Boulevard
Central Milton Keynes, MK9 2BE
www.authorhouse.co.uk
Phone: 08001974150

This book is a work of non-fiction. Unless otherwise noted, the author and the publisher make no explicit guarantees as to the accuracy of the information contained in this book and in some cases, names of people and places have been altered to protect their privacy.

First published by AuthorHouse 1/9/2008

ISBN: 978-1-4343-1979-1 (sc)
ISBN: 978-1-4343-1980-7 (hc)

Printed in the United States of America
Bloomington, Indiana

This book is printed on acid-free paper.

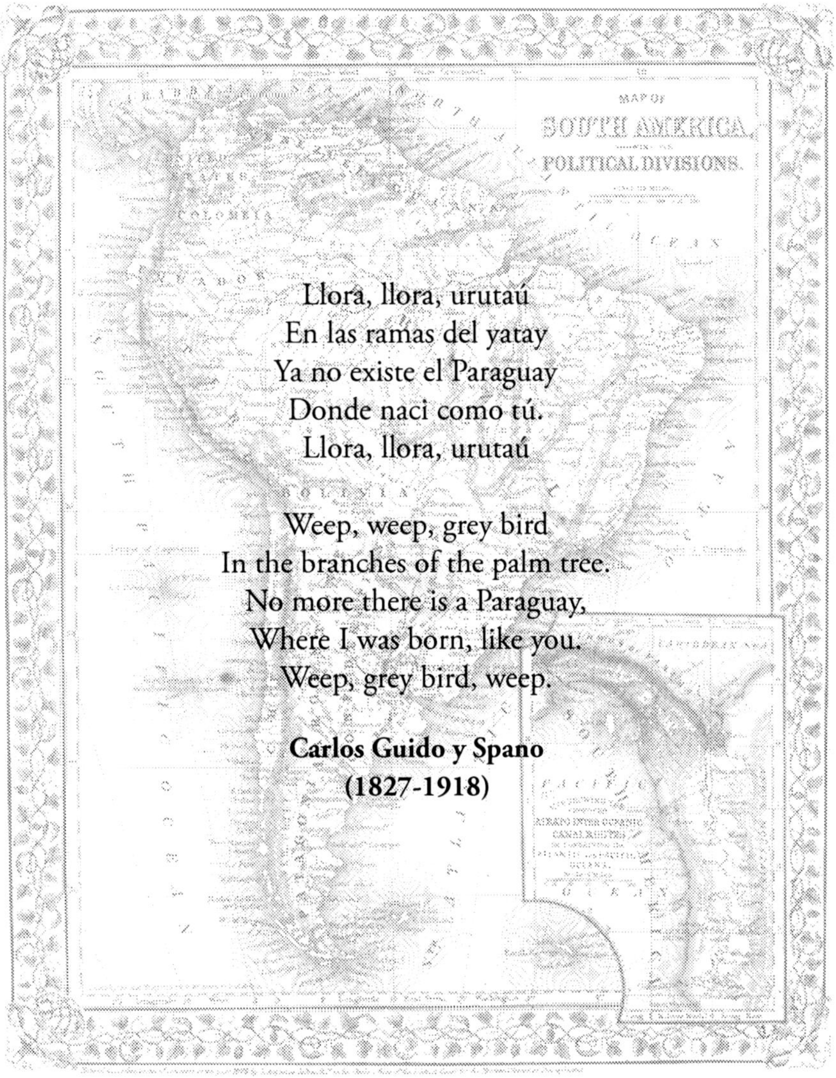

Llora, llora, urutaú
En las ramas del yatay
Ya no existe el Paraguay
Donde naci como tú.
Llora, llora, urutaú

Weep, weep, grey bird
In the branches of the palm tree.
No more there is a Paraguay,
Where I was born, like you.
Weep, grey bird, weep.

Carlos Guido y Spano
(1827-1918)

Contents

Part 1: The Vanished Arcadia

Chapter 1 3
Chapter 2 15
Chapter 3 21
Chapter 4 29
Chapter 5 39
Chapter 6 53
Chapter 7 61
Chapter 8 69

Part 2: Humaitá

Chapter 9 81
Chapter 10 101
Chapter 11 111
Chapter 12 121
Chapter 13 129
Chapter 14 137
Chapter 15 145
Chapter 16 151
Chapter 17 159
Chapter 18 167

Part 3: The Tiger's Paw

Chapter 19 177
Chapter 20 187
Chapter 21 197
Chapter 22 205

Chapter 23 223
Chapter 24 233
Chapter 25 241
Chapter 26 253
Chapter 27 269
Chapter 28 273
Chapter 29 281
Chapter 30 287
Chapter 31 295
Chapter 32 301

Part 4: To Cerro Cora

Chapter 33 311
Chapter 34 323
Chapter 35 341
Chapter 36 349
Endnotes 369

Part 1:
The Vanished Arcadia

Chapter 1

In September 1867, Mr. C.Z. Gould, Secretary to the British Legation in Buenos Aires sat at his desk and composed a report on the situation in Paraguay, a nation at war. "The whole country is ruined and all but depopulated," he wrote. "Everything is seized for the Government. The cattle on most estates have entirely disappeared and many estates have been altogether abandoned. The scanty crops raised by the women are monopolised for the supply of the troops. The women have been obliged to part with all their jewels and gold ornaments, although this extreme measure has been called a patriotic offering on their part. Three epidemics, measles, smallpox and cholera, besides privations of all sorts have reduced the population of this unfortunate country by more than a third...the mortality amongst the children is dreadful, and both scurvy and itch are very prevalent....The Paraguayan forces altogether amount to about 20,000 men of whom 10,000 or 12,000 at most are good troops, the rest mere boys from twelve to fourteen years of age, old men and cripples, besides from two to three thousand sick and wounded. The men are worn out with exposure, fatigue and privations. They are actually dropping from inanition. They have been reduced for the last six months to meat alone and that of a very inferior quality. They may once in a way get a little Indian corn; manioc and salt are so scarce that I fully believe they are only served out of the hospitals. In the whole camp there is absolutely nothing for sale. There must be, from what I saw, a great scarcity of drugs and medicines, if not a total want of them for the sick, whose number is rapidly increasing.

"Cholera and smallpox, which exist to a certain extent in the Allied Camp, are spreading very much amongst the Paraguayans. The horses have nearly all died and the few hundred which yet remain are all so weak and emaciated they can scarcely carry their riders. The last eight or nine hundred mares in the whole country have, however, just been brought in. The draught oxen are in a dreadful state and cannot last much longer. The cattle in the camp, some 15,000 or 20,000 head are dying fast for want of pasture.... Many of the soldiers are in a state of near nudity, having only a piece of tanned leather round their loins, a ragged shirt and poncho made of vegetable fibre." [1]

To this appalling condition had Paraguay and its once fine army been reduced by nearly three years of war. Gould' s report, like others that he wrote during the months of August and September, told of a nation facing not just defeat but extinction. Paraguay, a small insignificant country whose affairs were of little concern to the rest of the world, was dying. It was dying in the creeks and marshes of the south where its soldiers fought their hopeless war and dying in the vermin ridden huts called hospitals where dirt and lack of care completed what battle had begun. It was dying in neglected fields and far off villages where starving women searched for food and children cried for milk that would never come. It was dying in prisons, rotting in chains for unnamed crimes and imagined wrongs. It was dying alone, slowly and painfully, but silently and with a courage and love of country that was almost sublime and it was dying for a cause that was already doomed.

There was no hope that Paraguay could win this war. It was fighting against the combined forces of Brazil, Argentina and Uruguay, cut off from the sea by six hundred miles of enemy territory, and there was not the slightest prospect of another country coming to its aid. But there was to be no ending yet.

For nearly three years the pointless, futile slaughter would go on, becoming more, not less intense until it reached a climax of heroism and horror that, even a hundred years later, in an age hardened to the misery of war, seems almost unbelievable. By 1867, the war, as Mr. Gould saw only too clearly, was lost. But to the Paraguayans the fight had only just begun.

There was nothing in Paraguay' s history to account for the extraordinary patriotism which its people displayed in the war against their three neighbours. Far from being warlike, the Paraguayans had always had a reputation for mildness, and it was the peaceable character of the original Indian inhabitants that had encouraged the Spaniards to settle there in the first place. On the other hand, Paraguay had always been different from the Spanish colonies, and after breaking away from the mother country, it continued to develop in a way that was quite unique. It was in the growth of Paraguay in colonial times and in its first years of independence that at least part of the secret of its fantastic achievements in the war of the Triple Alliance are to be found. The Spaniards first arrived there in search of an alternative route to the gold and silver mines of the Andes, but this hope proved to be an illusion. The first expedition under Juan de Ayolas reached a point on the River Paraguay somewhere near the present day border between Brazil and Paraguay in 1536 and established a fort called Candelaria, but an attempt by Ayolas to march westward to the mountains with some of the expedition resulted in the disappearance of the whole force. Despite this, the Spaniards continued their attempts to reach Peru from the east, and they decided to establish a permanent settlement from which future operations could be directed. Such a base had in fact been established in 1536, when a fort was built on the site of what is now Buenos Aires, but the Indians nearby proved so fierce that the Spaniards were unable to make this toe-hold secure. On the way to Candelaria, however, Ayolas' expedition had come across Indians who were far more friendly, offering the white men food and making them welcome - to the extent of offering them their wives and daughters.

There was on both sides a certain amount of self interest in this friendship: the Spaniards wanted a base, and the Indians wanted allies to help them fight the fierce Indian tribes who lived on the west bank of the River Paraguay. On August 15th, 1537, the Spaniards established their settlement and called it Asuncion: it was a thousand miles from the sea, and was to remain for two hundred years the centre of Spanish power east of the Andes. The Indians who had welcomed the Spaniards so warmly were Guaranís, members of a great tribe that spread across the central portion of South America. Those living around Asuncion were primitive compared to the Incas of Peru, peaceful agriculturists living a semi-nomadic lifestyle before moving on after a few years, as they thought the land became exhausted after one crop. Their loosely-knit tribal structure made them vulnerable to attack, and it was fortunate that the leading figure of the early Spanish settlement was Domingo Martinez de Irala, a man of whom it has been said: 'No European of any race of nation, not even William Penn, deserves so high a credit for justice towards (the Indians).' [2]

Irala had been left at Candelaria by Ayolas, and after his leader's death had been confirmed by reports from Indians, assumed command of the new colony. By this time Buenos Aires had been abandoned to the Indians, and Irala, with only 600 men under his command, realised that although the fertile land around Asuncion would enable the colony to live independently of supplies from Spain, they could only do so if the goodwill of the Guaranís was retained. To ensure that this happened, he deliberately encouraged his men to marry Indian women, reasoning that a blood-tie between Spaniard and Guaranís would be the surest way of avoiding friction.

This policy was spectacularly successful. By 1579, according to a report submitted to King Philip 11 by the Treasurer, Montalvo, ninety per cent of the population of Asuncion was of mixed Spanish and Indian blood[3] and the Indian element was so important that the *mestizo* population even spoke Guaraní rather than Spanish as its first language. To this extent the Indians absorbed the Spaniards: in other ways the Spaniards absorbed the Indians, organising them into large estates called *encomiendas,* giving them a political cohesion that their own tribal system had lacked, a social structure that was basically Spanish, and the Roman Catholic religion. At the same time, the old dreams of opening a second route to the Andes faded : Irala managed to hack his way through jungle and hostile Indians to Peru, only to be driven away by the Spaniards who were already there, and after this the nature of Asuncion changed, from a base for exploitation to a colony of settlers who came increasingly to regard Paraguay rather than Spain, as their home.

It is in this period that the Paraguayan race has its origin. By the end of the century Paraguay already possessed some of the attributes of a nation, and was the one place in Spanish South America where the native Indians played an important part in society. The Paraguayans were distinct enough for Irala's grandson, Ruy Diaz de Guzman, to describe them as if they were already a separate race: "They are generally good soldiers, of great spirit and valour, expert in the use of arms, especially in that of the musket...excellent horsemen... the women generally are of an elevated and honest character. virtuous, beautiful, and of gentle disposition.'[4]

The success of the Paraguayan colony on a social level probably saved it from being abandoned as an economic failure, for the lack of a productive link with the Andean mines, and the absence of any precious metals in the colony itself meant that the Spanish government never gave it more than cursory attention. Throughout the colonial period, the colonies east of the Andes remained the poor relations of the Spanish colonial empire: despite the havoc the influx of gold and silver caused the economy, the Spanish government continued to consider America mainly as a source of precious metals and a market for Spanish goods. Paraguay produced no gold, and by the time Spanish goods had reached the colony by way of Panama and Lima they were so expensive that few people bought them anyway. The isolation that resulted helped to foster the gradually awakening sense of Paraguayan nationalism.

Despite the neglect, the colony grew. New towns and villages were established in the hills beyond Asuncion, and then settlers began to turn south again, to the open pampas of what later became Argentina. Corrientes and Paraná were established in 1558, and in 1580 a colony was again established at Buenos Aires by an expedition from Asuncion which significantly consisted of 10 Spaniards and 63 *mestizos*.[5] By 1600, despite all the disadvantages of its position, the Paraguayan colony was established, and its *mestizo* inhabitants and newcomers from Spain along the River Paraná and River Plate had created a series of other settlements. It was in this period that a second element was introduced that was to have an important effect on the later development of Paraguay and the Paraguayan character: the Jesuit missions. The first priests in Paraguay had been mainly Franciscans, who combined their zeal for converting Indians with a willingness to operate within the framework of the civil government. In this way they played an important part in spreading and maintaining Spanish authority, but the government in Asuncion was less enthusiastic about the activities of the Jesuits, who first arrived in 1588 and soon deve loped an even greater talent for proselytising than their ecclesiastical rivals. While the Franciscans generally operated under the aegis of the Spanish civil authorities, the Jesuits concentrated on areas well away from the settled areas and achieved such remarkable success that for 150 years, in the heart of South America, they ruled over one of the only theocracies that has ever existed. At its peak, this state within a state consisted of about thirty towns, each containing around 4,000 people, 100,000 horses, 800,000 cattle and 200,000 sheep.[6]

Although Catholic in religion, the missions were socially essentially communist and the Jesuits made the establishment of an egal itarian society one of their prime objectives. Each town, or *reduccion*, was a replica of its neighbour. A church, college and cemetery stood on the north side of the central plaza, or square. Elsewhere there would be a school, hospital and home for the aged. The inhabitants all lived in identical houses, all wore the same white cotton clothes, did the same work, and received the same rewards.

Each *reduccion* was run by two Jesuits, assisted by a handful of Indian officials appointed by them, and the word of the priests was absolute. Their rule was efficient and fair, but quite autocratic, and they treated the Indians as children, incapable of regulating their own lives. The Indians, who were by nature peaceable and submissive, seem to have accepted this paternalistic regime without protest, and whatever its drawbacks, life in the *reducciones* was undoubtedly preferable to the hideous fate of the Indians who were forced to work in the mines of Upper Peru. The Jesuits also protected the Guaranís from the slave raiding *mamelucos*, who came up from the Portuguese settlements in Brazil, and according to Jesuit estimates, seized 300,000 Indians between 1629 and 164-6. The authorities in Asuncion showed little enthusiasm for stopping these raids, and little ability when they tried: the Jesuits, on the other hand, armed the Indians and so organised them that the slavers were driven off and the raids ended. This success did little to endear the priests to the civilians, and the Jesuits' success in other fields increased the friction.

The Jesuits had established their missions in south-east Paraguay and the territory between the Rivers Paraná and Uruguay, which is now the Argentine province of Misiones. This was closer to Buenos Aires and the new settlements on the Plate estuary than Asuncion, and this and the excellent organisation of the Jesuits meant that the Paraguayans were deprived of the one market that existed for their agricultural produce and their economic isolation increased. Feelings were not soothed by the fact that the Jesuits enjoyed free labour and paid no tithes or taxes. This resentment flared up into revolt in the 1720s and1730s.

Apart from its anti-Jesuit motives, the revolt was to some extent an expression of Paraguayan resentment at the indifference of the Spanish government and the decline in their country's economic position. It could also be seen as an early manifesto of Paraguayan nationalism, for José de Antequeras y Castro, the rebel leader, had preached strange ideas about the power of the crown being subordinated to the wishes of the community, and the rebels fought the troops sent against them as Paraguayans fighting foreigners rather than fellow Spaniards with different beliefs. In 1767 the Paraguayans gained some sort of revenge. As a result largely of political events in Europe, the Jesuits were expelled from Spain and Spanish South America and the Paraguayan missions came to an end. Within twenty years the population of the reducciones had fallen to 70,000, by 1797 to 50,000 and within a few years nearly all the towns had been abandoned. Opinions differed greatly about the Jesuit colonies.

To some the missions represented a "vanished Arcadia"[7], while to others the Jesuit regime was "the worst government ever devised by the perverted ingenuity, selfishness and bigotry of man".[8] Both views, however, generally agree that the Jesuits did nothing to develop any sense of initiative among their charges, and on the contrary did everything they could to instil in them a sense of unquestioning obedience to authority. When the Jesuits went into exile the Indians were gradually absorbed into the lay Paraguayan state, taking these submissive attitudes with them. Although in other ways the Jesuits' influence soon faded this characteristic remained and the civil governments did nothing to eradicate it. As the colonial period drew to its close, therefore, Paraguay was already developing certain attitudes that made it distinct from other Spanish colonies : its docile and obedient population was basically *mestizo* speaking its own Guaraní language. In 1825, according to the Swiss naturalists, Rengger and Longchamps, the population of Paraguay was 200,000 of whom only 800 were white.

This gave its citizens a linguistic and racial homogeneity, which was fostered by Paraguay' s position at the extreme end of the link with Spain. Earlier in the colonial period, all contact with the mother country had to be made through Lima. Later, when Buenos Aires was allowed to trade directly with Spain, Paraguayan trade went via that port, but the country remained an economic dead end, isolated from the mainstream of life in the Spanish Empire, an unproductive backwater in a continent that, as far as Spain was concerned, existed only to provide what was demanded and take what was sent. This decline in Paraguay's status had been inevitable ever since the re-forming of the settlement at Buenos Aires in 1580, and the fact that Asuncion remained the centre of Spanish power east of the Andes for so long was the result not of its advantages but of the indifference of the Spanish government. Once Spanish policy changed and Buenos Aires was given an opportunity to develop the port rapidly took over from Asuncion as the most important Spanish town in the south-eastern part of the continent. The first indication of change had come in 1617 when Buenos Aires, previously administered from Asuncion, was given its own governor, but it was not until the latter half of the next century, that the city really began to grow, mainly as a result of reforms introduced in the reign of Charles III (1759 - 88), the last capable ruler produced by the Bourbon monarchy.

The first change came in 1774, when restrictions on inter-colonial commerce were lifted. Two years later the old Vice-Royalty of Peru, which had included the whole of Spanish South America, was divided into two, with a new Vice-Royalty of La Plata being created from the colonies east of the Andes with its capital at Buenos Aires. In 1776, Buenos Aires was allowed to trade directly with ports in Spain. These developments led to a dramatic change in the port's position. Until the late eighteenth century, Buenos Aires had had little to offer the Spanish economy: it had no precious metals, and its agricultural products could hardly compete with those of other parts of the continent since they had to go by way of Peru and Panama. The lifting of restrictions on the use of the River Plate's natural route to Spain, via the Atlantic, enabled Buenos Aires to grow, although it did little to encourage the economy of Paraguay. In 1778 Buenos Aires had exported 150,000 hides. Two years later this total had risen to 800,000 and by 1783 had topped 1,400,000.[9]

The new prosperity was reflected in the growth of Buenos Aires' population - from 26,000 in 1776 to 40,000 in 1800, making it easily the largest city in Spanish America east of the Andes. Asuncion had only about 7,000.[10] Although Paraguay benefited less than most, the reforms of Charles III had resulted in Spanish America enjoying the greatest prosperity it had ever known. But during the reign of his successor Charles IV much of the progress that had been made was undone, and the largest empire in the world was brought to the edge of revolution. Charles was an amiable nonentity, dominated by his wife's lover, a young guard's officer called Manuel Godoy. Forgetting the moral issues involved, this regal *ménage a trois* might have governed Spain without causing too much damage, had it not been for the impact of the French revolution. Godoy, whom the Queen had made prime minister at the age of 25, first led Spain into a popular war against the French regicides, and as a result lost the island of San Domingo. Realising that Spain could not resist France, Godoy then became a French ally, and for the rest of Charles' reign Spain was little more than a puppet of Napoleon.

This policy proved equally disastrous, since, although the alliance gave Spain the support of the French navy, it also brought them up against the British Navy. A series of naval reverses, culminating at Trafalgar destroyed the Spanish fleet, and left the Spanish American colonies at the apparent mercy of the British. The British thought so too, and in June 1806 an expedition under Sir Home Popham, which had just taken the Cape Colony from the Dutch, crossed the Atlantic and appeared off Buenos Aires. The Spanish Governor, the Marquis de Sobremonte, regarded resistance as hopeless, and fled inland, but the citizens organised a defence, and two months later the British were forced to surrender.

However, the glowing reports and loot that Popham had managed to send back to London made the British government decide to make another attempt. Reinforcements, which had arrived too late to save Popham, had occupied Maldonado, across the river in what is now Uruguay, and in January 1807 an army under Sir Sidney Auchmuty took Montevideo. But a fresh attempt to re-capture Buenos Aires in June resulting in another ignominious defeat at the hands of the *porteños*, the citizens of Buenos Aires, and the British were glad to agree to an evacuation. With their departure the British attempt to take control of the Plate estuary ended, but it was with the successful defence of Buenos Aires that the revolution against Spain really began. For years the policies of the Spanish government had resulted in the colonists suffering considerable inconvenience. The outbreak of war against Britain had led to the foreign trade of La Plata declining from 5.5m pesos in 1796 to 335,000 pesos in 1797[11]; but even before that, the economy of mainland Spain had been so weak that it was not capable of supplying all the colonies' needs, nor of taking all their produce. Illicit trade through the Portuguese settlement of Colonia, across the Plate, had been going on for some time - and although the colonists had fought them so venomously, the merchants who had come in the wake of the British invasions had shown what many *porteños* had already realised - that Britain, not Spain was the trading partner of the future.

At the same time, the fact that the British were able to seize Buenos Aires so easily was clear proof of the impotence of the Spanish government to defend its own dominions, and the British had ultimately been defeated not by Spain but by the colonists themselves. If events in La Plata served to arouse discontent, the increasingly disastrous consequences of Godoy's policy in Spain helped to turn that discontent into open rebellion. In 180S the favourite announced that he had uncovered a plot by Ferdinand, Charles' s son, to dethrone his father and kill his mother. This split in the royal family itself was too much for the patience of Napoleon, who sent his troops into Spain and, after deposing both father and son, replaced them with his own brother, Joseph Bonaparte. On May 2, 1808, the people of Spain rose against the French, and the Peninsular War began.

Although the French action had the effect of uniting the Spaniards in a patriotic war, the sordid way in which the Bourbons had brought their country to catastrophe tended to make the colonists wash their hands of Spain itself, and at the same time it destroyed the tie between the home country and the colonies. This had always been a very personal link with the King, rather than his government or Spain. Since the colonists refused to recognise Joseph, and Ferdinand and Charles were prisoners and obviously unable to govern themse1ves, there was a vacuum at the top. But the colonists refused to recognise the authority of the Cortes which had been established in Spain to organise the resistance to the French, since that would not only have been impractical, but would also have implied that the Americas were in some way subordinate to Spain itself.

On May 20 1810, soon after the last Bourbon strongholds in Spain had fallen to the French, the *cabildo abierto* , or town meeting, of Buenos Aires appointed a junta to rule the country on behalf of Ferdinand VII. This was a purely theoretical formula: in effect, Buenos Aires had declared itself independent of Spain. This revolt came at roughly the same time as similar events elsewhere in Spanish America, but although the colonists in Mexico, Venezuela, Colombia, Peru and elsewhere were to have to wait more than a decade before their independence was confirmed, the Spaniards made no serious attempt to recover their control over La Plata - probably because it was well down their list of priorities.

Even so, the assumption of self-government in 1810 did not mean that the viceroyalty's problems were over, and as soon as the news of the declaration of May 20 became known, it began to split into its component units. Despite the dreams of men such as Bernardo Rivadavia, Mariano Moreno, Manuel Belgrano, and other leaders, the provinces of the Vice-Royalty had never had very much in common except their allegiance to the throne. Now that this was gone - or at best in abeyance - the differences between them came to the fore. Bolivia (then known as Upper Peru) had been included in the Vice-Royalty of La Plata since the reorganisation of the previous century, but it still had closer ties with the colonies on the Pacific coast, and its economic and other interests were orientated in that direction. As soon as the link with Spain was broken, Upper Peru reverted to the ambit of Peru and ceased to play an important part in the affairs of La Plata.

The Andean provinces, such as Tucuman, Salta, Jujuy and La Rioja were mainly agricultural communities with small domestic industries supplying the mines of Upper Peru. Most of them had been founded by expeditions from Peru and had little contact with Buenos Aires, and if anything feared it as an economic competitor. Buenos Aires had learned the advantages of free trade and looked forward to a rapid development of its links with Britain and the United States, but the Andean provinces believed that foreign competition would ruin their own economy. The Litoral provinces, such as Santa Fe, Corrientes, and Entre Rios were in favour of more trade with the outside world, but they were jealous of the dominant position which Buenos Aires, the most important city and port in the Vice-Royalty, would inevitably hold. Many of the cattle men and *gauchos* who lived in the plains beyond Buenos Aires feared that the city would grow fat on the customs dues that their hard work would bring in.

The citizens of the Banda Orientale del Uruguay (the east bank of the River Uruguay) especially felt this. Montevideo, their chief city, had been founded largely as a military outpost to prevent the Portuguese in Brazil from gaining control of the area. The Portuguese settlement at Colonia, a short way Up the River Plate, had only been ceded to Spain a few decades before, and everyone in Uruguay was aware that the Portuguese, and especially their Brazilian colonists, coveted the rich cattle plains in the north of their country. At the same time, Uruguay was very much a junior partner in the Spanish colonial system. The Montevideans saw independence as an opportunity to shape their own destiny.

Even in Buenos Aires itself, the colonists were divided, some favouring a continuation of the theoretical link with Spain, others preferring outright independence and the declaration of a republic, others favouring the creation of an independent monarchy. The net result of these conflicting opinions and interests was anarchy. In 1816 the provinces of La Plata finally declared their independence of Spain, but the confusion continued, governments rose and fell, coups were followed by counter-coups. Only one province established itself independent with relative ease and a stable regime, and that was Paraguay.

Chapter 2

The citizens of Paraguay had shown little interest in the stirring events taking place in Europe and the other provinces of the Vice-Royalty. For two centuries it had been one of the most turbulent of Spanish provinces, but after that Paraguay entered a period of decadence. It lay almost forgotten, three months sail up the River Paraná, a land whose importance had gone and was now ignored and isolated, introspective and lonely. The Spanish governor of Paraguay was Bernardo de Velasco, a popular, kindly man with a deep interest in the welfare of his province. He was more aware than most of Paraguay's inhabitants of the events taking place in the Spanish Empire and saw that the action of the Buenos Aires *junta* was only a beginning. But as a Spaniard he was unwilling to take the responsibility for something that would have a decisive effect on Paraguay's future.

He called a council that met on July 24 and, after some discussion, decided to remain loyal to the Regency Council set up in Spain by Bourbon supporters, to establish relations with the *junta* of Buenos Aires but not to recognise its authority over the rest of the Vice-Royalty. The Buenos Aires junta had assumed that once it raised the standard of liberty the other provinces would follow. Anyone who did not do so was, according to the *junta's* definition, still in the grip of reactionaries. Paraguay, whose enthusiasm for the cause was clearly less than complete, was obviously a case in point, and so Manuel Belgrano, one of the leading lights in the junta and who had already failed to 'liberate' Upper Peru, was sent to Paraguay with an army of 1,000 men. His paradoxical mission was to free the province from the domination of the king whom the *junta* itself professed to serve. He entered Paraguay in December 1810, but as he advanced north it became clear that the opposition was far stronger than the *junta* had realised. Early the next year the Paraguayans defeated him twice, at Paraguarí and Tacuarí, and Belgrano was soon in retreat. But before doing so he sent messages to the Paraguayan camp, pointing out the indignities the Paraguayans and other *criollos* had to suffer at the hands of the Spanish *peninsulares*, and emphasising that the causes of Buenos Aires and Paraguay were the same. Although Velasco was personally still loyal to Spain, Belgrano's diplomacy split the Paraguayans into factions, in which the anti-Spanish element soon became dominant.

Events then moved so rapidly that on June 17, 1811, disdaining the semantic delicacies observed in Buenos Aires, a special congress at Asuncion declared itself completely independent of Spain, the first province in Latin America to take this step. The chief figure in the congress, and the leading advocate of independence was Dr. José Gaspar Rodriguez de Francia, who had first urged it at the congress of July 24 the previous year and was now selected as one of the five-man junta appointed to direct the new state's affairs. Within four years he had made himself absolute ruler of Paraguay, and remained so until his death in 1840. In that time he converted a neglected province into a nation.

Nobody could be further removed from the stereotype of the Latin American dictator than Dr. Francia. The son of an immigrant from the Brazilian province of São Paulo, he was tall, lean and ascetic in his habits. He never married, disdained pomp and pageantry and ruled with absolute and complete authority. That he was able to rule for so long, and die in power, is an indication that despite the severity of his regime he enjoyed a considerable amount of support. In fact, most Paraguayans were terrified of him. Francia, who soon became known as El Supremo, did offer his country certain benefits that were lacking elsewhere. In the first place, and in his eyes most important of all, he not only gave Paraguay independence, but also made the mass of the population feel a sense of separateness from the rest of South America and of identity with each other.

The country's isolation, the Indian ancestry of most of its people, the Guaraní language that was spoken by everybody were all influences that helped in this. But in the colonial period power had tended to be concentrated in the hands of the small Spanish and middle class element, many of whose political sympathies were with the mother country or the other provinces of La Plata rather than Paraguay itself. Elsewhere in Spanish America, men of this social elite had led the revolution and were the ones who profited most from it, while the peasantry and the native Indians remained in the same miserable condition as before. The secret of Francia's success, compared with other dictators of his time, was that he based his power on the peasant rather than the middle class and landowners. In 1814, even before assuming complete power, he signed decrees forbidding Spaniards and Argentines from marrying anyone except *mestizos*, and he exiled a hundred of them from the country. The brutal methods he adopted, including execution and torture, did little for Francia's later reputation, but it is doubtful whether the rest of Paraguay objected too strenuously, for in the long run Francia's policy helped to create a society that was almost classless. Francia was not personally avaricious, and although he controlled most of the state's revenues, he did not use them for his own benefit. Paraguay was poor compared with other states, but at least everybody was poor. There were none of the glaring contrasts that bedevilled social in other countries, and thanks to Francia the bulk of the population came to have a vested interest in the revolution.

His task in winning the support, or at least the acceptance, of the Guaraní peasantry, was helped by their subservience, which had been bred into them ever since the time of the Jesuits. Although they had been expelled from Paraguay more than half a century before, their influence seems to have lingered for a long time. Francia exploited this tradition of obedience and strengthened it, instilling into the Paraguayans a sense of blind obedience to government that was to have tragic consequences two decades after his death. Although Francia was virtually unchallenged at home following the crushing of the plot of 1820, in other fields his policies were not so successful. The *porteños*, having failed to bring Paraguay back into the fold of the United Provinces - the first name of modern Argentina - by war and by diplomacy, next tried to do so by imposing economic sanctions on Paraguay's trade. The lucrative tobacco trade with Buenos Aires was ruined when imports from Paraguay were prohibited, and when Francia tried to develop trade with the outside world his ships were frequently captured by pirates from the Argentine provinces bordering on the River Paraná. Realising that Paraguay was too weak to force Argentina to open the rivers to Paraguayan commerce, Francia simply turned his back on the world. Foreigners were expelled from the country, and trade came to an end.

From the 1820s until his death Francia contented himself with resisting attempts by Argentina and Brazil to take territory that he regarded as Paraguayan, and making the country as self-sufficient as possible. He tried to insulate it from the outside world, turning it into a South American Japan: it was in a sense the logical conclusion towards which everything in Paraguay's history had been leading. While events in Paraguay were taking this bizarre turn, elsewhere in La Plata anarchy was continuing. The liberals of Buenos Aires continued to believe that the old Vice-Royalty, could be maintained politically intact long after events in Bolivia, Paraguay and Uruguay had proved this to be a delusion. Their efforts to create a centralised government based on Buenos Aires alienated those who wanted a new nation, but believed it should be based on a loose, federal constitution. These two theories led to the development of the two factions that were to dominate Argentinean politics for more than fifty years, the *unitarios*, mainly liberal intellectuals and businessmen in Buenos Aires who believed in central government and the *federalistas,* who represented the provincial landowners and cattle interests and wanted the provinces to retain much greater powers. Although Buenos Aires had led the revolt against Spain, the provinces were too strong for the city to assume the dominant position to which it aspired.

More than 70 per cent of the country's population of around 400,000 lived in the Andean provinces and they soon fell under the control of petty *caudillos*, whose power was based on the wild, undisciplined *gauchos*, the cowboys of the pampas who came to play such a key role in Argentine politics and mythology. By 1820, a year in which Buenos Aires alone had 24 governors, the attempt to form a centralised government had failed, and the constitution created in that year was a federal, rather than unitarian one. As if the anarchy prevailing in Argentina proper was not enough, the government was also deeply involved in the problems of Uruguay which, having disposed of the king of Spain, seemed likely to fall under the control of the emperor of Brazil. Even before 1822 Uruguay had been the scene of fierce fighting, with the Portuguese trying to take advantage of the collapse of Spanish authority to seize a province that it had always coveted. In 1816 Portuguese troops had invaded Uruguay, driving José Gervasio Artigas, the patriot leader, into exile in 1820. For several years in the 1820s Uruguay was administered as part of the Brazilian Empire under the name of the Cisplatine Province, but in 1825 a group of 33 patriots, backed by the authorities in Buenos Aires, landed and war broke out again. This soon developed into a struggle between Argentina and Brazil, but after the decisive defeat of Ituzaingo in 1827, the Brazilians recognised Uruguay as an independent state: in effect, the two sides had agreed to create a buffer state of 60,000 people.

Shortly after this precarious compromise was reached, the government of Buenos Aires in which the leading figure was Bernardo Rivadavia, a *unitario* still trying to create unity even though the provinces were firmly federalist, finally collapsed. Federalist opposition centred around Manuel Rosas, a successful rancher and landowner from Buenos Aires province who typified the *gaucho* and *caudillo* faction and was bitterly opposed to the principles for which the *porteño* liberals stood. As the government crumbled, Rosas organised his forces, and in 1829 drove Rivadavia into exile and took over the reins of government. For the next two decades he dominated the affairs of Argentina and La Plata.

Although he had come to power as the champion of the federalists, this party was little more than a coalition of factions with the same diverse interests that had led to the fragmentation of the vice-royalty after the revaluation. Its chief link was hatred of the unitarios of Buenos Aires, and Rosas maintained and encouraged it, adopting a blood red ribbon as the symbol of the federalists and. banning the national blue and white. Like his predecessors, Rosas still dreamed of restoring the unity of the Vice-Royalty, and the chronic anarchy of Uruguay gave him plenty of scope for interference. The accord that had been created at the time of the treaty of 1828 broke down rapidly, and led to more or less continuous civil war in the next decade. One faction, under the leadership of Fructuoso Rivera, a former colleague of Artigas, called itself the Colorado party, adopting red as its colours. The other group, led by Manual Oribe, one of the leaders of the rising against Brazil, adopted white, and became known as the Blancos. In 1838 Oribe was forced to flee the country, and he took refuge in Buenos Aires. In general the Blancos represented the conservative, land-owning faction, and as such were favoured by Rosas. With his support, Oribe was able to return to Uruguay and start the civil war over again. It culminated in the nine-year siege of Montevideo, the stronghold of the Colorado party, and throughout the 1840s the politics of Argentina and Uruguay were inextricably intertwined. With Paraguay Rosas adopted a different strategy.

He refused to recognise the country as independent, but on the other hand made no attempt to assert Argentinean authority over it. Francia bitterly resented the condescending way in which Rosas continually referred to Paraguay as a 'province', but he was not one to make a major issue out of a choice of words: as long as Argentina made no move against Paraguay, Francia swallowed his pride, and continued his policy of splendid isolation. By 1840, the year in which Francia died, Paraguay was the forgotten country of South America.

Chapter 3

Francia's death, on September 24, 1840, left a vacuum at the head of Paraguayan affairs. Although, according to some versions, he was so hated that his body was dug up from its grave in the cathedral of Asuncion and thrown into the river,[12] the Paraguayans generally were so cowed that they were incapable of acting for themselves. Policarpo Patino, who had been Francia's secretary for years, organised a junta with himself as secretary, but he lacked personal power, and early in the new year was thrown into prison, where he committed suicide. In January 1841 the junta was overthrown by an army coup, and a triumvirate installed. But while it struggled with the unaccustomed problems of government, two men were already plotting its downfall, Mariano Roque Alonso, the commander of the army, and a former professor of theology named Carlos Antonio López. A month after the formation of the triumvirate these two men overthrew it, and in March 1841 were both nominated consuls by a specially called national congress. Three years later López, the dominant partner in the duet, came to supreme power when he was elected president by the compliant congress. With his rise to power Paraguay entered a period of tremendous change that was to give the country the tantalising glimpse of greatness that ultimately destroyed it.

Carlos Antonio López turned his country from the hermit state of South America into the most progressive state on the continent.

Although Francia's ruthless dictatorship had had its benefits, his policy had led to stagnation. López reversed it completely, believing that Paraguay must play an active part in the affairs of South America, and that the country must take advantage of the great progress that was being made in the outside world. This was a bold policy, which meant transforming Paraguay from the most insular to the most progressive state in the continent almost overnight, but López set about it with a great deal of energy, and a good deal of intelligence. The system that he had inherited from Francia helped in some ways, since his control over the country was never seriously challenged, and the power of the state was already paramount. López had been born in 1787 at the small town of La Recoleta, just outside Asuncion. His father, Cirilo López, was apparently a tailor of humble, and possibly disreputable origins, but his mother came from a family of moderately well off landowners. Carlos Antonio had originally planned to be a lawyer but Francia's system did not encourage such professions, and López ultimately became professor or theology and philosophy at the College of Asuncion, before this was closed down by Francia. López married the stepdaughter of a wealthy landowner called Lazaro Rojas, and through her came into a sizeable fortune. He lay low during the dictatorship, but fell into disfavour during the last two years of Francia's life, and was sent to live on his estancia at Rosario. Like Francia, he hated the small Spanish element that in colonial times had dominated Paraguay, and continued Francia's persecution of them. López was himself a *mestizo*, who took pride in his Guaraní ancestry, and he allied himself firmly with the poorer classes. The death of Francia was in other ways like the opening of a curtain, and even while a consul, López inaugurated a spate of reforms, clearing away the atmosphere of gloom and terror that had descended on Paraguay in the last years of Francia's life. About 600 political prisoners were freed from Francia's jails and the system of spies which he had built up, while maintained, was softened: López was a disciplinarian who took his insistence on complete obedience to such lengths that he ordered the men of Asuncion to wear hats so that they could take them off when he passed in the street, but he preferred his mailed fist to be inside a velvet glove.

Economically, Paraguay was on a fairly sound footing. The country in 1840 probably had a population of 220,000[13] most of them concentrated in the small, extremely fertile area around Asuncion. Because the land-owning class had never been able to gain political control of Paraguay, the lot of the peasantry was generally good and there was little social unrest. Paraguay had few minerals, and its long isolation had destroyed the once flourishing tobacco trade, but on the other hand, Paraguay was by 1840 so self-sufficient that imports were also minimal. As a result, López had no adverse trade balance or other economic millstones hanging round his neck, and was able to develop Paraguay's economy according to the country's own interests. Its chief asset was yerba maté, the South American tea. The best yerba maté was said to come from the hills around Caaquazu in Central Paraguay, and López soon built up a flourishing export trade to Buenos Aires. In 1846 the government established a monopoly of this trade[14], buying yerba from the farmers at ls an arroba (25 pounds) and selling it for between 24s and 32s[15]. Other exports included oranges, cotton and tobacco. There was an export tax of 5 per cent on all exports, and higher duties on imports[16]. State control of the economy extended to control over most of the country's production as well, and in 1854 of 80,000 planks of timber exported, 50,000 were government owned[17]. By the end of his life, López had brought around 50 per cent of the country into the possession of the López family[18], for Carlos Antonio was a firm believer in nepotism, one of his most celebrated coups being the appointment of his brother Basilio as Bishop of Asuncion.

The wealth that flowed into the national treasury from the profits made on foreign trade meant that other taxation was unnecessary, although trade did not really expand until the Argentine blockade imposed by Rosas was lifted in 1851. After that it grew rapidly. The total foreign trade of Paraguay amounted to 1 million dollars in 1851; the next year it doubled, and by 1861 had reached 4 million dollars annually. In the same year 404 ships docked at Asuncion, compared with 120 in 1851[19]. The wealth this trade brought to Paraguay was in general used for the benefit of its people. Francia had frowned on education, since he feared it might encourage opposition, but López saw that Paraguay could only become a modern progressive state if it had an educated population to lead it.

As early as 1844 López had persuaded Congress to agree to send young Paraguayans to Europe for advanced education, but it is an indication of the lamentable level of education in the country when Francia died that it was not until fourteen years later that suitable students could be found. The choice of subjects showed the practical outlook of the president - chemistry, pharmacy, designing, law and medicine. One of the 53 students who benefited from this far-sighted generosity was José Chrisostomo Centurión, who was born in 1840. Years later, Francisco Solano López, Carlos Antonio's son and successor, told him that the parents of most of the students thought the whole idea was a waste of time. Children who were destined to become shopkeepers and clerks had no need of such sophisticated education and, even when the students began sending home essays in French and English, their parents obstinately refused to believe that they were the work of their offspring but assumed they had been composed by their teachers[20].

To improve the general ignorance that prevailed in the country, López launched a programme of primary school building, and in 1861 ordered local magistrates to see that children of nine and 10 went to school, if they had no excuse for staying away. By 1862 Paraguay had a total of 435 schools, with 25,500 pupils[21]. A small enough percentage, considering that Paraguay's population at that stage had risen to more than 500,000 but still it compared favourably with many of Paraguay's neighbours, and as one historian of Paraguay says 'not until forty years later was Paraguay again to reach even this low level'.

Socially the oppressive atmosphere of Francia's day was lightened under López. On November 24, 1842, a decree was passed declaring that all children of Negro slaves born after June 1, 1843, would be born free. Although slavery had never been a strong institution in Paraguay, the fact that López abolished it at all is an indication of his identification with the lower classes. He further ingratiated himself by starting a deliberate policy of bread and circuses, encouraging fiestas and dancing, jollifications that had been rigorously suppressed by the puritanical Dr. Francia. These reforms helped to rouse Paraguay from its long sleep, but López knew that industrialisation was essential for really decisive progress, and although its agriculture was strong, the technical knowledge that was necessary to build up industries could only come from abroad. In 1845 he granted foreigners the same civil rights as natives, and his first effort to secure foreign investment came in the same year, following the visit of Edward A. Hopkins, a young Vermonter who was sent to Paraguay to investigate the possibilities of diplomatic recognition by the United States. Hopkins won López's confidence and on his return to the United States formed a company to trade with Paraguay that became known as the Rhode Island Company. In 1851 Hopkins managed to get himself appointed United States consul to Asuncion, and arranged for a steamer filled with machinery and other goods belonging to the new company to be sent there, but the ship was wrecked off the coast of Brazil and its cargo declared a total loss. Hopkins went on to Paraguay, and in 1853 acquired some land at San Antonio, twelve miles below Asuncion, where he established a sawmill, as well as a cigar factory in the capital itself.

Francisco Solano Lopez inherited from his father the most peaceful and progressive country in South America. Within less than a decade he destroyed it.

In the same year, López sent his eldest son, Francisco Solano, to Europe, to make Paraguay's name known in the capitals of the west and to encourage technicians and craftsmen to emigrate to Paraguay. This voyage to Europe was as crucial to Paraguay as the visit of Commander Perry was to Japan in the same year of 1853. It opened the country to modernising influences of Europe in the way that Carlos Antonio López had hoped it would, and from then on a steady stream of foreigners made the long journey across the Atlantic to seek adventure and fortune in Paraguay.

Count Franz Wisner von Morgenstern left Vienna and the Austro-Hungarian army to take up a military position in the republic, and according rumour, to escape from an unpleasant scandal. Mr. Fischer von Truenfeld came from Germany to establish a telegraph system. The arts were not neglected and so M. de Cluny arrived to establish an Academy of Music and teach French, and Luisa and Dorotea Dupart came to Asuncion to establish a finishing school on the lines of those of Paris. A well-known Spanish actor, Ildefonso Bermejo, made the journey with his wife to develop the nation's educational resources and to establish a national theatre. Some immigrants came in groups. As a result of the friendly relations established with France, a group of five hundred settlers from Gascony were shipped out to establish a colony in the Chaco, the almost unexplored area of swamp and forest that lay across the river from the mainland of Paraguay.

They were one of the largest national groups to arrive in Paraguay, but the most important of all were the British, most of whom went out on contracts arranged by J. and A. Blyth of Limehouse. Even at their peak, they never numbered more than a few hundred, but their skills were to lay the foundations of the modern state of which Carlos Antonio dreamed. Mr. William Keld Whytehead came to build an arsenal, and Mr. Padison to build one of the first railways in South America. Messrs. Valpy and Burrell came on the same mission, as did George Thompson, who was to achieve fame in a quite different field. There were medical men, like Dr. William Stewart who had originally emigrated to the nearby Argentinean province of Corrientes with a Scottish colonising venture, and moved on to Paraguay when it failed. He became the personal physician of Carlos Antonio and according to rumour was paid the highest salary of all the foreigners in Paraguay. Charles Twite, a geologist, set off for the cordilleras to hunt for iron, the key commodity in nineteenth century industrialisation. A young apothecary, George F. Masterman, left his home in Croydon to seek adventure. Alonzo Taylor left Chelsea to build a new capital for López and Thomas N. Smith came to build a new fleet for a country that was a thousand miles from the sea. John Watts, a marine engineer, came to serve on it. With the aid of these men and others, López intensified his modernisation programme.

In 1859, using 5,000 Paraguayan soldiers as workmen, the English engineers began work on the railway that was to connect Asuncion with the cordilleras, and on October 21, 1861, López himself opened the first six miles stretch between the capital and Trinidad. The line was later extended to Paraguarí 45 miles away. Great changes were made to Asuncion, which in López's time was a city of about 20,000 people. Francia had made an attempt to rebuild the capital, but with somewhat disastrous results, and López considered it necessary to start the job again. As early as 1842 he pulled down the old cathedral and erected another, and other early projects included the construction of stone embankments along the river front, to eliminate the threat of flooding, a new opera house, and the laying of cobblestones in some of the main streets. The English builders who arrived on contract from Blyth's were given other tasks, and worked on the railway station and a new mole in the harbour. Alonzo Taylor built several bridges and finally began a grandiose new palace by the river for López's son Francisco Solano.

Carlos Antonio did not live to see his capital rebuilt, and eight years after his death it still had a curiously incomplete look, with many of the buildings being only half finished. Even so the promise was there, and Asuncion probably compared favourably with Montevideo and Buenos Aires, neither of which greatly impressed foreign contemporaries. Other important projects begun at this time included a shipyard, part of Whytehead's arsenal, where the first iron-hulled ship ever built in South America was completed in 1856. Two 500-ton steamers were under construction as early as 1857, and a foundry was established at Ibicuí 90 miles south of the capital where a little iron was mined. It all added up to the beginning of a dazzling transformation, particularly in view of Paraguay's previous backwardness, although López's innovations probably made very little change to the lives of the average Paraguayan. It was what they promised that mattered: under López Paraguay reached a point where a remarkable future seemed to be almost within reach, a future which might have seen Paraguay as the leader and chief beneficiary of an industrial revolution.

The one threat came from outside. Francia's relations with Paraguay's neighbours had been almost non-existent, but the problems remained. Paraguay's future depended on how López dealt with them.

This engraving from the Illustrated London News shows Asuncion in 1865.

Chapter 4

On coming to power López saw that the greatest diplomatic problem facing Paraguay was the republic's relations with Rosas, the Argentine dictator, but unlike Francia he was not content simply to withdrawn into his shell and pretend that Argentina and the rest of the world were unnecessary. He realised that Rosas controlled Paraguay's access to Europe, and was determined to maintain his country's rights. Despite the odds against him, he did not shrink from a direct challenge to Rosas' domination and in 1841 antagonised him by signing a treaty of friendship with Corrientes, which had been in revolt against the dictator since 1839. Three years later, since Rosas still refused to recognise Paraguay's independence, López made a fresh treaty, which virtually recognised Corrientes as an independent state.

Rosas predictably retaliated by denying Paraguay the use of all Argentinean ports, ignoring the protest of Brazil, which with Paraguay had declared the great rivers open to international shipping, and was giving López secret encouragement in his stand. Oribe, the Blanco leader in Uruguay, backed his friend Rosas and López decided to settle the matter by resorting to arms. In November 1845 he made another treaty with Corrientes, agreeing to provide a force of 10,000, men in return for recognition of Paraguayan claims in the disputed Misiones region.

Early the next year Francisco Solano López, a general at the age of 19, led a Paraguayan army across the Paraná to support General José Paz, the commander of the rebel troops from Corrientes and Entre Rios. But before they could join them, the rebels were decisively defeated by Justo José de Urquiza, the pro-Rosas governor of Entre Rios, the province immediately south of Corrientes. The Paraguayan contingent retreated without firing a shot, and López's first attempt to resolve his differences with Argentina had ended in fiasco. For a time, indeed, it seemed as though matters could become even more serious. The Brazilians, who had used López as a pawn in their own struggle against Argentina, refused his suggestions for an alliance, virtually abandoning him to his fate. It was fortunate for López that Rosas was involved in a dispute with Great Britain and France, who had instituted a blockade of Buenos Aires, but even so, Rosas persuaded his congress to grant him unlimited funds with which to reincorporate Paraguay into Argentina. Fortunately, Rosas' power had passed its peak. He had originally been accepted as the one man who could end Argentina's anarchy, but the provinces had remained in a state of continual unrest and individual liberty had disappeared. For some time opposition had been growing, particularly in Buenos Aires where the remnants of the old unitario party had never completely given up their opposition. Many of them had fled abroad, where they plotted and hoped and planned for the day when they would be able to return. Among them were men like Bartolomé Mitre, a soldier/writer who had served in Rivera's army against Oribe and Rosas in 1839, and had then taken refuge on the Pacific coast, where be was achieving fame as a writer. With him was Wenceslas Paunero, another *porteño* who had served in the Uruguayan wars, and Juan Bautista.

Alberdi, a celebrated jurist and political analyst was another exile. Domingo Faustino Sarmiento, although from the inland province of San Juan, was another liberal who loathed what he regarded as the barbarism of the provinces and hated Rosas as its champion. He had achieved fame with his book 'Facundo' an indictment of the *caudillo* and *gaucho* mentality. The decisive moment came in 1851 when Urquiza, who had been Rosas' most important provincial supporter during the previous decade declared Entre Rios to be a sovereign federal province and withdrew the powers that had been ceded to Buenos Aires. Urquiza could himself provide an army of 10,000 men and this rapidly became the nucleus of an international army whose aim was to destroy Rosas. A contingent of 5,000 men joined him from Corrientes, 2,000 from the Colorados of Uruguay and 4,000 from Brazil. In November 1851 Mitre, Sarmiento, Paunero and other exiles arrived from Chile on the frigate *Medicis*, and the coalition was complete. The only obvious absentee was Paraguay.

Although Urquiza's revolt was exactly what López had been hoping for for so long, when the moment came he failed to recognise it, partly because the request for troops sent by Urquiza in May was accompanied by a demand for the return of territory in the Misiones that had been occupied by Paraguayan troops. López also mistrusted Urquiza personally. López's foreign adventures had not been marked by success, for the fiasco of the invasion of Corrientes had been followed by a quarrel with Brazil over a disputed boundary. By the time he received a second invitation to join the alliance in October, López had overcome his suspicion of the Urquiza-Brazil alliance, but it was too late to take an active part in the dramatic events that followed. After first ending the nine-year siege of Montevideo, and enabling the Colorados to take power, Urquiza led his army back into Argentina proper and early in the new year shattered Rosas' forces at the battle of Caseros.

Although Paraguay had given moral support at best, the victory achieved at least some of López's ambitions. The blockade was lifted, and in June of the same year Paraguay's independence was recognised by the new Argentine Confederation. Even so, the negotiations of the previous year had shown that the new rulers were not willing to concede the disputed territory so easily, and by not playing an active part in the alliance, López had forfeited the gratitude of the other Plate republics and the chance to put them in his debt. For the decade following Rosas's overthrow however, the internal problems of the new Argentine Confederation prevented its government from trying to enforce a settlement. Even before Caseros, the old divisions had begun to reappear. Urquiza, although a genuine patriot sincerely wanting unity was still a federalist jealous of the potential power of Buenos Aires, and when he entered the capital early in 1852 he wore the hated red hatband, symbol of Rosas' old party, rather than the blue and white colours of the unitarians. Friction also arose with men such as Mitre and Sarmiento who felt that they deserved a greater say in the government than he was willing to allow. He believed, with some reason, that they had only returned to Argentina as a result of his efforts, and that if anyone was entitled to reap the rewards of victory it should be himself.

In May the provincial governors selected Urquiza as provisional director of the nation, nationalised the customs revenue which had previously been the prerogative of Buenos Aires, opened the Paraná and Uruguay rivers to free navigation and negotiated trade treaties with the United States and the European nations.

All of these measures were a direct threat to the monopolistic trade position which Buenos Aires had hold for so long, and when they were ratified at San Nicolas, Buenos Aires was the only one of Argentina's 14 provinces to vote against them. Led by Bartolomé Mitre, the province broke away from the rest of the Confederation, and Urquiza moved his capital to Paraná, the capital of his own province of Entre Rios. This split was regarded by both parties as a temporary rather than permanent state of affairs, but neither side was willing to give in: the province and city of Buenos Aires by this time had 400,000 of Argentina's million people, the port controlled the nation's customs revenues and was geographically the only sensible site for a capital.

Without it the Confederation was really a never viable proposition. On the other hand, Urquiza and the federalists regarded the *porteños* as narrow-minded and selfish and feared that unity on Buenos Aires' terms would mean giving in to demands that would damage the nation's interests. Despite these internal problems, inconclusive efforts were made to settle the boundary differences between Argentina and Paraguay. These centred on two areas, the Misiones and the Chaco.

Paraguay claimed the Misiones, the thin strip of land where the River Paraná and the River Uruguay swing almost together, because it had once been settled by Jesuit missionaries and late in the colonial period had been administered as part of Paraguay. The Argentines claimed it was simply an extension of their province of Corrientes, and even at their most generous were only willing to recognise Paraguayan claims to the area north of the watershed between the two great rivers. Paraguay's interest in the region, which was largely uninhabited, was partly strategic: it gave the republic access to the Brazilian province of Rio Grande, and made it less vulnerable to the economic blockades which had been exerted by Argentina in the reign of Rosas and his predecessors.

The Chaco, although economically useless, was vaguely claimed by Argentina, Bolivia and Paraguay. Paraguay's interest there too was largely strategic, for the Chaco lay directly across the River Paraguay from the inhabited part of the country and by controlling both banks the republic would be able to exercise a much greater control over the river. López claimed the area north of the River Bermejo, and in 1855 had installed the new French colony at Nueva Buerdeos, just across the River Paraguay from Asuncion to stake his claim. The Argentines however insisted that the Chaco was theirs as far as the River Pilcomayo, a hundred miles north of the Bermejo.

In 1852 a compromise seemed to have been reached, under which Paraguay gave up its claims to the Misiones in return for effective recognition of the Bermejo line, but the Argentine Congress refused to accept the treaty, and the whole issue remained unsettled.

Paraguay's disputes with Brazil were equally old-established and concerned the northern frontier with the Brazilian province of Matto Grosso, and the boundary in the east on the river Paraná. The dispute had theoretically been settled in 1777 when Portugal and Spain signed the treaty of San Ildefonso, carefully defining the boundaries between their American possessions. Unfortunately, cartography in the eighteenth century was so vague, and knowledge of the area in question so limited, that in the words of Pelham Horton Box 'the statesmen who drafted that remarkable document did not themselves know what it meant.' It was scarcely surprising then that the treaty served only to confuse matters, and that both sides managed to interpret it in such a way that its ambiguities favoured their own case.

As with Paraguay's dispute with Argentine, López's interest was partly strategic. In the north, the Brazilians claimed the River Branco as the boundary, while Paraguay claimed the River Apa. The land between was swampy and difficult country for an attaching army to cross and in López's view would help protect Paraguay from an attack from Matto Grosso.

He maintained his country's claims with considerable spirit, on several occasions during the time of Rosas sending troops to drive Brazilian soldiers from outposts on territory claimed by Paraguay. Brazil had not retaliated strongly because she wanted López's aid against Rosas. But once he was gone, the Brazilians became less inclined than ever to settle the border question on terms that were favourable to López, and as relations worsened, so López decided to use his only important card: Paraguay's control of the River Paraguay, Brazil's link with Matto Gross. In 1855, after Brazil had again tried unsuccessfully to establish forts in the disputed territory, López blockaded the river. When Brazil sent a fleet of ships to force his hand he threatened to fire on it from a minuscule fort on the island of Cerrito, at the confluence of the Rivers Paraguay and Paraná. The Brazilians hesitated, and then agreed to negotiate in Asuncion.

López and his son Francisco handled these discussions so adroitly that the Brazilian negotiator, Pedro Ferreira de Oliveira returned to Rio de Janeiro with a treaty by which López in effect exchanged navigation rights for recognition of his territorial claims. Pedro II, the Emperor of Brazil promptly refused to sign it.

The following year negotiations were reopened. López sent his foreign minister, José Berges, to Rio to arrange a settlement with his Brazilian opposite number, José Maria da Silva Paranhos. Although Berges, an astute man who gave his country valuable service, made out a good case, the Brazilian arguments were backed by the veiled but definite threat of force. The treaty signed in April 1856, while acknowledging Brazilian rights to free navigation on the River Paraguay simply deferred the boundary dispute. Commissioners empowered to negotiate the borders were to be nominated within a period of six years. López agreed to this treaty reluctantly, and did his best to be obstructive to Brazilian shipping. But shrewd bargaining by Paranhos secured the co-operation of the Argentine Confederation and Uruguay in declaring the great rivers of the Plate free to international shipping, and finding himself diplomatically isolated López finally accepted Brazil's terms. In 1858 a Brazilian steamship company began regular monthly services to the Matto Grosso.

In addition to these quarrels with his neighbours, López also became involved with disputes with countries further afield. The Rhode Island Company, which López had hoped would help Paraguay take its place with the modern industrial nations of the world, soon turned out to be a major disappointment. Hopkins, its originator and leading light was a glib opportunist with a touch of arrogance, and although his business prospered, Paraguay saw few of the profits. López, who had lent Hopkins 10,000 dollars to help get established, became progressively more disenchanted with his protegé and late in 1854 he ordered Hopkins' saw mill at San Antonio to be closed. At this point Lieutenant Thomas J. Page, commander of the United States ship *Water Witch* entered the story.

He had been in the River Paraguay since June, exploring the Chaco tributaries and was at Corrientes when he heard of Hopkins' difficulties. He immediately went to Asuncion and after some argument managed to arrange for Hopkins and his party to leave the country. The incident seemed closed, but López, like all his countrymen, was a patriot first and foremost. In retaliation for Page's action, he forbade foreign warships to pass through Paraguayan waters, an action that was obviously aimed at the *Water Witch*. On February 1, 1855, the situation became even more serious when the garrison of the Paraguayan fort of Itapiru fired on the vessel, by then under the command of Lt. William N. Jeffers. One man died from wounds received.

Lt. Page had also been given the task of exchanging ratifications of a treaty of friendship, commerce and navigation between the two countries, but the trouble over the Rhode Island Company had prevented him from doing so. The firing on the *Water Witch* resulted in the United States government taking up the case of the company, and when a special commissioner, Richard Fitzpatrick, was sent to Asuncion to exchange the ratifications, he told López that the United States government considered Paraguay liable to pay Hopkins compensation. López showed little enthusiasm for this view, and stubbornly refused to exchange ratifications.

In 1859 another commissioner was sent to Paraguay, this time backed by a naval force of 19 ships, which at last induced López to apologise for the attack on the *Water Witch,* pay compensation for the death of the sailor, and sign a new treaty.

The Rhode Island affair, however, dragged on. López sent José Berges to Washington to discuss compensation to the Rhode Island Company, but he argued his country's case so well that the commission examining the matter decided that Paraguay had no case to answer. This failed to satisfy the American government. Charles Ames Washburn, the American commissioner in Asuncion from 1861 was asked to discuss the matter with López, but nothing was achieved. The American government tried to reopen the matter again in 1885, but the Paraguayan Chamber of Deputies twice refused to pay anything, in

1887 and 1888, and after that the matter was finally allowed to drop. While this was going on, López was also involved in a dispute with France over the fate of the 500 colonists who had gone to Paraguay after Francisco Solano López's visit to Europe.

López had used these colonists as a pawn in his dispute with Argentina over possession of the Chaco, but none of the rosy promises made to them ever materialised. They found themselves dumped in the middle of a jungle and abandoned. Despite the protests of France, López did nothing to help them, until at the end of 1855 he suddenly ordered the 50 per cent who had survived disease and starvation to leave the country within a week. Finally, the French government arranged for the survivors to be shipped home, broke off diplomatic relations for two years, and eventually López was obliged to pay compensation to a man named Dorignac who had been driven mad by his sufferings.

López, having antagonised France and the United States, also became involved in an argument with Britain. This arose from the measures he took to put down the one challenge to his rule that ever came - or is said to have come - from his own countrymen. Although Francia had almost extinguished all traces of independence among the middle classes of Paraguay, a few dissidents still remained. In 1859 a member of the Decoud family, one of the leading families in the country, who was López's agent in Buenos Aires, swindled the government out of a million dollars and fled to Europe. This resulted in accusations of conspiracy and a wave of arrests. Among the men who were thrown into jail was James Canstatt, a merchant who, though born in Montevideo, was technically a British subject. The evidence against him was extremely slim, and the British government immediately took steps to protect him: the similarities between this case and the notorious Don Pacifico affair of 1850 were not entirely coincidental. Lord Palmerston, who was Foreign Secretary then, was prime minister in 1859. G.A. Henderson, the British consul, demanded a public trial, but López with his customary stubbornness, refused.

At this point, the fragile truce between Buenos Aires and the Argentine Confederation broke down, and López sent his son Francisco Solano to arbitrate between Urquiza and Mitre. He accomplished this task with considerable success, and was returning home in triumph on board the *Tacuarí*, a gunboat he had purchased in Europe when the British acted.

The River Plate was the only place outside the Empire where ships of the Royal Navy were permanently stationed, and Edward Thornton, the minister at Buenos Aires, instructed the South Atlantic Fleet to intercept the Paraguayan gunboat. Two vessels, aptly named *Grappler* and *Buzzard* gave chase. The *Tacuarí* managed to reach Buenos Aires, and the younger López escaped ashore. But shortly afterwards the *Tacuarí* was taken in tow, and López senior was informed that it would be retained until such time as Canstatt was released with compensation. It was a humiliating position, but López had little choice but to give in: the *Tacuarí* had cost 150,000 dollars and was his only warship. Reluctantly he ordered Canstatt to be freed.

In all three of these adventures López showed an alarming lack of appreciation of the determination and long reach of the great powers, but he avoided serious trouble by always backing down before the situation became really serious. Nevertheless his entanglements with so many foreign governments and particularly the failure to settle Paraguay's disputes with Brazil and Argentina made him pay far more attention to the country's defences than Francia had ever done.

The geographical position of Paraguay made the country virtually impregnable against attacks by any route other than the Rivers Paraná and Paraguay, the approach used by the Spaniards in the sixteenth century, and the way followed by Belgrano in his attempt to unite Paraguay with Argentina in 1811. López's dispute with Rosas, and the ease with which Paraguay was blockaded, showed how vulnerable the country was to an attack from this direction. The construction of the arsenal, with its shipbuilding facilities, helped to make Paraguay less reliant on outside supplies, and in the 1850s López began work on the fortress that was designed to protect the country against the invasion even of a country with overwhelming naval power.

It was situated at Humaitá, a small village, on a bend of the River Paraguay, about thirty miles above its junction with the River Paraná at Tres Bocas. In the previous decade this had been simply a *guardia*, one of a chain of armed customs posts built along the left bank of the river to control trade and check the occasional raids of the Indians living in the Chaco opposite. Humaitá was unusual in that it was one of the few patches of firm ground for nearly 200 miles, and the way in which the river curved enabled any guns situated there to dominate the river for several miles above and below. In 1851 López asked the Brazilian government to provide advisers for the army, and one of the officers sent, Lieutenant Joao Carlos de Vilagran Cabrita, was asked to draw up specifications for improving Humaitá's defences. Wisner von Morgenstern was put in charge of the construction of further defence works. Even before, this work had begun. López had started building up his army, which for the last twelve years of Francia's government had been maintained at 5,000 men. When López quarrelled with Rosas in 1845 he was able to offer Corrientes 10,000 men and Francisco Solano's expedition comprised 4,000 men. In 1857 López increased the army to 18,000 men, with another 46,000 in reserve, and organised a fleet of 11 steamers. By the time of his death in 1862 Paraguay's standing army had been built up to 25,000 men, twice the size of the United States army before the outbreak of the Civil War, and larger than the army of Brazil.

It is difficult to see what López planned to do with this force, which must have been a considerable strain on Paraguay's economy, and which he certainly did not intend to use offensively. Its formation was partly due to the Paraguayan's innate sense of insecurity and of suspicion of the ambitions of Brazil and Argentina, and partly due to the prompting of Francisco Solano whose influence over his father became dominant towards the end of Carlos Antonio's life. When Carlos Antonio died, on September 10, 1862, he left his son a reputedly impregnable fortress, a bulging treasury, a sound economy, the largest standing army on the American continent and a number of unsolved disputes with his two largest neighbours. It was to prove a fatal legacy.

Chapter 5

With the accession of Francisco Solano, López a new force entered the complex and volatile world of South American politics. The consequences of López's rule were so tremendous, so appalling, that although more has been written about him than almost any other figure in the continent's history, nearly every writer has adopted an extreme attitude, seeing him either as a monster, motivated by insane ambitions, or as a patriot fighting to defend his native land against the greed and jealousy of two mighty neighbours.

As with most historical controversies, the reality must fall somewhere between these two extreme views, but both contain elements of truth. López was a man of contradictions, a hero and a coward; a faithful lover and a treacherous friend, a realist, who lived for his dreams; a nepotist's son who turned against his family; a man of culture and a bloodthirsty sadist; a patriot who destroyed his country. Even those who knew him frequently saw only one side of his complex personality, the Dr. Jekyll who charmed his admirers or the Mr. Hyde who appalled his enemies.

López was born on July 24, 1826, the eldest of a family of five children. Washburn, the American Minister to Asuncion, maintained that he was actually the son of a landowner called Rojas who had bribed Carlos Antonio to marry the mother and say the child was his, but Washburn was such a bitter opponent of López that this story can be virtually dismissed. Certainly Carlos Antonio never treated him as anything but his son, and he was the chief beneficiary of the profligate nepotism that was Carlos Antonio's most obvious failing.

Francisco was made a general in the army at the age of 17, his brother Venancio a colonel at 13, and Benigno, the third son, was made first a major and then an admiral while also in his teens. All three, and the two daughters, Innocencia and Rafaela, were thoroughly spoiled and given great privileges.

The daughters specialised in financial dealings, buying torn paper money at 6 cents in the dollar discount and then exchanging it for its full value. All the children were given large estates and were allowed to export yerba maté without any dues. Naturally enough, all became extremely wealthy.

All three sons were notorious womanisers. Venancio was reputed to concentrate on girls of the lower classes, while Francisco preferred the daughters of Paraguay's more prominent citizens. Julia Pessoa, of Villa del Pilar in the south of the country was his mistress for some time and bore him a son called Emiliano. The daughter of José Berges was also said to have been his mistress for a while, as well as the sister of Vicente Barrios, who later married his own sister Innocencia and became one of his most reliable soldiers. There were several other Paraguayan mistresses by whom López had several children.

There was nothing particularly reprehensible in all this. The López boys were merely exercising what they no doubt considered to be their legitimate *droits des seigneurs* and since the girls in question were presumably reasonably willing, no great harm was done. More ominous were the stories told of what happened to girls who did not return Francisco's affection. Pancha Garmendia, the daughter of an Asuncion merchant, and apparently as beautiful as she was virtuous, refused to become Francisco's mistress, and as a result was so persecuted that she was forced to take refuge in a convent.

Another girl, Carmelita R --, was engaged to marry Carlos Decoud, a member of the family that fell into disfavour at the time of the Canstatt affair. Despite her engagement, Francisco tried to persuade her to become his mistress, but she refused. One night shortly before her wedding Carmelita heard the sound of horsemen galloping past her house and when she went out on to the porch found the body of her murdered lover lying naked on the steps. This discovery drove her mad, and several years later George Frederick Masterman, the young English apothecary, came across her late one night praying beside a wayside crucifix near La Recoleta, and heard the whole story from his friends. Carlos Antonio for a long time ignored these activities and their indications of a streak of ruthless savagery. For years the whole López family had lived in the shadow of Dr. Francia, and Carlos Antonio may have regarded his sons' misdeeds as a natural reaction to years of repression. He was so indulgent towards them that he may have been blind to faults, which his own negligence as a parent no doubt encouraged. At all events, he treated Francisco from the start as his heir apparent, and gave him increasing responsibilities, starting with the command of the Corrientes expedition in 1845. That this ended in anti-climax was no doubt fortunate - an encounter with Urquiza's battle-trained army would have been far more uncomfortable than the meek withdrawal that actually took place - but it did not stop Francisco complacently coming to the conclusion that he was already a great soldier. He told the Chilean writer, Federico de la Barra, during the campaign: 'The military art has no secrets for me. General Paz cannot teach me, nor have I anything to learn of his science.' General Paz, the commander of the Correntino forces, was then regarded as one of the greatest military experts in South America, while Francisco had yet to see a shot fired in anger.

Arrogant though his son may have been, Carlos Antonio remained confident enough of his military talents to send him off to occupy the Misiones in 1849 during the crisis with Rosas. Soon after this venture Francisco was appointed Minister of War and Marine, but Carlos Antonio, who preferred diplomacy to real war, remained in control of affairs and Francisco had to content himself with a minor role. In1853 he was sent to Europe.

Rosas's fall had enabled Paraguay to venture into the outside world once again, and Francisco was given the double task of making Paraguay known to the rulers of the European powers and securing the equipment and technical experts who alone could turn Paraguay into the modern state of which the Lópezes dreamed.

During his trip, López visited England, France, Spain, Germany, Italy and the Crimea, where the war against the Russians was under way. He was received by the Emperor Napoleon III, the nephew of the great Napoleon whom López admired greatly, and as far as making Paraguay known was concerned, the tour could be regarded as moderately successful. But López excelled himself in the second part of his mission. The contacts he arranged in France and England, particularly with the Blyth company of Limehouse, were to form the basis of the great material progress made in Paraguay during the next decade. Although his father had originally planned these developments, we can perhaps see behind their implementation the youthful, dynamic figure of the younger López, already dreaming of a future greater and more glorious than the cautious and more practical visions of the ageing Carlos Antonio.

On his return to Paraguay at the end of 1854, Francisco resumed his post at the ministry and continued to play an important part in other aspects of national affairs, negotiating with the Brazilians, and going to Buenos Aires to mediate successfully between Mitre and Urquiza after the battle of Cepeda. In view of the abuse that was to be hurled at him during the next few years (and indeed ever since his death) it is interesting to note the generally favourable impression López created abroad at this time, particularly in the capitals of the River Plate.

One Buenos Aires newspaperman wrote of him in 1856: "Receiving that evening he was in elegant civilian attire, and it was noteworthy the freedom with which he wore his fashionable clothes, that might have come from Bossi or Gaumy in Buenos Aires, such was their cut, and such was the distinctive manner in which he wore them. Both his body and his clothes were well proportioned to each other, and the effect was distinguished. In manner General López is very affable. He was in a jovial light mood all evening, and talked interestingly of world affairs without dwelling too long upon matters which might be controversial." The public men of the Argentine Confederation were equally impressed by him following his successful arbitration in 1859 and the people of Buenos Aires presented López with a special album of thanks, signed by many prominent people, including Mitre. On the other side, Urquiza was also delighted with López's contribution, and sent him the sword he had worn at the battle of Cepeda.

It is difficult to see in this urbane and sophisticated diplomat the vindictive sensualist who drove girls mad, or the tyrant of later years, and it is impossible to believe that the glowing tributes paid to López during this period were the products of sycophants or diplomatic hyperbole. Yet the diplomat and the sadist are one person, two aspects of the same personality, in which the one side was temporarily on display, while the other was waiting its turn to emerge.

During the last years of his father's rule, López seems to have been a constant source of interest to the Press of Buenos Aires. He was young, handsome and personable, the obvious successor to the presidency of one of the most stable and yet most intriguing states in the continent - a state which many people in the anarchic provinces of the Plate estuary envied and admired. But López owed some of this attention to another of his European acquisitions, a young Irish beauty called Elisa Lynch, one of those extraordinary Victorian women who escaped from the stifling conventions of her sex and times to live a life of adventure and romance. She went on to share in a history filled with tragedy, despair and death.

South American Pictures/ PYGB0028s2
PARAGUAY young Eliza Lynch (1835-1886) consort of President Francisco Solano Lopez

Elisa Lynch. The photograph was probably taken early in the 1850s, while she was embarking on her career as a courtesan and before she left for Paraguay with Lopez. Her blonde beauty, poise and sophistication ensured that the women of Paraguay hated her.

She is, like López himself, a person who has inspired vehement controversy, and many of those who have defended López have tried to shift the blame for the disasters that befell Paraguay on to Elisa Lynch's shoulders. The one point on which all accounts agree is that she was a woman of quite outstanding beauty, who so dazzled the Paraguayans that 'when she landed in Asuncion the simple natives thought her charms were of more than earthly brilliance, and her dress so sumptuous that they had no words to express the admiration they both excited.' [22]

Elisa was born in Cork in 1835 and later claimed that her father's side of the family had produced several bishops, while one of her mother's family was a vice-admiral in the Royal Navy who had fought at Trafalgar with his four brothers. All of her uncles, she stated, had been officers either in the British army or the Royal Navy. Her immediate family, however, seems to have been less fortunate, and were in such dire financial straits that at the time of the potato famine in 1845 they left Cork and emigrated to Paris. When Elisa was only 15 she met a French military veterinarian called Xavier Quatrefages. He immediately fell in love with her and asked her to marry him. She was too young to do so under French law and so the couple eloped to England and on June 3 1850 were married by Church of England rites at Folkestone Parish Church.

Shortly after this, Quatrefages was sent to Algeria (a reason, perhaps, for his desire to marry quickly) and although Elisa went with him, within a year the marriage was effectively over. She returned to Paris and tried to earn her living as a teacher of languages: in fact, she embarked on a promising career as a courtesan. She was well-connected socially and had become friendly with Princesse Mathilde, the cousin of the Emperor Napoleon III.

She was introduced to López through José Brizuela, the Paraguayan *chargé d'affaires* in Paris, and they became lovers almost immediately. Had she been free to do so, it is certain that they would have married but she was unable to obtain a divorce from her husband. Under French law he was not legally married at all and since he had no desire to live anywhere else but France, Quatrefages saw no reason to go through a court proceeding simply to oblige Elisa. This was to have severe consequences for her, but nevertheless, her love affair with López was to last for the rest of his life. During that period he had a few minor affairs with various women - Juana Pessoa was not finally discarded until 1865 - but none of them was able to usurp Elisa's position as virtual queen of Paraguay, the lover, confidante and ultimately the only friend of its dictator. Despite her dubious position as official mistress, her impact on the relatively sophisticated *porteños* seems to have been quite as dramatic as it was later on the Paraguayans. She was 19 years old, a graceful, sophisticated blonde at the height of her beauty. Years later, the Argentinean journalist Hector Varela described her in the following extravagant language: 'She was tall and of a flexible and delicate figure, with beautiful and seductive curves. Her skin was alabaster. Her eyes were of a blue that seemed borrowed from the very hues of heaven, and had an expression of ineffable sweetness in whose depths of light Cupid was enthroned. Her lips were indescribably expressive of the voluptuous, moistened by an ethereal dew that God must have provided to lull the fires within her, a mouth that was like a cup of delight at the banquet table of ardent passion. Her hands were small with long fingers, the nails perfectly formed and delicately polished. She was evidently one of those who make the care of their appearance a religion."

In Asuncion, Madame Lynch - the name that she used in Paraguay - was immediately hated by all the women who passed for high society. The López family frowned upon Francisco's liaison, which was obviously far more serious than any of his previous flirtations and the rest of the capital followed their example willingly. Varela, who visited Paraguay in 1856, wrote: "I was struck by the deep dislike and rancour that all the Paraguayan ladies showed towards Mme Lynch because of her handsome physique, superior education, modishness and elegance. Particularly did they resent as mortifying and humiliating to themselves her role in Asuncion. They disliked to think of the even more prominent position which she would occupy when López succeeded his father."

In short, the ladies of Asuncion were jealous of someone who excelled them in all the qualities they held most dear. The men were less critical. Another Argentine journalist said that her home in Asuncion was exceptional for the taste and skill of its interior furnishings. "The luxury, elegance variety and dignity of its furnishings makes its reputation as the rendezvous of foreign visitors understandable. Many of the brasses and porcelains are museum pieces and the French tapestries and Oriental rugs are distributed with excellent taste and in a manner to delight the eye."

Masterman, who considered that her 'evil counsels' were largely to blame for the war which followed, hated her, but even he admitted that in 1862, when he first knew her, she was 'a tall, stout and remarkably handsome woman, although age and the rearing of many children had then somewhat impaired her beauty.' He regarded her as 'clever, selfish and most unscrupulous,' but at the same time admitted that her 'somewhat showy education' enabled her to speak 'English, French and Spanish with equal facility, she gave capital dinner parties, and could drink more champagne without being affected by it than any one I have ever met with.'

The general impression is of a courtesan of more than ordinary accomplishments and beauty - not to mention toughness - and the qualities which she possessed in such abundance were exactly those which one would have expected to impress a man like López, who yearned to emulate the glitter and worldly splendour of the European capitals. She was to be accused of having exploited her position in Paraguay to build up a fortune, of having for her own selfish ends encouraged López to embark on policies that ultimately proved disastrous. There may have been truth in some of this, and one would not expect a courtesan used to the delights of Paris to have gone to such an out of the way place as Paraguay with any reason other than plunder in mind.

Yet there was another side to Elisa Lynch's character. Before and during the war she showed frequent acts of kindness, particularly to the British residents in Paraguay, and although she may have dreamed of becoming the leading lady of a South American version of the Second Empire (after all, the Empress Eugenie was herself only the grand-daughter of a Scottish wine merchant) her affair with López was a genuine love match, rather than a union based on calculated self interest. Years after, when her dreams, whatever they may have been, lay in ruins and Paraguay itself was dying around her, she could have escaped to the safety and relative comfort of Europe. Instead she stayed with her lover and as tragedy closed in she was to behave with a dignity and loyalty that compels admiration.

Like López, she tended to keep her innermost thoughts to herself. Throughout her seventeen years in Paraguay she played a central role, but rarely dominated the centre of the stage. People were in awe of her, and afraid of her, because in her they recognised the power of López. Dr. Stewart wrote years later to his brother in Scotland: 'One never felt at ease in her presence,' and this feeling seems to have been general. Because nobody could ever accuse her of anything definite, they came to see her as an extension of López rather than a personality on her own and probably over-estimated her influence on him. Masterman believed that Mrs. Lynch 'virtually was the ruler of Paraguay,' but it seems on the contrary that she exerted too little rather than too much influence. She was the only person in Paraguay who always kept López's complete confidence, and she did so by shrewdly agreeing with him when it was clear he would tolerate no opposition and only attempting to win him round if a favourable opportunity presented itself. Occasionally she did help those who had fallen from favour, but more often than not she simply abandoned them to their fate.

There can be no doubt at all of Elisa's love for Solano Lopez. She was hated during her lifetime and detested afterwards, but she was never accused of infidelity and she demonstrated her love by providing him with a large healthy family. Their first child, who was christened Juan Francisco Lynch de Quatrefages, was born on the voyage to Paraguay in 1854 and in all they were to have seven children. The second, and their only daughter, was Corina Alicia, who was named after Elisa's sister and mother, was born in 1856. She died the following year and her death must have be a great blow to her mother. By then she knew that the Lopez family would never accept her and she was determined that her child should be given a proper burial. She was placed in an ornate tomb situated in the middle of the main path leading into La Recoleta, the main cemetery in Asuncion. Any one entering the cemetery must go past Corina's tomb and in a way it symbolised Elisa's determination not to be crushed by the hostility surrounding her. On the tomb she had engraved (in English) a short verse by Samuel Taylor Coleridge. It reads:

Ere sin could blight or sorrow fade
Death came with friendly care
The opening bud to Heaven conveyed
And made it blossom there.

Perhaps because the verase was carved bya local stonemason who could not read or speak English, perhaps because Elisa's own memory was at fault, the verse that was carved contains some mistakes. But there can be no doubting the sorrow that Elisa felt at the loss of her second child and only girl.

Other children followed. Enrique Lopez was born in 1858, Federico Noel in 1860, Carlas Marcial in 1861, Leopoldo Antonio in 1862 and Miguel Marcial during the war.

The entrance to La Recoleta, Asuncion's cemetery. The grave in the centre of the path is that of Corina, the only daughter of Eliza Lynch and Solano Lopez.

By 1862, the initial impact of Mrs. Lynch's arrival in South America had passed and the originally favourable impression that Francisco Solano had made upon the Plate republics had faded. The dashing young man of the 1850's with his European sophistication, slowly turned into a vain, ambitious, would-be tyrant, a man to be feared rather than admired and nervously derided rather than praised. In Paraguay itself the excesses which had led to his vicious treatment of Pancha Garmendia and Carlos Decoud had made him dreaded by those who knew him well and this hostility spread to neighbouring countries, particularly as Paraguay's power increased.

Physically López had changed, inheriting from his father a tendency to put on weight that in later years was to make him fat to the point of obesity. Washburn wrote. 'In person he was stout and short. His height was about five feet four, and though always inclined to corpulency, his figure in his younger days was very good. He dressed with great care... his hands and feet were very small, indicating his Indian origin. His complexion was dark, He was proud of his Indian descent, and used frequently to boast of it... Before going to Europe he dressed grotesquely, but his costume was always expensive and elaborately finished. After his return from Europe he adopted a more civilised costume, but always indulged in a gorgeous display of gold lace and bright buttons. He conversed with fluency and had a good command of language, and when in a good humour his manners were courteous and agreeable. His eyes, when he was pleased had a mild and amiable expression; but when he was enraged the pupil seemed to dilate till it included the whole iris.'

The older López grew, the greater became the basic split in his personality, and once his worst side had been seen his good qualities receded into insignificance. George Thompson, the railway engineer who was perhaps the most reliable and impartial eye witness of the Paraguayan tragedy regarded him as 'a monster without parallel' but although he knew López better than any other foreigner except perhaps Dr. Stewart, he confessed that it was not until the end of 1868 that he learned his true character. 'His manner was such as entirely to dispel and throw discredit on any whispers which might be uttered against him,' he wrote, almost apologetically. Martin T. MacMahon, who succeeded Washburn as United States Minister, became a close friend of López, and defended him stoutly on his return to America.

López's vicious nature was generally buried beneath a layer of civilised good manners, which he produced whenever the occasion demanded. Even when angry he rarely raised his voice, and except on extreme occasions never betrayed the slightest emotion. This facade was so well controlled that visitors to Paraguay, who had heard nothing but bad about him were astounded to find him charming and reasonable, the very opposite of what they had been led to expect, and usually came away convinced of the rightness of his cause. Those who had witnessed, or worse still experienced the reverse side of his character could never understand how such people had allowed themselves to be so deceived.

Masterman wrote: 'His manners when he was pleased were remarkably gracious, but when enraged, and I have twice seen him so, his expression was perfectly ferocious. The savage Indian broke through the thin varnish of civilisation as the Cossack shows through the angry Russian....' His anger was the more terrifying because it was so rare and then so well controlled. His sudden manias and the brutality of his vengeance were terrifyingly sadistic, but carried out with an icy calm.

During the last few years of Carlos Antonio's life, the darker side of Francisco's character seems to have become widely known. Carlos Antonio had been grooming his son for the presidency, but it seems that the old man began to have doubts about his son's fitness for the task. According to Washburn, Carlos Antonio's will provided for a triumvirate, and it is possible that at one time he added a codicil nominating Benigno López, his favourite son, as his successor in preference to Francisco.

Illness, old age, and finally death prevented him from making this plan effective. By 1862 he was 69, and his energy was failing. As he lay dying in Benigno's arms, with the British doctors Stewart and Barton beside him, watched by Father Fidel Maiz, the family confessor, he called Francisco to him and warned him against trying to settle Paraguay's outstanding border disputes by force of arms 'particularly with the Empire of Brazil'. It was his last attempt to avert the tragedy that he feared would follow his death, but it made no impact on Francisco.

As soon as he was sure that his father was dead, he seized his private papers, including the will and later announced that, since he had been named vice-president by Carlos Antonio, he was entitled under the constitution to take over the supreme office until Congress could be summoned to elect a new president.

On October 16, Congress met, and a man named Varela, who was reputed to be the richest landowner in the country outside the López family pointed out that under the constitution López was not eligible for the presidency, since a clause said the office could never become hereditary. Nicholas Vasquez, a former foreign minister, overcame this legal quibble nimbly by saying the this merely meant that the presidency could not be handed down from father to son against the will of Congress. Congress, on the other hand, could name anyone it liked.

Varela accepted this explanation, and Congress unanimously proceeded to vote López president for ten years.

He was still not satisfied. Varela was immediately arrested, and a purge of officials and others embarked upon. The chief justice, Pedro Lescaño was jailed and later died in prison, while Benigno López was sent into the interior of the country under house arrest. Father Maiz, generally regarded as one of the most able young Paraguayans, and a man of liberal sentiments was also arrested and thrown into prison.

Two days after the election Doria, the British chargé d'affaires, wrote to Lord Russell, the foreign secretary: 'His Excellency was not free from anxiety, and in conversation expressed to me that his position was one surrounded with difficulties but he hoped to be able to silence his opponents. I heard from a confidential source that Don Benigno, his youngest brother, was the leader of a party against the president who had opposed his election to the presidency."

Many years later, when he was an old man and the events of López's lifetime were a little more than a recurring nightmare, Father Maiz claimed that there had been a plot to limit López's power by reforming the constitution. 'I was acquainted with how he had been humoured with authority from the earliest age.... the young military man, supreme commander in the flower of his youth with the consciousness of his dignity and great zeal for the stability of the public order could scarcely compromise with any idea that might be open to interpretation and neither would he distantly tolerate opposition to himself, much less to the established system of government..'

The conspiracy, if it could be dignified by such a description, was a feeble effort, if it existed at all, but the measures taken to eliminate even potential opposition showed that López aware of his unpopularity in certain quarters, and the insecurity that he felt at the start of his presidency never entirely left him.

All Paraguayans felt isolated, lonely and nervous when they faced the outside world, but López was never completely at ease even within his own borders: arrogant, vain and ambitious, but at the same time suspicious and afraid he sought to strengthen his position by ruthlessly destroying anyone who seemed dangerous. For many Paraguayans, particularly those close to the López family, it must have seemed as though the darkest days of Francia's dictatorship had come back again.

In August, 1863, Washburn wrote to Seward, with prophetic foreboding: 'The lower classes have been indulged in a manner they never dreamed of before, and the fear among many is that this is but a stroke of policy on the part of the president to ingratiate himself with the masses prior to acts of severity against those who have in any way become obnoxious... he evidently desires reputation abroad as well as at home, and he must be aware that he can only get the respect of other people by using his power for the public advantage and prosperity. And yet the people here are full of doubt and apprehension in regard to the future. I trust that what they now fear will never be realised, but from what I have observed I must say that they have reasons for their anxiety and uneasiness, and I fear lest I may have occasion to write another dispatch ere long that will be a dark chapter in the history of Paraguay.'

Chapter 6

The deficiencies of López's character, although ominous, at first only affected the lives of a small minority of Paraguayans, many of whom prepared to leave the country while they still had time. They included men such as J.F. Decoud, another member of that ill-fated family, and the Saquier brothers, Carlos and Fernando, who had once been very friendly with López but later fell into disfavour.

Although this was a symptom of discontent, the vast majority of the population were completely loyal to López, and, looking at it from their point of view rather than that of the upper class exiles, and with a knowledge of the fate awaiting their country, the first years of Francisco Solano's reign can be seen as the culmination of Paraguay's golden age, a brief spell of twenty years at the most during which the Paraguayans were happier, and more contented than any other nation in South America.

What the population of Paraguay was at this stage is still a matter of conjecture, with estimates ranging from around 400,000 to 1,337,449. The latter figure is one of the most frequently quoted, partly because of its apparent precision, partly because it is the largest, and therefore makes the consequences of the war that was to ruin Paraguay seem all the more dramatic. In fact it is wildly inflated - it was the 1859 estimate of a Frenchman commissioned by Carlos Antonio López to write a book extolling the delights of the country - and most authorities favour a much lower total. Sir Richard Burton, who became British consul at Santos in Brazil in 1864 and twice visited Paraguay, estimated the population in 1865 as being 450,000, including 110,000 men between the ages of 15 and 55, and 150,000 between 12 and 60. Masterman selected a round million as his estimate. Dr. Stewart chose 400,000. Gould, the British diplomat who visited Paraguay in 1867, put the total at between 700,000 and 800,000. Edward Thornton, in 1864, was told that the population was 2,000,000, but did not himself believe it to be more than 400,000. Selecting one of these figures (or deciding on a different one) is largely a matter of guesswork, but it seems safe to assume that Paraguay's population in 1864 was probably around 500,000, with a total of 600,000 as the absolute limit.

There is less dispute about the nature of the Paraguayans. All accounts seem to echo Washburn's opinion that they were 'a people the like of which never existed before and never can exist again.' Compared with their neighbours they were remarkably homogeneous. In their physical appearance, the Guaraní element predominated; they tended to have flat faces, round rather than long, and in stature were short and rather squat. Among themselves, particularly in the country areas, they invariably spoke Guaraní, using Spanish only in the city, and then generally only for the benefit of foreigners.

The population of Asuncion, the capital, was about 20,000 in 1864, but no other town had even half this total, and the vast majority of the population lived in the country, particularly in the hills east of the capital. Here the soil was so fertile that when Paraguay was affected by a famine in the 1820s Francia solved the problem by ordering the farmers to plant their crops twice a year instead of once, a practice which had been maintained ever since. The result of the country's renowned fertility was that nobody in Paraguay was really in need, just as nobody was really wealthy (and even if they were, fear of the López family stopped them from any displays of ostentation).

With a climate that was almost perfect - the *viente del norte,* which made people so bad tempered that the murder rate was said to go up when it was blowing, and a south wind that in winter could send the temperatures suddenly tumbling towards freezing point were the only disadvantages. Paraguay was in short a land ideally suited for Lotus Eaters, which is what most of its inhabitants seem to have been. Thompson wrote dryly: 'As to most Paraguayans the idea of the sum of human happiness is to lie down all day on a poncho in the shade and smoke and play the guitar, they may be considered to have been very happy,' as they had little else to do.' Historical factors, such as the deadening influence of the Jesuits, and the general ease of life all tended to make it easier for the government to run the country without disturbance from the people. There were no wealthy landowners, flaunting their riches and making the rest of the people jealous and discontented. There were no *caudillos*, hacking their own private fiefs from the body of the state, or looting *gauchos* to upset the peaceful routine of every day life. There was no famine, and there were no tax collectors to extort money from the poor. For all of these blessings the people could, and did, thank the government. That the government, in return, demanded instant respect and obedience was to most Paraguayans a small price to pay, and something which had in any case been a tradition in the country for longer than anyone could remember. The *porteños* and *Orientales* of the Plate estuary spoke loftily of freedom and the rights of man, and many of them pointed accusingly at Paraguay where such rights were denied. But to the Paraguayans words like freedom, democracy, and liberalism meant, if they meant anything at all, only the anarchy and civil disorders that had prevailed in Argentina ever since the Spanish Empire collapsed.

The idea of disobeying the government simply did not occur to the majority of them and this had social as well as political consequences. 'Probably in no country in the world has life and property been so secure as all over Paraguay during his (Carlos Antonio's) reign', wrote Thompson. 'Crime was almost unknown, and when committed immediately detected and punished.' Masterman, who lived in Paraguay for seven years, only came across one serious crime, when a jealous young man at a dance stabbed a girl and her lover and then immediately gave himself up to the police. Having abandoned the responsibility for running the country to those who wanted to do so, the citizens of Paraguay concentrated on living. Although their intense nationalism made them suspicious of foreigners, they were gentle people, exceptionally hospitable, always offering visitors the best that their house had to offer and refusing to accept any payment. Even the poorest among them seemed to have a grace and charm that made Masterman feel ashamed of the English artisans recruited by Blyth's, many of whom responded to the unaccustomed ease of life in Paraguay by drinking themselves to death. Although the old Spanish customs were still influential, their rigidity had mellowed in Paraguay. Girls went to dances with their mothers, or a *duena* as chaperone, but their vigilance does not seem to have been particularly strict.

Women smoked (cigars) as much as the men, and although they were loyal to their husbands when married, there seems to have been a fairly free and easy attitude towards relations between the sexes beforehand. The foreign residents were all intrigued by the peculiar phenomenon of the *peinetas de oro,* girls of the lower classes whose wealth consisted of golden combs which they wore in their hair. They appeared at the dances and fiestas, were 'tolerably loose in their morals' according to Thompson, but do not seem to have been greatly frowned upon by the rest of society. Even Washburn who was something of a prig admitted that they constituted a very large part of the female community of Asuncion and were less depraved and abandoned than women holding such relations usually are in other countries.' Both Lópezes saw that the people's fondness for enjoying themselves could be exploited, and Francisco in particular arranged fiestas, bull fights, dances and other festivities. These were often arranged to coincide with some national celebration, such as López's birthday, or the anniversary of his accession to the presidency, and the celebrations would frequently go on for weeks; on one occasion the birthday celebrations, which began on July 24, merged with those for his accession on October 16. Elisa Lynch was always the star and chief organiser of these events. When she first arrived in Asuncion she found the women not only smoked cigars but also went to dances and festivals without shoes on. She set out to change this, encouraging the more fashionable ladies to get their gowns from Buenos Aires or Europe, herself setting the style in clothes and etiquette. During the lifetime of Carlos Antonio she was ostracised by many women, but later on, and especially after 1862 Mrs. Lynch became the undisputed leader of society.

The easygoing nature of the Paraguayans, combined with a lack of initiative that was a consequence of their subservience to authority meant that despite the modernising efforts of the López family they were never really efficient. They had to be led, and were not really interested in the projects that were promising to transform their country. This does not mean that they were not happy - rather the reverse, perhaps - and Masterman admitted that 'those who could see nothing of the strings and hand which moved the puppets would have said that the Paraguayans were indeed the happiest of people, and López the greatest and most beneficent of rulers.' But it did mean that the Paraguayans were at the mercy of the man who ruled them. Where he led, they would follow; what he did, they would applaud; those whom he opposed, they would fight. Juan Andres Gelly, who had been Francisco Solano's secretary during his trip to Europe in 1853, summed up his countrymen's character at this period: 'I think he is not gifted with that bold, weak and impetuous courage which provokes and looks for danger and death and is therefore little appropriate for an offensive war. But he has without doubt that serene, immobile intrepidity which sees the danger and death without moving excellent qualities for the defensive, and which put into practice, can be fearful even in the offensive.

'The Paraguayan is firm, constant, tenacious in his intentions; if in that which he begins he is crossed he prefers death, but does not give in or desist; he is insensible to the stimulation and seduction of immoderate wishes... he is on guard through education and the example of his elders against everything that is not of his country, and so submissive to authority that his obedience amounts to the most complete abnegation.'

This was the Paraguayan exactly, as time would prove, but in 1862 nobody could be sure of it since apart from a few border skirmishes Paraguay had not fought a war since 1811, and in the intervening years had shown neither desire nor aptitude for doing so. But within months of López's accession events began to move towards the climax that within two years would enable the cheerful, child-like, peace-loving Paraguayans to prove their talents as soldiers and patriots.

As relations with his neighbours deteriorated, López began to strengthen his grip on Paraguay itself, impelled by the feeling of insecurity that had been with him ever since his father's death. As a result, the carnival air, which had so impressed foreign visitors, began to flag. The celebrations and fiestas became less spontaneous. The police and spy network, which Carlos Antonio had inherited from Francia and moderated, were again strengthened. The Church, which since the time of Francia had always been subject to state interference, was made completely subservient to López's authority. After the death of Bishop Basilio López in 1859 a stopgap replacement named Juan Gregorio

Urbieta was appointed. He died not long afterwards, and López then made one of his cronies, a 35-year-old parish priest of outstanding ignorance called Manuel Antonio Palacios bishop in his place. He proved to be a willing tool, obeying López with a cringing servility even to the extent of adding the secrets of the confessional to the reports of López's extensive spy system. He was, said Washburn, "never accused of a good act," and was believed to have been the man who betrayed Father Maiz and the other men arrested at the time of López's accession.

Although the effects of these actions were not felt widely, Edward Thornton, the British minister in Buenos Aires visited Paraguay in September 1864 and was so shocked at what he saw that he wrote a confidential despatch to Lord Russell, which gave a bleak and depressing picture. 'The government,' he wrote 'has certainly become more tyrannical since [Francisco Solano López] came into power.... the number of spies is immense.... Families are well aware that their servants pay constant visits to the Police Office for the purpose of giving an account of all that passed in their house, and they know that any remonstrance on their part would immediately be followed by false denunciations which might endanger their liberty and expose them to the severest punishments. Even in the presence of their children they dare not give expression to their thoughts.

'The town is filled with police who peer into every house, and at night even interrogate any solitary passer-by as to whom and what he is, whence coming and wither going ... The prisons are filled with so called political prisoners, many of them of the best families.... the most obnoxious of them, Father Maiz, is represented as a man of considerable-talent and was at school with the President to whom he was invariably superior. This man has been kept in confinement ever since, loaded with fetters, and the miserable food which is allowed is thrown to him on the ground. Several ladies, too, who have been banished to distant villages inhabited only by Indians and one unmarried lady so exiled has been forced to live without any shelter but that of a tree.'

The President, Thornton continued, directed everything, to such an extent that it was even necessary to get his permission to marry. 'His Excellency's system,' he wrote, 'seems to be to depress and humiliate; if a man shows a little more talent, liberality of independent of character, some paltry excuse is immediately found for throwing him into prison;

if there be a chance of enriching himself, means are always at hand to impoverish him. With the exception of the President's family no one possesses even a modest fortune, and one of his own brothers who has incurred his displeasure is in vain attempting to get rid of his property at any sacrifice.[23]'

For the Asuncion bourgeoisie, at least, the golden age was nearly over, and even the carefully organised festivities were becoming forced. Thornton wrote sadly: 'The President's birthday was on 24th of July last. Ever since that day [his despatch was written on September 6] the population of Assumption [Asuncion] and many other towns in the Republic have been forced to devote themselves to banquets, balls and other festivities, and the Diplomatic Body and other foreigners are asked to believe that these are spontaneous effusions proving the enthusiasm of the people in favour of the President. A few days ago a Mass was celebrated at the expense of the ladies of the town for the prosperity and welfare of the President, and on the same evening a Ball was given in honour of His Excellency. At the Mass a sermon was preached by the Bishop in which an amount of eulogium and adulation was heaped on the President amounting almost to blasphemy, indeed the adoration due to His Excellency is the principle if not almost the only topic of the preaching of the clergy.

'At the ball speeches were made to the President by several of the Ladies, the flattery contained in which was beyond description. To defray the expenses of these festivities, all classes were called upon to subscribe, even the Political prisoners were not forgotten, and these unhappy men, hoping that by this means their release might be hastened to put down their names for large sums. They too were induced to go through the mockery of having a Mass solemnised, at which they prayed for the happiness of the Chief Magistrate who had condemned them to perpetual misery. No Ladies had the courage to absent themselves from the Ball, two were there whose father had died the day before, but this did not serve to excuse them...'

Thornton's report, a picture of gloom and misery from beginning to end, should be read with some reservations. In the first place, during his brief visit to Paraguay he mixed almost exclusively with the upper class elements in Paraguay - the ones who had suffered most at López's hands and were most hostile to him - secondly, Thornton was himself on bad terms with López, dating back to the time when he had ordered the Royal Navy to seize the *Tacuarí* in 1859, thereby ruining López's moment of glory after his peace mission to Argentina. When he went to Asuncion In 1861 López had treated him with pointed rudeness, and there had been further friction over the López's treatment of a British merchant named Atherton, a friend and business partner of the Saquier's who had been thrown into prison for a while. Thornton also wrote his report at a time when the Paraguayan army had been mobilised, throwing the economy and social life of the country into a state of great upheaval.

But Washburn, who attended the great ball in honour of López's birthday me, recalled years later 'the sad face of a lady who was one of the chorus, as, with a breaking heart, she repressed her tears and forced her tongue to swell the strains in praise of López. Poor woman! Her husband for some cause known only to López had been thrown into prison a few weeks before and loaded with fetters...' Even the poorer classes were by this stage affected, either being called up into the army or else being forced to work on the grandiose building schemes initiated by López and his father, or on projects connected with defence.

By the latter half of 1864 in fact, the structure of Paraguayan life was beginning to creak under the strain of López's ambitions. Paraguay was in many ways a fortunate country, but in other ways was sadly deficient: it had no minerals, except for a little iron and its developing industrial revolution depended entirely on supplies from the outside world. In addition, its manpower was already stretched. If Paraguay was to continue to develop, peace was essential. Instead, López was about to plunge his country into possibly the most catastrophic war ever fought.

Chapter 7

Ever since gaining its independence, Paraguay had been suspicious of its two powerful neighbours, Argentina and Brazil. The Empire still claimed large areas of Paraguayan territory, and in any case its greed for land, worthless or otherwise, was already notorious.

It would have been natural for Paraguay to turn to Argentina, Brazil's traditional enemy, for support, especially since geography already made Paraguay reliant on Argentinean good will for its economic lifeline. Unfortunately, Paraguay was if anything more suspicious of Argentina than of Brazil. The ambitions of the unitarians, and their refusal to recognise Paraguay's independence encouraged the belief that the Argentineans still wanted to absorb Paraguay into a sort of republican Vice-Royalty and although Rosas had been overthrown and Urquiza had recognised Paraguay as independent in 1852, the Paraguayans correctly believed that many Argentineans still nursed the old dreams. Domingo Sarmiento, the provincial who had allied himself with Mitre and the *porteño* liberals, had made his own plans for the future clear, in a book called Argiropolis, published in 1850 while still in exile in Chile. In this he envisaged a federation of Argentina, Uruguay and Paraguay, in which all three would have equal rights, with the capital city being built on the island of Martin Garcia, where the Rivers Paraná and Uruguay joined to form the River Plate. It was full of high ideals and noble sentiments, but it ignored the fact that Paraguay had no wish to form such a union - as had been made clear to Belgrano nearly 40 years before.

Internal problems meant that Argentina could not have put such a project into practice, but many Argentineans still believed in the recreation of the Viceroyalty with as much faith as the Byzantines under

Justinian dreamed of the reconstruction of the old Roman Empire. As late as April 24, 1865, Thornton was reporting to Lord Russell a conversation with Rufino Elisalde, the Argentinean Foreign Minister, in which the latter had told him that one day he hoped to see Argentina, Paraguay, Uruguay and even Bolivia united in a confederation. [24]

López's spy service extended to Buenos Aires, and he was well aware that this ambition still lingered. As early as 1857 he had told Varela, the Argentinean journalist: 'I know that Brazil and you Argentineans covet Paraguay. We have here sufficient means to resist both, but I do not believe in waiting for you to made the attack. It will be I who will make it. In other words, on the first pretext they give me, I will declare war on the Brazilian Empire and the Plate who, if they continue to live in distrust of each other, will have to unite in order to fight.'[25]

Carlos Antonio López was as conscious as his son of the menace of Paraguay's two neighbours, and during his lifetime had shown a spirited resistance to any attempts to seize land which he considered Paraguayan. The difference between him and his son was that Francisco was willing to consider an offensive war. Within weeks of his accession, indeed, he was asking Washburn for details of the American ironclad *Monitor*, which had fought its celebrated action with the *C.S.S. Virginia* on March 9, 1862, and the minister, catching the point quickly, assured him that if he wanted to whip Brazil or any other of his neighbours, the Yankees would furnish him the tools to do it with greater despatch, on more reasonable terms, giving at the same time a more efficient article than could any other nation or people.

López was not actually planning a war, but the fact that he was even considering it was a great deal more than Carlos Antonio had ever done, and this difference in outlook was made all the more serious by the fact that during few the last few years the development of the Paraguayan armed forces had given López the means to embark on such a venture. As long as the delicate balance of power, which had existed in the River Plate, continued, all of this would remain only a distant possibility. But López's attitude meant that should a crisis arise, then Paraguay would no longer automatically remain aloof and in the troubled world of the River Plate such crises had a habit of developing with monotonous regularity.

López's mission to Buenos Aires in 1859, though temporarily successful, had not succeeded in permanently uniting Argentina's squabbling provinces. Buenos Aires, after being given considerable concessions, had rejoined the confederation. In 1860 Urquiza's term of office came to an end, and Santiago Derqui, his own nominee succeeded him as president. Within a few months, however, trouble came again when a revolt in San Juan was put down with brutal force by the Confederation army under Colonel Juan Sáa. The *porteños* were outraged and in 1861 war broke out once again. Urquiza, the most powerful man in the confederation although no longer president, was named commander in chief of its forces, and met Mitre at Pavon in August. The battle was militarily indecisive, but apparently despairing of ever uniting Buenos Aires with the rest of the country, Urquiza withdrew to Entre Rios, leaving Mitre in command of the situation. In 1862 the *porteño* champion was elected president of the Argentine Confederation, with Urquiza's tacit approval, and for the first time for decades the country was united, although the power of the provincial *caudillos* was to cause unrest throughout Mitre's presidency and for many years to come.

The nation that Mitre nominally at least controlled was potentially strong, but its long history of civil unrest had hindered its economic development. Argentina's population in 1864 was around 1,500,000, with perhaps 100,000 of them in the city and 400,000 in the province of Buenos Aires. During the last three decades of the century, Argentina was to make dramatic progress, developing the potential of the pampas, constructing railways, which helped bind the provinces together, and encouraging the immigration of hundreds of thousands of European settlers. But Rosas, preoccupied with political rather than economic matters, had done little to develop the country, so that in the twenty years of his dictatorship the population of the country rose by only 200,000.[26] Wheat and cattle were to be the foundation of the country's future wealth, but the first wire fencing was not introduced to the pampas until 1844.[27] As late as 1865 there were only 373 square miles of tilled land in the whole country,[28] and Argentina still imported grain in 1875[29]. Its first railway, a six-mile stretch running south from Buenos Aires, was not built until 1857[30] and by 1867 there were still only 319 miles completed.

Mitre set about tackling the problems facing the country with energy and determination. A national bank was formed and the most turbulent of the caudillos crushed. Immigration was encouraged, and 100,000 Europeans entered the country during Mitre's six-year term[31]. The 1869 census showed the population to be 1,800,000 of whom 212,000 were foreign born. Trade also increased, from 45,000,000 pesos in 1862 to 72,000,000 in 1868.[32]

As far as Paraguay was concerned, this was not a welcome development. Even when it was most divided, Argentina had refused to give way on the boundary question. Many of its leading politicians still yearned for an even greater Confederation embracing the neighbouring republics and now that the country's internal problems were on the way to being solved the chances of Paraguay forcing a settlement on favourable terms were even more remote. In fact, although Paraguay had to some extent set the pace in modernisation, by the 1860s Argentina was embarking on its own economic revolution and within a few years, no matter what happened, would have forged past Paraguay for the same reasons that had led to the latter's economic and political eclipse in the colonial period. Francisco Solano López could see clearly enough that time was not on Paraguay's side, and that the gap between Argentina and Paraguay could only grow wider. This knowledge was to have some influence on later events: he already half-believed that a war was coming, and he was coming to the conclusion it would be better to fight it sooner rather than later.

By the 1860s, Brazil had also overcome the most pressing of its internal problems, and was embarking on a period of considerable economic growth. The empire sprawled across more than three million square miles of South America, and by 1864 had a population approaching 10,000,000. Its great size meant that the Spanish speaking republics scattered along its borders were constantly nervous of the empire's intentions. Brazilian independence was indirectly the result of French aggression in the Iberian peninsular. In 1808 the Portuguese court was forced to flee to Rio de Janeiro when Napoleon's troops invaded Portugal. They enjoyed Brazil so much that King John VI did not return to Portugal until 1820, leaving his son Pedro to govern in America. He advised that if Brazil demanded independence he should grant it – but should put the crown on his own head. In 1822 Pedro did so, declaring Brazil an independent monarchy with himself its first emperor, Dom Pedro I. His initial popularity soon faded, however, and to save the dynasty he abdicated in 1831 in favour of his five-year old son, who became Pedro II. Throughout Pedro II's minority the country was threatened by a series of provincial revolts, particularly in Rio Grande do Sul, Brazil's most southerly province, where the Farroupo revolt, an independence movement, was not finally crushed until 1845.

After this, the empire's economy began to develop, led by such men as Irineu Evangelista de Souza, Baron Maua, who created a private banking empire and developed roads, railways, ports and other commercial enterprises. Pedro II encouraged these developments.

A handsome man six feet three inches tall, he was studious, kind-hearted and liberal, a bibliophile with a keen interest in science. He admired the constitutional monarchy of England, but in his heart was not really a convinced monarchist at all. He declared on one occasion that he would rather have been president than an emperor, and also stated that had he not been born a monarch he would have been a republican.

Pedro was aware that Brazil had many problems, and many faults, and it would be many years before the society of which he dreamed could ever be created. He rejected a programme of hasty reform, which he believed would prove disastrous to the empire's hard won unity, and instead used his considerable influence behind the scenes, encouraging rather than forcing changes.

Of Brazil's 10,000,000 people, perhaps as many as six million were Negro slaves and only 1,000,000 were whites. Slavery was not nearly so onerous in Brazil as it was in the United States, but it was still bitterly controversial, and was to have an influence on the empire's relations with foreign powers, as well as in internal politics. Pedro was personally opposed to slavery, but saw that immediate abolition would be economically and politically disastrous. Slavery was to be one of the greatest issues in Brazilian politics in the latter half of the nineteenth century, but in the 1860s its full impact was yet to be felt. In general the country had recovered from its internal difficulties and was making steady progress. But like Argentina, even at the height of the civil troubles of the 1840s, Brazil consistently maintained its claims to the

Paraguayan border territories. This was ominous, but no more than that. The most direct threat to the peace of the nations of the Plate came not from the overt ambitions of Brazil, Argentina or Paraguay, but from the continued anarchy that reigned in Uruguay. All three nations had reason to be interested in what was happening there and events determined that all three should become involved in its destinies.

Although Brazil and Argentina had recognised Uruguay as an independent buffer state in 1828, both continued to meddle in Uruguayan affairs. This was made more excusable by the way Uruguayan politicians continually beseeched one power or the other to intervene in the endless feuding and bickering that passed for political life there. By the end of the 1830s these quarrels had taken a fairly definite shape, with one faction uniting behind Fructuoso Rivera, who had been elected President in 1830, the other behind Manuel Oribe, who had succeeded him in 1834. Oribe, while in office, decreed that the army and public employees should wear a white emblem bearing the words Defensores de las Leyes. Rivera's supporters responded by adopting first the pale blue Argentine colours and then, when they found that these tended to fade into white, switched to blood red.

The two factions soon became known simply as Blancos and Colorados. The differences in their policies were less easy to discern. Rivera began a revolt against Oribe in 1836 and the resulting civil strife culminated in the 'Guerra Grande' in which the Colorados were besieged in Montevideo for nine years. In 1851 Urquiza brought it to an end when he defeated the Blancos, Rosas's allies, before moving into Argentina and overthrowing the dictator himself, but the anarchy continued, and the patched-up coalition between the two factions collapsed, largely due to the scheming of Venancio Flores, the Colorado Minister of War. After the lifting of the siege, Brazil had shown its customary interest in Uruguayan affairs, extorting agreement to a treaty which gave her control of the disputed border territories, and granting a loan to the Uruguayan government was guaranteed by Uruguay's customs receipts. In 1854 Brazilian troops were again sent into the country at the request of the government, and with their backing, Flores was able to get the Blancos ousted and himself made president. Within a few months however he had lost Brazilian support and the Blancos, who were backed by Urquiza, resumed control. Flores went into exile in Buenos Aires, where Mitre, an old friend from the days of the siege was Minister of Government and Foreign Affairs. Flores supported him ably at Cepeda and commanded the cavalry at the decisive battle of Pavon, which enabled Mitre to become president of the Argentine Confederation.

Immediately afterwards, Flores wrote to his old friend to remind him of his promise. Mitre was conscious that there was a debt to pay. Unfortunately, the only way he could help Flores to achieve his ambition would be by supporting him in another revolt against the Blanco government headed by Bernardo Berro, an able and moderate man who was trying to end the bitter rivalry of the traditional factions. At the time of Pavon he had abandoned the normal Blanco support for the Argentine federalists and followed a policy of strict neutrality, which Mitre, the beneficiary, recognised and applauded. Yet this was the very man that Flores was asking him to help overthrow.

Mitre endeavoured to get the best of both worlds from this dilemma. The Uruguayan government soon learned that Flores was planning a new revolt, and asked Mitre to put a stop to it. Mitre offered to intern Flores if proof of such scheming could be produced, but when it was, did nothing at all. Thanks to this friendly turning of a blind eye, Flores was able to complete his arrangements and on April 19, 1863 landed at Rincon de las Gallinas with two companions.

Chapter 8

Argentina and Brazil reacted to Flores' invasion cautiously, but not antagonistically. Mitre had his debt of gratitude to pay, and in any case could see definite advantages in having a friendly government in power across the River Plate. On the other hand, he was reluctant to become too closely involved with Flores' operations for fear of upsetting the provincial *caudillos,* who, like Urquiza, still the most powerful man outside Buenos Aires, were generally sympathetic towards the Blanco cause. Mitre was prepared to support his friend behind the scenes - but not at the cost of civil war in Argentina.

Brazil was also slightly favourable to Flores, who had once been their puppet, and might be so again. The Blancos, truculently nationalistic, were generally anti-Brazilian and the Imperial government looked forward to their fall from office with some pleasure. In addition, the Brazilians still yearned for the wide prairies of Uruguay, which had once been Brazil's Cisplatine Province and there were also more recent reasons for taking an interest in Uruguayan affairs. The republic was a favourite refuge for runaway slaves, and its continual anarchy was a constant threat to the neighbouring province of Rio Grande do Sul, which, ever since the Farroupo revolt, had been a cause of anxiety to the Imperial authorities.

By virtue of climate and geography, this province had a great deal in common with Uruguay. Both were cattle producers and the great ranchers of Rio Grande had extensive business interests in the republic - including rustling. There were an estimated 50,000 Brazilians living in Uruguay[33], who claimed the protection of the Empire every time there was a threat of civil disturbance. The government was also urged to take an active role in Uruguayan affairs by men such as General Felipe Netto, the leader of the Rio Grande magnates, who had made a fortune supplying cattle to Oribe during the siege of Montevideo and saw further opportunities for personal enrichment in the present disturbances.

It was traditional enough for Brazil and Argentina to dabble in Uruguayan affairs, and, since both countries were anxious to avert a major crisis, the whole affair might have passed off comparatively smoothly had it not been for the emergence of a new force, eager to take its part in the affairs of the River Plate - the Paraguay of Francisco Solano López.

It was perfectly understandable that Paraguay should be interested in what happened to Uruguay, and López had as much right as Mitre and Pedro II to interfere. Argentina's position astride the River Paraná already meant that Paraguay's link with the outside world was at Mitre's mercy and the continued presence of Urquiza in Entre Rios meant that he would be unlikely to impose the sort of blockade that had been established in the past by Rosas. Like Urquiza and the Argentine federalists, the Paraguayan government had always tended to favour the Blancos of Uruguay rather than the Colorados. The victory of Flores, a pro-Mitre, pro-Brazilian puppet, could only make Paraguay's strategic position worse, since it would give the traditionally anti-Paraguayan forces control of both sides of the River Plate. It was therefore logical that López should regard Flores' invasion as a threat.

The Uruguayan Blancos, conscious of their isolation, had realised the basic similarity of Uruguayan and Paraguayan interests long before the invasion. In March 1863, Dr Juan José de Herrera, the Uruguayan foreign minister, sent Dr. Octavio Lapido to Asuncion to suggest an alliance.

López however hesitated, and was to continue to hedge until it was too late either to save the peace or make an effective alliance with the Blancos, and the manner in which he conducted his diplomacy during the next months indicates that the interests which should have motivated him were perhaps less important than other factors.

López's true ambitions during this period are still a matter for debate, but it is clear that he was thinking not simply of defending his country's legitimate interests, but in actively advancing certain ambitions of his own. Had he been interested solely in protecting Paraguay's rights, he would have concentrated on preserving the status quo. He would have given his support to the moderate Blancos under Berro, tried to win Urquiza to a similar position, and then used the strength that these alliances gave him to force a settlement. If the worse came to the worst, such an alliance would give the Blancos an opportunity of defeating the revolt, for Mitre would have hesitated to continue supporting Flores if it meant taking on Paraguay and a coalition of rebel provinces. But at no time did López make any real attempt to adopt such a course.

Paraguay's neighbours, and many people within Paraguay itself, had been suspicious of López's ambitions long before he succeeded his father as president. It was widely assumed that these involved territorial expansion, and the creation of an enlarged Paraguay with López at its head. This was not such an impossible dream as it might appear to be: the Argentine Confederation was still a fairly loosely-knit organisation, and the provinces along the River Paraná, Paraguay's highway to the outside world, were traditionally hostile to the porteños. Corrientes and Entre Rios, in addition, had historical and cultural links with Paraguay, and in the north of Corrientes many people spoke Guaraní and looked upon the Paraguayans as kinsmen. The bond of common interest between Paraguay and Uruguay has already been mentioned, and some sort of political structure built around these regions could possibly have been created.

More extraordinary was the rumour, widely believed in Buenos Aires and the other capitals, that López ultimately planned to make Paraguay a monarchy with himself as Emperor. In November, 1863 Washburn informed Seward, the Secretary of State, that López had recently told him that Pedro II had advised him to do so, and that he was negotiating with Napoleon III to secure French support for such a step. Masterman, who also believed that López had monarchical ambitions, saw Elisa Lynch as the chief culprit: "She had two ambitions: the first to marry him, and the second to make him the Napoleon of the New World." Others believed that López intended to marry Princess Isabel, the elder of the Emperor Pedro II's two daughters[34], reasoning that a princess of the House of Braganza would carry slightly more weight in the royal circles to which he aspired than the courtesan daughter of an Irish emigrant.

How much truth there was in these rumours is not clear, but the fact that they were so widely believed - and from what is now known of López's ambitions and character were so eminently believable - is an indication of the suspicion about his intentions that existed at that time.

While López may have had a plan for establishing a monarchy at the back of his mind, he never actually did so. Even so, his accession to power was followed by a series of new regulations, which illustrated the vanity and self-esteem that was such a dominant feature of his personality. He began issuing decrees forbidding others to sit when he was standing; he made it known that etiquette now forbade people from turning their backs on him, and as a result dances such as the quadrille had to be rearranged. The tributes of the *Semanario*, Paraguay's only newspaper became so fulsome that they amounted to idolatry. The total impression is of a man whose head was being turned by the absolute power which he had inherited and whose sense of proportion was becoming dangerously distorted. The Flores' crisis had the effect of diverting López's attention from his position in Paraguay to his role in the affairs of the continent as a whole. But his policy bore very little relation to the interests of Paraguay; he had made himself a great figure in his own country, and the sycophantic adulation heaped upon him by his courtiers confirmed his impression that he was destined to shine on an even larger stage. His ambition, in fact, was to play the leading role; the subject of the play was almost unimportant.

López's greatest concern in the months ahead was that the crisis should pass over without Paraguay ending it. It was in this frame of mind that he viewed the progress of Flores' invasion - mindful of his country's interests, but above all desirous of intervening in a way that would bring the greatest possible glory to himself.

The invasion, in fact, was following the established pattern of Uruguayan civil wars. On landing at Rincon, Flores headed straight for the Brazilian border, where the power of the Montevideo government was weakest, and rapidly built up a force of cavalry that enabled him to dominate a large section of the countryside. The government however still maintained firm control over the capital and the larger towns, thanks to its superiority in artillery and infantry. Stalemate soon approached - the same sort of stalemate that had resulted in the nine-year siege of

Montevideo during the time of Rosas. If this was annoying for Flores, it was embarrassing for Mitre, who wanted a swift victory for his *protegé,* so that the whole matter could be forgotten in Argentina as soon as possible. Instead, he found himself gradually being sucked into what had all the makings of another nine-year civil war.

He continued to deny that he was assisting Flores, but it soon became obvious that the Argentine government was offering the rebels more than sympathy. In June 1863 the Blancos seized an Argentine ship in Fray Bentos that turned out to be loaded with arms and other contraband bound for Flores. Only the offer of arbitration by Italy averted war on that occasion, but the secret aid to Flores continued - and continued to be discovered. In November a government expedition surprised 41 rebels and a store of arms and ammunition on an island in the River Uruguay: the Argentine government claimed the island was Argentine territory and another incident arose. Meanwhile Mitre was fortifying the island of Martin Garcia, which lay at the mouth of the Rivers Uruguay and Paraná and was in an excellent position for aiding Flores - and stopping someone like Urquiza from helping the government.

As if this was not enough, the Blancos were also faced with a growing threat from Brazil. Felipe Netto, the Rio Grandense leader, was in Rio de Janeiro, complaining about the way in which Brazilian subjects were being treated in Uruguay, and demanding intervention. He was backed by Baron Maua, the financial genius who had also been born in Rio Grande, and their campaign, together with the old Brazilian ambitions for Uruguay, soon began to have an effect. When the Uruguayans protested against the fortifications on Martin Garcia in December 1863, the Brazilians shrugged and did nothing. The government which met in January, 1864 was dominated by Liberals, the more jingoistic of Brazil's two main parties, and Zacharias y Goes, the prime minister was unable to resist the pressure on him to take action on behalf of the 50,000 Brazilian exiles now said to be suffering at the hands of the savage Blancos. Ostensibly to stop aid reaching Flores, the army was sent to the Uruguayan border.

At this point, with pressure building up from three sides President Berro's term of office came to an end. He had proved to be a moderate of considerable ability, and had there been no invasion the bitter divisions of Uruguayan politics might have been ended. But he was succeeded in March by Atanasio Aquirre whose policy was based on winning the alliance of the federalists of Argentina - and above all, of López of Paraguay.

In May, the Brazilian government finally bowed to the pressure of Netto and the Rio Grande party, sending José Antonio Saraiva to Montevideo to demand reparations for damages inflicted on Brazilian settlers and ask for guarantees for the future. Since the country was convulsed by civil war the government was clearly in no position to give any such assurances, although the demands were backed up by the arrival of a squadron of five ships under the command of Vice Admiral Joaquim Marques Lisboa, Baron de Tamandaré.

Like Argentina, in fact, Brazil had slowly lurched into a position from which war was only a short distance away, and although the Blancos were still successfully holding Flores' forces, their position was daily growing more precarious. In their isolation, they saw in López the knight in shining armour who would come to save them from the dragon of Brazil, and they redoubled their efforts to win him over.

Throughout 1863 López had rejected Blanco offers of an alliance, but he had shown himself to be not uninterested in the developments in Uruguay by ordering a general mobilisation in February 1864. The Paraguayan army at the end of Carlos Antonio's life was already the largest in South America: López's mobilisation, which called upon all the available reserve units, more than doubled it.

Within weeks 30,000 men were training at Cerro Leon, a vast camp in the hills east of Asuncion, 17,000 were at Encarnacion, on the Paraná, 4,000 at the capital, 3,000 at Concepcion, half way up the River Paraguay between Asuncion and the Matto Grosso border, and a further 10,000 at the key fortress of Humaitá. The total force amounted to 64,000 men, a huge total in relation to the population of Paraguay and one that was achieved only by calling to the colours almost every available man - many of them, even at this stage, grandfathers or children. It put a great strain on Paraguay's resources, and from a purely logistical point of view was a mistake. Even more serious was the simple fact that it existed: López, obsessed with dreams of playing a great role in the world was probably at this point thinking of repeating his 1859 success as an arbitrator. But once the army was formed it proved to be a constant invitation to play an even more active role.

This mobilisation encouraged the Blanco extremists - it showed that Paraguay had the ability to help them, even though the desire to do so was still lacking - and in May 1864 Herrera sent José Vazquez Sagastumé to Asuncion as new minister, with instructions to emphasise the common danger threatening the two republics. In June, with López still hesitant and Brazil's demands still unmet, Sagastumé formally asked López to mediate between the two powers. This was the moment that López's vanity had been waiting for - a chance once again, to juggle with the destinies of nations - and on June 17 he sent a messenger to Brazil to announce that he had accepted. Unfortunately events had already overtaken him.

Some weeks before, Thornton, the British minster in Buenos Aires, had been asked to accompany Rufino Elisalde, the Argentine foreign minister, to Montevideo to try to ease the strained relations between the two countries. Once in Montevideo, however, the two men began trying to settle the differences between the Blancos and Colorados - the cause of the whole crisis. After some hesitation, Herrera and Aguirre agreed to negotiate and on June 10 decreed an amnesty to the rebels as a sign of good faith. On June 16 Elisalde and Thornton met Flores at Monzon, 120 miles from the capital and found him so convinced that he could not win the civil war that he too agreed to a compromise. It seemed, therefore, that peace was assured and López's offer of arbitration was not needed. With some relief, since the last thing the Brazilians, Argentineans and Flores wanted was the intervention of Paraguay, López's offer was politely declined. This refusal, however justified by events, infuriated López, who regarded it as a personal snub. The result was that he lost interest in arbitration as a means to personal glorification and from this point on began actively to consider war.

In this he was encouraged by the extreme wing of the Blanco party, notably Antonio de las Carreras, the most militant of all, a fanatic who had been responsible for the massacre of Cesar Diaz and his men in 1858. Carreras and his supporters were utterly opposed to any compromise, and in the face of their opposition, Aguirre rejected the proposals that could have ended the civil war and brought the long crisis to an end. Saraiva, who had joined Elisalde and Thornton in their peace making efforts, offered Aguirre armed support against the extremists, but on the evening of July 6 Aguirre refused to appoint the suggested moderates to his cabinet, and appointed one that consisted entirely of extreme Blancos.

This virtually meant the end of the peace mission that had once seemed to be on the brink of success, and the whole affair had served only to make matters worse. Flores was determined to continue the fight, the Blancos had decided to bank everything on López coming to their rescue, López himself was contemplating salving his injured pride in the balm of war - and on July 11 Saraiva met Mitre and for the first time suggested a joint Argentine-Brazilian intervention on behalf of Flores.

Because of the situation within Argentina, Mitre would not agree to this, but he did make it clear that he would not object to Brazil acting alone. This was just the assurance that the Brazilian war party had been waiting for, for with an army on Uruguay's northern border and a fleet in the harbour of Montevideo, the Empire was prepared in every other way. On August 26 the Uruguayan ship *Villa de Salto*, taking supplies to the town of Mercedes, which was besieged by Flores, was forced to turn back by Tamandaré's squadron, and the Uruguayan government promptly retaliated by expelling the Brazilian minister. On September 14, Brazilian advance guards crossed from Rio Grande into Uruguay.

This action was taken with the knowledge of Mitre, but it completely ignored López. Carreras, who had been hammering home the old Blanco theme of the threat to Paraguay from Brazil and Argentina, did his work so well that on August 30 Berges, the Foreign Minister, sent the Brazilian minister Vianna de Lima a note in which Paraguay disclaimed all responsibility for what would happen if Brazil were to invade Uruguay. Berges' note was followed up by hints that it was the composition of the Uruguayan government that prevented more open support.

Carreras dashed back to Montevideo on August 28 with this welcome piece of information, and succeeded in bringing down Herreras, who was still hoping for peace. He took his place as foreign minister, and took on the additional responsibilities of minister of finance and minister of war and marine - a mixed bag that emphasised the dominant position he now held in the government of his country. On October 16 the

Brazilians showed their opinion of the Paraguayans by ordering their main army to cross the border and go to the aid of Flores.

But still there was no formal protest, no move against the invaders by Paraguayan troops. Outwardly, relations between Brazil and Paraguay were the same as ever, and on November 9 the 300-ton steamer *Marques de Olinda* arrived at Humaitá on her way to Matto Grosso. The steamer belonged to the Brazilian steamship company that under the agreement of 1858 had been allowed to operate a service of eight sailings a year from Rio. On board was Carneiro de Campos, the new governor of Matto Grosso. Two days later she arrived at Asuncion, took on coal, and at 2pm resumed her journey. Everything still appeared to be normal and there is no reason to believe that at this stage López was at all worried by what appeared to be a routine voyage by the Brazilian ship. But Sagastumé knew that something was different and he hurried to Cerro Leon, where López was busy training his army, to pass on the news. He had learned from agents that the *Marques de Olinda* was loaded with a cargo of arms and ammunition.

This was the worst possible news for López. He was already fearful of developments in the River Plate, which threatened to turn into war at any moment. The last thing he wanted was to see the Matto Grosso turned into an armed camp, with a well-armed garrison ready to attack from the north whenever they were ordered to do so. He decided to act. That evening the *Tacuarí* left in pursuit of the Brazilian vessel. The next day she was intercepted 150 miles above the capital and brought back to Asuncion in triumph on the 13th. To give this piratical action some semblance of legality, Berges sent Vianna de Lima a note dated November 12 which said that Paraguay was acting in accordance with the measures outlined in the note of August 30, and that diplomatic relations were broken off.

For better or worse, war had come to Paraguay.

Part 2:

Humaitá

Chapter 9

During the diplomatic manoeuvrings that preceded the attack on the *Marques de Olinda* López had suffered several set-backs: his offer of arbitration had been turned down, and he had seen Brazil and Argentina, the two arch-rivals, come to an agreement which gave Brazil a free hand in Uruguay. Even so, his position was still fairly strong, and his support for the Blanco government, however hesitant, had established him in most eyes as the champion of the Spanish-speaking republics against Brazil. It is difficult to disagree with the opinion that "had López chosen to go directly to the aid of the Blanco government, he would have been acclaimed a hero, a defender of the Plate provinces against the hated Lusitanian neighbours."[35]

Had he done so he could have carried others with him: ever since Cepeda, López had been on good terms with Urquiza, and they had been corresponding closely since Flores' invasion. It was in the interests of both to prevent him from gaining power, and Urquiza was certainly opposed to anything that would put Uruguay under the control of Brazil. It was believed, with reason, that this was still a Brazilian ambition and on September 19, James Watson Webb, the United States minister to Brazil wrote to Seward about a visit from "a gentleman connected with the government who manifestly came for no other purpose than to enquire of me what the government of the United States would think of the conquest and annexation of Uruguay."[36] Any Paraguayan intervention, moreover, would prove acutely embarrassing to Mitre, who would find it difficult to support Brazil without splitting the Confederation.

From a military point of view, an immediate retaliation might have been López's best bet. The Blancos still had considerable military strength, but obviously the intervention of Brazil had swung the balance heavily against them, and it was only a question of time before they defeated. It was therefore in López's interests to go to their aid sooner rather than later.

While López delayed, Flores acted. Although he was at first reluctant to accept Brazilian aid, the impossibility of winning without it soon persuaded him to arrange concerted operations with Tamandaré, who directed Brazil's operations in Uruguay after the return of Saraiva to Rio in September. This co-operation soon achieved results. On November 28 the town of Salto on the River Uruguay surrendered to a Brazilian army under Brigadier Joao Propicio Mena Barreto, and the next month 12,000 Brazilians and Coloradores united in an attack on Paysandu, another town on the River Uruguay, and the only Blanco stronghold left in the west of the country. With a population of 9,000,[37] Paysandu was a comparatively large town and its importance was made greater because its garrison of 1,900 men. It was commanded by Leandro Gomez, an extreme Blanco. All South America watched the epic that began to unfold, the vast majority willing Gomez to hold out, anxiously waiting for the Paraguayans to arrive. The mistake they all made was to assume that López was going to arrive at all.

The reasons for López's failure to aid the Blancos at Paysandu were, as usual, complex. One factor was his lack of interest in the Blanco cause as such. The second reason was more down to earth. López knew that Paraguay was not prepared for war.

The strength of the Paraguayan army in 1865, like the population of Paraguay itself, is still a matter of debate. Contemporary estimates range from around 50,000 to 100,000 officers and men. Thompson, the most reliable witness of the military aspects of the war, put the figure at 80,000 but even this seems rather too high. Modem opinion tends to put the total at around 60,000. Even so, this total still represented a formidable army that outnumbered the combined forces of the three Allies. But unlike its enemies, the Paraguayan army in the first year of the war was at its peak, and had been formed only by ruthlessly stripping the country's farms and industries of their available manpower.

Once the guns began firing and the soldiers began to fall the total began to decline, for the reserves of manpower were never sufficient to fill the gaps in the army's ranks. Even before the war broke out, 6,000 men had died during training[38], partly because of the severity of army discipline, partly because the sudden withdrawal of the labour force put the Paraguayan economy on the verge of collapse. In civilian life the men ate maize, mandioc and oranges, but in the army the staple food was meat, since beef cattle did not require much attention and could be moved easily when the army was on the march. This sudden change in diet led to severe health problems, particularly dysentery, enteric fever and diarrhoea. In fact, the army began dwindling away before the war had even started, and the total of 60,000 men that existed in late 1864 represented a peak that was never reached again.

Although the army had for long held a central position in the Republic's hierarchy - even judges were obliged to take off their hats to ensigns - Paraguay had no real military traditions. Apart from a few border clashes with the Brazilians and Argentineans and Francisco Solano López's march into Corrientes in 1845, the army had done nothing since the battle of Tacuarí more than fifty years before. Consequently, there were no officers with experience of practical soldiering and no one could really tell what would happen when they came up against the enemy.

The officers themselves had all risen from the ranks, and their promotion was generally based on ability rather than family connections: in fact, government policy, with its anti-aristocracy bias, had actively discouraged the formation of an exclusive officer class and until 1866 there were no officers in the army with a rank higher than colonel. Even after that promotions tended to be handed out meagrely. Relations between officers and men had a paternalistic and idiosyncratic quality. The men would salute by standing rigidly to attention, cap in hand. They referred to their superiors as "My father", while López himself was known as *Taita guasu* or *great father.* The officers never returned salutes, and called their men "my son."

In view of the penalties involved it is a wonder that any offences were ever reported, but when punishment was administered, which presumably was often, it was never resented The soldiers accepted everything with their customary resignation, never protesting, rarely questioning the rights or wrongs of the decision that led to it. "A Paraguayan never complained of an injustice and was perfectly content with whatever his superior demanded," wrote Thompson. "If he was flogged he consoled himself by saying 'If my father did not flog me, who would?'"

About 40,000 of the men were in the infantry, which was composed of 48 battalions each containing about 800 to 1,000 men[39]. Most battalions had six or more companies with 120 men in each. The 40th Battalion, for example, which was recruited in Asuncion, had 1,050 men at this stage,[40] who were said to include the cream of the capital's society. The 6th and 7th Battalions, which had taken part in the Matto Grosso campaign, were veteran units, who had spent several years working on the railway line to Paraguarí.

The cavalry, numbering between 10,000 and 15,000 men, was divided into regiments arranged in four squadrons of 100 officers and men. Generally speaking, a lieutenant would command a regiment. The cavalry's chief weakness lay in its horses. There were about 100,000 of them in Paraguay at this time, but many of them had a spinal disease which prevented them from galloping more than two or three miles.

The artillery had between 300 and 400 guns. The horse artillery had four batteries of six guns, and the other guns were used in the field, while heavier pieces were installed at Humaitá and other fortifications. All three sections wore uniforms consisting of red blouses *(camisetas)* and white trousers and all except the senior officers went barefooted. The army had no separate transport command and each unit was supplied with bullock carts and was responsible for its own movements.

The medical staff was headed by Dr. Stewart and the senior doctors were all British. They were a devoted team, but the facilities with which they were provided proved hopelessly inadequate. Drugs were running out even before the war began, and the majority of Paraguay's losses were due to lack of treatment and general physical debility and the lack of salt and vegetable food in particular cost thousands of lives. Pay was also something of a rarity: it ceased completely once the war began and during the entire struggle the men had to make do with three 'gratifications' each equal to about one month's money.

Despite its size, therefore, the Paraguayan army had many weaknesses, most of them as yet still hidden, but all important. It was a tragic coincidence for the isolated Republic that the crisis had arisen at a time when arms and armament were changing more rapidly than at any time since the invention of gunpowder, a situation which was entirely to the Allies' advantage. Had the war been fought ten years earlier both sides would have been equipped with weapons similar to those carried at Waterloo; ten years later, they would have fought with equipment not very different from that used at the battle of the Marne. As it was, Paraguay had to make do with the former, while the Allies were able to arm themselves with the latter.

López himself was fully aware of this weakness. He developed into an ingenious and resourceful commander, with a far quicker grasp of the potential of the modern weapons being introduced in the 1860s than any of his opponents. Max von Versen, the Prussian observer, said that he saw the implications of the Dreise needle-gun more quickly than anyone else in South America[41]. His interest in the clash between the *Merrimack* and *Monitor* has already been noted, and during and after his trip to Europe he made several unsuccessful efforts to import modern weapons. During 1864 he commissioned the Prussian Fischer von Truenfeld to construct a telegraph from Asuncion 240 miles south to Humaitá and Paso de la Patria on the Paraná opposite Corrales with the result that the Paraguayan war was the second in history in which the telegraph was used. López's extraordinary vacillation in the months leading up to the war was partly prompted by his knowledge of Paraguay's military weakness. In the early 1860s he ordered a number of modern armoured warships from yards in Europe and he was hoping that they would arrive before war broke out. In this he was to be disappointed.

As far as the infantry were concerned, the ones who had guns of any sort were in the minority. Thompson estimated that at least half the men carried only knives and lances. Masterman said that only forty per cent were armed with muskets. Four battalions carried smooth-bore muskets with percussion locks and three Witton rifles but the remainder were armed with old flint-lock muskets, some German, most of them Brown Besses still bearing the Tower of London mark. These weapons, which had been used by, the British army throughout the Napoleonic Wars, could kill a man at 500 yards, but they were so inaccurate that the effective range was only 100 yards.

Rifling the barrel improved the musket's performance, although early rifles took longer to load and were not used by line regiments during the Napoleonic Wars. In the 1840s experiments by the French Captain Claude Etienne Minié led to the general adoption of a conical bullet which expanded under the impact of firing, filling the grooves inside the barrel so tightly that none of the propellant gas was wasted in 'windage', the gap between the projectile and the inside of the barrel. The result was an increase in velocity and accuracy that tripled the effective range of the weapon and completely outclassed the musket.

The Springfield and Enfield rifles, both derivatives of the Minié, were used extensively in the American Civil War and had an effective range of up to 600 yards, although they could kill at 1,000. At 200 to 300 yards the rifle was generally deadly. Weapons of these types were introduced into the Brazilian army before the Paraguayan War broke out and meant that the Allied infantry had a weapon that could shoot accurately at more than three times the range of the Paraguayan smoothbores. Some of them, moreover, were Prussian-made Dreise needle-guns, Spankers and other breech-loading models, which could be reloaded lying down. The Paraguayans had to load their muskets with a ramrod, which could only be done properly standing up and exposed to enemy fire. Breech-loaders also had a far higher rate of fire than muskets - the Spencer, for example, carried eight shots, and during a test its inventor fired at a rate of 21 shots a minute.

This quality gap also applied to the artillery. The vast majority of the Paraguayan guns were smooth-bore muzzle loading guns so old that Burton thought that most of them resembled streetposts, and, he noted with amazement, that one gun found at Humaitá had been cast at Seville in 1681 and another in 1684. Most of them, Thompson said, had originally been taken to Paraguay as ships' ballast.

Ten years before this would not have been a serious weakness since the design of cannon had not greatly changed since the seventeenth century. As an example, during the American Civil War, which ended four days before the Paraguayan attack on Corrientes, the standard field gun used on both sides was the 12 pounder muzzle-loading smooth bore. This weapon, the 1857 'Napoleon' 12 pr, was lighter but otherwise very similar to the field guns used in the Napoleonic wars and its maximum effective range, using solid spherical shot weighing 12.30

pounds was about 2,000 yards. The range fell off rapidly when different projectiles were used. Explosive shell, which was lighter, carried less than a mile. Spherical case, a shell containing 78 musket balls (also known as shrapnel) was used at ranges between 500 to 1,500 yards. When firing against troops at point blank range - 350 yards and less - the gunners switched to canister, a metal container holding 27 cast iron balls weighing .43 ounces, the overall effect being like a giant shotgun. The smoothbore was in many ways a crude weapon. Powder was inefficient; the shot did not fit completely tightly in the barrel - otherwise it could not have been loaded - and consequently much of the propulsive force of the explosion was lost in 'windage'. None of them had an effective range of much more than 3,000 to 4,000 yards, and the fuses and sights available at the time further reduced their effectiveness.

In such a context the Paraguayan army's artillery would not have been unimpressive. Its best weapons were 48 8-inch guns weighing 65 cwts, which were similar to the 68-pr guns still being used by the British army. These could fire solid shot a maximum of 3,250 yards and although the firing cycle normally took two minutes, in an emergency they could fire ten rounds in eight minutes. Other weapons included 100 guns ranging from 24 to 34prs, and between 150 and 200 smaller guns whose calibres ranged from 2 to 12prs. In addition, one of the horse artillery batteries was armed with steel rifled 12prs, and another rifled 12pr was installed on one of the gunboats. But apart from the latter weaponry, all of these guns were obsolete when the war began.

It was not until the middle of the nineteenth century that industrial techniques improved sufficiently to enable engineers to introduce rifling and breach loading in artillery. Not surprisingly, the impetus came mainly from the Crimean War.

In 1854 a Tyneside civil engineer named William Armstrong introduced a 3pr rifled breech-loading gun made up of thin wrought iron layers shrunk on to an inner tube. This was technically a great advance on earlier guns, which had been made of cast iron, since it enabled more powerful explosive charges to be used. The rifling principle was equally important, since it resulted in greater accuracy and longer ranges. Another engineer, John Whitworth, was also working on ways of improving artillery, and devised a breech-loading gun with a hexagonal bore that fired a mechanically fitting projectile. Both guns were tested in Britain in the late 1850s, and during that period the principles of rifling and breech loading, were established. Similar experiments were being made in Germany, with the Krupp gun and in France, where the rifled La Hitte was adopted.

Because the mechanisms tended to be cumbersome, breech loading did not increase the rate of fire of these early rifled weapons, but the rifling and strength of the barrel soon resulted in dramatic improvements in performances. A rifled Whitworth 12pr, for example, could fire a shell up to six miles and it and the Armstrong were said to be more than fifty times more accurate than the standard British smoothbore at 1,000 yards. By the 1860s Whitworth and Armstrong guns were being built that were capable of hurling projectiles of 150 pounds, with far greater force than smoothbores of similar calibre, because windage was greatly reduced.

These guns were far from perfect. Nevertheless their performance was far superior to that of any of the smoothbores used by the Paraguayans, and they were, of course, readily available to the Allies. In March 1864, the Brazilian government purchased its first ten Whitworth guns and during the next few years bought hundreds more, as well as Krupp and La Hitte guns. Paraguay's geographical position meant that if a war broke out with Argentina or Brazil, it was almost certain that the River Paraná would be blockaded and Paraguay would be cut off from the outside world. The longer a war lasted, the ability of Paraguay's enemies to buy arms abroad meant that this gap in weaponry would inevitably increase.

But the enemy's biggest advantage lay in manpower. None of the Allies was fully prepared for war - except possibly Uruguay - but their potential superiority was enormous. The Brazilian army in 1864 consisted of 16,834 officers and men, most of them stationed in the threatened province of Rio Grande. It was organised into 22 battalions of 800 men each, and its composition reflected the many races that made up the Empire. Generally the cavalry were whites, mostly from Rio Grande, while the rank and file infantry were Negroes, mulattos or *mestizos*, many of them descended from slaves. In addition to the regular troops there were about 200,000 men in the Guarda Nacional, a semi-police force that was not allowed by law to serve outside the province in which it was raised. This technicality however could be circumvented without difficulty and when a call for volunteers was issued in January 1866 the Guarda represented a considerable pool from which soldiers could be recruited.

The Guarda was also able to take over normal duties from regular units. Although Brazil's population including several million Negro slaves, who would not normally have taken part, in November 1866 the government granted freedom to any who volunteered for the war, thereby tapping another source of manpower for the armies. A further temptation, under the decree of January 1865, was a grant of land to volunteers. Thanks to these measures, and the initial patriotic enthusiasm for the war, the Brazilian authorities received more volunteers than they could cope with, and although this enthusiasm soon died away, the Brazilian army more than tripled in strength during 1865.

López was fully aware of the odds against him. As late as October 1864 he had instructed Bareiros, his agent in Europe, to ask Lord Russell, the British Foreign Secretary, for permission to buy an ironclad warship in England (nothing came of this) and during the next few months shipments of weapons and ammunition increased. Knowing that war would probably result in at least a temporary blockade he wanted to get as much equipment as possible before it was clamped down.

It was this desire for weapons and ammunition cattle that prompted López's next move, which otherwise is almost inexplicable. For while Gomez at Paysandu was hanging on in the expectation of imminent help from the Paraguayans, López struck in the opposite direction - at the inviting vastness of the Brazilian province of Matto Grosso.

The Matto Grosso covered an enormous area of jungle, mostly unexplored, and had a population of 90,000 concentrated in a few small towns long the River Paraguay and its tributaries. It was 1,500 miles to the east coast, where Rio and the other chief towns of Brazil were situated, and by land convoys of pack-animals and carts usually took up to three months to complete the journey. Consequently, the only practical route was by river, which meant going through Paraguayan waters. Both the Brazilians and the Paraguayans were aware of the province's vulnerability to an attack from the south and over the last few years the Brazilian government had taken steps to improve its defences by sending in considerable quantities of arms. It was the presence of these weapons that chiefly interested López, although he probably also saw an opportunity to remove the threat of an attack from the rear.

Colonel Francisco Isidoro Resquín, who visited the province in the guise of a Paraguayan planter[42], had surveyed the best means of approach earlier that year, and preparations for an invasion had been going on ever since the seizing of the *Marques de Olinda.* On December 14, 3,000 men under the command of López's brother in law Colonel Vicente Barrios left Asuncion on five steamers escorted by three schooners, while Colonel Resquín led 2,500 cavalry and a battalion of infantry overland from Concepcion to seize a number of small villages near the Paraguayan border.

This two-pronged attack proved highly successful. On December 26 Barrios' flotilla anchored at a point three miles below the fort Coimbra and demanded its surrender. Portocarrero, the Brazilian commanding officer, refused and after a bombardment the Paraguayans attacked the next day. This was an expensive failure but during the night Portocarrero and his troops abandoned the fort, leaving; all their stores behind - an action which resulted in his arrest when he reported to his superior officer. From Coimbra, the Paraguayans moved on to the abandoned towns of Albuquerque and Corumba, the capital of the province, taking 23 cannon and considerable supplies of ammunition.

Resquín, meanwhile, was enjoying an almost leisurely promenade through the border country, capturing the outpost of Dourados on December 29 and the village of Miranda on January 12. The Paraguayans left small garrisons in the major towns and returned to Asuncion with their plunder, the rigging of their ships decorated with the ears of Brazilian sailors killed on board a steamer captured during the campaign.

From the view of material, the whole affair had been a stunning success. A total of 67 brass guns, was sent down to Asuncion, but even more important were the enormous stocks of gunpowder and ammunition. The Matto Grosso, Thompson said, provided Paraguay with "almost all the stores it consumed during the war".

The only disturbing feature about the campaign was that it had done nothing at all to help the Blancos of Uruguay. Indeed, by the time the heroes of the Matto Grosso returned to Paraguay the war in Uruguay had come to a bloody and dramatic close. Throughout December, Gomez and his dwindling band had been holding the Brazilian and Colorado forces at bay with a heroism that aroused the admiration of thousands of neutral Argentineans. The defenders of Paysandu became symbolic figures in what was regarded by many as a straightforward Spanish-Portuguese clash of the traditional type - which, since Flores' contribution consisted only of 600 men, was not very wide of the truth. The Entre Rianos could watch the whole thing from the other side of the river, and the refugees had already spread the story of the town's suffering across Uruguay and Argentina. Mitre found himself under increasing pressure to intervene, and although Urquiza managed to restrain his followers, several Entre Rianos, including his son Waldino, crossed the River Uruguay to join the Blanco cause.

However, the help that came was not enough, and the failure of López to march meant the end of Paysandu. On January 2, 1865, after a bombardment lasting 52 hours, Gomez was finally forced to surrender. At his own request he was handed over to the Colorado contingent as a prisoner of war and promptly murdered by an enemy officer, apparently to avenge an old insult to the officer's mother[43].

This atrocity roused the anti-Brazilian feeling in the Litoral provinces to fever pitch and although the fall of the town was militarily a serious blow, it gave López an opportunity for an intervention that would have made him the champion of Spanish America, and would have given him the support of several Argentine provinces. Urquiza although unwilling to take the lead in backing the Blancos, told Sir Richard Burton later that, had López struck at this time, he would have joined him.. This would not only have given López a secure base from which to operate, but would have gained him the support of several thousand skilled cavalrymen. At the same time, Mitre would have found it even more difficulty to take action against them, since the murder of Gomez was being blamed on the Brazilians and an intervention in their favour would have been regarded as an act of treachery against his own race.

For the moment, therefore, and in spite rather than because of his own diplomatic skills, López was in a position to safeguard his country's interests and achieve the personal glory that he craved, at a minimum of risk. With almost unbelievable folly, he proceeded to throw the opportunity away.

In a sense, the key figure in the situation immediately after the fall of Paysandu was Mitre. Paraguay and Brazil were at war, certainly, but the course of that war depended largely upon the attitude adopted by Argentina, since the only effective way the belligerents could attack each other was by crossing Argentine territory. The Paraguayans' most obvious move was to attack the Brazilians in Uruguay or Rio Grande, but the first would mean crossing the provinces of Corrientes and Entre Rios, and to accomplish the second the Paraguayans would have to cross the disputed Misiones territory.

During and immediately after the siege of Paysandu López could have probably managed either without bringing Argentina into the war against him, but as the weeks passed the memory of Gomez's murder faded. López's delay left the field clear for Brazil whose negotiations were in the capable hands of José Maria da Silva Paranhos, probably the greatest statesman of the empire, who had been sent to the Plate late in December 1864 to take over from the bungling and undiplomatic Tamandaré.

His aims were as clear-cut as López's were vague: to win Argentina over to an alliance with Brazil and Flores, and to end the Uruguayan civil war as soon as possible. Although still reluctant to make his country a vassal of the Empire, Flores saw that he needed the Brazilians to win final victory. At the end of January he signed a treaty of alliance by which he agreed to join Brazil in the war against Paraguay and pay compensation for losses suffered by Brazilian citizens in Uruguay.

Carreras and the Blanco die-hards were by this stage almost beyond reason. Lettsom, the British minister in Montevideo, believed that Carreras was 'as mad as any patients in Bedlam,[44]' and Carreras told him that the Blancos intended to blow up the city of Montevideo and die in the ruins rather than surrender. Fortunately for Montevideo, Aguirre's term of office was due to expire on February 15, and despite the intimidation of the Blanco fanatics, the government's military leaders, who knew the situation was hopeless, gave their support to Thomas Villalba, a moderate who immediately got in touch with Flores to negotiate a settlement. By its terms Flores took over the government and an amnesty was granted to all except the extreme Blancos, most of whom fled to Entre Rios. The relatively amicable end of the civil war was a considerable relief to Paranhos, who feared that the bloodbath that Carreras had been planning would have resulted in the Spanish republics finally declaring war against the Empire. The triumph of Flores was similarly gratifying to Mitre who had been doing his best to cool the anti-Brazilian tempers of his countrymen for the past few months.

Meanwhile, López had finally decided to act. At the end of January he sent an envoy named Luis Caminos to ask Mitre for permission for Paraguayan forces to cross the province of Corrientes "in case this country is compelled to such a course by the operations of the war in which she is engaged with the Empire of Brazil." Of all the possible moves open to López, none could have played more completely into Mitre's hands than this request. All he had to do was to say no - which was done on February 9 - and López was at once converted from the champion of Spanish America to the potential destroyer of the Argentine Confederation. Urquiza, who knew of López's plans before Mitre, tried to suggest that the action proposed would not be as serious as it appeared, but the request, as Mitre pointed out, would have led to an Argentine province becoming a battlefield between two foreign powers, a situation that no self-respecting government could condone.

What made the request even more absurdly tragic was that it was not even necessary. Paraguay did not need to cross Corrientes to reach Rio Grande do Sul and as Washburn, whose observations during these months were far shrewder than his subsequent activities would indicate, wrote: 'If instead of asking permission of Mitre to send troops across the Misiones he (López) had actually done so there would have been no other result than a long diplomatic correspondence. The people of Buenos Aires were very strongly opposed to any act that might lead to war... the passage of an army of 10,000 or 20,000 men through a tract of country almost uninhabited would not have been regarded either by Mitre, his government or the people of Buenos Aires as sufficient cause for declaring war on Paraguay.'

Mitre's refusal, however predictable, took López by surprise, but although simple common sense should have made it plain that to continue with his preparations for invasion would force the two greatest powers in South America into an alliance against him - the eventuality that, above all others he should have tried to avoid - he refused to change his plans.

In fact, after months of hesitation, López had cast all caution aside. His behaviour was so irrational that it is perhaps true, as Thompson suggested, that his policy towards the government of Argentina was influenced by the hostile attitude of the Buenos Aires press, which sneered at him and Mrs. Lynch and ridiculed his pretensions. More likely, he simply decided that it was already far too late to turn back without losing face. His only chance of victory was to strike before the enemy was fully mobilised.

The only thing that now held him back was the imminent arrival of two shiploads of arms from Europe. On March 23 Mitre, still hoping for peace, allowed the *Salto* to proceed, and the next month similar permission was given to the *Esmeralda*. On April 16 large transactions on the Buenos Aires stock exchange, instigated by Paraguayan agents on López's orders, threw the capital into a panic, but it was not until the next day that Mitre learned the worst: on April 14 Paraguayan forces had attacked and captured the important port of Corrientes. Like Brazil, the year before, Argentina had been plunged into war with Paraguay.

The Paraguayan attack on Corrientes led to a predictable outcry in Buenos Aires, where angry crowds demanded immediate retaliation and cheered loudly when Mitre promised them that Argentinean troops would be in Asuncion within three months. Then, when the initial excitement was over, he and the Brazilian and Uruguayan governments set about planning how this should be accomplished.

Thanks to the treaty Flores had signed in February, Brazil and Uruguay were already allied and Francisco Octaviano de Almaida Rosa, the Brazilian Ambassador, had no trouble in getting Flores' consent to the terms of a draft treaty. Octaviano then took it over to Buenos Aires, where Mitre had already obtained the agreement of the Confederation's leading figures, including Urquiza, to an alliance with Brazil.

The precise terms took some time to settle, since the Argentineans were reluctant to agree to the Brazilian stipulation that Paraguay should not be annexed. Despite this, both sides were conscious of the need for haste. López's army was expected to burst upon them at any moment and on May 1 Elisalde, Carlos Castro, the Uruguayan Foreign Minister, and

Octaviano signed on behalf of their respective countries the document that became known as the Triple Alliance.

Although the small size of Paraguay inevitably gained it support as the under-dog, the way in which the war had begun gave the allies a certain amount of sympathy as the aggrieved parties. But the alliance which they signed, although full of declarations that their quarrel was with López rather than the Paraguayan people, was so harsh that the allies themselves decided to keep it secret. When its terms were revealed the following year by the British government, for whom Lettsom had obtained a copy, a storm of protest resulted throughout South America and, in Pelham Horton Box's opinion, the treaty "goes far to explain the desperate resistance of Paraguay. The Guaraní people were thereby convinced that their national existence was at stake." Thompson, the only Englishmen to join the Paraguayan army wrote: "When the secret treaty was published it gave me further zest to fight for Paraguay, as I believed from the terms of the Protocol that she must fight or be absorbed."

Thomas J. Hutchinson, who was British consul at Rosario during the war wrote: "No greater error could have been committed than making such a covenant as this... it appears to everybody a complete illustration of counting one's chickens before they are hatched. Moreover I am inclined to believe that there is no possibility of effecting a peace between the belligerents until this treaty has been repealed."[45]

The first clauses of the treaty[46], however, were harmless enough, and dealt with the organisation of the Allied forces, with Mitre being named as commander in chief. Clause 6 set the tone for the rest of the Agreement. It stated: "The Allies bind themselves solemnly not to lay down their arms, unless by mutual consent, until they have abolished the present Government of Paraguay, nor to treat separately with the enemy, nor sign any treaty of peace, truce or armistice, or any convention whatever to put to an end or to suspend the war, unless by the common consent of all."

The key phrase here was the reference to abolishing the present *government* of Paraguay, a direct reference to López. It meant that the Allies were insisting on López resigning the presidency and going into exile before any peace could be considered. This would have been a presumptuous demand in any circumstances, but in view of López's pride, his love of power, his absolute authority in Paraguay - all of which were known to the Allies - it was a grievous tactical blunder. There was no indication that the Paraguayans wanted anyone else as their leader and the clause was as insulting to the Paraguayans as a demand by López that Dom Pedro must abdicate would have been to the Brazilians. The same article prohibited any of the Allies from making a separate peace, which in practice meant that Brazil, the dominant partner, was able to drag Argentina and Uruguay in her wake long after their enthusiasm for the cause had subsided.

The treaty went on to state loftily: 'The Allies moreover bind themselves for five years to respect the independence, sovereignty and territorial integrity of the Republic of Paraguay. Consequently the Paraguayan people may elect their own Government and give it any institutions they think fit; none of the Allies incorporating it, nor pretending to establish any protectorate as a consequence of the war.' This all sounds fine enough until one reaches the clauses that define Paraguay's boundaries.

Argentina claimed several thousand square miles west of the River Paraguay and territory to the east. This would not only deprive Paraguay of the Misiones but also the whole of its territories in the Chaco. The Brazilians claimed several thousand square miles between the Rivers Apa and Branco in the far north of Paraguay and territory to the east. In other words, the Allies guaranteed Paraguay all its territory - except the parts they wanted. If carried out, this section of the treaty would have reduced the republic's territory by half.

Another article, establishing the principle of free navigation of the Rivers Paraná, Uruguay and Paraguay was fair enough, but the Allies then moved on to the question of reparations. Paraguay, it was agreed, should pay all the expenses that the Allies incurred in the war, and would also be expected to pay compensation for the damage caused to public and private property in Allied territory. Perhaps even more unacceptable than any of these clauses, however was the Protocol mentioned by Thompson which was tacked on to the end of the treaty almost as an afterthought and seemed intended to emasculate a nation that, under the earlier clauses would already have been dismembered. The fortress of Humaitá, which dominated the mouth of the River Paraguay and was regarded as the key to the republic's defence, was to be demolished and no fortifications of a similar nature were to be permitted in its place. Furthermore, the government that was installed in place of López, would be deprived of "any arms or elements of war."

The clauses regarding territorial cessions were hard: the demand for reparations was savage: but the Protocol was intolerable - it would have meant the Republic giving up any power to control or influence its own affairs and abandoning itself to the mercy of its enemies. It was small wonder, in fact, that the secret treaty of the Triple Alliance, signed so enthusiastically that day in May, ensured that the Paraguayan war became not only the longest but also the bloodiest war in South American history.

While the terms of this document - which would have made the negotiators of the Versailles agreement blink a little - were being hammered out, the Paraguayans were preparing to attack. Although it had taken López a disastrously long time to decide to act, once the Argentinean government had rejected his request for permission to cross Corrientes he moved rapidly, and on February 26 he summoned a special meeting of the Paraguay congress to rubber-stamp a series of measures and endorse his actions so far. The Congress met on March 5, under José Falcon, who had been Foreign Minister in the mid-1850s and during the course of the next few weeks enthusiastically did everything that López told it to do. His salary as President was increased to 60,000 dollars a year, and he was declared the country's first and only Marshal - a title that owed something to Napoleonic precedent.

On March 18 a more serious step was taken, when Congress was told that Mitre had refused permission to cross Corrientes, was conspiring with Flores, and had allowed the Buenos Aires press to print libels about López. As a result, war was officially declared, and the earlier action against Brazil was approved. This decision was however kept secret, since López was still waiting for his arms shipments to arrive. It was not until April 13 that five Paraguayan steamers entered Corrientes and Paraguayan troops boarded and captured the *25 de Mayo* and the *Gualequay,* two ancient Argentinean warships that were in the port at the time. The next day, with the Corrientinos still only partly aware of what was happening, the Paraguayan fleet reappeared with General Wenceslas Robles and an army of 3,000 men, who were disembarked without incident. They were joined that night by 800 cavalry who had landed further up river at the town of Corrales and then advanced overland.

López's next moves show signs of some careful planning, and indicate that he was still hoping that the Correntinos would join him in an alliance. Robles was armed with a list of friendly citizens, compiled by a spy called Miguel Rojas who had been living in the town since the previous year, posing as a cattle buyer, and as soon as the bridgehead was secure Berges and a triumvirate of renegade Corrientinos were sent over to establish a puppet government. The townspeople themselves were treated with great tact, with all those who objected to the Paraguayans' presence being allowed to leave for the south, to where the Governor Lagrana had already departed - his information enabling the Argentineans to intercept and capture the *Empedrado* with her cargo of arms. Once the new government was more or less established Robles left a garrison of 1,500 men and then began to advance south along the river, his army being built up by reinforcements brought daily by the fleet until it reached a total of 25,000 men.

At the same time, a second Paraguayan army was preparing to invade the province of Rio Grande. For several months the Allies had known that something was afoot there: as early as September 1864, Paraguayan and Argentinean soldiers had clashed in the disputed Misiones region, Brazilian and Argentinean scouts had reported Paraguayans there in large numbers, and by April 1865 rumours of an imminent invasion were rife. On April 24 the commander of the Brazilian lst Light Brigade reported that 10,000 men were massing at San Carlos in the Misiones.

These reports did not disturb the 68-year-old Brazilian commander General David Canabarro, an old Farroupo rebel and friend of Flores, who had been assigned to defend the Misiones frontier with a force of 5,000 men. As late as May 13 he was forecasting a Brazilian invasion of Paraguay rather than the other way round, and the surprise was considerable when on June 10 12,500 Paraguayans under the command of Lieutenant Colonel Antonio Lacu Estigarribia suddenly appeared on the banks of the River Uruguay, crossed by means of 20 canoes brought all the way from Paraguay, and captured the town of San Borja in Rio Grande itself.

This meant there were two Paraguayan armies on Allied territory, both marching steadily southwards towards the province of Entre Rios, the fief of Urquiza, whose personal loyalty was still uncertain. The Paraguayans at San Borja claimed that Urquiza was going to join them, and the pattern of the double-headed advance seemed to indicate that López was probably banking on the great *caudillo* abiding by some previous agreement. If this happened, the whole Allied position east of the Paraná would be in jeopardy.

López's immediate target was Brazil, the most powerful of his opponents. Neither of the Empire's two allies matched her contribution to the war. Mitre could count on about 10,000 men at the outbreak of war, most of them from Buenos Aires. The troops in other provinces were in practice the private armies of the local *caudillo*, and their participation in the war against Paraguay depended on the attitude of their local leader.

Since the *caudillo* himself was just as likely to lead his men against the forces of the Confederation as against the Paraguayans, no more than half the Argentinean army was ever available for service against Paraguay at any one time and its operations were frequently almost paralysed by revolts in the provinces. The Argentinean army never rose to much above 15,000 men, and many of these were foreigners.

The Uruguayan contingent was even smaller, and consisted of the hard-core Colorado supporters who had helped Flores gain power, about 1,500 men, formed into three battalions, and were led by Flores himself

As far as experience went, all the Allied armies had seen more fighting than the Paraguayans, even though much of it consisted of civil wars. The Brazilians had seen action in Uruguay, and the Farroupo and other revolts of the regency period had been serious affairs that were only crushed after heavy fighting. These had given their senior officers considerable military experience. Osorio, who was born in Rio Grande in 1808, had fought against the Argentineans at Ituzaingo, in the Farroupo revolt, and against Rosas at Caseros. Another veteran of all three was Manoel Marques de Souza, Barão de Porto Alegre, who had retired for health reasons in 1856 but was recalled when the Paraguayans invaded Rio Grande to take command of the Brazilian forces in that province. He had commanded the Brazilians at Caseros. The most respected of all Brazil's soldiers was Luis Alves de Lima e Silva, the Duque de Caxias, who was 61 in 1864, and had been one of the chief supporters of the crown during the troublesome days of the regency, and had been instrumental in breaking the Farroupo rebels. In 1864 he was out of favour with the government since he was a noted Conservative. The presence of a body of experienced senior officers was another factor to be added to the list of Allied advantages over their opponents, and apart from their initial manpower superiority, it was difficult to find one definite advantage which the Paraguayan army possessed. That, of course, ignored one of the most important factors of all, morale, but at this stage in the war nobody could safely, forecast how this would be apportioned. What was clear to the Allies was that in time the odds would swing slowly in their favour. The first essential was simply to weather the storm now breaking over them from Corrientes and Misiones.

Chapter 10

The Allied military leaders met in Buenos Aires in May and decided that the main Allied armies would concentrate at Concordia, a town in Entre Rios on the River Uruguay about half way between Paysandu and the Brazilian border. It was a convenient rendezvous for the Brazilians in Rio Grande, the Uruguayans and the Argentineans, who could be transported by ship from Buenos Aires. It was far enough away from Corrientes to be safe from an immediate attack, but well placed to act as a springboard for a counter-offensive towards Robles' army, or up the River Uruguay towards Misiones, where scouts were reporting almost daily the second Paraguayan build up. An important role, according to Mitre's plans, was to be played by Urquiza, who had promised to raise 10,000 men. Although the proposed concentration of forces was strategically sound, it did nothing immediately to help the citizens of Corrientes province, where the Paraguayans had so far been allowed almost a free hand. Berges worked with some success at placating local opinion, while Robles continued his march down river with the main body of the Paraguayan army. In the interior Governor Lagraña and General Nicanor Caceres, a local *caudillo*, had managed to raise about 6,000 men, all recruits, but this force could hardly have stopped Robles on its own, and Mitre realised that he could not simply abandon an province while the Allied army was concentrating. On April 24 the first Argentinean troops left Buenos Aires for Bella Vista, a small river town about 90 miles south of Corrientes.

The total force consisted of around 4,000 men under the command of General Wenceslas Paunero, an old colleague of Mitre's who had once owned the printing press in Bolivia on which Mitre printed his newspaper *La Epoca*.[47] Once at Bella Vista he made rapid contact with the loyal Correntino troops, who had had their first clash with the advancing Paraguayans on May 2. This was not enough to stop Robles, who left his camp at the River Riachuelo on May 11 and pushed south again and so the Allies resorted to the only trump card they held at that time - the Brazilian fleet.

Soon after Robles entered Bella Vista on May 20 Paunero embarked 2,000 men, including 350 Brazilians, on board two Argentinean transports and the vessels of the Brazilian fleet, which had left Buenos Aires on April 13. On May 25 - chosen because it was Argentina's national day - the fleet suddenly appeared off Corrientes, which was held by 1,500 Paraguayans. Covered by the heavy guns of the fleet, the Allied troops disembarked at the Arroyo de Poncho Verde, a dried up stream that crossed the town. The Paraguayans formed up to defend a small stone bridge across the stream, despite being caught in a murderous cross fire from the river and the troops on shore, who were supported by two small 6pr field guns. The fighting went on all afternoon and was bitterly intense: the Allies found to their consternation that the Paraguayans did not seem to realise when their position was hopeless, but kept on fighting until they were either killed or a victorious.

Burton, who spoke to Allied eyewitnesses, wrote: 'The Paraguayans fought with a rare ferocity. "*No tengo orden* (I have no order to)" replied a solitary soldier resolved to die when asked to surrender. Another swarmed up an orange tree and had to be shot down like a bird. *Quiero morir* (I want to die)' cried a disabled man, cutting at those who wanted to save him. The Brazilians did not help matters, according to Thompson, by showing for the first time 'a peculiarity in their tactics which consists in firing whenever they have any guns to fire with, no matter whether they kill friend or foe or both together which last was usually the case.'

By the late afternoon, the Paraguayans had lost 400 men and at length abandoned the bridge and the city. Paunero, whose own troops had suffered 350 casualties, entered it and announced that all civilians who wished to leave would be taken away on the Allied ships. The next day, knowing that Robles' main army would be able to annihilate him if he delayed, he re-embarked his men and the civilians who wanted to leave and sailed back down the river. It had been a gesture of defiance, intended to revive spirits at home rather than to intimidate the enemy. In fact, the events that it set in motion were to have a decisive effect on the outcome of the whole war.

During the early months of the war López had remained in Asuncion, but on June 2 he announced that he was going to lead the army in person and at dusk on June 8 he was rowed across to the *Tacuarí*, the flagship of the Paraguayan fleet, while the crew of HMS *Doterel*, a gunboat which was in Asuncion to protect the interest of British subjects manned the yards. At midnight the *Tacuarí*, leading five other steamers crammed with troops, left Asuncion for Humaitá.

López had seen at once that although the immediate effects of the attack had been negligible, the threat it had implied was considerable, for the Allies had with complete impunity sailed into the most important point held by Paraguay in Allied territory, captured it, and then sailed away at their leisure. The next time they came they might have an army of 50,000 not 2,000 and if that happened Robles and his men would be trapped and Paraguay itself laid open to invasion.

All this had been made possible by the existence of the Brazilian fleet, and although Paunero and his men had returned to Entre Rios, the fleet still lay at anchor a few miles south of Corrientes, neatly severing water-borne communications between Robles and his base. The elimination of this fleet would not only solve the problem of the blockade and remove the threat to Robles' army, it would also immeasurably aid the Paraguayan advance. Although the Brazilian navy had 45 ships[48], many of them were unsuitable for river use, and it would be weeks, probably months, before they could send another fleet to the Paraná. In the meantime all of the Argentine Confederation's great cities - even including Buenos Aires - would be at the mercy of the Paraguayan fleet. A few judicious blows might very well spark off a revolt or two in the provinces, and the fate of Paunero's army in southern Corrientes could almost be regarded as sealed.

The only trouble with the plan was that the Brazilian fleet, snugly anchored off the mouth of the Riachuelo, the small stream beside which Robles' men had camped the month before, was a good deal more powerful than anything the Paraguayans could muster. López knew that his fleet was weak and obsolete and he had attempted to overcome this by ordering new ships from yards in Europe. These included five armoured coastal defence battleships of over 1000 tons displacement, all equipped with defensive armour plate and armed with Whitworth rifled guns. Unfortunately, the ships were not built until 1865-1866 – too late to be delivered to Paraguay in time for the war.

To help him in his deliberations, López called upon John Watts, the English engineer of the *Tacuarí*, who had served in the Brazilian fleet during the expedition against Paraguay in 1859 and was regarded as something of an expert on their tactics and efficiency[49]. Watts' opinion of his former comrades was not high. He told López that it would be an easy matter not only to defeat the Brazilians but to capture their entire fleet. He suggested sailing down to the Riachuelo under cover of darkness and then, as dawn was breaking, going alongside and boarding. In this way, he said, the Brazilians would be taken by surprise and easily overpowered.

This was exactly the type of plan that appealed to López, offering a glittering prize for very little cost, and he at once decided to risk everything on the attempt. On June 9 the tiny flotilla reached Humaitá and, after the reinforcements for the garrison had been disembarked, a handful of other ships were rounded up, and the whole squadron put under the command of Captain Pedro Mesa, who had skippered the *Tacuarí* on her journey from Europe to Paraguay a decade before. This appointment was made in the face of plaintive opposition from Mesa himself, who according to Washburn was not only fat, but old and sick as well. More important, he was pessimistic about the expedition's chances of success, and terrified of what López would do to him if he failed.

Nevertheless López insisted that he take command and at 2am on June 10 the ships slipped away from Humaitá and began their journey down river, headed by the *Marques de Olinda*, whose capture the year before had started the war against Brazil. There were nine of them altogether and in the whole fleet only the *Tacuarí* was a genuine warship. She carried six guns, and had a displacement of 421 tons, making her roughly the same size as a Royal Navy gunboat of that period, although she was already obsolete. She was more than ten years old, wooden built and paddle driven. Although paddles were reasonably efficient propulsion units, they were easily damaged by enemy fire and took up space which could have been used for guns

In addition, the huge wheels, projecting from the sides of the ships, made it difficult to get alongside another vessel, and were therefore a great hindrance to boarding, which was the essence of the Paraguayan plan. The same was true of most of the other ships. The iron-hulled *Paraguarí*, built in England under the Blyth contract and delivered only the year before, at 627 tons was the largest ship in the fleet. She carried four guns, which, like all the Paraguayan weapons, except one, were smoothbore muzzle-loaders. The *Ygurei* (548) tons) had five guns and the 205 ton four. The *Marques de Olinda* carried four guns and was commanded by Esequial Robles, brother of the general. The final paddle steamer was the 120-ton *Jejui*, which mounted two guns.

The remaining vessels, the *Salto Oriental* (250 tons, four guns), *Pirabebe* (120 tons, one rifled gun) and the *Ybera* (300 tons, four guns) were all screw driven ships. The most serious defect of all the Paraguayan ships, except the *Tacuarí*, was that their boilers were situated above the waterline. This made them very vulnerable to enemy fire - and there was every likelihood of there being a lot of that.

The Brazilians, under the command of the Portuguese born Admiral Francisco Manoel Barroso de Silva, who had been in command of the 1855 expedition, had nine ships, the same number as the Paraguayans. But they were far bigger and, since they were designed as warships, all had their boilers situated below the waterline, more or less safe from enemy fire. The only paddle steamer was Barroso's flagship, the six-gun *Amazonas*. Three of the other ships, the *Belmonte* (eight guns), *Mearim* (eight) and *Araguari* (three) were wooden screw-driven ships that had been built in 1857-8 after the crisis with Paraguay had revealed the limitations of the Imperial navy. The other ships included the *Biberibe* (eight guns), *Iparanga* (seven) and *Iquatemi* (five). In addition to their crews, which ranged from 187 for the *Mearim* to 79 for the *Iparanga*, all the Brazilian ships carried infantry. In firepower the Brazilian vessels mounted 59 guns against the Paraguayans' 34. Most of them were rifled, and they included several 120pr and 150pr Whitworths while the Paraguayan guns were all 14pr smoothbores, apart from two 32prs.

The balance was evened up to some extent by the presence of a 22-gun shore battery of the 2nd Regiment of Horse Artillery under Colonel José Maria Bruguez, who had been sent from Robles' army to harass the Brazilians and prevent any repetition of the raid on Corrientes.

The Paraguayan ships also towed with them eight *chatas*, each armed with an 8in gun, but these proved to be nothing but a nuisance. They were difficult to manoeuvre and slowed down the rest of the fleet. They were really a product of López's indecision: the extra firepower of the *chatas* would only be useful in a long-range gun battle, but López had already decided that the best chance of victory was to board. To add to Captain Mesa's worries, the *Ybera*, one of his most powerful ships, soon developed mechanical problems. By 5am, instead of being poised for the attack, the fleet had only reached Tres Bocas. The *Ybera*, her propeller broken from the shaft, was eventually abandoned, but by then it was 7.30 and all hope of surprise was apparently gone. Yet this is exactly what the Paraguayan achieved.

The Brazilians, who were anchored on the Chaco side of the river, had not seen an enemy ship since leaving Buenos Aires, and had come to the dangerous conclusion that, because they had so far made no move, the Paraguayans had already conceded them control of the river. They were so confident that they had not even posted lookouts and when the Paraguayans' ragged collection of cargo ships came into sight, (at about 8.30 am), none of the Brazilian ships had steam up. Unable to move, their crews could only watch in stupefied horror as Mesa's vessels churned down on the current towards them.

At this point López's desperate gamble seemed about to pay off. The Brazilians were at Mesa's mercy and all he had to do to win a victory that would have given López control of the whole River Paraná and make Paraguay secure from invasion was to smash straight into the enemy before they could manoeuvre. But López had told Mesa that he must prevent any of the enemy from escaping by getting below them, and Mesa, who had never wanted the job, was afraid to disobey. Paralysed into indecision he allowed the fleet to sail past the stationary Brazilians and on down the river, and with this missed opportunity, the odds swung heavily back in the Brazilians' favour.

As the Paraguayans passed them the Brazilians were at least able to fire their guns. In the bombardment one shot hit the boiler of the *Igurey*, killing 20 men, and another shell disabled the diminutive *Jejui*. A mile below the Brazilians, Mesa ordered his fleet to heave to and called a conference of his captains to decide what to do next. While it was in progress, Watts, who had already seen one plan ruined, appeared with the unnerving information that the Brazilians had at last got steam up and were moving down river. At any moment, he said, they would attack. To forestall them he suggested sinking the damaged *Jejui* and the *Pirabebe* in the channel and using the heavy guns of the *chatas* to bombard the enemy from a distance. This would give time for Bruguez's shore battery to move into position and join in the attack. Mesa was by this time, however, so nervous that he was unable to make any decision at all. While he dithered, while Bruguez's men heaved their guns into position, Barroso's fleet swept down the river towards him. In fact attack was the last thing that Barroso had in mind. He had still not fully recovered from the shock of seeing the Paraguayan fleet loom out of the morning mist, and was fully convinced that, far from having blundered, Mesa had passed the Brazilians with the purpose of cutting him off from Buenos Aires and safety.

With both admirals convinced that defeat was inevitable, it seemed possible that sheer paralysis might have allowed the two fleets to pass without actually coming into contact. But at this point the river was only 500 yards wide and in their efforts to pass the Paraguayans two Brazilian ships struck a sandbank. The *Jequitinhonha* stuck fast and immediately became a target for Bruguez's battery, which was only a few hundred yards away. She continued firing but could not be moved. The *Paranáiba* had only touched the edge of the shoal, but while she was struggling to free herself the *Tacuarí* came alongside, and Paraguayan soldiers began scrambling on to the enemy ship. The *Marques de Olinda* soon joined the *Tacuarí*, followed by the *Salto Orientale* and although they were handicapped by the absence of grappling irons - which had been forgotten - and the large paddle wheels, the Paraguayans were soon swarming exultantly over the ship's decks, while her crew fled below and secured the hatches. Another Brazilian ship, *Belmonte*, had to run aground after being hit below the water line, and it seemed that the Paraguayans were about to gain an astonishing victory.

Then once again, the course of this extraordinary battle suddenly turned. The Brazilians, who had escaped disaster once, now faced it again. It was left to Bernardino Gastavino, the son of an Italian immigrant to Corrientes, to save the Imperial fleet. As the pilot of the flagship *Amazonas* he saw that the *Paranáiba* was doomed unless she was saved at once and although by this time the remainder of the

Brazilian fleet had almost passed the Paraguayans and reached open water, he turned the flagship round and went to the rescue. Aided by this intervention - the *Amazonas'* heavy guns were soon carving swathes around the Paraguayans fighting on the *Paranáiba's* decks - the stranded ship managed to go astern and slip from between the ships that were attacking her. Within a matter of minutes, Gastavino converted rescue into victory. Using the superior weight of the *Amazonas* to good effect he rammed the *Paraguarí*, forcing her on to a sandbank, where she lay stranded, her guns still blazing defiantly. The helpless *Jejui* was sunk as well and after being struck by a shell the exposed boiler of the *Marques de Olinda* exploded, killing most of her crew. Another shot smashed the boiler of the *Salto* and with the *Ygurei* already crippled the Paraguayan fleet had been reduced to four ships. Meanwhile Mesa had been wounded in the shoulder while on the bridge of the *Tacuarí* and Watts tried to save what was left of the fleet. The *Tacuarí* escorted the damaged *Ygurei*, the *Pirabebe* and *Ypora* up river, fighting off the pursuit of the *Amazonas*, while Bruguez's gunners battered away at the rest of the fleet. The *Paraguarí*, still stuck on her sandbank, continued firing, but by this time there were only 12 men left, the most senior of them being the English engineer, a man named Gibson. The Brazilians demanded his surrender. But when Gibson lowered the Paraguayan tricolour the survivors dived overboard and swam to the Chaco. Gibson followed, and the party soon met other survivors from the battle. The victorious Brazilians sent a boat to take them, with the result that its crew were killed themselves and the boat captured, but this hardly affected the main issue. The Brazilians had won, and their control of the river was secure. They made no attempt to follow up their success. They had lost 300 men, all of their ships were damaged - the *Paranáiba* had 13 holes around the water line - and they had experienced an even greater fright. On June 13 Barroso ran down river past the wreck of the *Jequitinhonha*, and anchored just above Bella Vista.

Despite this, the Paraguayans did not relinquish control of the rivers without a fight, and soon after the battle they began to hit back at the victors. Bruguez, whose shore batteries had caused so much damage - on June 18 an ambush killed the commander and some of the crew of the *Belmonte* - was reinforced, and two months after the battle marched south along the river to Bella Vista, where the Brazilian fleet was still licking its wounds. The news of his arrival was enough to make the Brazilians, who had also been reinforced with two steamers, up their anchors and sail further down river, suffering heavy casualties in the process The Brazilians stopped six miles below the battery but the same night the aggressive Bruguez shifted his guns to Cuevas, immediately below the new anchorage, and the Brazilians ran the gauntlet again. Compared with the defeat at the Riachuelo, these encounters were only of minor importance but the aggression showed by Bruguez had significant results. The Brazilians had taken a severe battering and although the Paraguayans were never again able to challenge the surface strength of the Allied naval forces, the Allies themselves never managed to shake off the fear of the Paraguayan shore batteries that was born in those few days in June and August.

The immediate effect of Bruguez's action was to clear the river of Brazilian ships for the next eight months. This enabled the Paraguayans to salvage two 68prs, four 32prs and five 5ins howitzers, together with the mainyard of the *Jequitonhonha*, which was taken to Humaitá and turned into the central column of a dancing rotunda. The wrecked *Paraguarí* was also recovered, and although she was too badly damaged to be made serviceable, the iron in her hull and engines was of great value later in the war when metal became extremely scarce.

After this experience the victorious Barroso retired from the fray, with promotion and the title of Baron das Amazonas. Gastavino was given 500 ounces of gold and the commission of lieutenant colonel. Watts, who had saved the Paraguayans from an even greater defeat, received an award in the new Order of Merit. Three days after the battle Gibson made his way back to Humaitá from the Chaco with other survivors, including three English engineers, two of whom, named Bagster and Spivey, died a few days later from scalds received when the boilers of their ships were holed. They were buried in a special Protestant cemetery not far from the church, complete with its own wall and an ornamental gate. Gibson, who had tried to surrender, was jailed for three months.

Mesa received neither medals nor sympathy. Hearing that he was lying in hospital wounded, López sent a message saying that he wished the captain a speedy recovery so that he could have him executed.

Mesa wisely managed to die that night, the first time he had ever dared disobey his president.

López's despair was justified. At the battle of Riachuelo Paraguay had suffered a complete and quite irreversible defeat. This 4½-hour naval battle fought six hundred miles from the ocean severed Paraguay's lifeline with the world and ended forever López's dreams of an empire in the heart of South America. Without control of the river he could only wait, cut off from all outside help and unable to purchase modern weapons, for an attack that must inevitably come, from an Allied army that must with equal inevitability grow stronger while his own grew weaker. Less than three months after the signing of the Triple Alliance, the war had reached its turning point. To make matters worse, the warships that López had ordered in Europe soon ended up in the hands of the Brazilians. Because Paraguay was unable to pay for them, six coastal defence ships, largest being the 1330-ton *Lima Barros*, were sold to the Imperial navy. They arrived too late to take part in the battle of the Riachuelo, but served in the latter stages of the war. Had the Paraguayans possessed these ships at the battle they would probably have won a decisive victory.

But this blow was not only one that López had to face that day. For while his fleet was being destroyed at the Riachuelo, General Wenceslas Robles and the army at Goya had, quite against orders, begun to retreat.

Chapter 11

López's immediate conclusion was that Robles, a favourite officer who had presided over the tribunal which sentenced Father Maiz; was betraying him. He therefore sent Colonel Resquín, a ruthless, brave and sadistic man whose complete loyalty to López never wavered, to act as second in command and report on what was going on. Colonel Paulino Alén, another trusted soldier, who had accompanied López on his European trip, was made chief of staff, with instructions to spy on both of them.

By this time the army had retreated by a series of forced marches to Empedrado, thirty miles south of the town of Corrientes and Robles, who had been in contact with the Brazilians for some time, realised that he was under suspicion. He tried to cover himself by sending all the letters he had received to López and at the same time wrote to the Brazilians agreeing to surrender his army, providing the price was right. López was not convinced by Robles' protestations of loyalty and on July 23 his brother in law, Vicente Barrios, arrived at the camp. Before Robles could conclude his bargain he was arrested and forced to walk behind Barrios's horse for nine miles to where a boat was waiting to take him back to Humaitá. The official version was that Robles was planning to let the Brazilians in on the following day, July 24, under the cover of the celebrations for López's birthday. At Humaitá, Robles was kept in solitary confinement and periodically tortured and beaten up while López decided what to do with him.

Resquín was then put in command of the Corrientes army, and marched back down the river to Bella Vista. This was little more than a gesture of defiance. The Allied fleet was at Goya and to have gone any further would have been an invitation to another disaster. Although the Brazilian fleet had withdrawn in the face of Bruguez's battery, the battle of Riachuelo had destroyed the Paraguayans' tenuous hold on the river, and sooner or later the Brazilians would back. What with one thing and another, June 10 was an eventful day for Paraguay: it had lost a fleet, one army had retreated, and 200 miles to the southeast, Estigarribia's had crossed the River Uruguay and entered Brazil. Although Estigarribia did not at that stage know of the defeat at Riachuelo, as soon as the news became known at Humaitá López should at once have ordered him to retreat. The whole two-pronged offensive at its best was a risky operation, depending upon Paraguay retaining control of the Paraná, and since that control was now lost - although the Brazilians seemed reluctant to accept it - both the Rio Grande and the Corrientes armies were in considerable danger of being cut off. But one of López's greatest failings as a general was his stubborn refusal to alter his plans to meet changed circumstances and so Estigarribia and his 12,000 men were allowed to continue a march that had lost all chance of success even before it begun.

At San Borja, the feeble resistance of the garrison encouraged the illusion that the invasion would be a promenade, but in fact Estigarribia was heading straight towards the Allied assembly point at Concordia, and Canabarro, with his covering force of 5,000 men, did nothing to hinder the advance, although the Paraguayan route was marked by looted villages and similar outrages. For this he was later called upon to face a court-martial, although his inactivity was strategically the correct policy.

Meanwhile the Allied armies were gathering. On June 17, Mitre handed over political matters to his vice president Marcos Paz, and set off for Concordia, which he reached a few days later. Early the next month Flores arrived with 6,000 men, including the Uruguayan contingent and some Brazilians. Great hopes at this stage were still being put on Urquiza, who had raised 10,000, and by the end of June had reached Basualdo, near the Corrientes border. He left his men there and rode on alone towards Concordia to confer with his fellow generals. On the way he was overtaken by a messenger with the disconcerting news that on July 3 his army had mutinied, and most of them had already gone home. Their lack of enthusiasm for the Allied cause was perhaps understandable: they had been brought up to regard the *porteños*, symbolised by Mitre, as their rivals and the Brazilians were their traditional enemies. Paraguay, on the other hand, had always been, if not a friend, then at least an inoffensive neutral. Throughout July, Estigarribia's advance continued. Soon after taking San Borja he divided his force into two columns, the main body, under himself, marching down the left bank, while 2,500 men under Major Pedro Duarte kept pace along the opposite side the two columns_keeping in touch by canoes.

On August 4 Canabarro evacuated the town of Uruguayana, about thirty miles from the Uruguayan border. Estigarribia entered it and finding a considerable amount of stores decided to halt the advance for a while. Duarte at the same time garrisoned the town of Yatai on the opposite bank.

So far, the invasion had been uneventful, but in fact the Paraguayan's position was already giving Estigarribia cause for some concern. Despite the arrival of 400 reinforcements, injuries and sickness had reduced his total strength to only 10,500. He was 200 miles from Encarnacion, and a similar distance from the Paraguayan army in Corrientes, which was separated from him by a shimmering morass of impassable lakes and swamps called the Laguna Ybera, the shining lake. Retreat was still possible - but López's orders had been to advance, and Estigarribia could not consider retreating without even fighting a worthwhile battle. And so he did the same as his colleagues at Bella Vista: he dug in, and waited for the enemy to make the next move.

While the great invasion was fizzling to a halt, the Allies were already preparing a counter-attack. In the middle of July Flores began to advance on Yatai with 13,000 men, half of them Brazilians. Another column of 2,000 men under General Carlos Castro was sent off to Misiones to cut off Estigarribia's route to Encarnacion. Duarte's cavalry scouts spotted the long columns of men winding towards them, and he appealed to Estigarribia for help, also sending a messenger across the swamps to Resquín in Corrientes. This messenger was captured by troops from another Allied force under Paunero which was converging on Uruguayana, while Estigarribia could do little for his colleague but send words of encouragement: the Allies already had some small boats on the river and it was impossible for the Paraguayan leader to send sufficient reinforcements. On August 17 Flores and Paunero reached Yatai and invested the town.

Duarte drew up his men behind the houses of the small town, with their backs to the river. Immediately Flores attacked his troops advancing in columns that were soon under heavy fire. Duarte's handful of cavalry charged repeatedly, but the enormous difference in manpower began to tell. The Paraguayans were soon broken up into individual groups who continued fighting with the savage desperation that their countrymen had displayed at Corrientes. Only 300 prisoners were taken, including Duarte himself, most of them wounded. More than 2,000 Paraguayans were dead, but in Washburn's words "they had fought with valour never surpassed, not even at Thermopylae."

The victory had cost Flores nearly 2,500 casualties, but the sacrifice was worth it. In one battle Estigarribia had lost nearly a quarter of his entire force, and he was now virtually cut off. There was still one slight possibility of escape, by retracing his steps along the eastern bank of the Uruguay, but although he had heard nothing from López since the middle of June, 1 he eventually decided that his orders obliged him to stay put. He contented himself with strengthening the town's defences. This decision simply handed the initiative to the Allies and meant that, unless a Paraguayan relief force was already on the way (which it was not) then the army was doomed. On August 25 Mitre left Concordia with the main Allied army, marched north and crossed the Uruguay to begin the siege of Uruguayana with a total force of 30,000 men opposed to only 8,000 defenders. Estigarribia again considered retreat and again decided against it, although by now the prospect of succeeding in such a venture had really vanished altogether. Taking advantage of a sudden rise in the level of the river - the whole campaign had been conducted in miserably wet and cold weather - Tamandaré brought four gunboats up to assist in the siege, ending all hope of successfully re-crossing the river which separated the Paraguayans from Encarnacion and home. After the experience of Yatai, the Allies knew that an attack on the town would be costly, and so they tried to persuade Estigarribia to surrender by pointing out the obvious hopelessness of his position. They offered to let him and his men march out of the town with all honours of war, and even return to Paraguay if they wished. Estigarribia refused. On September 2 the Allies again offered terms and on September 5

Estigarribia sent his reply, a long bombastic piece of rhetoric composed by a priest who acted as his secretary, in which he pointedly referred to Allied claims to be offering Paraguay its freedom and wondered if this would also be extended to the Empire's millions of slaves. He compared himself and his men to Leonidas and the 300 Spartans and concluded that 'if fortune should decree us a tomb in this city of Uruguayana our fellow citizens will preserve the remembrance of those Paraguayans who died fighting for the cause of their country, and who, while they lived, did not surrender to the enemy the sacred ensign of the liberty of their nation.'

On September 5, Pedro II, the Emperor of Brazil, arrived with his new son-in-law, the Comte d'Eu, to witness the closing ceremonies. The Allies were still determined not to waste lives needlessly, and prepared to pound the Paraguayans into submission with their heavy guns: besides those on the gunboats they had 42 modern rifled weapons, some of them brand new 150pr Whitworth breech loaders. The Paraguayans had five small smooth-bores. In addition, Estigarribia's provisions were dwindling. By the middle of September the bullocks had gone, and the garrison was reduced to eating the horses. On the 17th Estigarribia began making rafts, with the forlorn idea of ferrying his troops across the river, but soon gave up the idea as hopeless. The next day the Allied troops took up positions ready for the attack and at noon sent a curt demand that Estigarribia surrender within four hours. Faced with the prospect of certain defeat following the devastating barrage of the enemy artillery, Estigarribia agreed. By four o'clock the final terms had been settled, and the 6,000 men who still survived marched out of Uruguayana to surrender. Nine hundred of them were sick and the rest on the verge of starvation. About 5,000 stands of arms and 231,000 cartridges were taken. Of the five captured guns, two were more than 70 years old, and another dated back to 1679.

Although the surrender of Estigarribia was inevitable, the news took López completely by surprise. "In the Paraguayan army", wrote Thompson, who was at Humaitá at that time, "the battle of Yatai was considered of little or no importance except to show the Allies what sort of people they were dealing with and that they would fight to death rather than given in. But the news of the fall of Uruguayana fell like a thunderbolt on López, though he must have known that his division was doomed, besieged as it was by the whole of the Allied armies, either to die to the last man or surrender. On receiving the news López was very savage with Estigarribia. He sent for all the officers in the garrison at Humaitá and told them of it, saying that Estigarribia had sold the garrison for 3,000 doubloons, and holding him up to their execration as a traitor. This was the only reverse in the whole war which affected López at all, although he did not show it in public. For three days he was so savage that even his son, on whom he doted, was afraid to go near him."

As the awful consequences of the defeat sank in, López realised that all ideas of conquest must be abandoned and that from then on Paraguay would be fighting a war of survival. He had come face to face with reality in the most abrupt and brutal fashion and it was natural that he should believe that Estigarribia had turned traitor. Robles, the great favourite who had been trusted completely, had set a precedent, and if he could be bribed, then so could Estigarribia - and this was a more acceptable theory than the only alternative, which was that Estigarribia had fallen a victim of López's own incompetent strategy.

Ironically, despite his doubts, was right about Robles, and despite his certainty was equally wrong about Estigarribia. Later on in the war the Allied generals told both Washburn and Burton that Robles had been plotting to sell army, but denied that Estigarribia was planning to do the same. The erroneous belief that Estigarribia was a traitor like Robles made López fear that he was surrounded by treachery. He became obsessed with a fear of assassination and a double cordon of sentries, later increased to a treble one surrounded his house at Humaitá.

In this atmosphere, Robles' fate was soon decided. In January 1866 he and several others, including Martinez, who had been in command at Corrientes at the time of Paunero's raid, were shot, to the satisfaction of most of his colleagues who had long hated him for his cruelty and shared López's belief in his guilt.

The unpleasant rumours about López's youth were well enough known for many of his officers and officials to view such actions with alarm, knowing that in his disappointment López was quite capable of taking a terrible revenge on whoever was conveniently at hand. As if to make the point absolutely clear López issued a warning at a *beso mano*, a *levée*, a few weeks after the capitulation at which Bishop Palacios concluded his customarily fawning speech with some hesitant references to Robles and Estigarribia. López heard him impatiently and then, speaking in a loud voice, completely different from his normal tone, he said with savage passion: 'I am working for my country, for the good of you all, and none help me! I stand alone I have confidence in none of you - I cannot trust one among you!

Clenching his fist and white with tension he stepped forward and shouted: "*Cuidado*! But take care! Hitherto I have pardoned offences, taken pleasure in pardoning, but now from this day, I pardon none!"[50]

He stormed from the room, and Masterman, who was there, saw "many a blanched face among [the officers], for they knew he would keep his word." For the moment, however, the army had more immediate problems and in October Resquín's army began to retreat north towards Corrientes, sweeping before it a vast herd of 100,000 cattle and taking as much loot as it could carry. Five steamers were sent to bring back the battery at Cuevas that was still keeping the Brazilian fleet at bay, and on October 31 the Corrientes army began to cross the Paraná into Paraguay. This should have been the Allies' opportunity to complete the work that had been begun at Uruguayana and Riachuelo, since the Paraguayan steamers could not have resisted a serious challenge by the Brazilian fleet. But although gunboats came up to see what was happening they did not interfere and by November 2 the remnants of Resquín's army were safely across. It then became possible to count the hideous cost of the failure of López's grand design.

The original strength of the Corrientes and Rio Grande armies had been nearly 40,000 men. The total that a crossed the Paraná to Paso de la Patria at the end of October was 14,000, together with 5,000 sick. About 8,500 had died on Argentinean soil. In addition, thousands more had died at Humaitá and other camps: dysentery and diarrhoea, both largely the result of the change of diet, were continual scourges, and the army was also hit by epidemics of measles and smallpox. Masterman believed that by the end of the year more than 50,000 men had died from one cause or another, and although this figure is probably too high (Masterman estimated the strength of the army at its peak as 100,000 men, which is certainly an exaggeration and Thompson put the total at 40,000), the losses had been staggering. As a chemist, and later surgeon, at the main hospital in Asuncion, Masterman was well placed to see how the Paraguayan army died its slow and lingering death, and although he had served for a time on the medical staff of the British 82nd Regiment the misery that he saw moved him deeply. The wounded and sick "came up, poor fellows, in the half crippled steamers from the front after a journey of three or four days, and as a rule did not get a morsel of food on the way; by that we must understand half or a third of those who were put on board, the rest had died and been thrown overboard. The condition in which they arrived was shocking beyond description, and I saw their sufferings with an indignant pity which frequently overpowered me completely. Almost or quite naked, with their wounds untended, dirty and famished, and so emaciated that when dead they dried up without decomposition, they were carried up from the pier to the hospitals; and then had to lie perhaps for a week or till they died, on the ground; but one never heard a word of complaint: they bore all with a silent heroism which won them our heartfelt sympathies."

The General Hospital, the largest of the three in Asuncion, was a former cavalry barracks on a hill west of the town. It had originally been designed to hold 300 people, but by the end of 1865 was housing 900 wounded men or more. The luckier ones were accommodated within the building, two in each bed or else lying on the damp, uneven tiled floor; but hundreds more were placed under the colonnades surrounding the hospital, their only protection from the sun which in the summer sent the temperature up to 100 degrees or more, and from the cold of the winter, when the normally mild weather occasionally plummeted to freezing point. Many would lie there for a week. Few had clothes: even fewer had blankets. Up until the outbreak of war, Masterman had led a comfortable and privileged existence. His duties as chief apothecary were not strenuous and once he had learned Spanish he became professor of materia medica at the college of Asuncion, lecturing to a class of about forty students, which was not a very demanding task either.

The war changed this way of life as it changed everything else in Paraguay. The blockade resulted in the supply of drugs drying up completely and within a few months Masterman had no more pills to pound. He tried to find native substitutes, with some success, but the most important drugs, such as opium, were irreplaceable. As a result there was very little he could do in his official capacity, and after watching helplessly while Dr. Rhind and Dr. Fox carried out operation after operation on the wounded soldiers he finally wrote to Stewart at Humaitá asking if he could help them. Stewart spoke to López who appointed Masterman a Ciruiano del 2do clase - an assistant surgeon - and Masterman began his duties "by amputating a leg above the knee, ten minutes after my commission."

For months his routine was unvaried. In the morning, he would go to the dispensary and prepare what medicines he could. After breakfast he went into the hospital and began his tour of the wards. The first one measured about 100ft by 25ft with a dirty stained roof of massive tiles supported by palm and bamboo: the wounded lay on beds, some with a sack of moss as a mattress, the rest simply resting as best they could on bare thongs that cut into their flesh. Visitors, wives, daughters and mothers, surrounded many of the beds, talking in low voices to the injured men. The windows were closed – the orderlies insisted on doing so every night – and the air heavy with the smell of medicine, bodies and death. Masterman first examined the newcomers, with time to see only the most seriously wounded. and as he walked between the beds other patients would reach out, begging him to hold their hand, as though his touch alone was some sort of talisman that would miraculously cure them. Others would ask him "Shall I get better?" and if he was forced to shake his head they "would but reply 'Esta bien' (it is well) in a tone of sad but uncomplaining resignation."

Masterman had lunch and rested between twelve and two and then in the afternoon would help the 'skilful and kind hearted' Rhind perform some operations or else carried out some of his own: despite his lack of experience, Masterman developed into an able surgeon, certainly far better than the Paraguayan assistants, who had never received any training. Then, having done what he could for the hundreds of casualties lying around the hospital, Masterman would settle down for night duty.

Between them these three men had to try to save the lives of up to 2,000 soldiers lying in the General Hospital and the two smaller hospitals of San Francisco and Estanco. All of the injured needed close attention, most needed urgent treatment as soon as they arrived: few could hope to receive it and so small cuts festered into hideous sores, minor wounds turned gangrenous and wounded men died. The men who were sick as opposed to wounded - and there were thousands of them - were sent to the old training camp of Cerro Leon, where it was presumed that the cooler air of the mountains would be beneficial to them. But the English doctors could not be spared and so consequently little was done to help them recover. Masterman saw that the problem was not so much the lack of medicine, as the treatment they were receiving, in particular the inadequate food. It generally consisted solely of meat, the worst possible diet for men suffering from dysentery and enteric fever, and one to which the Paraguayans were not accustomed. Although the hospital patients received more salt than most other people, the supply of even this essential item virtually ceased after the war began.

Appalled at the suffering and death around him, Masterman took the opportunity of a visit to Humaitá to appeal to López for a more humane and sensible treatment of the patients, in particular pointing out the unnecessary deaths being caused by bad diet. López, who always acted as though he had millions of men at his disposal and showed little concern over losses, said sarcastically: "If you have no better advice as a medico to give me than that, do not come to me again." And so the slow wasting away of the manhood of Paraguay continued. The wounded lay quietly in their own congealing blood beneath the colonnades of Asuncion, hungry, thirsty, tortured by flies and pain, lashed by wind and rain and roasted by the sun. Masterman wrote: "Day after day the actors changed, some few restored to health, others, and they more numerous than all, passed to the bare cemetery on the hill; but the same drama went on."

It was to do so for another four years.

Chapter 12

With the failure of the two Paraguayan offensives, the initiative passed to the Allies. Various plans for invading Paraguay were considered, including an attack from the Matto Grosso, the northern part of which was still held by Brazil and another through Encarnacion, the port from which Estigarribia had launched his disastrous campaign. But although neither plan was completely abandoned, neither was really feasible as a major invasion route: the Matto Grosso was too far from the rest of Brazil, and could not support a large army, while the Encarnacion route would mean leaving the River Paraná and striking inland towards Villa Rica and Asuncion - which would leave a long and vulnerable supply route and threaten an Uruguayana in reverse.

The problem of supplying the army was in fact one of the major ones facing the Allied commanders. The roads of Corrientes, the neighbouring Argentine provinces, and southern Paraguay itself were either non-existent or else quite inadequate for the movement of large bodies of men and supplies. Although some railways had been built in South America, there were none within several hundred miles of the war zone. That left only one other means of transport, and that was by water. Thanks to the battle of Riachuelo, the Allies had already gained control of the River Paraná as far as Tres Bocas, and from November onwards began building up their army and stores of equipment along the southern bank of the river, using Corrientes as their main base. From there they were well placed to invade Paraguay by means of the River Paraguay, which led more or less straight to Asuncion and afforded a splendid highway on which the Allies could carry all the men and equipment they would need. The only trouble was that a few miles from Tres Bocas the Paraguayans had built the fort of Humaitá - and until that fort was either destroyed or captured, no Allied supply ship could hope to reach Asuncion. Since Asuncion was two hundred miles away, and the country in between was almost deserted, an invading army could not live off the land, and it did not take the Allied commanders long to decide that before they did anything else they must remove the cork that was bottling up their supply fleet. In other words, Humaitá must be captured. Their next conclusion was that the batteries - the raison d'être of the whole fort – were too strong to be attacked frontally. They would have to land an army on the north bank of the Paraná and then march across the twelve miles or so that separated them from Humaitá and take the batteries from the rear.

In the years that followed, the name of Humaitá was to spread to the other countries of South America and then across the Atlantic to the United States and Europe, becoming a heroic symbol of resistance to overwhelming odds. Journalists seeking for a comparison that would appeal to their readers, wrote of the Sebastapol of the South, conjuring up images of a vast fortress of stone, bristling with guns, and crammed with men. This was colourful and quite inaccurate: the whole point about Humaitá was that as a military stronghold it was a sham. Thompson, who did more than anyone else to build up its defences, regarded it as 'the weakest position of any that the Paraguayans held.'

As the war dragged on, the Paraguayans did improve the fort's defences and make the reality to some extent approach the myth, but in 1865, when the Allies were so carefully preparing to burst down the back door they were unaware that they already possessed the key that could have opened the front. The eight batteries at Humaitá contained ninety guns when the war broke out, all of them smoothbore muzzleloaders. The largest were the 8in guns, weighing 65 hundredweight, there were several 32prs and the rest were smaller pieces. This total was rather less than the number of guns carried by the *Victory* at Trafalgar.

By the end of 1865, however, it had been drastically reduced. Guns had been taken from Humaitá to Corrientes earlier in the year, and others were moved to Paso de la Patria on the north bank of the Paraná ready to resist the expected Allied invasion. Probably no more than fifty guns were left elsewhere in the river batteries and because of pressure elsewhere the number was never substantially increased. The guns themselves, as we have seen, were no match for the rifled weapons possessed by the Allies and in Burton's opinion: 'The works were utterly unfit to resist the developed powers of rifled artillery, the concentrated discharge from shipping and even the accurate and searching power of the Spencer carbine.'

The first of the batteries, as noted by Burton in 1868, was the Bateria Cadenas (Chain Battery) which mounted 13 guns. As a further defence, Carlos Antonio López had had a chain stretched across the river at this point which could be tightened when necessary to prevent ships from passing. Francisco Solano added two more at the beginning of the war. They were suspended on canoes and three pontoons, and protected by floating mines and rows of piles driven into the riverbed. Immediately below the Chain Battery was the Bateria Londres, which had 27 feet thick brick walls and embrasures for 16 guns, although when Burton saw it eight were blocked up because the earth-covered roof was in danger of collapse. The other batteries, from north to south were Tacuarí (3 Suns), Coimbra (8), Octava (3), Pesada (5), Itapiru (7) and the Humaitá redoubt with one 8in gun - a total of 48 guns in all, little more than half the original total. Gould, who visited Humaitá in 1867, counted 46 guns in the river batteries, including an 80pr, four 8ins, eight 32prs, and an assortment of smaller weapons.

Except in the Londres battery, all the guns were mounted *en barbette*, that is, they were placed on a flat platform without embrasures or a parapet to protect them: this enabled the guns to be manoeuvred easily to fire in any direction, but left the gunners completely exposed to enemy fire. However, the batteries would still have been a considerable obstacle to the type of fleet that could have been expected in the mid-1850s when they were built. The river was only 700 yards wide at Humaitá, and in normal times could only be navigated by ships with a draft of 12 feet or less: this meant that only relatively small ships could approach the batteries at all.

Since ships at that period carried most of their guns broadside, they would have been under fire from the batteries long before their own guns could be brought to bear, and the narrowness of the channel would have made it difficult for them to manoeuvre effectively.

Up until the Crimean War, the capital ships of all the world's navies were wooden sailing vessels similar in design to the *Victory* and not greatly different from the ships that had been in use two hundred years before. Although iron was being used in merchant and passenger vessels, it did not offer many advantages to naval architects: the wooden walls of the larger fighting ships could absorb a terrific amount of punishment without the ship sinking, and between 1688 and 1815, when the Royal Navy did more fighting than at any other period, only two ships of the line were actually destroyed in battle. The reason was that wood tended to close up after being hit, while in iron ships the hole remained. Steam power was another comparative rarity in the 1850s. Although the Royal Navy had its first steam vessel in 1822 (a tug), as late as 1845 its 87 ships of the line were all sailing vessels.

Apart from conservatism, this was partly because paddlewheels took up valuable gun space and the need to carry large supplies of coal restricted the ship's range. The Crimean War showed the advantages in manoeuvrability given by steam and the invention of the screw propeller got round the problems associated with paddle wheels. By the end of the 1850s the principle of steam was well established and propellers were taking over from paddles as the favoured means of propulsion. These developments in Europe were followed elsewhere in the world and in Brazil the desire to strengthen the fleet was fostered partly by the quarrel with Paraguay in the late 1850s but particularly by a quarrel with Britain over slavery. The Royal Navy throughout the middle of the nineteenth century was involved in a zealous attempt to stop the slave trade from Africa to the America and signed various agreements forbidding the trade. Brazil had proved unwilling or unable to stop it altogether. In 1862 this led a to a serious breach between the two countries which was ended in true Palmerstonian fashion when Britain sent a fleet to threaten Rio de Janeiro. The humiliation of this event made the Imperial government determined to build up its naval strength and by the outbreak of war the fleet of 45 vessels included 33 steamers.

Steam power did not in itself threaten Humaitá. The ships themselves were just as vulnerable, and were no bigger than their sailing predecessors, although they could of course be manoeuvred more easily since they did not rely on a favourable wind. The really important feature about the Imperial Navy was that it included ironclads. The first of these was the *Brazil*, which arrived in December 1865. She had a crew of 145 and a central armoured battery containing four 68prs and two 32prs. By March 1866 three other armoured ships had joined her at Corrientes. They were the *Tamandaré*, which had a crew of 120 men and the same number of guns as the *Brazil*, the *Barroso*, which carried four 68prs and four 32prs (according to Thompson her armament included a 120pr Whitworth) and the *Bahia*, a 1,000 ton vessel built by Laird's of Birkenhead, with two 150pr Whitworth guns mounted in a revolving turret built on the principle drawn up by Captain C.P. Coles of the Royal Navy. These vessels were all protected by armour plating ranging from 4in to 4½ins thick.

The Brazilian ironclads were not elegant vessels. John Codman, an American traveller who saw some of them in Rio in 1867 called them 'the veriest absurdities of naval architecture. It is just to other foreigners to say that the contractors who furnished them are English.' Burton was also unimpressed and called them 'floating coffins, equally vile for living in as for fighting.' The Brazilian sailors themselves later in the war complained to Commander A.J. Kennedy of the British gunboat *Spider* about the awkward size and clumsy steering of the ships and Kennedy sympathised. But all of these disadvantages were outweighed by one crucial fact - the Brazilian ironclads were virtually immune to the guns of Humaitá.

That the Allies possessed ironclads at all was another of those cruel ironies that dogged Paraguay throughout the war, and as with all the other technical innovations that helped the Allies so much, it was entirely coincidental, resulting not from developments in Brazil, Argentina or Uruguay but from events in Europe and the United States. In the years following 1815 the French naval authorities were continually trying to find ways of reducing the vast gap in naval power that existed between them and the British, but since they could not hope to match Britain in numbers they tried to do so by technical innovations. One of their most important developments was the invention of the Paixhan gun, which for the first time enabled exploding shells to be fired from wooden ships: previously there had always been a fear that the ship doing the firing would blow itself up.

Although the shell-gun was invented in 1838, it was not until 1853 that its advantages over conventional solid shot weapons were demonstrated, when a Russian fleet armed with Paixhan guns wiped out a Turkish fleet at Sinope. Providing it hits its target, in fact, the Paixhan shell could hardly go wrong. If it exploded on impact it blew an enormous hole in the side of the ship, which could result in the ship sinking if it was anywhere near the water line. If the shell exploded inside the ship it would cause great damage, and probably start a fire - the greatest battle threat to wooden ships. And if it simply went straight through the other side of the vessel, then it had done at least as much damage as a conventional solid shot.

It was clear that wooden ships were doomed after this battle, and in 1855 the French cancelled a programme to build 40 wooden ships of the line and turned to other materials. Experiments with armour plating had been going on for some time before the Crimean War, but the war gave these efforts a greater impetus. In 1855 the French built three floating batteries each plated with 4in armour and sent them off to bombard the fort of Kinburn, which covered the estuaries of the Bug and Dnieper rivers. Although the Russian 24prs hit the batteries 137 times, none of them penetrated the armour plating and within four hours the forts were battered into surrender. Although no British batteries took part in the Crimean campaign, tests made in England confirmed the French experience. It was clear that armour plating was the answer to the Paixhan shell since the shell's penetrating power was less than that of solid shot, while an explosion on impact would do little damage to the plates. Both Britain and France embarked on a programme of ironclad building. The appearance of the French *La Gloire,* the world's first ironclad warship in 1859 was followed in 1860 by the launching of *HMS Warrior.* The following year Britain gave up building wooden capital ships and from then on armoured vessels rapidly became standard. There were at least 100 ironclads under construction in various parts of the world in 1862 when the famous battle of the *Virginia* (or *Merrimack*) and *Monitor* demonstrated dramatically the superiority of amour plating to the guns in use at the time. Its significance was not lost in South America. López himself ordered a number of ironclads from Blyth's of Limehouse, but the order was cancelled when the war broke out because Paraguay was unable to send money to Britain to pay for them. Eventually the Brazilians purchased them. The famous battle in Norfolk Roads came in the middle of their quarrel with Great Britain, and the government included ironclads in its plans for strengthening the fleet. The outbreak of the war with Paraguay gave this programme fresh impetus, and ironclads began to arrive in numbers just when they were most needed.

By then the development of rifled guns, such as the Whitworth, had made armour plating less impregnable than before, but that did not affect the campaign in Paraguay: the Paraguayans did not have any rifled guns, while the Allies did have armour plating. It meant that they held not only all the aces, but the trumps as well.

López realised that the Humaitá batteries were not impassable and while the Allies were concentrating he had a second battery constructed at Curupayty, about six miles from Humaitá, to keep the Allied fleet so far away that they could not bombard the batteries with their heavier and longer ranged weapons. But neither Curupayty nor Humaitá could have resisted a serious attack by the Allied fleet once the ironclads arrived.

By March 21 when it left Corrientes for Corrales, the fleet included 18 steam gunboats and four ironclads, and mounted a total of 125 guns. Although the Paraguayan 8in guns did occasionally penetrate the armour plating of the Allied ships, there were only a handful of them in both batteries, and the other guns were unable to penetrate the armour at all. It should have been a simple task to put these guns out of action - since the Whitworths of the fleet outranged the Paraguayan guns this could have been accomplished in perfect safety - and then move in for the kill, using the ironclads as the spearhead of the attack. The firepower at the ships' disposal would have prevented the Paraguayan army from interfering, and any attempt by the remnants of López's navy to resist would simply have resulted in a repeat of Riachuelo. Once the batteries had been destroyed and the Paraguayan fleet eliminated the whole river approach to Asuncion would have been open to the Allies. Since the Paraguayans were just as reliant on the river as the Allies for their supplies, López would have been forced to abandon Humaitá altogether and retreat north by land to a position nearer his bases in central Paraguay. The Allies, however, made no attempt to challenge the myth of Humaitá. They accepted, without so much as a reconnaissance, that the batteries both at Curupayty and Humaitá itself were too strong to be attacked - although the experience of the American Civil War should have shown them that river fortifications, however strong, could always be reduced by armoured warships with powerful guns. They estimated that Humaitá alone mounted 120 guns in the river batteries, including rifled Lancaster guns[51] - a gross exaggeration both of the numbers and the quality of the fortress's armament.

Their reluctance to find out exactly how strong Humaitá was (which could only be done by actually going there) was partly conditioned by the activities of Bruguez and his flying batteries in the months following Riachuelo. His 32prs had severely punished the gunboats of the Brazilian fleet, and had given the Allies a healthy respect for Paraguayan marksmanship.

The *Amazonas* was hit 41 times at Cuevas, the *Iyahi* 22 times and the Argentinean Guardia *Nacional* 27 times, and all suffered severe casualties. But none of them was an ironclad and despite the punishment they received, none of them was sunk. The Allies should have come to the conclusion that the batteries were not impassable, and then set out to pass them. Instead, they chose to attack from the rear - and by doing so committed themselves to a campaign that lasted years.

Chapter 13

Apart from the batteries, the defences of Humaitá in 1865 were rudimentary. Because of the lack of suitable building materials, no stone was used, and the whole system on the landward side was made up of earthworks. In 1865 the fortress consisted of a 14,000-yard long perimeter trench which ran from each end of the 2,500-yard cliff on which the batteries were built enclosing an area roughly 4,000 yards by 2,000 yards. The trench, about eleven feet wide and six feet deep, served the same purpose as a moat in medieval fortifications, and was strengthened by a parapet on the inside. At intervals of about 250 yards, special redans were built into it from which guns could sweep the front of the trench. Other field guns were mounted at intervals along the parapet itself. The total number of guns installed along this perimeter was probably not much more than 100 at this stage, and Humaitá was never envisaged as a real fortress but as a series of batteries and an entrenched camp for the army.

This engraving, also from the Illustrated London News, shows Humaitá in 1865. It was then only a small and isolated customs post. Later it became the main Paraguayan fortress in the war.

Masterman remembered Humaitá as a "dreary place, flat and marshy, the soil a retentive clay so that a heavy rain makes a lake of it. On all sides stretch the dismal *esteros,* with narrow, bad roads winding through them. A little raised above the general surface would be a few neglected fields. a grove of ragged old orange trees, and a poor rancho. Nothing else between the low parapet on the land side and the distant hills, a blue line on the horizon. Within the works there were long ranges of barracks, mere sheds of adobes and thatched with reeds, a single-storied brick house, where the President resided, he at one end, the bishop at the other, and Mrs. Lynch between them, and a few squares of tiled rooms for the officers.

"The church was rather a favourable specimen of native architecture, gaily painted outside, and with a double row of life sized wooden saints within. The tower had been built so badly that they dared not suspend the bells within it, so they hung from a beam outside. The batteries were hidden by a belt of trees from the lines, and none but those having business there were allowed to go near them.." The church, which had only been consecrated in 1861 and was dedicated to San Carlos Borromeo, was in the north-east corner of the camp. Other important buildings included the arsenal, customs house and a soap factory, all to the west of López's house. The barracks for the artillerymen were just behind the batteries they manned, while the infantry barracks, with room for 12,000 men were to the south west. The hospital was in the rear of the batteries.

From the cliffs, a ridge of comparatively firm ground ran south for six miles to a point called Paso Pucu (the 'long pass' in Guaraní). Curupayty was about six miles to the south west, although because of the bends of the liver was twice as far by water. These three points, Humaitá, Paso Pucu and Curupayty, enclosed a rectangle of relatively firm land about six miles long and four wide. South of Curupayty and north of Humaitá, the firm ground abruptly gave way to areas of swamp known as *carrizal.* In the rainy season this was always under water, and the banks of the river could only be picked out by the long lines of palm trees that grew along them. The mud, thick, black and glutinous, made movement almost impossible. This helped the Paraguayans, since the Allies were unable to position heavy artillery there. The Paraguayans were further aided by the thick forests of palms and other trees that screened the high ground at Paso Pucu and Curupayty.

Elsewhere the view was always the same. To the north, south, east and west one saw "the meadow-like pampas beyond, covered with short dry turf, scarcely green in the foreground, except shortly after rain, grey then blue, as the plains recede to the horizon and save for the shadow of a passing cloud, without one interruption to the gradual change of tint; and as silent and unpeopled as when they first rose from the bottom of the sea.[52]" Much of the land was marked by *esteros* mentioned by Masterman, shallow lakes and rivers that spread for miles, usually no more than six feet deep, but made almost impassable by a floor of mud and thick rushes called *piris*. When these esteros dried up, the soil turned into grey dust, full of cracks, covered with wiry grass and low shrubs. Patches of higher ground, never more than a hundred feet or so above the level of the river, rose here and there like islands, often covered with the twenty feet high *yatai* palms, swaying gently in the wind, or the orange groves that seemed to grow everywhere in Paraguay. A few roads wound from island to island, meandering lazily across the swamp. The largest of these *esteros* was the Estero Bellaco, the western tip of the great Néembucu swamp which covered most of southern Paraguay as far as Encarnacion. The Bellaco split into two separate branches east of Humaitá, and entered the River Paraguay several miles below the fort by means of the Laguna Piris, which also drained off several esteros south west of Curupayty. The northern Bellaco was only two miles beyond Paso Pucu, and was marked by numerous islands, swamps and palm forests. The southern Bellaco, two miles wide in places, was another mile or two beyond that, the area in between being known as Tuyuti. South of the southern Bellaco was another area of reasonably firm ground which included the visage of Paso de la Patria, and beyond that the ground fell away suddenly into another mile wide stretch of carrizal before the River Paraná was reached. After some hesitation - he was not sure whether the Allies would attack Humaitá or Encarnacion and toyed with the idea of making his camp at Santa Teresa, half way between the two - López decided that Humaitá was the most threatened point and in October he sent Thompson off to make a survey of the ground between the fortress and the River Paraná.

Thompson's career was an interesting one. He had gone to Paraguay under contract to build the railway, and worked on it for about six years before the war broke out. He was probably only about 20 years old when he arrived with William Padison. He decided to join up, as he put it, 'for a change of air,' sharing the common Paraguayan misconception that it would be a brief and bloodless promenade after which life would get back to normal. He was given the rank of major, and at first played very little active part. Later, when the war entered its defensive phase he became more and more important to the Paraguayans. Wisner von Morgenstern was supposed to be the chief engineer but he was ill for most of the war and his duties fell upon Thompson's shoulders. Although he had previously had no experience whatsoever of military engineering, he found two books on the subject, MacAulay's 'Field Fortifications', and 'The Professional Papers of the Royal Engineers', swotted them up and devised his own system of surveying. In time he became so skilled and such an able officer that Washburn believed López was more indebted to him than any other man in the army.

Although Thompson's motives for joining the army were scarcely idealistic, the publication of the treaty of the Triple Alliance convinced him that Paraguay was fighting for its survival. He was the only Englishman to join the army, but he fought for the Republic with skill, courage and an unwavering devotion that makes him one of the most admirable of all the figures who played an important part in the war. It did not take Thompson long to decide that Paso de la Patria was the best position. The carrizal to the west could not be held in force since no heavy guns could be placed there and it would in any case be dominated by the Brazilian fleet. The ridge at Paso de la Patria was about forty feet above the level of the carrizal. By fortifying this position, the Paraguayans would dominate the carrizal through which the Allies would have to advance, and the position itself could not be outflanked. Further to the west there was a small fort called Itapiru - the fort which had fired on the Water Witch so many years before which was too small to do much, but could act as a further check. The front was further protected by a stream called the Carraya, which was normally six feet deep but could be made deeper if dammed up. On November 25 López moved his headquarters to a house on the ridge, and Thompson began work.

The main feature of the position was an 11 feet wide, six feet deep trench running along the crest of the high ground. It was about a mile long, and by the time it was finished roughly 100 guns had been positioned there. To man it López stripped the frontier posts of troops, reduced the garrison of Humaitá to a minimum, converted several cavalry regiments into infantry, and scoured the training camps for men. In this way he managed to build up a force of around 30,000 men. Compared with the fine army that had existed a year before, this was a pathetically small total, but Thompson at least thought that it would be adequate for the task. The position could hardly be better: the men's morale was as high as ever; their guns were old fashioned, but most of the men had weapons of some sort, and there was still plenty of ammunition. By the end of 1865, a year that had begun with victories in the Matto Grosso, and had then been marked by defeat after defeat, Thompson was feeling confident.

The Allies had a fairly good idea of what they were up against (or thought they had) and were in no great hurry to tackle it. And there was no real reason why they should be. Time was on the Allies' side, and Mitre saw no reason to attack until he was ready.

By the new year, 62,000 men were under arms, 40,000 of them Brazilians, 18,000 Argentineans and 4,000 Uruguayans. Of these 50,000 were concentrated around Corrales, a small port directly opposite Paso de la Patria, although Corrientes remained the main supply base. Another 12,000 Brazilians, under Porto Alegre, meanwhile marched from Rio Grande to Candelaria, opposite Encarnacion, with vague ideas of invading Paraguay from a different direction. López sent 3,000 men and 12 guns under the command of Major Nuñez to keep an eye on them, and continued to dig in at Paso de la Patria.

While the troops worked on the defences, López did his best to boost their morale - not a difficult task, since the Guaraní soldiers remained in good spirits despite the calamitous consequences of the year's campaigning. López was a master of psychology, and like the Napoleon whom he admired so greatly, he could mingle easily with the rank and file, chaffing them, telling them jokes in Guaraní, generally convincing them that he was one of them and shared their trials and sufferings. He soon discovered a way of channelling their desire to do something more positive than dig trenches. Early in December, when the Allied troops were moving into Corrales, he noticed some Correntino troops on the opposite bank of the Paraná, and sent over a few optimistic shots from a 12pr. When these missed he sent over four canoes, each carrying twelve men, to drive the enemy away.

This succeeded so well and proved so popular with the troops that the raids became almost a daily occurrence, with up to 200 men at a time frequently taking part. These raids put the Allies in a state of nervous apprehension that twice led to rumours that the whole Paraguayan army had landed and surrounded them. On February 20, in a final flourish, 1,000 Paraguayans landed at Itati 24 miles from Corrales and attacked the 5,000-strong Uruguayan contingent, which fled in such haste that the Paraguayans were able to sack and burn their camp.

During these raids the Paraguayan morale was always astonishingly high. The troops would march down to the river dancing and singing, accompanied by one of the army's splendid bands and the women of the camp. Elisa Lynch, whose personal courage had already won her the admiration of the soldiers, would hand out cigars and presents and wish them luck as they paddled off into the darkness. The thought of death never seems to have worried the Paraguayans, and on occasions it could even be regarded as a source of amusement, as Thompson noted: 'If a Paraguayan in the midst of his comrades was blown to pieces by a shell they would yell with delight, thinking it a capital joke, in which they would have been joined by the victim himself had he been capable.'

The Paraguayans rapidly came to realise that man for man they were superior to their opponents, and despite the reverses they suffered they never lost this self-confidence. Their attitude towards the Brazilians at least was accompanied by a good deal of racial prejudice. The Brazilian rank and file were drawn from the poorer sections of the multi-racial empire and were mostly Negroes. Many of them, in fact, were ex-slaves, since the war was so unpopular that the Imperial government was forced to offer freedom to any slaves who volunteered for the army. The Paraguayans sneered at them as the 'cambas' or blacks and 'macacos' or monkeys. The Allied troops, who, especially as the war dragged on, were often recruited against their will, were badly led and badly treated, and although they sometimes showed great bravery they never rose to the fanatical heights displayed by the Paraguayans.

But the raids, although they raised Paraguayan's morale and terrified the Allies, did not stop the build up at Corrales. On February 25 Tamandaré, the Brazilian admiral, finally arrived at Corrientes, after having spent a year on his way to the war and on March 21 he moved his fleet up to Corrales. It included eighteen gunboats, the four ironclads and behind this impressive screen the Allies had assembled thirty transport steamers, thirty floating piers, 150 canoes and an enormous quantity of supplies and equipment. The long awaited invasion was about to begin.

Chapter 14

It was not in López's nature to sit back meekly and wait for the enemy to set foot in his country, and as the Brazilian fleet prepared to transport the army across the Paraná he organised his first counter measure. Canoes carrying rocks were sunk in the channel directly off Paso de la Patria, the *Gualequay*, one of the Argentinean ships captured at Corrientes, was armed with two 12prs, and on March 22 a *chata* armed with an 8in gun was towed half a mile below Itapiru and began blasting away at the fleet. Since this consisted of more than twenty warships with 125 guns between them, this was not exactly a fair match, but the Paraguayan gunners hit Tamandaré's flagship four times before the Brazilians could get near them. The *chatas* were ideal for this type of action. Their low freeboard made them almost impossible to hit, and their lack of manoeuvrability was not such a disadvantage as it had been at the Riachuelo. From the Paraguayan point of view the whole incident was eminently satisfactory.

The *chata's* crew dived overboard as soon as the Brazilians got too close and swam ashore. Then, when the Brazilians tried to take the *chata* in tow a hundred infantry hidden in the reeds on the shore opened fire on them and eventually the enemy had to be content with setting the *chata* on fire. Even then the Paraguayans managed to salvage her gun.

López watched the whole thing from his headquarters, and on March 27 a second *chata* was towed to the same place and took on three of the ironclads. Although most of her shots shattered on the armour plating, one ball went through the porthole of the *Tamandaré*, killing four officers and wounding 14 men.[53] After this the Brazilians withdrew and next day the battle was resumed. The *Barroso* was holed four times, and her 120pr Whitworth cut in two, but eventually the Paraguayan gun was destroyed, and the ten members of her crew dived overboard and swam ashore. López ordered another *chata* to be towed down from Humaitá the next day, but she was captured by the Brazilians.

Meanwhile, the Paraguayans were still firing from the *Gualeguay* and the fort at Itapiru. This fort, in Hutchinson's opinion, was 'no fort in the common acceptation of the word; for it consists of a breastwork of clay and stones about twenty yards in length, on which two 42prs and a mortar are mounted, a small rancho (hut), a *galpon,* or shed, of like dimensions, and a flag staff on which the Paraguayan banner is mounted.'

Nevertheless, the fort kept up a brisk and annoying fire. Hutchinson, who watched the proceedings from Corrales half a mile across the river, said he could tell when the fort was firing for the Paraguayan guns 'had invariably that sharp ringing crack which tells of good gunnery.'

The Allies took the threat of Itapiru so seriously that on April 5 they set up a battery of eight guns on a sandbank that had appeared within rifle range of the fort the previous November. These guns, aided by twelve rifled 12prs and some 13in mortars at Corrales began a vigorous bombardment. So far López had shown good sense, goading the Allies into unnecessary attacks, and generally disrupting their plans, but five days later he allowed himself to be goaded in his turn, sending Lieutenant Colonel José Diaz with 1,300 men to attack the battery and the garrison of 2,000 men. They landed at 4am and fought with ferocious bravery, but the alarm was given, and the fleet arrived to pour round after round of devastating canister into their ranks. The Paraguayans lost about 500 dead, and gained nothing.

After this, although the *Gualequay* and the gunners of Itapiru kept up their David and Goliath duel with the ironclads, López made no serious attempt to impede the invasion, and on April 16 Osorio and Flores landed half a mile up the River Paraguay with 10,000 men. A second wave of 10,000 Argentineans followed, and a half-hearted Paraguayan counterattack was beaten off. By nightfall the bridgehead was secure, and the next day the Paraguayans abandoned Itapiru: it had served its purpose, but was too isolated from the main Paraguayan positions to be of any further use. The next day the Allies took possession of it, and Mitre, the commander in chief, crossed to Paraguayan soil. He was optimistic that the easy crossing meant that the Paraguayans were weakening, and he told Hutchinson before he left Corrales that he was hopeful that the war would soon be over ('An opinion in which I regret that I cannot coincide,' the consul wrote).

The lack of resistance was however deceptive. The Paraguayans had all along planned to make their major stand at Paso de la Patria, which by then had been converted into a position of great strength. Burton considered that López could have held the position "for months, if not for years. Upon this subject both Paraguayans and Argentineans agree." Thompson believed that the Allies would probably 'never have been able to take the trenches.' It was therefore a pleasant surprise for the Allies when López suddenly decided not to hold Paso de la Patria after all. While the Brazilian fleet was moving into position to bombard the trenches, López suddenly mounted his horse and rode off to the north.

A general exodus followed this precipitate departure. More than 1,000 women with the army were sent off just as the bombardment was beginning. Shells crashed all around them, but no one was hurt, and during the day Resquín ordered the evacuation of the infantry, while Bruguez and the artillery commander Lieutenant Colonel Hilario Marcó held the trenches with a rearguard.

The Allies bombarded the trenches all day long with the fleet and 40 guns of Mitre's artillery, and killed or wounded only six men. As Thompson had predicted, the earthworks had proved almost impregnable to the Allied fire. The Whitworth shells, although accurate, buried themselves in the soft ground before exploding, and the blast was muffled by the earth. Damage to the parapets could easily be made good, and in any case, artillery alone could not take the position: all the Paraguayan guns were intact, and were as capable as ever of repelling any attempt by the Allied infantry to storm the trenches.

Since the Allies themselves were astounded to have taken it so easily, friend and foe alike tried to find some explanation for López's decision to abandon Paso de la Patria and for most of them the answer was simple: López was a coward who had run away because he was afraid of the Allied guns. López came to be so hated that his cowardice became an integral part of the mythology surrounding him. But it is too simple an explanation to be really accurate. Nobody saw López under fire so often as Thompson, and his opinion was that 'he possessed a peculiar kind of courage: when out of range of fire, even though completely surrounded by the enemy, he was always in high spirits, but he could not endure the whistle of a ball.' This does not make López a hero - but it does give the customary verdict a different emphasis. López's terror of gunfire was certainly extreme - on the day after he fled from Paso de la Patria Thompson saw him move even further from the front because two shells burst a mile away. But the occasions when fear got the better of him, while spectacular, were rare, and although he was not a brave man it seems that López's aversion to gunfire took the form of a phobia, similar to the fears that other people have of heights, or rats. Paso de la Patria was the first time in his life that he had experienced artillery fire, and he panicked at the prospect of being subjected to a sustained bombardment. Having run, his pride and fear prevented him from going back - and so the defences his army had been working on for months were surrendered without a fight.

That, at any rate, is the theory favoured by those who hated López. There is, however, another possibility. Despite its defensive merits, Paso de la Patria was a long way from Humaitá, the key to the whole Paraguayan position. If the Allies, using their armoured ships as a battering ram, were to launch an attack on Humaitá the Paraguayans would find it difficult to move troops from Paso de la Patria in time to prevent them from capturing the fortress. If that were to happen, the army would be trapped and Asuncion and the rest of the country would be completely defenceless. The Allies would have won the war.

Whatever the reason, López decided to make Humaitá his main base. The river defences were relatively strong, but there were no defensive works on the landward side. Later in the day, Mrs. Lynch and the Bishop, who had been abandoned along with everyone else, found him on a hill three miles behind the lines, and that evening López started planning his next position. He spent the next day riding over the land around Estero Bellaco, and Thompson was again called upon to make sketches and maps of the area.

This investigation showed that the strongest line was north of the northern branch of the *estero*, and on April 22 the army marched to new positions at Paso Gomez, one of the fords that led through the marshes.

The next day orders were given for the final evacuation of Paso de la Patria. The gallant *Gualequay* was scuppered - only to be found and refloated by the Brazilians a few days later - and the town was burned and evacuated. The Allies, who had been expecting a bitter struggle, occupied the trenches, the same day, confident that the war would soon be over. They had had a year of victories so far and the Paraguayans had scarcely lifted a finger even in defence of their homeland. In Paso de la Patria they had secured a firm base, and the majority of their army was ashore. A huge armada of ships, 54 steamers, 11 smaller steam vessels and 48 sailing ships, were ferrying guns, equipment and supplies across from Corrales and Corrientes and things were generally going so smoothly that on 8 May Dom Pedro wrote to a friend that "the Allies will march into Humaitá and I hope the war will soon be ended."

But six days before the Emperor's letter was written the march to Humaitá came to an abrupt halt: 5,000 Paraguayans under the command of Diaz made their way quietly through the woods and caught Flores' vanguard completely by surprise. The infantry gave the enemy artillery time to fire only once before charging across the earthworks and killing or capturing the startled gunners. Three Uruguayan battalions fought bravely but were virtually wiped out as 1,000 Paraguayan cavalry joined in the attack.

The Brazilians and Argentineans in the vanguard suffered equally, and while they fell back Diaz sent four brass rifled guns back to the Paraguayan lines - the first trophies of the campaign. Flores' tent was taken, and the general himself was only rescued when Osorio marched to the relief with a battalion of Brazilians. At this stage the Paraguayan victory was almost complete, and Diaz, who had too few men to do any more, should have returned to the safety of his own position. Instead he went on and his troops were severely punished by Mitre, who was moving up with reinforcements. The Paraguayans suffered 2,300 casualties - nearly fifty percent of their force - and had to abandon the other guns they had captured. Even so, the moral victory rested with Diaz. Allied losses had been about the same, and the Uruguayans in particular had suffered very heavily. The Florida battalion (which had fought at Yatai) was left with only 40 men and eight out of 27 officers, while the 24 Abril lost 9 officers and 200 men. Altogether the vanguard had suffered 1,600 casualties.

Flores at any rate was in no doubt about the result of the battle. The following day he wrote to his wife, Maria: 'Yesterday the vanguard, under my orders, sustained a considerable defeat, the Oriental Division being almost completely lost. Between twelve o'clock and one o'clock my camp was surprised by a powerful column of Paraguayans of the three arms. It was impossible to resist forces triple the number of ours...' The battle gave him an excuse to give vent to his feelings on the war generally, and after this frank admission of defeat, he proceeded to blame it on Mitre: 'I comprehended the bad position of our encampment. Some day before the event, Marshal Osorio and myself went in person to the General in Chief to show him the advantage of removing the camp, but Mitre answered thus: "Don't alarm yourself, General Flores: the aggression of the barbarians is nil, for the hour of their extermination has sounded." If therefore anyone is responsible for the occurrence of May 2, General Mitre is that man.'[54]

The truth of the matter was that Flores was out of his element in the swamps of Paraguay. He was a *gaucho*, a swashbuckling horseman who saw warfare as a succession of cavalry charges across the wide open plains of the *pampa*. 'What is passing here does not suit my temper at all', he confessed to Maria. 'Everything is done by mathematical calculations, and the most precious time is lost in drawing lines and looking at the sky...meanwhile, some of the corps have had nothing to eat for three days. I don't know what will become of us and if to the critical situation we are in you add the constant apathy of General Mitre, it may very well happen that in going to seek for wool we ourselves may be shorn.'

Compared with the situation in the Paraguayan camp, the predicament of the Allies scarcely justified the pessimism shown by Flores, but his letter reflected not only his unease with the type of warfare necessary in Paraguay, but the unhappy state of the Uruguayans. As a result of the battle of May 2 their contingent was almost eliminated, and the losses had to be made good with Argentineans.

This merely confirmed what had for a long time been evident, that Uruguay was by now such a junior partner in the war that the wishes of its president and leading general scarcely counted. Since the war had broken out because of the situation in Uruguay itself, the irony of his position must have done little to cheer Flores up. A further embarrassment was provided by 700 Paraguayans who had joined the

Allied armies after being captured at Yatai and Uruguayana. They had been armed, fed, given fine uniforms and a position of honour among the first troops to set foot in Paraguay when the invasion began. And as soon as they were ordered into the attack they dropped their banners, kept their guns, and promptly rejoined Diaz and their fellow countrymen. Quite apart from its military results, therefore, the battle of the Estero Bellaco had made the Allies a little more thoughtful. They moved cautiously across the southern *estero* on May 20 wondering if Humaitá was quite so near as it had seemed.

Chapter 15

López did not attempt to stop the Allied advance. He had decided to make his stand at the northern Bellaco, and so the Allies were able to move forward in three columns and take possession of the lonely and unlovely stretch of marsh called Tuyuti, which only a year before had been unknown to all but a few herdsmen and the cattle that fed on the lush grasses that grew there.

On May 20, the same day that the Allies moved to Tuyuti, López established his headquarters at Paso Pucu, conveniently close to the Bellaco, Curupayty and Humaitá. On the same day the indispensable Thompson began work on a new trench covering the ford at Paso Gomez, where the high road from Paso de la Patria to Humaitá crossed the Bellaco. A few other fords crossed it at various points and fortifications were constructed there as well.

South of the stream was an area known as Potrero Sauce, a mass of tangled jungle and *carrizal* so thick with trees, shrubs and creepers that it was impossible to see more than twenty yards. In the centre was a natural clearing, and the position was so difficult to penetrate that López decided to hang on to it as a threat to the Allied left flank. The only opening to the south was closed by building another trench and a road was cut through the woods from the clearing to the main Paraguayan positions. About 25,000 men and 100 guns held the line, which extended from Potrero Sauce to Rojas, about two miles east of Paso Gomez.

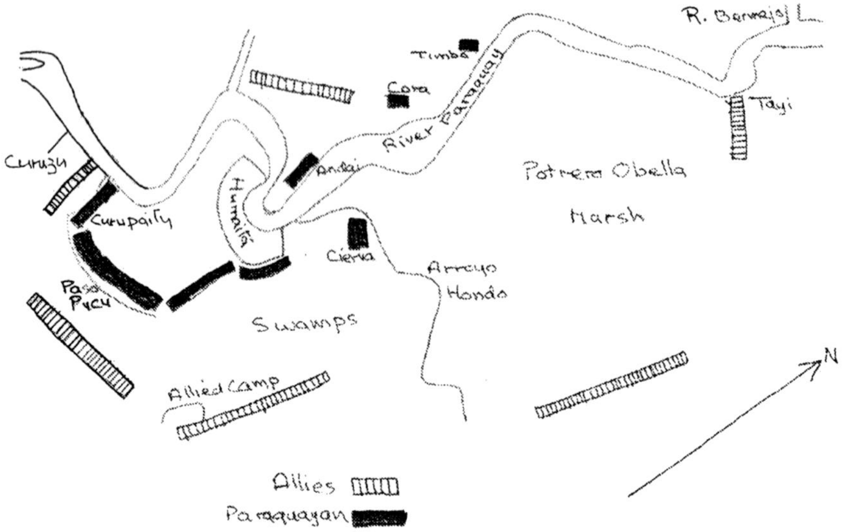

This map shows the position of the armies around Humaitá at the beginning of 1868. The Allies had troops on both sides of the River Paraguay and also had warships above and below Humaitá. Despite this, the Paraguayans managed to cross the river, march fifty miles north through the Chaco and then re-cross the river before the Allies realised they had gone.

The Allied army facing them consisted of 45,000 men. Flores, still the commander of the vanguard, held the centre with the remnants of the Uruguayan forces, some Argentinean cavalry, two Brazilian infantry divisions and 34 guns. Osorio and the Brazilians were on the left, and the Argentineans on the right. These troops were commanded by Paunero, Emilio Mitre, the commander in chief's brother, and General Juan Gelly y Obes: he was born in Asuncion and it was his father who had been secretary to López during his visit to Europe. The Allies occupied a front of three miles, along which 150 guns had been placed and they immediately built two redoubts to prevent a repeat of Diaz's attack.

The Paraguayans skirmished incessantly, watched the Allies dig in, and waited. There was no need to do anything else. To get to Humaitá, the Allies had to cross the Bellaco, and it was reasonably safe to assume that they would try to do it by Paso Gomez: if they moved towards the passes on the east they would become hopelessly bogged down in the mud and lay themselves open to a flank attack. Knowing this, the Paraguayans had made their plan, which was simple enough. As soon as the Allies were committed to a frontal assault on an entrenched position, 10,000 men would be sent into the Potrero Sauce by means of the newly cut road. This led right to the edge of the trees, but the last few yards had been left uncleared to screen it from the Brazilians opposite. It was assumed that they would be watching the natural opening in the trees, so that an attack from the hidden road would take them by surprise and roll up the whole line.

With a bit of luck (and by then the Paraguayans must have felt they were due for some) the Allies would be forced back beyond the southern Bellaco and possibly right out of Paraguay. López would have gained the stunning, crushing, once-and-for-all triumph that he had been dreaming of since before Riachuelo.

But there was a problem. On May 20 Tamandaré had sent his fleet of ironclads and gunboats up to Curupayty. They had given the batteries a cursory inspection and then retired a few miles down river to Palmas where they anchored and did no more. Even so, it was disturbing, because apart from the batteries Curupayty was almost undefended, and if the Allies should land an army there they would find the path to Humaitá wide open. A year later López told Thompson that he had heard that Mitre planned to attack on May 25. He said: 'Frankly I did not like the plan and resolved to prevent the execution of it by attacking him beforehand."'

Rumours of an impending assault on the batteries were circulating in the Paraguayan camp on the 20th and López kept several battalions of infantry at Paso Pucu ready to hurry west if anything should happen there. It is probable that it was these rumours that López was referring to when he spoke to Thompson and although they were false, they were convincing enough to make López abandon his plans and decide on an attack. The plan itself was ambitious. López was banking on a knockout blow, not just a victory and skated over the fact that the Paraguayans were outnumbered by two to one, were poorly equipped and would be attacking well-armed men in entrenched position across flat ground dominated by enemy artillery.

Barrios, with 8,000 infantry and a handful of cavalry was to move into the woods of Potrero Piris (beyond Sauce) on the right wing, Diaz to attack the centre with 5,000 infantry, and Resquín, with 7,000 cavalry and 2,000 infantry, was to cross the Estero Bellaco by the passes on the far left. All the troops were to move into position during the night of May 23 and, when a signal rocket was fired at 9am on the 24th, would hurl themselves on the unsuspecting Allied lines. Resquín's cavalry would overwhelm the Argentineans, pour round the rear of the Allied army and link up with Barrios. The enemy would then be surrounded, and the battle won.

This was the plan and it began to go wrong even before the battle was started. Barrios's men, who had the furthest to go, got ensnared in the woods and it was not until 11.55am that the signal rocket finally soared into the sky. By then the Allies were already drawn up ready for a reconnaissance in force ordered by Mitre in preparation for a major attack planned for the following morning (López had been right about the date of the attack but had got the place wrong). They were thus in some sort of order when the Paraguayans suddenly emerged from the woods and attacked.

The impact was devastating. The Paraguayans came out of the swamps and forests, charged through rifle bullets and shells and flung themselves against the Allied defences with complete disregard for losses. On the right Barrios's troops drove the Brazilians to the edge of the southern Bellaco before Osorio could rally them and they did it twice more, overwhelming superior numbers by fanatical courage. But they could not capture the Brazilian artillery. Secure behind a trench, 28 Whitworth and La Hitte guns blasted away at the red-shirted ranks with fuses cut to a minimum. The men in the trench suffered terrible losses, but they held on gallantly and as the afternoon wore on the Paraguayan attacks began to fade.

On the far left Resquín's cavalry came from behind its screen of palm trees and swept away a detachment of 200 Correntino cavalry under Caceres. Colonel Ignacio Rivas, one of Paunero's best officers, charged the Paraguayans in an attempt to stem the tide only to be overwhelmed in his turn. This left the Argentinean artillery exposed and the Paraguayan troopers, giving their whooping Indian war cry, rode over them, lancing the gunners and capturing 20 guns.

But this proved to be the limit of their success. Resquín lacked reserves, and while his men were trying to bring back the captured weapons the Argentineans rallied. Mitre sent a division of infantry to hold the line and then the cavalry counter-attacked. Caught in the open and without support the Paraguayans were surrounded and the guns re-taken. The Paraguayan infantry were sent forward in a forlorn attempt to retrieve the situation but were driven back by withering artillery fire.

There was just one chance now of Resquín joining up with Barrios, and that lay with a few cavalry regiments who had been sent further to the left to cross the swamps by the Minas pass, but by the time they were ready to attack the Argentineans had stabilised their line, and the Paraguayans were again forced back. Only one regiment, under the command of Major Olabarrieta, cut its way through and reached the rear of the Allied army. But by this time Barrios's final attack had failed and Olabarrieta finally arrived at the Potrero Sauce badly wounded and almost alone after having fought his way round the entire Allied army.

In the centre, Diaz's attack was a failure from the start. Flores' men were well armed and could use the full power of their modern weapons against men advancing through cloying mud and waist-deep water. Many of the Paraguayans were new recruits who had received little training, and they herded together like sheep and were blown to pieces by the Allied guns.

López watched the first stages of the battle from the cemetery at Paso Pucu, five miles away, and when the firing began went to Paso Gomez with Thompson and Bishop Palacios. By then the battle was raging on all sides and the whole field was hidden by smoke. The marshal and his party moved on to the woods near Rojas, but could still make out very little. Later in the afternoon it became obvious that the attack had failed.

At 4.30 pm, although still uncertain of the exact losses, López gave orders for the attack to be called off. After dark he made his way to Bruguez's house, where Barrios and Diaz arrived soon afterwards, and spent the night discussing the results of the battle. It soon became clear that the Paraguayan army had suffered a catastrophic defeat.

Of the 22,000 men who had charged forward the previous day 6,000 were dead. A further 7,000 were wounded, most of them still lying where they had fallen or struggling back through the woods. Another 350 men, all wounded, had been captured. The other 9,000 were scattered and disorganised, exhausted and almost incapable of defending themselves.

The Allies, although victorious, had suffered heavily themselves. Osorio and Paunero were both wounded, and casualties had totalled about 8,000. The Brazilian General Antonio Sampaio, who had defended the artillery on the left, was mortally wounded, and his 3rd Division had lost 1,033 men. One battalion, the 4th, had gone into the fight with 490 men and come out with only 200 uninjured.

Still, the Allied losses were bearable. They still had more than 40,000 men left at Tuyuti and if necessary Porto Alegre's 12,000, who were still at Encarnacion, could be brought to the Humaitá front as reinforcements. By contrast the Paraguayan army had ceased to exist as an effective force. It would be days before the remnants could be re-organised, and weeks before fresh troops could be brought down from Cerro Leon and the other training camps.

Even then, most of them would consist of old men and boys because the cream of Paraguay's soldiers had already died, either of sickness, lack of treatment, or in the string of defeats that had been going on for a year and of which Tuyuti was the disastrous culmination. Yet it was at this moment, with the war apparently lost because of his own blunders, that López began to prove himself a general.

Chapter 16

Although he was jeered at for his fear of gunfire, López never panicked at defeat. In fact he recovered from the battle of Tuyuti far more rapidly than Mitre although he was in no doubt whatsoever about the critical position he faced. Even when the scattered troops were re-formed he would have only about 10,000 men to fight an Allied force of four times that number. Curupayty could scarcely have resisted a serious attack. The whole left flank at the Bellaco was open, and the trenches at Humaitá were undefended. The cavalry, which had never been strong, was almost destroyed, and 'aides de camp and commanders of corps were mounted on jades with nothing but skin and bones and which could not possibly go beyond a poor walk- and they frequently stopped on the road not being able to move another step.'[55]

This desperate situation was made even worse by the fact that Paraguay was already teetering on the verge of economic collapse, a product of months of war and López's insistence on cramming every available man into the army. Agriculture and industry had both suffered as a result, and the spectre of mass starvation was looming on the horizon. As far as the army was concerned the supply situation was already acute. Originally the troops' rations had consisted of one bullock among 80 men, but as the winter of 1866 approached this had already been reduced. The huge herds that had been brought back from Corrientes the previous year had been almost wiped out by poisonous plants to which the animals were not accustomed. The difficulties of supplying Humaitá were considerable and all of the troops were suffering from malnutrition and dietary deficiencies. Thompson noticed that the bodies of the men who had died in the battle did not decompose in the normal way but simply shrivelled up and the Allies, who tried to dispose of the piles of dead before their trenches by burning them complained that the Paraguayan soldiers were so thin that they did not catch alight. The hospitals, which had been under terrific strain for months, found the task of coping with the new influx of wounded men beyond their control, and the mortality rate soared despite the efforts of Stewart and his fellow doctors.

The country had perhaps 150,000 men between 15 and 55 available for service when the war broke out and by June 1866 probably a third of these were already dead. Although conscription was extended and intensified, the ranks could only be filled at the expense of other sections of the economy, starting a vicious circle from which there was no escape.

In the long run this situation could only lead to defeat, but it would take time. The purely military situation was a far more immediate threat, and López began trying to cope with it even before he knew the full extent of the disaster. On the evening of May 24, when the wounded were still crawling back to the Paraguayan lines (they were still coming in three days later) López gave orders for the trenches to be manned in case the Allies tried to follow up their victory, and instructed the military bands to play stirring music, to encourage the survivors and also to deceive the enemy into believing that the Paraguayan situation was not so serious as it seemed. The Paraguayans also began aggressively patrolling the swamp and forest between the lines, to keep Allied scouts from finding out the true situation.

Behind this screen, López dug in. Thompson was commissioned to construct new trenches at Paso Gomez and the lines were strengthened by the addition of 37 cannon ('everything which by a stretch of courtesy can be called a gun,' in Thompson's view). Artillery was also put in the woods of the Potrero Sauce and in the middle of June began bombarding the Allied vanguard, where the unfortunate Flores twice had his tent blown up by a well-aimed shell. To improve communications, telegraph lines were laid from Paso Pucu to Curupayty, Humaitá, and Potrero Sauce and eventually to all sections of the perimeter.[56]

The shortage of manpower was the greatest problem of all and López tackled it with his usual energy. Although Carlos Antonio López had abolished slavery, his decree only applied to the children of slaves, and several thousand slaves still lived in Asuncion and the surrounding district. In view of the gravity of the situation, López had 6,000 of them brought down to Humaitá and distributed among the depleted battalions manning the perimeter. More reinforcements came in the shape of 200 Payagua Indians, members of a semi-civilised tribe that lived near Asuncion and was already threatened with extinction; they were drafted into the heavy artillery, which did little for their chances of survival, and proved to be admirable soldiers. These measures proved so effective that by the end of June the army had been built up to about 20,000 men, and López was already feeling confident enough to contemplate fighting another battle. He had, however, learned from the debacle of May that modern weapons had given the defence a great advantage over the attack, particularly if the defending troops were positioned in well-constructed earthworks. Instead of attacking recklessly, he therefore tried to goad the Allies into attacking him and on July 10 sent two battalions of infantry to attack the Argentineans at Yataity Cora, an island in the Estero Bellaco. This battle went on for two days before López called it off- the Allies had failed to rise to the bait, and all he had done was lose about 500 men.

He next switched his attention to the opposite flank and sent Thompson off to extend the Paso Gomez trench through the Potrero Sauce woods towards Potrero Piris: this would threaten the flank held by the Brazilians and would make the Allies hesitant about an attack on the centre of the Paraguayan line. This trench had just been completed when the Allies attacked on July 16. Heavily outnumbered., the Paraguayans withdrew from the trench into the woods and kept up a harassing fire, and although the fighting went on all day the Allies made no further impression. They had lost 2,000 men, but the next day the bombardment continued, and on the 18th Flores ordered an attack on the trench guarding the entrance to the Potrero Sauce. This attempt was beaten back, and after that the Allies gave up their belated attempts to take the Sauce position. They had lost 5,000 men in three days, twice as many as the Paraguayans, and had gained nothing except a few yards of useless trench.

Like the Paraguayans, the Allies had learned that brave men in well entrenched positions could hold superior numbers at bay, and like the Paraguayans they dug in, building new batteries and redoubts while the

Paraguayans perfected their trenches until the line of parapets and gun platforms ran from Paso Gomez to the Laguna Chichi on the extreme right.

The way in which López was able to restore an apparently hopeless situation was a great tribute to his tenacity and talents as a defensive fighter - it was a tragedy that he chose to demonstrate those talents so late - but the Paraguayan recovery was also due to the failure of the Allies to exploit their victory.

There were several reasons for this, but among the most important were the continued divisions in the Allied high command, and the growing war-weariness affecting their armies. While the Paraguayans were retreating these factors had to some extent been hidden by the prospect of imminent victory; the battle of Tuyuti had, paradoxically, convinced many of the Allies not that the Paraguayans were beaten, but that the real war was only just beginning. Thompson wrote: 'Their ardour for the war was spent. The soldiers had seen their comrades killed around them by thousands, the attack always having been made by the Paraguayans, and they had only advanced where the field had been purposely left to them; now that the Paraguayans had made a real stand their leaders vacillated, and instead of advancing, entrenched themselves.'

The heavy losses of the battle and the savageness of the fighting had been a severe shock for the Allies, and the unhealthy climate of southern Paraguay, damp and mosquito-ridden resulted in many more lives being lost through disease. Within weeks of the battle, the effective strength of the Argentinean army had been reduced from 15,000 men to 9,000 and the strength of the army as a whole had shrunk to 30,000 fit men.

Even more seriously, the Allied commanders were in considerable disagreement about what to do next. Mitre, who was one of Argentina's greatest statesmen but not ruthless enough to be a great general, refused to consider an immediate attack on the Bellaco position, and believed that the best a course would be to build up the army at Tuyuti while Porto Alegre and the Brazilian 2nd Corps drew off the Paraguayans reserves by operations in the Encarnacion area. This policy was negative to say the least, and the Brazilians began to chafe under Mitre's ineffectual control. Tamandaré, always fishing in troubled waters, and Osorio favoured an attack on the outpost of Curupayty, where the Allied fleet could take part. 0n June 30 a council of war agreed that the attempt should be made.

This decision was not at all what Mitre had had in mind but there was little he could do about it, for shortly before the council met he had been astounded to receive a letter from Porto Alegre saying that he was coming to the Tuyuti front. At the council, Mitre discovered that the suggestion for this move had come from Tamandaré. But since it received the approval of Flores, Osorio and General Polidoro da Fonseca Quintanilha Jordao, commander of the Brazilian lst Corps, and the Brazilians supplied two thirds of the army's manpower, Mitre found himself in a minority. He accepted the decision, and there was a military lull while the Allied waited for Porto Alegre to arrive - a lull that the Paraguayans made good use of.

Porto Alegre arrived at Paso de la Patria on July 12. He had 2,000 cavalry with him, and during the next few days 14,000 men, 14,000 horses and 50 guns followed. Two days before he landed, on July 10, Polidoro took over from Osorio as commander of the Brazilian forces - a promotion that was due partly to Osorio's wound, partly to political manoeuvres in Rio - and Porto Alegre arrived just in time to see the failure of the attack on the Potrero Sauce trenches. Although Polidoro had initiated this attack, it was in a sense a product of the strategy Mitre was advocating, and its failure seemed to prove the wisdom of the Curupayty approach. The preparations for the great attack occupied most of August. Tamandaré and Porto Alegre first quarrelled over which of them was to command the operation and on August 28 the admiral announced that Porto Alegre was under his orders when working with the navy and under Mitre only when the commander in chief was directly involved in an operation. This neatly annexed the responsibility (and hopefully the credit) for the expected triumph to Tamandaré and Brazil, since Mitre would presumably be with the main army at Tuyuti while Curupayty was being taken.

While the Allied generals were haggling over rank, and dithering over what to do next, López was rebuilding his army and digging in at the crucial Bellaco position. Once this had passed the test of July 16 - 18 he turned to Curupayty. In August he established another battery at Curuzu, two miles below, to defend Curupayty in the same way that

Curupayty defended Humaitá. It was surrounded on three sides by *carrizal*, and was connected to Curupayty by a narrow path along the riverbank. Inland, the marsh ended in a lagoon about four feet deep, and a 2,000 yard long trench was dug between this and the river as a protection against a land attack. As long as this position was held, Humaitá was reasonably secure.

On September 1, Tamandaré's fleet (it by then included nine ironclads) began its long-delayed bombardment, but without doing a great deal of damage. In fact the Curuzu battery probably came off best, scoring several hits and causing a few casualties. The next day the fleet resumed firing, and the ironclads moved closer to the battery, banking on the protection of their armour. The Paraguayans answered furiously with their three heavy guns and, after her 4in plates had been holed twice by the 8in gun, the *Rio de Janeiro* suddenly sank: a huge hole had been blown in her hull by a floating mine, and she went down with the loss of her captain and 54 of the crew. This success had a profound effect on the Brazilians: they already feared the Paraguayan batteries, but the introduction of the ironclads seemed to have given them a means of challenging the shore guns without serious injury. The loss of the *Rio de Janeiro* showed that not even ironclads were safe and it was to inhibit their movements for many months.

For the time being, however, the Brazilians pressed ahead and under cover of the bombardment Porto Alegre's 2nd Corps was landed in the carrizal below the Paraguayan trench. The next day, with the fleet again joining the battle, Porto Alegre formed his men up for an attack.

The Paraguayans prepared to receive a frontal attack on the trench, and although they were worn out from the long bombardment and an enemy shell had dismounted the 8in gun, they were confident of driving the Brazilians back. Porto Alegre, however, ignored this line of approach and marched his men through the four-foot deep lake that protected the left of the trench, pushing on through a furious hail of musket fire until he had outflanked the position. This section of the Paraguayan line was held by the 10th Battalion, a unit which had been on garrison duty in the Matto Grosso until the losses of Tuyuti necessitated their recall, and had never before been in action. Perhaps the long months of relative idleness had sapped their discipline, but at any rate the surprising Brazilian move and the courage with which it was pressed home unnerved them, and as the enemy poured into the trench the soldiers broke and began streaming back through the swamps towards Curupayty.

This astonishing and almost unique collapse enabled the Brazilians to push on up the Paraguayan trench, which had already taken a severe battering from the ironclads, and after some desperate hand to hand fighting Diaz ordered the survivors to retreat, leaving all their guns in the hands of the Brazilians. Diaz managed to make a stand halfway between Curuzu and Curupayty with the 1,800 men who remained of his force, but it was a make-shift position that could scarcely have held up Porto Alegre for long had he followed up his attack.

Fortunately Porto Alegre contented himself with occupying the Paraguayan position and camping there under the cover of the guns of the fleet. In so doing he lost the chance of marching into Curupayty and perhaps ending the war. He later excused himself by saying that he had no information about the Paraguayan defences there and the terrain made further attack too difficult: in fact, the garrison of Curupayty at that time consisted of only 50 soldiers and one gun.[57] Despite this, he had with one blow opened up the Paraguayan line at its weakest point: at the very moment that the Bellaco front had been restored, another gaping hole had thus been opened.

A few days after the battle, López heard that two Argentinean divisions were being sent to join Porto Alegre presumably in preparation for a renewed attack, and his gloom deepened. In eighteen months he had seen his hopes of making Paraguay the supreme military power of South America dwindle into a fight for survival against odds that were already enormous and were growing daily. Since the conquest of the Matto Grosso his armies had not won a single major success and despite all the efforts made since May 20 it seemed that the war was heading for an early and ignominious finish, Wherever López looked he could see nothing but defeat, disgrace and humiliation, and in a moment of profoundest depression he confessed to Thompson: "Things could not look more diabolical than they do." It was one of the few occasions on which he admitted the pessimism that defeat had created and to make an example of the troops who had panicked he ordered every tenth man of the 10th battalion to be shot. The officers drew lots, and the ones who picked the long piece of grass were marched off and executed in the same way. The others were reduced to the ranks and the whole Battalion broken up, its men being divided up among the other units. This demonstration showed that López had no intention of surrendering, but he knew that the odds were very much against him and Thompson believed that 'he was quite persuaded that the Allies were about to give him the coup de grace.'

On September 8 he called a council of war at Paso Pucu to consider a defensive prepared a few days before by Wisner de Morgenstern. It was approved by everyone except Diaz, who said that while it was very impressive on paper, in practice it would not work. López supported Diaz, who was sent back to Curupayty to prepare the defence, which consisted primarily of a 2,000-yard long trench designed by Thompson. This proved to be more difficult to dig than anyone had imagined. The clay was hard, and the woods in front of the position had to be cleared to give a good field of fire and because timber was needed to make gun platforms. With the exception of a small rearguard, Diaz's force, which had been reinforced to 5,000, was brought back at night to the new position, but the operation resulted in complete confusion that was not sorted out until daylight.

It all seemed to prove that the Paraguayan army was nearly a broken force, and on September 10 López sent Captain Francisco Martinez, the husband of one of Elisa Lynch's great friends, to the Allied lines with a white flag: he had decided to try and make peace.

Chapter 17

López's initiative was well timed, and although he was hoping to delay any further Allied attack, it represented a genuine desire for an end to the war. Selfish and ambitious as he was, López was a sincere patriot, and he knew quite well that he could not win the spectacular victories he had dreamed of little more than a year before. It was equally obvious that a prolonged war could only result in the destruction of Paraguay and the complete triumph of its enemies. To prevent this López realised that he must try to end the war while Paraguay still had an army and the bargaining power that went with it and López was intending to bargain, for the terms of the treaty of the Triple Alliance had been published earlier in the year, and they were quite unacceptable. There seemed to be a chance of some sort of settlement being reached because sympathy for Paraguay was stronger at this stage than at any time since the war began. The publication of the Treaty by the British government had resulted in neutral opinion swinging behind López, and the west coast republics, led by Peru, had officially protested at its harsh terms. In Buenos Aires opposition to the war was growing daily, and only two important papers were still in favour of continuing a campaign that was widely regarded as being of benefit solely to Brazil. One paper, *La America*, was so hostile that it actually reprinted articles from the *Semanario*[58], the Asuncion weekly newspaper, and the provinces were almost solidly opposed. López calculated that with these pressures building up against him, Mitre would be prepared to talk.

In his first attempt to reach the Allied lines, Martinez was accidentally fired on, but on September 11 he was allowed through and was able to deliver the message to the Allied commander. After conferring with Polidoro and Flores, Mitre accepted López's offer, and fixed the meeting for gam the next day at Yataity Cora. Marshal López prepared for it carefully, putting on a splendid new uniform, grenadier boots, shining spurs and a magnificent scarlet poncho with a collar of gold lace. Accompanied by his brothers Venancio and Benigno, his brother-in-law Vicente Barrios and fifty staff officers, he rode to the Bellaco trenches in his wheeled American carriage. There he mounted his favourite horse, and set off by a roundabout route for the meeting, officers strung out behind him 'like a flock of sheep,' according to Thompson. He was so tense - and possibly frightened at being ambushed – that he had to stop half way for a dose of medicinal brandy, but at length the Paraguayans reached Yataity Cora and saw Mitre riding towards them, escorted by 20 lancers. The Allied commander in chief was a considerable contrast to López- he was wearing a frock coat and an old hat called a Jim Crow, which Thompson thought gave him 'a Quixotic appearance.' As their escorts halted, Mitre and López rode forward and saluted and then dismounted and the conference began. Polidoro declined to attend, but Flores turned up, and López immediately accused him of being the cause of the war, because he had asked the Brazilians to intervene in Uruguay. Flores protested that he was an anxious as anyone to preserve his country's independence, and went off in a huff. He was not missed. His chief function in the war had been a to act as a catalyst and by this stage the importance of Uruguay had almost vanished. López then introduced Mitre to Barrios and his two brothers, but soon they also left, and he and Mitre were left alone. They talked for nearly five hours, sometimes sitting, sometimes walking, and decided nothing.

The day after the conference, Mitre reported to Marcos Paz, his vice president: 'In the course of our interview General López declared himself ready to treat on all questions that may have led to the present war, or may affect our tranquillity for the future, so as to satisfy (as he says) the legitimate demands of the Allied, including a definite arrangement of frontiers, without accepting any imposition, and least of all his retirement from command in the Republic of Paraguay. In this sense he manifested his readiness to arrange on bases, and even make a treaty, which, amounting to a negotiation not in harmony with the stipulations and objects of the Triple Alliance, I neither could nor ought to accept same - but confined myself to hearing what he had to say, so as to communicate it to the Allied governments, as is expressed in the annexed memorandum."[59]

This memorandum simply recorded López's views. Mitre refused to commit himself except to state that he could do nothing against the treaty. López replied that he could never accept the conditions the treaty contained and if they remained the only ones the Allies would consider, then he would resist them to the end. On this unsatisfactory note the conference virtually ended. The two presidents had brandy together, exchanged riding whips and parted, never to see each other again. The rejection of his overtures by Mitre was a crushing blow for López. Although he, of course, knew the terms of the treaty he probably hoped that a face to face meeting between himself and Mitre would lead to a softening of those terms, and perhaps even a separate peace with Argentina. Instead, he had clear proof that despite its unpopularity in Argentina, the Triple Alliance was still as strong as ever as far as Mitre was concerned.

As long as this remained the case, López knew the war was lost. Paraguay would be dismembered, Humaitá reduced to impotence; and this would happen whether he left the country or not. It was a situation that offered not the slightest glimpse of hope, for Paraguay's only chance lay in military success - and of this López had already despaired. He returned to Paso Pucu and the sympathetic consolations of Mrs. Lynch looking "very black"[60] and although it is not often easy to pity López, it is difficult not to fell some sympathy for him at this moment. He had offered Mitre peace on generous terms, and Mitre had simply demanded unconditional surrender. He claimed to have done so because the Triple Alliance tied his hands - but it was his own fault that the alliance was signed and he can hardly be excused on that score. He had offered no word of encouragement, made no offer to intercede with Dom Pedro; in fact he had offered López no real choice except to carry on fighting.

As the man on the spot, Mitre must take a large share of the blame for the failure of the conference of Yataity Cora but a far greater, though more remote, influence was Dom Pedro of Brazil. For all his humanity and liberal sentiments, the intellectual emperor was then, and always remained, the leading hawk on the Allied side. He contemptuously dismissed foreign protests about the war, and on October 9 he wrote to a friend: 'Peace is being spoken of in Rio de la Plata: but I shall not make peace with López and public opinion is with me. There is therefore no need for you to be worried over the honourable success of the campaign for Brazil. I fear some possible official intervention from Europe, but we shall know how to conduct ourselves with energy."[61]

The Brazilian obsession with López was shown when, on November 10, the Foreign Minister, Octaviano, wrote to Elisalde: 'In accordance with the thoughts of my government, which I have confided to you in showing you the latest confidential instructions I have received, I think you can authorise the General in Chief to make the following reply: "The Allied Governments are not conducting a war against the nation of Paraguay- it is being conducted against the policies and government of General Francisco Solano López; and convinced by experience that the continuation of this government represents a menace to peace in South America and to freedom of commerce and navigation along the Paraguay and Upper Paraná Rivers and their tributaries, *they cannot under any circumstances deal with that nation as long as the aforementioned General López remains on its soil."* Any changes to be made in the foregoing will be agreeable to me as long as the text contains the concluding phrase which has been underlined."[62]

It was typical of López that he should react to this crushing disappointment by an act of almost insane savagery - and act, incidentally, that did much to lose the sympathy that the failure of the conference should have gained him. Mitre, whose courteous reception of the Paraguayan leader had already received favourable comment, had announced a two-day truce to show his sincerity, and some of the Paraguayan exiles serving with the Argentinean forces took advantage of the lull to approach López's lines to talk to old friends. One of then, a man named Ruiz, agreed to return on the day after the conference with some of his colleagues, including Colonel Luciano Recalde, a member of a family that had been high on López's lists of particular aversions for a long time. When López heard that Recalde was coming, he ordered a Colonel Montiel to prepare an ambush. The next day, while Recalde, Ruiz and the others were chatting with their friends Montiel's group suddenly burst out of the long grass in which they had been hiding and after a struggle captured Ruiz and another Paraguayan exile called Soriano, both of whom were severely wounded. Recalde himself got away, but even so Thompson noted that "López was much pleased and had Ruiz and his companion flogged to death."

It was, of course, an appalling breach of the accepted conventions of the time. It made no difference that Recalde and Ruiz were traitors: they had gone to pay a social visit to their friends under flag of truce and they should have been allowed to return unmolested. Apart from its moral indefensibility it was a political blunder: it convinced Pedro II that the stories he had heard of his enemy's wickedness were all true, and meant that any future peace negotiations would be that much more difficult. López probably saw all this but it made little difference. As always he reacted against disappointment with a wanton act of petulant anger like a small child throwing china because it cannot get its own way. Unfortunately for Ruiz and Soriano, and the others who suffered similar fates, López had unlimited scope for the sadism which afforded him this therapeutic solace, and his desire for vengeance transcended all arguments of humanity, honour and even self-interest.

With the collapse of negotiations, it was obvious that the expected Allied offensive would be launched at any moment. The Argentine lst and 2nd Corps had embarked for Curuzu at Itapiru on September 12 the day of the Conference, and clearly Curupayty was to be the objective of the next Allied offensive. The Paraguayans had made prodigious efforts since the fall of Curuzu to strengthen the defences there. The troops worked continuously, in eight-hour shifts and a week after the conference at Yataity Cora the number of guns had risen to 49. Thirty-six of the guns were along Thompson's trench, ready to deal with the attack that was expected at any time. On the evening of September 21 López sent Thompson to inspect the trench, and he found the finishing touches were just being made. The trees fronting the position had been almost cleared and beyond the trench was a 25 yard wide *abatis,* lines of sharp stakes driven into the ground to serve the same function as the barbed wire entanglements of the First World War. The right of the trench rested on the river, and the left on a lake called the Laguna López: great care had been taken to continue the trench round so that the enemy could not repeat their tactics of Curuzu.

While this frenzied activity was going on in the Paraguayan camp, the Allied commanders were still deciding what to do next. On September 6 another conference was held at which it was agreed that a cavalry attack would be made by Flores at the Bellaco, while a frontal attack would be launched at Curupayty. Mitre, as commander in chief, decided to move to Curuzu, despite the protests of Tamandaré and Porto Alegre, who considered that he was trying to steal the credit and Mitre had to threaten to write to the Imperial Government before they agreed to co-operate. After the brief lull brought about by the negotiations with López, further details of the attack were worked out.

Tamandaré insisted that his fleet would be able to silence the batteries at Curupayty and destroy the Paraguayan earthworks, and although Mitre was doubtful he accepted this. Once the bombardment was over, it was decided, four waves of infantry would advance from Curuzu. This would coincide with Flores' cavalry attack and an artillery and infantry attack launched by Polidoro at Tuyuti. In this way the Paraguayans would be stretched to breaking point and would be unable to reinforce the Curupayty line. As the day of the attack drew nearer, doubts began to set in. First Tamandaré asked that the attack be postponed from the original date of September 17 because of heavy rain. Then Porto Alegre demanded that Polidoro's attack begin first. Finally Mitre put his foot down and insisted that the attack would take place on September 22: the delay had given the Paraguayans just enough time to complete their preparations. Early in the morning, the Brazilian fleet, led by the ironclads *Barroso* and *Brazil*, steamed up to Curupayty and began bombarding the trenches.

During the course of the day the fleet fired more than 5,000 rounds into the Paraguayan positions. Whitworth bolts smashed into the parapets and the air was filled with the curling smoke trails of percussion shells 'so pretty,' said Thompson, 'that it would be almost a consolation to be killed by one.' Other shells burst in the air, adding to the din and spectacle, but not doing a great deal of damage. And that was true of the entire bombardment: it was fascinating to watch, but almost completely ineffective. The Whitworth guns that were the Allies pride were effective enough against masonry, but in southern Paraguay the impact of the explosion was muffled. Because their fuses were badly set, many of the other shells exploded before they reached the Paraguayan positions. This did not stop Tamandaré from announcing to Mitre that he had, as promised, demolished the enemy positions and that the Paraguayans were already evacuating the trenches. At noon, 11,000

Brazilian soldiers and 7,000 Argentineans left Curuzu carrying *fascines* of rushes and cane to fill the trench and ladders to climb the parapet and began to advance across the 3,000 yards of *carrizal* that separated them from the Paraguayan lines.

Almost at once it became clear that Tamandaré's information was tragically inexact. The bulk of the Paraguayan artillery was untouched. Thompson had placed the guns with great care, and the closer the Allies, advancing in four columns, were to the trench the worse the fire became. The 8in guns, firing canister - like buckets of billiard balls - at a range of 300 yards or less began tearing huge gaps in the Allied lines. The Brazilians, advancing on the river side, had the firmer ground and made the better progress, but were unable to reach the trench, Further inland the Argentineans were trapped in the mud, and although a handful of mounted men reached the trench they had either lost or forgotten their fascines and scaling ladders. They were wiped out by Paraguayan infantry firing muskets at point blank range. Early in the afternoon it was obvious that the whole attack had been a disastrous failure, and Mitre, who had been watching its progress from the old Paraguayan trench at Curuzu, ordered the retreat. Elsewhere the great attack had been a complete fiasco. Flores had made some impact on the extreme left of the Paraguayan line, but withdrew as soon as López sent in reinforcements, and Polidoro had not even attempted to attack the centre - which was just as well, for the slaughter at Curupayty alone had been appalling.

The Argentineans admitted losses of 153 officers and 1,843 men, the Brazilians 200 officers and 1,700 men, but both figures were too low. The main hospitals at Corrientes alone held 1,100 wounded survivors and Thompson claimed that 5,000 Allies were left in Paraguayan hands. Altogether he estimated the Allies had lost 9,000 men. The casualties included hundreds of prominent Argentineans, and the cream of *porteño* society had been decimated at Curupayty in much the same way that Asuncion's elite had been wiped out at Tuyuti. Domingo Sarmiento, the only son of Mitre's old colleague, now serving as minister to the United States, lay somewhere on the field, dead at 21. Francisco Paz, the son of the vice president, who had joined the army in preference to going to study in Europe, had also been killed. Rivas was wounded. The Italian Charlone, who had taken part in the attack on Corrientes the previous year was dead. Up to 40% of the Argentinean forces taking part in the battle had been killed, wounded or captured.

As for the Paraguayans, out of a total force of 5,000 men they had lost just 54 dead, most of them killed by Allied snipers firing from the Chaco across the river. López made no attempt to follow up, for two years of bloodletting had swept away the trained reserves that could have turned the defeat into a rout that would probably have ended the war. But López was content with the smaller triumph. Almost unable to believe that the fortunes of war had at last turned in his favour he spent the evening getting drunk on Champagne with Diaz. Only six uninjured prisoners were taken - an indication of the blistering impact of the Paraguayan guns - and two of the Paraguayan deserters were hung on Diaz's instructions. That night and during the next day the victorious Paraguayan soldiers moved across the battlefield, plundering where they could - several battalions re-clothed themselves in uniforms looted from the Allied dead - and massacring most of the wounded. The Allies, who had themselves committed a few atrocities during the war, could do little more than express their horror, however, for there was no question of resuming the attack. Aware only that the war, which the day before had appeared to be rapidly moving towards a victorious conclusion, now seemed likely to go on for ever, Mitre and his Argentineans moved back to their trenches at Tuyuti and dug themselves in.

Chapter 18

The defeat at Curupayty was so crushing that many on the Allied side despaired of ever winning the war. The Argentinean deputy Manuel Augusto Montes de Oca recalled that Mitre was so pessimistic that he considered issuing a declaration to his partners that it was impossible to continue the war[63]. Three days after the battle, on 25 September, the Argentinean Council of Government agreed that Mitre should be authorised to negotiate peace with Paraguay. But the Emperor of Brazil remained implacable: the war must continue until victory was won; there could be no peace talks until López agreed to surrender. Venancio Flores was less belligerent. On 26 September he abandoned the front line and returned to Montevideo with 250 of his men, leaving General Enrique de Castro and a brigade of less than 700 soldiers to represent Uruguay.

As the summer wore on, more familiar faces disappeared. Caceres, the Correntino leader had gone home even before the Curupayty attack. Porto Alegre returned to Rio de Janeiro in December to explain what had gone wrong and recover from illness, and General Alexandre Gomes de Argolo, who had begun the war as a major, took over as commander of the Brazilian 2nd Corps at Curuzu. Osorio was sent to Rio Grande to build up a 3rd Corps and make yet another attempt at invading Paraguay by way of Encarnacion.

More significantly, Polidoro was relieved as commander in chief of the Brazilian forces and his place was taken by Luis Alves de Lima e Silva, Baron de Caxias, who took up his post in November. Then aged 63, he was the greatest military figure in the Empire, but had been kept from active participation in the war by the intricacies of politics:

he was a stalwart Conservative, and as such was anathema to the Liberal government of Zacharias. The political situation in Paraguay, however, made it necessary to subordinate party strife to the national good and so Caxias at last got his chance. He was already an almost legendary figure. He had risen to prominence in the 1840s when he had been given the task of ending the revolts that were threatening to ruin the Empire. By a judicious combination of military force and well timed amnesties he restored Brazil to internal tranquillity within a decade, receiving the titles and honours that were his due from a grateful monarch. Like Osorio and many other officer he had fought at Ituzaingo, and his arrival was eagerly awaited by the Brazilian troops. It proved to be an anti-climax. He ordered his officer to remove all distinguishing marks from their uniforms - the Paraguayans took a keen interest in sniping at the higher ranks - but then seemed to run out of ideas.

In December, to everyone's great relief, Tamandaré finally vanished from the scene. He returned to Rio and was replaced by Admiral José Joaquim Ignacio, who had once served under Admiral Lord Cochrane during that controversial Scotsman's period as commander of the Brazilian navy in the 1820s. A Portuguese by birth, he was expected to show more enterprise than his predecessor and do less talking, but all he did was to fire more shells.[64]

For Mitre, problems multiplied. The Argentineans, who had never been happy about their young men marching off to help the Emperor of Brazil settle his feud with López of Paraguay, were even more averse to having them slaughtered in idiotic charges against fortified lines. They expressed this concern in the normal Argentinean manner and began a revolt. On November 9 government buildings in the province of Mendoza were attacked, and rioting and civil disturbances followed in Corrientes, Salta, Jujuy and Cordoba. On January 5 a government detachment was defeated by rebel forces at Pocitos, high up in the Andes, and the revolt spread to San Juan, La Rioja and Catamarca. In January Paunero was sent off to suppress the revolt but in February, with the situation becoming worse daily, Mitre himself finally responded to the desperate pleas of Marcos Paz and returned to Buenos Aires, leaving Caxias in command of the Allied forces.

As the mild Paraguayan winter gave way to the heat of summer, the war entered a new phase. Yataity Cora had dispelled all hopes of a negotiated settlement, at least for a time, and after Curupayty the Allies had to abandon their dreams of a speedy victory. On the other hand, Paraguay was too weak and exhausted to take the offensive. The trenches and parapets of Humaitá, bolstered by gun emplacements, visibly growing stronger every day as the emaciated troops dug in, hid from Allied view the real condition of the country, but they did not alter the fact that Paraguay was bleeding to death and had already suffered injuries from which only peace could enable it to recover. The country lay behind its earthworks like a wounded beast, able to bite and claw anyone who approached its lair, but too weak to spring out and attack. Supplies of everything, it seemed, were coming to an end.

The bright red *camisetas* of the Paraguayan soldiers had long ago been turned to rags by the sun and rain, and those who had not been able to loot Argentinean or Brazilian uniforms on the plain of Curupayty dressed in leather loincloths and whatever scraps they could find. Carpets from the wealthier homes of Asuncion and other towns were cut up and made into *ponchos*, not very successfully, for after they had been soaked by rain they became stiff and stuck out like boards. Salt had vanished from all but a few privileged tables and some people made a substitute from the leaves of trees, which were boiled, ground up and mixed with ashes. Ashes were also mixed with boiled fat to make soap but the product was so caustic that it burned the skin. Ink was made from ashes mixed with the juice of berries and black beans: it was legible, but soon faded.

In March 1867 the troops of the garrison were provided with a new source of entertainment and information, a weekly newspaper called *Cabichuí,* which was edited by Captain José Chrisóstomo Centurión.

Mr. Truenfeld, the German director of telegraphs, experimented with paper made from cotton and the leaves of the wild pineapple plant, while Masterman, always resourceful, got in touch with Charles Twite, who was conducting a hopeless search for coal in the cordilleras east of the capital, and obtained some iron pyrites which he smelted down for sulphur. This was needed both in the hospitals and the arsenal, for gunpowder. Masterman had to answer a number of searching questions from officials who thought the gleaming 'fool's gold' was the real thing.

Food was short, inevitably. All over Paraguay the weaker ones, the women, the children, the old and sick, were beginning to die of starvation. In Humaitá rations were gradually reduced from one cow to 80 men to one to 500 and soldiers were being bribed to improve their diet with a mugful of Indian corn for every shell or heap of splinters that they brought in. Earlier in the year a track had been cut through the Chaco to Bolivia and a few adventurous traders came down it with salt and other items. But the route was hopelessly inadequate for military purposes, and the long blockade remained to all intents unbroken.

The Allies, for their part, were content to wait, or rather they waited because the prospect of again attacking the dreadful canister-belching, musket-bristling parapets of the Paraguayan stronghold was too hideous to be contemplated yet awhile. Mitre concentrated on turning Tuyuti into an Allied version of Humaitá, complete with shops and a theatre, and every day the Brazilian fleet of ironclads steamed timorously up river to a point where its guns could just reach Curupayty and lobbed in a few thousand shells that killed on average two men a day. Curuzu was fortified and armed with a battery of new Whitworth 32prs, which the Paraguayans called 'phews' because of the noise the shells made as they flew overhead.

The continual shelling made the Allies feel that they were achieving something, and Thompson wrote: 'The bombardments all round were a source of pleasure to everybody. The Allies liked the noise and thought they were doing immense execution. The Paraguayan soldiers liked them as they got a mugful of Indian corn for every shell or heap of splinters they collected. López liked them, as he got large supplies of different kinds of shot and shell and quantities of iron, which was sent to Asuncion and cast into shot....' Throughout the war the Paraguayans proved themselves to be masters of improvisation, and nowhere was this talent better demonstrated than in the field of artillery. The huge numbers of rifled guns, which the Allies were able to buy in Europe, completely outmatched the weapons used by the Paraguayans and López was, of course, unable to import any himself. A few guns were captured, but the only way that the Paraguayans could build up their artillery was to make the guns themselves.

Thanks largely to the work of William Whytehead, the head of the arsenal, the Paraguayans were well able to do this. Of all the foreigners who volunteered to work in Paraguay during this period, Whytehead was by far the most important. He was a serious, conscientious man, devoted to the mother and three sisters back home in England, who depended on him for their income. He was also a brilliant engineer and a dynamic organiser, whose influence extended far beyond the shipyard and arsenal that were his chief responsibilities. He was involved in the development of the railway and the blast furnaces at Ibicuí and was so successful in bringing the industrial revolution to Paraguay that his work was admired and envied throughout South America. Unfortunately, poor health and personal worries began to build up, exacerbated by the outbreak of war, which led to more and more work for him and his colleagues. At the same time, his relations with López began to deteriorate, largely because of his stubborn loyalty to old friends, such as the Laurent-Cochelets, the French consul and his wife, who were out of favour in presidential circles. In July 1865 his depression became so obvious that Barrios, the Minister of War, became concerned and sent Dr Fox to see what was wrong. He arrived at Whytehead's home to find him hanging from a beam in his bedroom.[65] He was given the equivalent of a State funeral and, such was the esteem in which he was held, it is significant that Thompson, Washburn, Masterman and others who wrote their memoirs after the war, all refrained from mentioning the cause of his death. It was as though they had all agreed to do nothing to diminish the memory of a man who had served his adopted country so well – and they all agreed that, whatever the reason, his death was a major disaster for Paraguay. Masterman wrote that "the country, strongly entrenched by nature, might have been made almost impregnable by the skill and ever-ready resources of Mr Whytehead."

Despite his, the craftsmen at Ibicuí mastered the art of gun making well enough to cast numerous weapons of all calibres, which were then taken to Asuncion to be bored out to fit the appropriate stock of enemy shells. One gun, called the *Christiano* because it was made from melted down church bells, weighed 10 tons and fired a spherical 10in shell. The ultimate triumph, however, was the *Criollo*, another mammoth 12-ton gun superbly cast at Ibicuí and bored out to take carefully gathered Whitworth 150pr shells, stocks of which ran into thousands. Like the *Christiano*, it was made of church bells and a special levy of all the copper saucepans and boilers remaining in the country. It was finished early in 1868. The Paraguayans also constructed a number of mines (then called torpedoes) which were either floated town river towards the ironclads or attached to underwater obstacles such as the chains at Humaitá.

Beyond the perimeter, watchtowers called *mangrullos* began to sprout among the swamp, grass and reeds, 60 feet high, with a small platform on top from which officers would gaze out across the dead land towards the parapets, counting guns and carefully noting the progress of the Paraguayan earthworks. These enabled the Allies to glimpse the defences, but not much more, and later on the Brazilians introduced a more novel means of aerial observation by importing a 15,000 dollar balloon, together with a Frenchman to fly it. Unfortunately the balloon caught fire before it could take off. Undeterred, the Brazilians imported two more balloons from Rio, and in June 1867 an American balloonist made the first ascent while straining soldiers hauled away on three ropes to prevent it from blowing away. By tugging on the ropes the soldiers eventually enabled the balloonist to examine nearly all the Paraguayan perimeter, although the Paraguayans lit fires piled with grass, to obscure their lines whenever a balloon was spotted. Since the Allied batteries were out of range of their smooth-bores, the defenders responded by blowing trumpets called '*turuturus*' which derisively blew what Thompson remembered as 'a horrible note which began at one end of the line and was successively taken right to the other end'.

The braying trumpets did no harm, but they infuriated the enemy, and frustrated them: if the Paraguayans treated the bombardment of their splendid European guns in this derisive fashion how could they he made to see the hopelessness of their position? They at times tried bribery, offering large rewards to Paraguayans who deserted to their side and the Paraguayans retaliated by putting captured Brazilian officers up on the parapets to persuade their compatriots to run away, all the time jovially prodding them with bayonets to encourage them to shout louder.

On the Paraguayan side there were the occasional losses and in January 1867 Diaz, the hero of Curupayty and great favourite of López was mortally wounded by a Brazilian shell that exploded over his boat while he was fishing. One of the English surgeons, Frederick Skinner, amputated his leg, but in February he died and Colonel Alén took over as commander of the Curupayty front. The loss of Diaz was a severe blow to the Paraguayans and to López personally. He was his closest friend, as well as one of his best soldiers, while his sister Isadora was the favourite companion of Elisa Lynch. Diaz was given an elaborate funeral service at the church in Humaitá and his body was then transported to Asuncion and buried in the cemetery of La Recoleta. None of these alterations to the *dramatis personae* of the war had much effect on the war itself. Curupayty had brought that to a standstill.

It was at this point that Mr. Charles Ames Washburn returned to Paraguay.

Part 3:

The Tiger's Paw

Chapter 19

Washburn had gone to the United States on leave in January 1865, and left Washington in September 1865, on his way back to Paraguay. It took him more than a year to reach his destination. First a quarrel with Admiral S.W. Godon of the United States Navy had resulted in the admiral refusing to provide Washburn with a ship for the last stage of the journey, and when this difficulty had been resolved the Allies refused to open the blockade and let the ship through. Washburn finally landed at Curupayty on November 5, 1866 and was given a warm welcome, which he dryly noted was "based on the hope that, the blockade having once been broken, the war must soon end." Washburn had first come to Paraguay as American Commissioner in 1861, at a time when the United States still hoped to clear up the loose ends left by the Rhode Island affair and in 1863 he was appointed Minister resident. Like many American representatives abroad, he owed his appointment not to his diplomatic talents but to his political activities.

A 45-year-old Republican from Livermore, Maine, he was a member of a family which wholeheartedly supported Abraham Lincoln. His brother, Elihu, a Congressman from Illinois, was a close friend of General Grant and was partly responsible for Grant's rise to the position of commander in chief of the Union army, since he had introduced a bill into Congress reviving the rank of Lieutenant General. This rank was then conferred on Grant. Charles Washburn had moved to California in the early 1850s and entered journalism, becoming editor of the San Francisco Times in 1858. Although stories of the situation in Paraguay had filtered through the blockade to the outside world, Washburn was still unprepared for the terrible changes that had taken place in his absence. Many of his Paraguayan friends had been thrown into prison, and when Dona Pancha Acuña, wife of the former postmaster of Asuncion, was released shortly after his return he went to visit her.

"She was a mere skeleton. Her voice was gone and she could hardly speak in a whisper. She seemed very glad to see me and undertook to tell me something of her suffering. I could only make out as she held up her bony fingers and motioned towards the prison where she had been confined. 'Eight months, eight months'. Those two words told me the whole story. The poor old lady had been in solitary confinement with no human face that she could look upon except the brutal soldier for eight months, and had only been let out of prison in time to die."

Equally alarming were the stories told about López by Dona Carmelita Cordal, another friend from before the war. Washburn said she 'used to frighten me with the stories she told me of his atrocities which she said were known to her acquaintances. She said that the hypocrisy among the people in their professions of devotion and loyalty was beyond belief, it was universal; and they were in such constant fear and anxiety that they would be willing to surrender everything in the world but life and health so that the López family might be driven from Paraguay. She said: "They have taken our husbands, our fathers and our sons. They have taken the greater part of our fortunes and will take all if allowed to remain. They are welcome to everything provided they will simply leave us our lives. But", she said, "López is a great tiger, we all fear for the last stroke of his paw. He will kill us all in his dying grasp."

'When I asked her how she could denounce her husband as she did, she said no Paraguayan would respect her the less for that, neither would her husband, if he were alive, and that the lives of herself and her three children were probably dependent on some such humiliating act.' The denunciation to which Washburn referred had appeared in the *Semanario* shortly after Tuyuti, and was typical of hundreds of others that had graced the heavily-censored columns of the government journal. Señora Cordal's husband had been a member of the 40th Battalion, the elite Asuncion unit that was virtually wiped out at the battle. He was wounded and captured, which in López's eye meant that he had turned traitor - Paraguayan soldiers were meant to die rather than surrender, no matter how badly wounded, and most of them did. Cordal finally achieved this patriotic destiny in the hospital at Corrientes, but nobody knew that at the time, and so his wife was ordered to condemn him.

While he was writing of his experiences in Paraguay, Masterman had some of these 'miserable letters' on his desk, yet he still found it difficult to believe the orgy of abuse that they expressed. 'In one,' he wrote, 'a mother bitterly curses her son. In another a man heaps imprecations on the head of his brother; a wife disclaims and vituperates her husband.... I saw this lady a few days after the letter appeared and as I knew her intimately ventured to ask her how she could have written it. "To save my children", she said, the merriest little woman I have ever met. "It is all false; you know that I love my husband dearly; but *señor*, what would you do?" For her the question was merely rhetorical, but with the advantage of hindsight, and from a safe distance of several thousand miles and a hundred years, one finds it almost impossible to understand how a people as brave as the Paraguayans could have allowed such things to happen, yet they did so throughout the war. On another occasion, López called Lieut. José Urdapilleta to his headquarters and told him: "I have just had your father shot as a traitor. Take care! Behave well for fear of the same fate."[66] The young man left without saying a word, or more to the point, without doing anything. When he told his sister what had happened she screamed at him: "Couldn't you pluck up courage to shoot the monster?"

It was part of Paraguay's tragedy that nobody could. López's merciless punishment of suspected assassins was unnecessary. The Paraguayans who willingly fought to the death against the Allies allowed López to torture them, rob them, imprison them and kill them without once lifting a hand against him even though during the bleak days of 1866, when total defeat seemed imminent, López began to intensify this persecution.

In view of the daily arrests, the terror of Washburn's Paraguayan friends was understandable. But what astounded him most, however, was the attitude of the foreigners in López's service. On December 22 the minister arrived at Humaitá and was "astonished to observe the great change that had come over not only Dr. Stewart but the other Englishmen at headquarters, Col. Thompson and the civil engineer, Mr. Valpy. Before I had left Paraguay, though they all knew that López was a tyrant capable of any atrocity they had never supposed that they were in any personal danger. But it was all changed now. They had seen that López was resolved that if he could not continue to rule over Paraguay no one else should, and was bent on the destruction of the entire people. They early warned me to be careful in my intercourse with him: and that if I could keep in favour with him my presence in the country might somewhat restrain his barbarities; but that were he to quarrel with me it would have been infinitely better for them all had I never returned. They all of them expressed the opinion that they would never leave the country alive and gave me the cheering information that my chance of escaping was little better than theirs." The Englishmen had plenty of reasons for their warnings, for during his previous service in Paraguay Washburn had shown a quite remarkable ability for upsetting the notoriously delicate sensibilities of the Paraguayan President. In 1863 he had led the Asuncion diplomatic corps in the Great Uniform Revolt - a well organised refusal to wear the elaborate uniform requested by López to his birthday ball and Washburn had taken great delight in ignoring the semi-regal etiquette that López had introduced into Paraguayan society at the same time. The minister did not see that this was an unnecessary provocation and that he was being as petty as López himself. On the contrary he toasted about his contempt for the President's decrees, and recorded in his memoirs with smug self-satisfaction: 'I took pains to show my disapprobation of them by openly disregarding them. It may not have been diplomatic, and certainly was not courtier-like, but I took a sort of malicious pleasure, when everybody else in the room was standing, to sit in a conspicuous place, indifferent to whether the President were standing or not.'

He soon showed that, despite all warnings and the evidence of growing despotism, he was determined to maintain this militantly independent attitude. On Christmas Day, 1866, he was talking to Thompson, Mrs. Lynch, General Bruguez and General Resquín in the orange grove by Thompson's house at Humaitá when he 'suddenly saw everyone around me jump up hastily and stand with a reverent air, all facing in the same direction. Casting my eyes that way I saw the President at a distance of several rods, strolling leisurely through the grove. For my part I let him stroll and kept my seat, which act of discourtesy would probably have cost the life of any other person in the group.'

It was exactly this type of needless aggravation that Stewart and Thompson had been afraid of, and with reason. For the privileged position of Paraguay's foreign colony had already been broken. In October, a month before Washburn's return, Masterman, Fox and Rhind were arrested. The cause was trivial in the extreme. On October 7, a telegram arrived from Paso Pucu ordering Dr. Fox and Dr. Rhind to visit Dona Juan, López's mother, who was ill. They were told to report to her at seven o'clock, but Fox was not in the hospital and by the time Rhind found him it was 8.30 pm. Furious at being kept waiting, the Lady Presidenta refused to see them, and they were again turned away the next morning. On López's instructions, Stewart then wrote to the two men asking them to explain why they were not at their posts: Fox's reply was regarded as unsatisfactory, and López ordered Juan Gomez, the mayor of Asuncion, to arrest them. When Masterman, who had been out riding, returned late on the afternoon of the 8th he found Rhind, who was already suffering from tuberculosis, in great distress. "I am certain they are going to put me in prison", the doctor hold him. "I cannot bear it. I shall never come out again."

That night Masterman heard both men had been imprisoned, and that he was now in charge of the Hospital General. Teniente Ortellado 'an old native practitioner completely ignorant of surgery and indeed of almost all else' was assigned to the capital's two other hospitals. Between them they were made responsible for the health of over 1,500 men.

It seems incredible that López should have deprived himself of the services of two such important men for such a petty reason - Dona Juana's illness, whatever it was, was obviously slight since she recovered without any treatment at all - and although Masterman worked night and day for the next two weeks, the dictator's petulant revenge undoubtedly condemned scores of patients to death. But worse was to come. On October 22 Masterman received a packet of letters from home which had reached Asuncion via Laurent-Cochelet, the French Consul. Some were for Rhind, and realising how pleased his friend would be to receive them - Masterman himself had not had any letters from England for more than two years - he went to see Gomez. The mayor, however, would not let him take the letters to Rhind and demanded that he hand them over. Masterman refused, insisting that the letters were private. Gomez looked at him angrily and said: "*Terrido*, (go) and do not trouble me again.'

That evening Masterman was stopped in the street by an officer who politely asked him to go back to the Mayoria with the letters, and thinking that Gomez had changed his mind, Masterman went straight there. As soon as he arrived he was arrested. During the next two days Masterman was interrogated and forced to give up the letters. After being threatened with being put in irons he reluctantly signed a deposition which was a gross travesty of the facts and was then marched back to his cell. He was not told how long he would have to remain them, nor what he had done. Months later he learned that he was suspected of having started a rumour that Atherton, the English merchant, who had died suddenly some years before, had been poisoned on López's orders.

Masterman lay in his prison all that summer. He was not badly treated, and after a while he was even allowed to have books and wine sent to him, but he was bored and worried about the effect that a long imprisonment might have on his health. In addition, there was the uncertainty of not knowing if or when he would be released, or whether on some perverse whim of the President he would be treated with the pointless, almost absent-minded cruelty that was inflicted on the other prisoners. For the screams and groans that had made Mrs. Lynch indignantly refuse the house next door to the prison were a daily ordeal for the young Englishman. Through the open door of his cell he 'often saw respectably dressed men taken into that dreaded courtyard, followed by a group of ruffianly policemen; and knowing what was coming I closed my ears with my fingers or buried my head beneath the bedclothes to exclude the agonising shrieks and groans which, after a shorter or longer time, would tell of the hellish deeds of the *verdugos* (guards). Some times I heard blows but frequently the cries of the victim alone told how they were torturing him.'

Sometimes the torture was more prolonged, as was the case with an Argentinean merchant named Capdavila who had been arrested soon after the war began. One day Masterman saw him put in irons. A month later he was marched off again, presumably to the police headquarter, and returned with two sets of fetters on his legs: each set probably weighed 25lbs. Three weeks after that a third set was added. As Capdavila passed Masterman's door he caught sight of the Englishman and pathetically tried to raise his hat. In doing so "he stumbled and fell. He was brutally kicked till he scrambled up again. His cup of misery was not yet full: after a shorter interval he was once more marched out, and, as several hours passed by, I made sure that he had been set at liberty, but to my grief and horror he returned late at night in a far worse plight than before. He still wore three bars, and so thick and long that he staggered under their weight and was more than half an hour crossing the patio inch by inch, and at length he crawled by my door on his hands and knees. Yet he did not die for several months afterwards..."

Fox and Rhind were both released after two months and resumed their duties at the hospital, which must have been a relief to the patients who had bean left to Teniente Ortellado's care for so long, but Masterman remained. Although friends sympathised with him, their desire to help was inhibited by the fear that any such attempt would result in them joining him rather than him joining them. Washburn had no such fears, but he had rather weightier matters on his mind than the fate of Masterman. At the end of 1866 the American Secretary of State William H. Seward had told the American Ministers in the South Atlantic, that the United States would welcome any requests for mediation in the Paraguayan war. Apart from considerations of humanity, he was motivated by commercial interests and a fear that the European powers might beat the United States to it, and in December, Seward suggested a meeting in Washington of representatives of the belligerents. This was well received by several papers in Buenos Aires (as the result of which they were suppressed by the government) and Asboth, the minister in Buenos Aires and Webb, the representative in Rio made several approaches to the Allied governments. Because of the blockade, Washburn received no official despatches about these initiatives, but he read about them in the newspapers, and decided to do what he could to help. On March 7 he travelled down to Humaitá.

Despite his victory at Curupayty, López knew that the long-term odds were still against him winning the war, and he received Washburn's offer with delight. He had been banking on foreign intervention for months, and had ignored the studied rudeness of the American minister in the hopes that an offer such as this would materialise.

On March 11 Caxias, the new commander in chief, gave Washburn permission to pass through the Allied lines and he set off, accompanied by Mrs. Lynch and her 14-year-old son Panchito: López wanted to know exactly what happened at the meeting. Caxias received Washburn courteously, but soon made it quite clear that the Allies would accept no offers of mediation until López agreed to leave the country. Washburn told him that the dictator was at bay and would fight to the bitter end, but Caxias was undismayed. The most he would do was to hint that López would be allowed to take as much money as he liked if he should decide to go into exile 'Always provided a golden bridge for a fleeing enemy', he quoted.

On March 14 Washburn returned to the Paraguayan camp, where López invited him to breakfast to hear what had happened. He was bitterly disappointed at the minister's failure: he had also banked on Mitre being overthrown and Washburn told him - incorrectly at this stage - that the Argentinean leader had regained complete control of the situation.

Speaking with unusual frankness López gave the American his view of the war: "He knew [his position] was very grave, but seemed to be confident that if the Allies were to attack him he could repulse them at every point, yet he showed that he felt his chances of final success to be very slight. The odds against him were very great and if the Allies could hold together long enough and sustain the enormous expense to which they were subjected by the war it was probable that sooner or later they might overrun and conquer Paraguay..." All of this was realistic enough, but as López continued talking it became apparent that he had exchanged his vision of a glorious life for the more macabre ambition of dying a glorious death. He told Washburn that "he would fight to the last and fall with his last guard. His bones must rest in his own country, and his enemies would only have the satisfaction of beholding his doom. They would never have the pleasure of seeing him a fugitive in Europe or elsewhere. He would sooner die than be a second Rosas. If the worst came to the worst it was to be no surrender, but all were to fight until they were killed; that he was prepared to resort to more extreme measures than anyone imagined, if necessary…"

Appalled at López's fanaticism, Washburn tried to persuade him to make peace while there was still a chance of doing so - and some

Paraguayans left to benefit from it - saying angrily that history would condemn the useless slaughter. The President refused. He continued in the same vein (as Washburn recorded in his diary that night), saying that 'he would if necessary crown his triumphs with an act of heroism and perish at the head of his legions. He had laboured so long for his country, and with such self-abnegation, had been sustained by his people so bravely and with such free and spontaneous will that all these things must justify him in history and give him a place such as no South American hero ever held.

He said that there was no future for him; he should leave no one in whom he had any interest; save only the children I saw around him (Mrs. Lynch's) there was nobody else in the world he cared anything for. Life was a mere nothing, a thing of a few years more or less. He had not lived very long, but he had lived much; it was better to fall at the pinnacle of honour than to live longer, a fugitive, his country given up as spoil to the enemy....' Despite this ranting, López had a right to feel bitter and desperate, and on March 19 Washburn wrote to Caxias to protest against the Allied insistence that López go into exile. 'The people of Paraguay have never evinced the slightest desire to change their form of government,' he wrote, 'this condition precedent to mediation is certainly so antagonistic to all ideas of self government that the undersigned believes it to be his duty to his government that never could have contemplated such a reply to its offer of mediation to protest against it ...'[67]

It was all quite ineffective, and rather pointless. Caxias was only the head of the Allied armies. Unlike Mitre, he had no political role and had never been authorised to negotiate any sort of settlement at all. The Allied governments were the ones who would make the decision about peace or war, and they did it promptly: American mediation was rejected by Uruguay and Argentina at the end of March and by Brazil on April 26. There was a brief flurry of optimism in May, when despatches arrived saying that the Allies might be willing to make concessions, but nothing came of it. The whole episode had done nothing except to raise Paraguayan hopes and then dash them to pieces. From then on Washburn's influence with López waned rapidly. The personalities of the two men would probably have prevented them from remaining on good terms for long, but now Washburn had failed to bring peace he was not even useful. López's basic dislike for the American, who was so pompous and proud, always giving him unwanted good advice, began to fester and as Washburn, blind to the danger, continued to aggravate him, dislike turned to hostility and hostility to hatred.

Chapter 20

While hopes of peace were evaporating, a new menace threatened Paraguay. Cholera, which had been marching westwards from Asia into Europe for the last few years reached Rio de Janeiro in February, came up the rivers on the steamers that were bringing the Allies their guns and ammunition and was reported at Paso de la Patria on March 26. By May 13,000 Brazilians were in hospitals at Tuyuti, and 2,400 died in Curuzu alone, but in the same month the disease crossed the trenches at Paso Gomez, and for weeks the undernourished Paraguayan soldiers collapsed and died at the rate of 50 a day. Resquín, Bruguez and Dr. Skinner were all affected, and on June 25 López himself was taken ill. He blamed it all on the doctors, but although two special hospitals were established there was little the medical men could do except try to contain the epidemic. In this they were surprisingly successful. An earlier outbreak of smallpox had been prevented from spreading when Dr Fox prepared large quantities of vaccines from cattle on the State Ranches near the capital.[68] In October 1867 Dr Rhind, the Italian pharmacist Domingo Parodi and the Paraguayan Dr Velilla prepared plans which were based mainly on improving hygiene rather than medical remedies (there were virtually no medicines left in the country by then).

On the Humaitá front, the cholera epidemic brought military action to a virtual close, but at the other end of the country the Paraguayans were facing an attempt to invade the republic from the north. This expedition had originated in early 1865, when the Brazilians were trying to find some way of striking at Paraguay without going through Argentinean territory. They decided to send a column overland from Rio to the southern Matto Grosso, and from there south into the disputed border territory beyond the River Apa. The first units left Rio de Janeiro on April 1, 1865. It took them four months to travel the first 280 miles, and the column did not reach Miranda, the village in the southern Matto Grosso where Resquín had found such a large haul of arms, until September 1866. By then the rigours of the long march had reduced the expedition's strength by a third. On January 11, 1867, the column finally left Miranda and marched south under the command of Colonel Carlos de Morais Camisao, a member of the garrison which had abandoned Corumba to the Paraguayans and who had since been trying to polish up his tarnished military reputation.

From the start, the march was dogged by ill luck. Camisao's 1,600 men were all infantry, and he had no way of finding out what was happening around him. Every so often Paraguayan cavalry scouts would be seen, red-shirted horsemen flitting between the trees, and occasionally the Brazilians would find a message nailed to a tree, jeering at Camisao's prominent bald head, and making it quite clear that the Paraguayans were ready for them. By April the Brazilians were on the verge of starvation, and in desperation Camisao marched to an estate called Laguna, where large herds of cattle had been reported. They arrived there on May 1 to find only a burning hut and another mocking message.

Unable to go any further, Camisao ordered a retreat, but as the Brazilians struggled back through the forest the Paraguayans closed in. López had been kept well informed of what was happening and sent Colonel Montiel (the author of the Recalde ambush) to head the Brazilians off, and these troops, and a detachment of cavalry under Major Urbieta harried the retreating column continually. Meanwhile cholera spread among the Brazilian troops; Camisao, his second in command, and the expedition's guide all died: others were burned to death in the brush fires which the Paraguayans thoughtfully started along the column's line of march. By June 11, when the Brazilians finally reached the port of Canuto on the River Aquiduauna more than 900 men had died. But the 700 survivors had managed to drag their useless, but symbolic guns with them and in their dreadful retreat had written a chapter of endurance and heroism that deserved to be remembered with the epics of courage provided by their enemies.

López, in any case, was given little time to celebrate for a month after the dramatic failure of the Matto Grosso expedition, the Allies at last showed signs of stirring on the vital Humaitá front. First, 5,000 men were marched from Paso de la Patria a few miles up the River Paraná. In the middle of the month, Osorio joined them, and then on July 22nd the whole force, totalling 30,500 men under the command of Caxias, crossed the Bellaco at Paso Frete and turned westwards towards Humaitá.

On the 29th, after a brief cavalry skirmish, this army occupied Tuyucué, six miles from Paso Pucu, and began to transform it into their new headquarters: from here their patrols were soon operating over the swamps that guarded the Humaitá perimeter on the north-east, and they established another outpost at San Solano, thereby cutting the high road from the fortress to Asuncion.

López did not try to stop this move. He had at most 20,000 troops left, barely enough to guard the long lines of trenches around the Humaitá position, and an attack on such a large force in the open field would have been suicidal, particularly as the Allies still had 13,000 men at Tuyuti and Curupayty. It was perhaps significant that this advance should be made just before Mitre returned to the front to take up his position as commander in chief on August 1. The Brazilians showed a marked reluctance to do anything when he was there, and most of the decisive Allied moves were made when a Brazilian was in charge of the army. In view of Mitre's limited abilities as a general, which had been so amply demonstrated at Curupayty, this attitude is to some extent understandable, and in any case Caxias' move was entirely successful. Humaitá was outflanked, and almost cut off by land. This did not mean that its fall was imminent. The River Paraguay was still open, and this had always been the fort's main link with Asuncion and the north. And although the Allied forces at Tuyucué were on the face of it better placed to move north than the Paraguayans, a major offensive was not really practical.

The Allied supply route ran from Paso de la Patria to Tuyuti and then through the marshes of the Bellaco, where it was in constant danger from Paraguayan raids. If the Allies advanced still further north they could find themselves cut off, and in any case the difficulties of transporting large amounts of equipment through the marshes were almost insuperable. This problem could only be solved if the River Paraguay were opened to the Allied supply ships, and that would only happen if the batteries at Curupayty and Humaitá were destroyed. The immediate objective, in fact, was still Humaitá, but López had seen this danger long before and had already prepared for it.

During the previous few months, the Curupayty battery had been linked to the Potrero Sauce earthworks with a trench that ran along the edge of the *carrizal* and Laguna Chichi, making a strong flank impregnable. Then, in March, 1867, Thompson had strengthened the Sauce-Paso Gomez line by digging a new trench further back in the woods: the Bellaco was dammed and diverted down the old trench to form a fast flowing, unfordable stream more than six feet deep along the most important sector of the line. When that was completed another rampart was constructed from the eastern end of the Bellaco trench (a point known as the Angulo) to the old perimeter at Humaitá. This line completed the encirclement of the whole Humaitá system, and towards the end of the year more entrenchments were built from Espinillo, a redoubt near the centre of this line, along the Paso Pucu ridge to the Laguna Chichi. If the enemy tried to attack from Tuyuti, they would consequently find three strong lines of trenches between them and Humaitá. Paso Pucu was the nerve centre of the quadrilateral. Von Truenfeld's intricate telegraph network radiated from there, and of 5,000,000 sods of earth used in the 56 kilometres of earthworks that eventually existed at Humaitá about 1,000,000 were used at Paso-Pucu. Since his headquarters was in range of the Allied guns at Tuyucué, López had a special earth barrier built, and when the bombardment was at its worst took refuge in a shell-proof bunker built for his exclusive use. Because the old telegraph line to Asuncion was threatened by the Allies at San Solano, López had another one built along the river's edge, although he had the old one repaired regularly to convince the Allies that it was still being used. His telegraph system enabled him to keep in constant touch with the capital and every sector of the fortress, and he formed a special reserve of cavalry, ready to move at an instant's notice if the Allies should threaten to over-run the defences at any point. By the time the Allies reached Tuyucué, the Paraguayans had about 380 guns in place along the trenches. Most of them were smooth bores of fairly small calibre, and in places the earthworks themselves were unimpressive. Burton complained: 'I came to believe that Humaitá was a 'hum' and that, with the rest of the public I had been led into believing the weakest point of the Paraguayans to be the strongest.'

Despite this, the debacle at Curupayty had cured the Allies of all ideas of a frontal assault. But there was still a chance that Humaitá could be taken by an attack from the river. Experience had shown that although the 8in guns could give the ironclads a severe battering, they could not sink them. There would undoubtedly be casualties, but the batteries could probably be forced, and if this happened, then Humaitá was doomed. It would be cut off by river as well as by land and any attempt to cross into the Chaco could be defeated by the ironclads alone - the Paraguayan canoes would be shot out of the water. Even if the Paraguayan army did reach the Chaco, it would sooner or later have to cross back. A break-out by land seemed equally hopeless: the Paraguayans were already outnumbered and were relying more and more on the protection of their earthworks. Out in the open they would be at the mercy of the Allied cavalry and with the river in their hands the Allies could ship troops north to Asuncion faster than López and his raggle-taggle bunch of skeletons could march. Mitre, whatever his faults, saw that the key to the whole war lay in passing the Paraguayan river batteries. He had frequently urged the Brazilians to make the attempt, but the naval men had always shaken their heads and talked about the dangers and the certainty of defeat. Mitre found, to his frustration, that he could not simply order them to do so. He may have been commander in chief of the land forces, he was informed, but that did not mean he could tell the Brazilian fleet what to do.

But in August the Brazilians finally agreed to make the attempt. On August 15 Admiral Ignacio dashed past Curupayty with ten ironclads. The Paraguayan gunners were prepared, but they were expecting the Brazilians to use the channel on the far side of the river. Instead, the ironclads suddenly veered over to the nearside, and some of the shore guns could not be depressed in time to hit them. Most of the ships were damaged, for the solid shot used by the Paraguayans slammed into the iron plates with such force that the thick wood to which they were fastened splintered and the splinters caused unpleasant injuries. The Tamandaré had 15 men, including her captain, killed or wounded when a shot entered a gunport, her engine was so damaged that she had to be towed, but even so the passage had proved surprisingly easy. In fact, although the Brazilians did not realise it (because they did not attempt to find out) the passage of Curupayty had opened up the route to Asuncion itself. The Paraguayans had strengthened the Curupayty batteries at the expense of those at Humaitá, and at this stage the Humaitá batteries contained only three 8in guns, and a few smaller pieces. Fortunately, the Brazilians contented themselves with anchoring just out of range and bombarding the Humaitá using the famous twin towers of the church of San Carlos Borromeo as a marker. Although they were in virtually no danger from the Paraguayans, the Brazilians soon began to feel exposed and Ignacio requested permission from Caxias to withdraw to the old anchorage at Curuzu (even though this would have meant running the Curupayty gauntlet once again). Caxias agreed, but when Mitre heard on August 27 he ordered the fleet to stay where it was.[69]

The danger of the fleet's sudden move was apparent to López, but he had prepared for it. He had begun building up stocks of cattle in the Potrero Obella, the huge stretch of carrizal that spread for fifteen miles north of Humaitá, and he also gave instructions for the Chaco opposite to be explored and a road built through to a point known as Monte Lindo, roughly opposite the mouth of the River Tebicuary, as an escape route in case it became necessary to evacuate Humaitá. He was not, however, planning to abandon the fortress yet, because to retreat at all would give the Allies a chance of destroying the Paraguayan army in the open, and there was nowhere between Humaitá and the hills south of Asuncion where a stand could be made. It would be far better if the Allies could be forced to withdraw from Tuyucué and sent back to Tuyuti where they could be kept under control more easily.

López was considering ways of achieving this when C.Z. Gould, the secretary of the British Legation in Buenos Aires arrived in Paraguay on the gunboat *Doterel*. Gould's mission was to arrange for the repatriation of the British subjects resident in Paraguay; he soon discovered that he could hardly have come at a worse time. He was staggered at the terrible conditions under which the Paraguayans were living and fighting (his assessment is quoted at the start of this book) and realised that with the Allies on the war-path again, it was hardly the time to ask López to allow his most valuable employees to leave the country. And of the value of the English to López Gould had no doubt. "It is largely owing to the exertions of this handful of Englishmen that Paraguay, reduced to its own limited resources, has, under the direction of President López, thus far been able to prolong the desperate struggle in which it has been engaged for upwards of two years. Hence the natural reluctance of his Excellency to part with men whose services are invaluable to him and whom he cannot possibly hope to replace under present circumstances," Gould reported. When Gould spoke to him on the evening of August 18, López was as courteous as he always was with foreigners. He was trying to impress, but he made it quite clear that "he could not, under the present circumstances, possibly dispense with the services of the British subjects in Paraguay, who were in his employment and bound by contracts." He told Gould that all the British in Paraguay were perfectly happy and as far as he knew none of them had ever shown any desire to leave the country. He gave Gould permission to talk to any of the British in the camp, whom he was sure would back up everything that he had said.

The next morning López called Dr. Stewart to see him, and told him of Gould's mission. As the doctor was leaving he warned him: *"Cuidado! Si yo sepe que algun Ingles diga que quiere salir del pais..."* Roughly translated this was a chilling threat as to what would happen to any Englishmen whom López heard saying that he wanted to leave the country. The British all knew López well enough by this time to know that this was not an idle threat and although Stewart, Thompson and some of the others managed to tell Gould what the real state of affairs was in Paraguay, none of them dared to make his views public, or to state that he wanted to leave.

Despite this setback, Gould persisted in his attempts to procure their release. Unlike the majority of foreigners who visited Paraguay during the war he did not allow a natural sympathy for the underdog and the well-exercised charm of López and Mrs. Lynch to influence his opinion unduly. There were several cases that worried Gould in particular: one was that of Valpy, the railway engineer, who had refused to join the army and as a result was being treated virtually as a prisoner. Although Dr. Fox had been released from prison several months before, his health was very bad and he, too, was anxious to leave Paraguay. Masterman, however, was still in prison and his position was so delicate that Gould considered it wiser not to mention him at all. During the course of his interview with López he had learned that the president 'considered he had a perfect right to treat Englishmen in his service (and he does not give them the option of retiring from it) just in the same way as he would his own subjects.' Several of the men employed at the arsenal had been jailed for trivial reasons, and others had been forced to work on the Paraguayan ships where they were in danger from the Brazilian ironclads. It was obvious that, if driven too far, López would not hesitate to kill the British, just as he killed his own people.

Since the chances of saving the British subjects seemed to be negligible while the war was at its present critical stage, Gould showed commendable resourcefulness and decided to try to end the war itself. Consequently he re-opened the negotiations which had been broke off after Washburn's failure. With the war apparently beginning to turn against him again, López agreed to a series of proposals that Gould volunteered to take to the Allies. The terms were a far cry from the harsh conditions of the secret treaty of the Triple Alliance and, if accepted, would be a good deal better than Paraguay could have hoped for. López agreed that arbitration or negotiation should settle the territorial disputes after the conclusion of peace. The two sides would give up their respective conquests, and prisoners of war would be exchanged. There would be no indemnity, and the Paraguay army would be disbanded, with the exception of the forces necessary for maintaining internal order. This amounted to a return of the *status quo ante* and the reference to disbanding the Paraguayan army was something of a blind, since it could always be argued that internal order could only be maintained by having an army as large as the one that now garrisoned Humaitá. The most remarkable clause however, was the last one: the President 'at the conclusion of peace, or the preliminaries thereof, will retire to Europe, leaving the government in the hands of His Excellency the Vice President.' López had thus agreed to the very condition that had led to the failure of the two previous attempts to negotiate peace.

On September 11 Gould went to the Allied camp where the proposals were well received. Caxias was so impressed that he sent his chief of staff off to Rio in a special steamer to present the terms to the Emperor and after two days Gould returned to Humaitá and told López of the success of his mission. To his amazement, he was told that López had changed his mind: he refused to go into exile, claiming, in a letter from Luis Caminos, the Foreign Secretary, that he had told Gould that this clause could not be considered, even before he went to the Allied camp.

This decision demolished all hopes of a peaceful settlement, and Gould boarded the *Doterel* and left Paraguay on the same day, September 16. He had with him three English widows and five children, the only British subjects that he had been able to save. His own health was causing considerable concern and in any case there was no point in staying longer. López's rejection of the exile clause meant the inevitable collapse of negotiations. The other terms of the secret treaty were negotiable: that one was not.

Although Washburn, still in Asuncion, but by now no longer on speaking terms with López, sneered at Gould's efforts as "feeble," the young diplomat had come closer than anybody to ending the war by means of a negotiated compromise. According to Thompson, López finally refused the exile clause because he had heard of another revolution in Argentina and believed that he could force a dramatic eleventh-hour victory. This may have been one factor. Another was López's own fantasy-dream of glory and immortality. The rambling talk of dying with his people, sword in hand, never surrendering, that had so horrified Washburn was not simple rhetoric, but an eventuality that López was seriously considering. Under the influence of Gould's skilful arguments and the Allied offensive, which threatened to make that alternative come true all too son, López's more rational side temporarily prevailed. It was when he tried to imagine life as a deposed dictator, skulking like Rosas on a farm at Southampton, or living in genteel poverty in one of the cheaper Paris hotels, that he changed his mind again. And from this point on what was important was not the avoidance of defeat - that could only be postponed - but the manner of defeat. It had to be memorable.

Gould, in addition to his official duty of freeing the British subjects and his self-imposed task of trying to make peace, also took the opportunity of learning a great deal about the comparative strengths of both armies. His estimate of the Paraguayan forces - 20,000 troops - has already been quoted. He reckoned the Allied army to consist of '48,000 men in the field and from 5,000 to 6,000 in hospital. Of these

45,000 are Brazilians, 7,000 or 8,000 Argentines and 1,000 Orientales (Uruguayans).'

Of this total 8,000 were cavalry, all of them well mounted, and fresh horses were arriving continually in large numbers, many of them from Urquiza whose last attempt to raise an army had by this time ended in failure. The Allied artillery strength was overwhelming. In addition to this, the Allies had ten Brazilian ironclads near Humaitá, and seven wooden ships stationed below Curupayty. In view of this enormous superiority - which was in fact even greater, since probably half of the Paraguayan forces consisted of old men and boys - it is difficult to deny Gould's conclusion that "it is only owing to the dilatory manner of proceedings of the Allies and their want of energy that he (López) is still able to prolong his resistance."

Since the ironclads were only a mile below the port, the few steamers left to López could only land cargoes at Humaitá at night. The garrison, according to Gould, consisted of roughly 16,500 men. Of these, five battalions, three of them made up of old men, one of boys and one of convalescents, were stationed at the batteries. Another 6,000 men were on the left flank - the new danger zone from Humaitá to the Angulo, and 5,000 men guarded the trenches from there to Curupayty. The reserve of 2,000 - 2,500 consisting of three battalions of infantry and a few regiments of cavalry, was based at Paso Pucu. This number was just about sufficient to defend the fortifications of Humaitá, but by this stage the war was moving north, away from the fortress towards the heart of the country.

Chapter 21

After the departure of Gould, López gave up all hopes of making peace. The Allies had rejected his efforts to reach a compromise settlement, and when it came to the point, López found it impossible to agree to the only terms that would interest them. Exile was out of the question, and if the only alternative was a fight to the finish and a hero's death, well, a hero's death it would have to be. He began to drink a little more heavily, became more suspicious of those around him, and took refuge in his dreams. But he did not forget the war.

The Curupayty guns were hauled back to Humaitá, so that when the Allies stopped congratulating themselves on passing them and decided to challenge Humaitá they would find the same guns waiting for them. As soon as the Allies moved to Tuyucué, López sent Lieutenant Colonel Nuñez and a few hundred men to the River Tebicuary, fifty miles north of Humaitá, to check any attempt to go further and throughout August and September the Paraguayans fought desperately against the Allied troops north of the Bellaco, ambushing their convoys at Tuyucué and fighting a series of cavalry actions. It was exhilarating, for a while, but it could not last. On October 21 Caballero found a regiment of Brazilian cavalry on the plain north east of Humaitá, and charged as the Paraguayans always charged 'not with the fine old Spanish war *cry "Santiago y a Elles"* but with a kind of *trille* here directly derived from the Red Indians. They exposed themselves with upraised blades, like Mamelukes, careless of what they took and determined only to give.'[70]

The Brazilians bolted, the Paraguayans followed, and suddenly found themselves in an ambush, surrounded by 5,000 enemy horsemen at Tatayiba, three miles from Humaitá and safety. Caballero hacked his way through somehow, but 400 of his men were killed and more than 130 were wounded and captured. In one battle the remnants of the Paraguayan cavalry had been wiped out. Caballero, who began the war as a sergeant in the Matto Grosso campaign had been promoted to Lieutenant-Colonel shortly before the battle and was made a full Colonel for his bravery immediately afterwards, but this was small consolation: the Allies had asserted themselves at last, and could probe north without worrying about ambushes and surprise attacks. Their first objective was a trench guarding the entrance to the Potrero Obella. The Brazilians had discovered this some time before during reconnaissance, and once the Paraguayan cavalry had been destroyed they prepared to take the trench. On October 28 General Joao Manoel Mena Barreto attacked with 5,000 men, and although the Paraguayans fought as well as ever, the 200 men holding the position were soon over-run. On the same day the Paraguayan steamers *Olimpo* and *25 de Mayo* were passing Tayi, a *guardia* just north of the Potrero Obella when they notice enemy troops near the town. These were patrols from Mena Barreto's army, who immediately started firing at the two ships with field guns. The Paraguayans fired back, and drove them off, and continued down river to Humaitá. López at once saw the seriousness of this action. Tayi was a vital objective, for it was the first firm ground between Humaitá and the Tebicuary, and if the Brazilians moved quickly they could establish a battery there that would close the river to Paraguayan ships.

He sent Thompson to build a strongpoint to protect the vital 400-yeard cliff and he arrived at Tayi early in the afternoon of November 1 find that the Paraguayans had won the race: the Brazilians' advance patrols were keeping an eye on the town from some nearby woods but their main army had not yet arrived. Even so an attack was clearly imminent, and Thompson hastily traced out the lines of the planned redoubt, while three steamers took up positions to cover the digging with their guns.

Mena Barreto approached the town next morning to find the Paraguayans still digging furiously, but the trench was still too small to give much protection and the Brazilians overpowered them. Mena Barreto then brought up his heavy artillery and sank the *25 de Mayo* and the *Olimpo* in quick succession. While the *Ypora* was scuttling down river to tell López of the defeat, the Brazilians began installing a battery of 14 guns and a chain was strung across the river, similar to the ones at Humaitá. To make sure that there was no chance of the Paraguayans re-taking the town, a garrison of 6,000 men was installed, backed by a further 10,000 at San Solano. The river line, Humaitá's most important link with Asuncion, had been cut, and the only one that remained was the 54-mile-long road through the mire and jungle of the Chaco. If and when the Allied fleet passed Humaitá, Paraguay's only army would be trapped, but López was still reluctant to abandon the position, and as he wrestled with a problem that became more serious daily, he saw one possible solution.

The steady Allied advance round the Paraguayan left flank had resulted in their army becoming spread in a wide arc between Curuzu and Tayi. The majority of this force was north of the Bellaco, with Tuyucué the focal point, but it still depended on the supply convoys that moved up from Tuyuti and Paso de la Patria. There was no chance of challenging the Allies at Tuyucué - but Tuyuti was a different matter. Although still strong, Porto Alegre's 2nd Brazilian Corps there had become a little too complacent. The Paraguayan patrols had retained control of the no-man's-land lying between the two fortified lines, and there was a chance, however faint, that a sudden onslaught at Tuyuti would catch the Allies unprepared. If this defeat were big enough it might result in the forces north of the Bellaco being recalled, and there need be no more talk of abandoning Humaitá. López had been considering this plan ever since the taking of Tuyucué, but had not done anything about it, probably because of the risks involved. The fall of Tayi made the situation at Humaitá so serious that the risks had to be accepted. Thompson was sent off to study the area, for since the first battle of Tuyuti, more than a year before, the Allies had greatly strengthened its defences. On November 2, with this report complete, López made his final plans for the attack.

Barrios was selected to command an assault force of 8,000 men - roughly half the total Paraguayan army. While he was attacking at Yataity Cora with the infantry, Caballero and the cavalry were to sweep round Porto Alegre's right flank. Apart from forcing the enemy to concentrate at Tuyuti, López gave instructions for as many guns as possible to be captured, particularly the Whitworth 32prs which had been proving very effective during the daily bombardments of

Paso Pucu. Because of the shortage of men, there was no intention of holding the position, if and when it was captured.

This plan, despite its risks, was sound enough: it recognised the limitations of the Paraguayan army, and did not expect the men to do more than was possible and the first stage of the plan went well. At dawn on November 3 the Paraguayans swept on the Brazilian lines, achieving complete surprise. They overran the first line of entrenchments without meeting serious opposition, and began setting fire to the camp and blowing up powder magazines. In the confusion that followed they swept on over the second line and started destroying that as well. The impact was so great that four battalions simply broke in panic and fled towards Itapiru, followed by camp followers, merchants, and the other human paraphernalia that several months of uneventful and static warfare had accumulated. Huge clouds of black smoke spewed across the blazing camp, clearly visible at Tuyucué and at Paso Pucu, where López was watching: another observer was Carneiro Campos, the governor of the Matto Grosso, who had been captured on board the *Marques de Olinda*. He became convinced that the whole Brazilian army was on the point of destruction, collapsed in despair and died three days later. It seemed for a while as though his pessimism was justified. The Paraguayan onslaught had broke a hole right through the 2nd Corps' line, and the troops who should have been defending it were pouring south in complete disorders. On the far right, Caballero's cavalry had stormed the first Brazilian redoubt and captured several hundred prisoners. They then pushed on and took two more redoubts before setting fire to the enemy barracks.

At this stage, the Paraguayans were on the verge of an even greater success than López had been banking on. About 250 prisoners had been taken, and the Paraguayans were also dragging away 14 guns, including one of the cherished Whitworth 32prs. But then the troops reached the Comercio, where the Allied stores and shops were located, they were given permission to loot, and as they flung themselves gleefully on to huge piles of supplies such as they had not seen for years, the whole attack came to a sudden halt. All discipline vanished as the troops gorged themselves on food, plundered the clothing stores, and got drunk on captured wine. While the Paraguayans were turning from an army into a mob, Porto Alegre was desperately trying to turn a mob back into an army. He managed to organise the defence of the citadel, the core of the Tuyuti defences, and his personal courage - he had two horses shot under him - and furious energy gradually pulled his army together and managed to halt the retreat. Some cavalry camped near the southern Bellaco arrived and charged into the Paraguayans in the Comercio and reinforcements began to arrive from Tuyucué just as Porto Alegre was on the point of trying to fight his way out to them. Soon the pressure became so great that the Paraguayans, by this time little more than a rabble of looters, were pushed back across the Bellaco. Fortunately Caballero had kept his men under firm control, and he charged the enemy repeatedly until the infantry were safely back in their own lines before joining the retreat. By 9am the battle was over.

It had been an extraordinary affair from the start, and both sides could obtain some sort of satisfaction from the result. The amount of booty brought back was enormous, Thompson recollected, and 'consisted of articles of every conceivable kind. The only artichokes I ever saw in Paraguay were brought from the Allied camp that day.'

The captured guns soon proved their worth. The Whitworth was sent off to Curupayty, where hundreds of Allied shells had been collected for it, and began firing at the Brazilian wooden fleet, which previously had been out of range. The *Belmonte's* 150pr Whitworth was dismounted, and 34 hits recorded before the fleet upped anchor and moved back down river to a safer berth. But none of this could really alter the fact that, although it had not been a complete defeat, the second battle of Tuyuti had not been a victory either. The Allies had suffered about 1,700 casualties, but the Paraguayans had lost 1,200 dead and a similar number wounded. The 40th Battalion had been reduced to a hundred men: the 20th went in with 460, and came back with 76; the 3rd lost 300 out of 400. It was a heavy price to pay for a few guns, and the first artichokes that Paraguay had ever seen. Most important of all, the Allies did not concentrate at Tuyuti: once the battle was over, the reinforcements Caxias had sent went back to Tuyucué, and the slow strangling of the Paraguayan army began all over again. López realised that the battle had been lost, even if nobody else did. It had left him dangerously short of manpower – only 15,000 half-starved men facing 50,000 - and he urged Thompson to finish digging m the new trench along the Paso Pucu ridge.

Once it was completed the 150 guns at the Bellaco were moved north. Advance guards were left at the Potrero Sauce, but the bulk of the army was sent to man the new line. Across the river in the Chaco, a new fort was started early in December at Timbo, a few miles up river from Humaitá and the southern end of the Chaco road. Caballero (by this time a general) was sent there to take charge of the army's only supply line. For the first time in more than a year the camp women - there were several hundred of them were given permission to go back to Asuncion. All of this was done with the object of making Humaitá itself more capable of resisting an attack and a siege. López had a new redoubt built at Cierva, a position on the banks of the Aroyo Hondo, a small river that separated Humaitá from the Potrero Obella. According to Thompson this was done largely as a diversion, but it did help to stop the Allies seizing the Paraguayan herds of cattle. It also served as a haven for the *Tacuarí* and *Ygurei*, which had been trapped south of Tayi by Mena Barreto's battery and were doing sterling work ferrying supplies across from Timbo and the Chaco road.

This road crossed five rivers - one of them 200 yards wide - and was at best nothing but a trackway cleared through previously impenetrable forest. Most of the time it was deep in mud, so that wagons and guns frequently stuck fast, cattle became trapped, vital supplies and stores were lost or had to be abandoned. At both ends there was a hazardous river crossing to be faced. It was the *Voie Sacrée* of Humaitá, and it was in danger.

As the Allied armies closed in, so the Brazilian fleet began to show signs of life. The ironclads started bombarding the pontoons that supported the three chains across the 700-yard wide river, and after three months persistent, if generally inaccurate shooting, finally managed to sink them all. The chains sank to the bottom of the river and were buried in two feet of mud, and all attempts to raise them on floats failed. The only obstacle consisted of the guns in the river batteries. Thanks to the lull granted by Ignacio after the passage of Curupayty, the Paraguayans had been able to install more guns there until they had 18 8in guns in place, nine of which the Allies had already passed at Curupayty. In addition, they had mounted a 130pr gun and the 150pr *Cristiano*. The guns were all well sited, the gunners excellently trained, but they knew, as the Brazilians should have known, that all their efforts were doomed. If the ironclads could pass Curupayty, they could pass Humaitá. The fortress hung by a single, slender thread. And whenever the Allies wanted to they could cut it.

Chapter 22

By the new year, the Humaitá campaign - and that meant the war itself - was approaching a climax, but it is doubtful whether this was completely clear to those at Asuncion two hundred miles to the north. The *Semanario*, as always, spoke only of victories, and although by reading between the lines the shrewd interpreter of government propaganda could tell that things were not going as well for Paraguay as might have been hoped, the whole drama was being played so slowly that for most people there was no drama at all. Indeed, the chief characteristic of life in the capital was monotony - and nobody was more bored than Charles Ames Washburn, the American minister. When he returned to Paraguay at the end of 1866, Washburn had been on fairly good terms with López - which was one reason why men like Thompson were so guarded when they spoke to him - but after the failure of his meeting with Caxias, had fallen steadily out of favour. In Paraguay, it was an accepted and necessary fact of life to be friendly only with those who had the approval of the President. As a result, Washburn found himself being shunned. This also meant that Washburn found it almost impossible to hear what was going on in the war and the outside world. The Allies, indignant at what they regarded as his pro-Paraguayan attitude, held up his mail, so that he was cut off from home for months on end. He learned what was happening at the front mainly from scraps of information passed on by the English engineers working on the Paraguayan river steamers.

Venancio López, nominally the Minister of War and Marine, but in reality a cipher, 'never knew anything, or at least would never speak of anything that had not been licensed in the *Semanario.* He would never speak of anything except his health and that of my family, the weather or some such matter that could not be construed to mean anything. He appeared to be in a chronic fright. Should I speak of any event that had been mentioned in the paper he would say "Yes, so says the *Semanario.*" But if I asked of any matter not yet officially promulgated, his answer was always the same: *"No se nada* - I know nothing."

Benigno López was more forthcoming - when he had had a few drinks, which seems to have been fairly often, he became almost too talkative - but his conversation was hardly reassuring. He once told Washburn that if he had the chance he would be happy to flee from Paraguay with nothing, and 'seemed impressed with the conviction that Francisco would sooner or later make an end of him.' Benigno's pessimism was not entirely misplaced. In December 1867, his brother-in-law, Saturnino Bedoya, led a delegation of eight prominent citizens to Humaitá, where they presented López with a laurel-leaf of gold and a sword of honour encrusted with 23 brilliants and other stones, set in gold, complete with a golden scabbard. This gift, magnificent though it was, was not unusual.

What made Bedoya's gesture different was that after it had been made he did not return to Asuncion. Somehow or other he incurred López's displeasure and was kept at Humaitá under arrest. Two of his companions died of cholera shortly after their arrival, and the other five were put in the army. If López could turn on his brother-in-law in this fashion, poor Benigno probably reasoned, then there was every likelihood that sooner or later he would direct his attentions towards his brothers. It was a prospect that had already made braver men than him feel more than a little depressed. By late 1867 the war was quite inescapable. It dominated the life of everyone living in Paraguay, whether they were soldiers or civilians, men or women, adults or children, near the front line or far away in the villages of the interior. In September 1867 the war even managed to ruffle the tranquil life of Alonzo Taylor, the stonemason from Chelsea.

Taylor had arrived in Paraguay in 1858 and liked the country so much that when his contract expired in 1861 he renewed it, this time for a period of four years, and arranged for his wife and children to come out and join him. Unlike many of the British workmen who went to Paraguay at this period, Taylor was a levelheaded, quiet person who enjoyed his work and did not let the excitement and prosperity of a well-paid job in a new country go to his head. So reliable was he that he used to look after the widows and orphaned children of the many men who became so fond of the local liquor that they drank themselves to death.

The war did not at first make a great deal of difference to his way of life. He had a pleasant home near the Customs House in Asuncion, into which he had built a fireplace and chimney, the first ever seen in Paraguay, and all round him he could see the results of his labours; the railway station, the foundry, the new mole in the harbour, and, grandest of all, the President's palace, which like most of the other buildings in the city, had been left unfinished when the war broke out. Since then Taylor had been working in the arsenal. On the evening of September 22, Taylor and his family were eating supper when there was a knock at the open door, and a man walked in. The children looked up and screamed with fright, for the stranger's thin face was so pale that it seemed almost transparent, his white hair and beard straggled together and reached below his shoulders, and his bright eyes appeared to be the only feature that was alive. They gazed at Taylor with a burning intensity that for a moment unnerved him. Finally he managed to move, and, going towards the stranger, said in Spanish: "What do you want, *señor*?'

The man, so weak that he was swaying and about to fall, replied in English: "Why, Taylor don't you know me?" Only when he heard the voice did Taylor recognise his visitor as Masterman, who had been released a few moments before after eleven months in prison. Compared with the sufferings of the other inmates, Masterman's period in the former Jesuit College that served as the capital's jail had not been harsh. But after six months or so the strain began to tell, and in the end his health threatened to collapse. Teniente Ortellado, who was still at the hospital, came in to see him, but when Masterman told him what medicine to prepare, the old man thought he was planning to poison himself, and refused. Fortunately, Narcisse Lasserre, a French distiller living in Asuncion, came to the rescue with three bottles of brandy and once he was released Masterman made a rapid recovery. The problem then was what to do in the future: although he wanted to help the sick and wounded soldiers, who were still pouring into the hospitals he could not bring himself to re-enter the service of a man who had treated him as callously as López had done - even his release from prison was conditional on his remaining in Asuncion. Masterman first tried to get a permit to start a private practice but this was refused, and then Washburn offered him a post as private surgeon, which could be changed to the more official title of Surgeon to the American Legation if López should threaten him again. Masterman accepted this offer gratefully, particularly since it included an offer of accommodation in the Legation itself. The Legation, once the home of Don Luis Jara who had died a short while before serving in the army, was an enormous, rambling building that occupied one side of the Plaza Vieja, the Old Square. It was built 'in the Moorish fashion, with a large yard or patio in the centre, with a corridor extending the whole length in front and other corridors within extending along three sides of the patio. It was finely furnished.'[71]

Masterman's release had been arranged largely through the intercession of Washburn. The minister's wife, who was expecting a child, was not well, and after conquering his aversion to having to beg favours from a fallen woman, Washburn asked Mrs. Lynch if she would speak to López about freeing Masterman so that he could give her treatment. Mrs. Lynch, who had little enough reason for doing favours for Washburn, nevertheless agreed and was able to catch López in a relatively benign mood. Apart from his desire to obtain competent medical attention for his wife - Dr. Rhind was the only competent doctor in the capital, since Fox had been packed off to Humaitá a few months before - Washburn also wanted to show López that he was not afraid of him. After the excitement of Masterman's release, however, life in the capital soon settled down. To break the monotony, and for the health of his wife and their infant daughter, Washburn moved to Rafaela Bedoya's house at La Trinidad where they remained as her guests for four months. In January 1868 cholera reached the capital in epidemic form, and wiped out a quarter of the population within a few weeks, but despite this new danger Washburn decided to return to the Legation early in February. Rafaela had already left the quinta and the tedium and uncertainty of life in the country, cut off from all news and the few friends that remained to him was more than the minister could stand.

Apart from cholera, he found that little had changed. Laurent Cochelet, the French minister had left in October and been replaced by M. de Cuberville, who immediately fell under the spell of López and remained one of his most devoted admirers. In December Lorenzo Chapperon arrived, after a march through the Chaco, to take up a new position as Italian consul. By this stage even the foreigners were becoming so alarmed that a group of them anxious to demonstrate their loyalty, started a subscription list for López and soon collected 54 names.

For the Paraguayans, the tension was growing daily. One of those who almost suffered as a result was Centurión, who was ordered to receive Chapperon and escort him to Paso Pucu. He somehow misunderstood his instructions and took him to Humaitá instead. As they neared the fortress, Centurión saw one of López's aides riding towards them. He asked Centurión where he was going and then, without waiting for an answer, told him to take the consul the Paso Pucu.

At the headquarters Centurión was ordered to dismount, his sword was taken away and he was arrested. That evening, Chapperon was taken to Humaitá, from where he crossed into the Chaco and was taken north to Asuncion. Centurión was released, given a lecture about obeying orders implicitly and told that no excuses for subsequent misconduct would be accepted. For some time afterwards he was given no work to do and despaired of his future and even toyed with the idea of deserting to the enemy.[72]

One reason why the Paraguayans and López in particular were so jumpy was that they knew they were living on borrowed time. At some point the enemy must attack. That would almost certainly involve an attempt by the Brazilian fleet, still being reinforced with ironclads, to challenge the batteries of Humaitá. If they tried to force their way past they would succeed, as the experience of Curupayty had shown. In Rio de Janeiro, the Minister of Marine Alfonso Celso, Viscount of Ouro Preto, wrote to Ignacio asking whether an attempt to pass the batteries might not be possible. Ignacio wrote back complaining of the great dangers involved. Other Brazilians asked similar questions. Were the Paraguayan defences really that strong? Sooner or later, the Paraguayans knew, Ignacio would be forced into action.

There was no indication that anything dramatic had happened when, on February 21, Washburn went off duck shooting in the marshes near La Trinidad with James Manlove, a 6ft 4in ex-Confederate officer who had managed to get into Paraguay in 1866 and tried to interest López in a scheme for forming a fleet of privateers for preying on the Brazilian fleet. López had not trusted him sufficiently to adopt this suggestion and since then Manlove had drifted round Asuncion rather aimlessly, unable to get out of the country, depending largely upon the charity of Washburn for his subsistence. They returned at dusk, and on the outskirts of the city met Henry Valpy and Percy Burrell, the two English engineers, who were both in a state of great excitement. They stopped the two Americans and told them the almost unbelievable news that three days before the Brazilian ironclads had passed the batteries of Humaitá. As they galloped back to Asuncion, Washburn and Manlove were in no doubt about the significance of the news. The minister was convinced that 'if the fleet had passed Humaitá then...López and his entire army were surrounded and besieged so effectively that they could never escape. The war must soon be over.'

Like Valpy and Burrell, and indeed most of the foreigners in Paraguay at that time, the two Americans hoped that this would prove to be the case. Washburn's relations with López were so bad that it was almost impossible for him to carry out his functions as United States minister. In January he had fact written home to request his recall, but it now seemed that the Allies would come to the rescue before the American government had a chance to act. Although they had been told the news in strictest confidence, Washburn and Manlove found the whole city in a state of near pandemonium when they reached the Plaza Vieja. People were rushing in and out of the American Legation, wondering what they should do, while out in the streets harassed officials were trying to organise hundreds of terrified people into some sort of order. A message from José Berges, the Foreign Minister, was waiting for Washburn, and when he reached the Government House Berges told him that the city was being evacuated. Four ironclads had passed the batteries and two of them had already reached Villa Francia, half way to Asuncion: they were expected to reach the capital within three days. Since there was virtually nothing to stop them, the authorities were preparing to evacuate the population of the capital to Luque, a small town that had been named as the new capital. In common with the other diplomats in Asuncion, Washburn was asked to prepare his Legation for the move, and was offered carts and other facilities to enable him to do so.

This request put Washburn in a difficult position. In view of the imminent arrival of the Brazilian ships, the Paraguayan government was obviously justified in moving the capital to Luque and since Washburn was the American minister it was his duty to follow. But Luque was twelve miles from the river, and since there were no reports of the Allied land forces having broken through it was unlikely that the naval expedition would be able to reach the new capital. By going to Luque therefore, Washburn would once more be putting himself at López's mercy. If, on the other hand, he remained in Asuncion it would only be a matter of days - probably hours now - before the Allies arrived and he was saved. Deciding that self-preservation - and he did after all have a wife and family to consider - was more important than diplomatic duty, Washburn told Berges that the Legation was American territory and 'that the Paraguayan government had no power or authority over me; and that if there were danger that the town might be taken by the Brazilians, that was a reason why I should remain in it.'

Washburn's decision was especially important because it influenced many other people. Nobody knew what was really happening down the river, but it was clear that Paraguay had suffered a major defeat and that Asuncion was likely to fall. Everybody in the capital therefore had to choose between going to Luque, or waiting for the Brazilians, and their decision would inevitably be regarded as an indication of their sympathies in the war. Once it became widely known that Washburn was staying put, he found himself a rallying point of those who, for various reasons, had decided to stay in the capital. One of the first callers was Antonio de las Carreras, the former Uruguayan foreign minister who had once vowed to perish in the ruins of Montevideo. Following the collapse of the Blancos, he had fled to Entre Rios, and then made his way to Paraguay. He was understandably afraid of what would happen to him if the Allies won the war, and months before had asked Washburn if he would give him protection. Since their victory seemed imminent he came to ask the minister to fulfil that promise, bringing with him Rodriquez the young former secretary of the Uruguayan Legation. Both were admitted. They were followed by four English engineers from the arsenal, among them Alonzo Taylor and John Watts. Washburn sent them to get permission from Colonel Francisco Fernandez, one of the López's closest aides, who was helping to organise the evacuation of the city and once permission was granted the engineers moved in with their families, a total of 22 people. The Calas family, Washburn's friends from Limpio, were also in the Legation on a visit, and decided to stay on until the situation was clarified. Masterman was already there, and Manlove and another American, called Porter C. Bliss, moved in from the small cottage they had been sharing on the outskirts of town. Within two days the number of people inside the Legation, including servants, rose to 42. In addition to these refugees, scores of other people, mostly Paraguayans, came to leave their valuables in Washburn's care, among them Mrs. Lynch, who called at the Legation on February 22 to leave property estimated at $200,000.

With some satisfaction, Washburn noted that she seemed very despondent, and when she asked him what he thought the Allies would do next, he told her that they would take Asuncion and the war was lost.

While the Legation group was preparing to welcome the Brazilians as deliverers, the civil government was trying to stop them arriving at all. After years of despotism, they were nervous of acting on their own. Communication with López was difficult. Messages had to be sent to the Tebicuary by telegraph, then taken across the river to Monte Lindo and carried down to Humaitá by horseman. This complicated and uncertain journey was far too slow for the emergency that faced Asuncion. The responsibility for action rested on the shoulders of a small group of men, nominally headed by Sanchez, the 82-year-old vice-president, of whom Carlos Antonio López had once caustically remarked: 'He can call himself what he likes, he will still be an idiot.' Berges, the foreign minister, and his deputy Gumesindo Benitez, the principal writer in the *Semanario* were members of the group, as was Francisco Fernandez. Although he had no official rank, as a friend of López he carried considerable weight. His wife was a close friend of López's sisters, and he was generally liked as a kind-hearted man who frequently granted requests. Another key figure was Captain Matias Sanabria, the chief of police and López's head spy, a cruel man who was widely feared. Both Benigno and Venancio López were in Asuncion at this time and their positions as members of the López family gave them an automatic authority.

This group heard of the approach of the ironclads on February 19. As soon as the message was received, Venancio López instructed Sanchez to call a meeting, which was also attended by Berges, Fernandez, Benitez, Benigno López, Carlos Rivero, Dean Bogado and two other priests named Ortellado and Espinoso[73].

The purpose of the meeting was to decide whether the town should be defended or not. Fernandez advised against on the grounds that supplies were so low that the Paraguayans could not resist for very long. The rest of the group were inclined to accept this view until Father Espinoso asked permission to speak and then delivered an impassioned speech in which he said it was their duty to fight, right down to the last cartridge. Sanchez supported him and it was agreed that they town would be defended while Sanabria organised the evacuation. Venancio was furious at this development. He ordered Sanchez to arrange a second meeting, this time at Venancio's house near the port and he again put the question: should they defend the capital or not? This time Rivero spoke in favour of fighting and the original decision was confirmed.

Even so, they all knew that their chances of stopping the Brazilians from taking Asuncion were virtually nil. Juan Gomez, the *mayor de la plaza,* commanded a handful of troops but most of the garrison had long ago been sent to Humaitá, and all that was left were a few cavalry and some field guns that were quite incapable of stopping an ironclad. The only useful weapon was the Criollo, the monster 12-ton gun made by the English engineers at the arsenal, which been completed a few days before. So far this had never been fired, but it was hauled off to a bluff overlooking the river and manhandled into position. Within a day or two, the evacuation of Asuncion was completed. The refugees were sent off to the mountains without food or shelter, and hundreds of them died of exposure as a result. The men who were hoping to defend the city, and the group in the Legation, who were praying for its fall, were left alone. The only others were a few policemen who patrolled the empty streets to guard the shuttered houses.

Then on February 24, rumours began to spread that the ironclads were approaching. To get the best possible view of the liberation, Washburn, Masterman and Cuberville went up on to the roof of the

Legation and looked south towards the bend round which the ironclads would appear. Meanwhile, in the battery at the far end of the street, they could see the Paraguayan soldiers struggling to haul the *Criollo* into position. Soon the three men saw thin wisps of smoke curling above the trees and then the grey shapes of two ironclads steamed round the bend. A shell whistled over the Legation and landed somewhere beyond the city, and at this point Cuberville announced that his horse would suffer from standing in the sun and vanished downstairs. The Paraguayan gun began to fire back, but its first shots flew well over the two enemy vessels. When the gunners tried to depress the barrel to get them in range, they found to their consternation that the hill on which the gun stood was in the way.

To hit the enemy they would have to cut away part of the hillside. But by then there was by no time to do this, and so after a few ineffective shots, the gun fell silent. The Brazilian shells continued to sail overhead. This went on for some time, and it dawned on Washburn and Masterman only slowly that the ships had not come any closer. Even the bombardment seemed to be slackening, and to their horror, the two men suddenly realised that the ironclads were turning and then were sailing away. Four hours after they had arrived, the two ships finally disappeared behind the point and the smoke of their funnels faded from the sky. The only damage, according to Masterman, had been `the destruction of a balcony of the President's palace, a slice off the front of the house and the demolition of a couple of dogs in the market place." That the Brazilian expedition would turn out to be a fiasco like this had never occurred to Washburn. Like everyone else, including the men handling the *Criollo* and the committee that had organised the evacuation, he had taken a Brazilian landing for granted. Shaken at this unexpected development, he and Masterman went downstairs and told the other occupants that the Brazilians had left. They hoped for a while that the two ships would return in a day or two, but instead they continued down river until they reached the Brazilian battery at Tayi, where they stopped and celebrated. Washburn and his guests were still convinced that the war was virtually over, since the action at Humaitá had obviously resulted in López and his army being trapped, but even so, he became increasingly uneasy as the days and then weeks passed.

The minister was coming to realise that his own position was now a good deal more precarious than it had ever been before. By refusing to go to Luque he had thumbed his diplomatic nose at López, convinced that the Brazilians would rescue him before the President had time to exact his revenge. But the Brazilians had gone away without him, and Washburn began to wonder fearfully what López would do.

The successful attempt to pass the Humaitá batteries had been the result of several factors. The sinking of the chain across the river was followed by an unexpected rise in the water level, which enabled the Brazilians to clear the mines and other underwater obstacles.

Secondly, three monitors that had been built in Rio de Janeiro passed Curupayty on February 13 and joined the other ironclads. These ships, the *Alagoas*, *Para* and *Rio Grande*, were armoured with 4in plates, powered by twin screws and had Whitworth guns mounted in the revolving turrets whose gunports were so well designed that they were very difficult to hit.

Thirdly, Mitre was no longer in command. On January 2 Marcos Paz, the vice president of Argentina died of cholera. Although Paz had continually complained about the difficulties of governing the country and begged Mitre to return to Buenos Aires, he had generally managed to cope, but his death meant that there was nobody able or trustworthy enough to take over the reigns of civilian government. Since Mitre's term of office as president was due to expire later in the year, political activity in Buenos Aires and the provinces would soon be even more turbulent than usual. On January 14, therefore, Mitre left Paraguay for Buenos Aires, handing over supreme command to Caxias. Once he was out of the way the Brazilians began to show more energy.

The Humaitá batteries were passed by the three monitors and the ironclads *Bahia, Barroso* and *Tamandaré.* While they were doing so the Allies began a furious bombardment of the perimeter trenches, although Thompson found it difficult to see the reason for these diversions 'as the 8in guns could not very well, at a moment's notice, have marched off to Espinillo.' At 3.30 am on February 18 the three large ironclads moved upstream each with a monitor lashed to her port side. The gunners at Humaitá were as accurate as usual, but the ironclads were not seriously damaged, although the lashings connecting the *Alagoas* to her monitor were shot away and she had to make her way past the battery under her own. At Timbo Caballero's men gave the six ships a drubbing on the port side, but again they forced their way past and reached the safety of Tayi, where they were covered by the Brazilian battery. The *Alagoas* had been hit 180 times and the *Tamandaré* 120, and these two and the *Para*, which had also been damaged, remained at Tayi to refit while the other three ships continued up river towards Asuncion. On the same day as the passing of Humaitá, the Brazilians took Cierva, after a heroic defence that was only ended when the Paraguayans ran out of ammunition. As a result of these two setbacks, López at last prepared to abandon Humaitá.

It is a tribute to his coolness as well as his courage that he should have waited this long. It is equally almost incredible that he should have been able to do so, for by all the rules the Paraguayan army was already hopelessly trapped, cut-off by an army that outnumbered it by four to one, a fleet, an enemy-controlled river, and miles of thick jungle and swamp. The only logical result should have been surrender. Instead the Paraguayans embarked on one of the boldest and most heroic episodes in the whole war, and it started with an act whose daring was to characterise the whole period.

It was apparent to all that the Allies depended largely on the fleet of ironclads which by now dominated the river above as well as below Humaitá. Paraguay could not obtain ironclads from abroad, and she lacked the facilities for building her own. An attempt to fix railway lines to the hull of the *Ygurei* had failed because the ship's timbers were too frail to bear the weight. The only way in which an armoured vessel could be obtained, therefore, was by taking one from the Brazilians. On the night of March 1, 24 canoes, slipped quietly down river towards the dark shapes of the *Cabral* and *Herbal*, two of the seven ironclads that had been left at Curupayty while the others passed Humaitá. The canoes were tied together in pairs and covered with branches, leaves and vegetation to make them look like *camelotes*, the huge floating islands of driftwood and water lilies that were a frequent sight on the river. It was a very dark night, and the canoes remained undetected until they gently bumped alongside their prey, and as the alarm was given, the Paraguayans scrambled up the sides and rushed on to the decks of the two ships.

The commander of the squadron and several other officers were caught and killed, but other Brazilians managed to get inside the gun-turrets or dive below. The party which had attacked the *Cabral* forced open the hatches with hand grenades and were fighting their way inside when two other ships in the squadron, aroused by the noise, got up steam and came to the rescue. Using grape and canister their heavy guns began to cut the Paraguayans to pieces, and swept the Cabral party off the ships just as the Paraguayans were on the verge of taking her. Ignacio, the Brazilian admiral, wrote: "I endeavoured to save some, ordering boats to be lowered for that purpose: but they refused any help and preferred to die." More than 200 men died in the attack and immediately afterwards the evacuation began.

It continued throughout March, helped by the almost inexplicable inactivity of the Brazilian ironclads. They were stationed at Curupayty, and controlled the river between there and the sea; others were at Tayi, and patrolled from there to the north. The only part of the river that they chose to ignore was the only part that at this stage really mattered - the few miles of water between Humaitá and Timbo. Although the Paraguayans did most of their work at night, the Brazilian ships made not the slightest attempt to investigate what was happening, nor to interrupt the evacuation, and they thereby let the whole Paraguayan army slip through their fingers and vanish into the forest of the Chaco.

It was an ironic commentary on the changes brought about by the war that the death of Flores the day after the passing of Humaitá should have had absolutely no effect on the course of events and was scarcely noticed by either side. By February 1868 he had already faded into insignificance and his death was an irrelevance. He died as a result of the vicious party politics that still bedevilled life in Montevideo. His own term as President was due to expire on February 15, and, despite the pleas of his son Fortunato, he refused to run again. Fortunato then attempted to seize power, but failed, and the extreme Blancos, under the ex-president Berro revolted in their turn. As soon as he heard of this Flores went to Government House to find out what was happening, but on the way he was ambushed, shot in the mouth and then stabbed to death. Flores himself could hardly have complained at such treatment; he was one of the leading exponents of violence in Uruguayan politics and his own career had been almost entirely disruptive. He was a victim of the anarchy that he had helped to create.

While all this was going on Thompson was planning the defences at the Tebicuary to which the main army was retreating. The Tebicuary itself was 560 yards wide where it entered the Paraguay. The land to the north and for thirty miles inland was marshy and cut off m from the east by an intricate maze of *esteros* that connected the river to the Laguna Ypoa, a shallow lake roughly fifty miles long. The roads were few and at best little more than tracks, and there were four main fords across the river, which were still being guarded by Nuñez and the handful of men under his command. Although the land was difficult, the line to be defended was too long, and the winding river veered south just before joining the Paraguay, making it a less suitable line that López wanted. Still, it was the only place for a hundred miles where a stand could be organised and López had decided to make for it. López spent the rest of the day at the tiny fort, which Caballero still commanded, giving orders to his officers and in particular to the men selected to remain in Humaitá.

For although López had decided to evacuate his main army he did not intend to abandon Humaitá completely. While it held, the Brazilians' wooden fleet and transport vessels would have to remain below Curupayty, and without these ships it was unlikely that the allied army would move north in any force. If secrecy could be preserved, moreover, it would be some time before Caxias realised that the bulk of the army had actually left - and those few days start, and the thorn of Humaitá still in the enemy's side, might be enough to save the army.

Once the army had reached the Tebicuary line, the Humaitá garrison of almost 3,000 men would be cut off by an Allied army that outnumbered it by more than ten to one, the Brazilian fleet and fifty miles of flooded countryside: the rise in the river which had helped the ironclads cross the sunken chains at Humaitá had resulted in flood water pouring over much of the low lying country that lay beyond the banks. The garrison's future, therefore, was bleak, and López was in fact asking it to sacrifice itself so that the rest of the army could escape.

The man selected to command this doomed contingent was Col. Paulino Alén, a brave and able soldier who had been a member of the President's party during his visit to Europe fifteen years before, and had been sent to Corrientes at the time of the Robles affair. Short and fat, with predominately Indian blood, he was regarded as a spy for López and for this reason was unpopular with many of the Europeans. His deputy was Colonel Francisco Martinez, one of López's favourite *aides de camp*. He had taken López's letter to Mitre on the occasion of the ill-fated peace conference of September 1866 and for years slept outside López's door as a bodyguard. His beautiful 24-year-old wife, Juliana, 'pretty, plump, laughing and heedless' according to Washburn, was a close friend of Elisa Lynch and was living at her *quinta* at Patino Cué, twelve miles from Asuncion. The two other senior officers were Gill and Ortiz, the naval captains.

The same evening, March 3, López and his party started on their journey north. Despite all the efforts that had been made, the Chaco road was three feet deep in mud in places and some of the numerous streams and lagoons that it crossed had still not been properly bridged. Even on horseback it took three days to reach Monte Lindo, but even though the retreat went on all through March, it was several weeks before the Allies realised that something was happening. On March 21 Caxias decided to risk an assault and General Alexander Gomez de Argolo Fernao, who had succeeded Porto Alegre some months before, managed to overwhelm the hundred or so men holding the trench at the Potrero Sauce. An attack by Osorio at Espinillo was driven back, but the next day the outer perimeter, which had resisted all Allied attacks for two years, was abandoned for good. The troops along the Paso Pucu line were also withdrawn, and the defence concentrated on the original trenches around the town of Humaitá itself. While this was being done, two of the ironclads at Tayi moved south and forced their way past Timbo, thereby cutting direct communications between Humaitá and the Chaco road. The *Ygurei* was surprised in mid-river and sunk, and, after landing her guns in the Chaco, the *Tacuarí*, which had played such a significant part in Paraguay's history, was scuttled by her own crew.

Had they done this three weeks before, the Brazilians could have trapped the entire Paraguayan army, but by the time they did act nearly all the troops had left. Barrios, Resquín and Bruguez, who had been supervising the last stages of the evacuation crossed into the Chaco by canoe and rode north to Monte Lindo. Alén was left with a garrison of 3,000 men and several hundred women who had refused to leave. Against this force, which had to man a perimeter 15,000 yards long, the Allies had massed 30,000 men. Guns were mounted at the old Paraguayan strong points such as Paso Pucu and Espinillo. Despite the ring of steel surrounding them, the Humaitá garrison could still contact Caballero by sending canoes to the small point directly opposite Humaitá, The Paraguayans had built a small redoubt there, and a narrow path ran north along the river bank to Timbo. During the day it was under fire from the Brazilian ironclads, but the Paraguayans were able to move supplies along it at night.

The Allies were still unsure what was happening at Humaitá, but at the end of April a reconnaissance convinced them that the fort was still too strong to be carried by a direct attack. Instead, they decided to cut its last link with Timbo and safety. On April 30 General Ignacio Rivas crossed the Riacho de Oro, a small river on the Chaco side that entered the River Paraguay between Humaitá and Curupayty, and advanced north with 1,200 Argentineans. At the same time the ironclads landed 2,500 Brazilians in the Chaco south of Timbo, and the two Allied columns began moving towards each other. Paraguayan patrols in the swamps opposite Humaitá soon told Alén what was happening, but there was little he could do. A small detachment of men sent to attack Rivas was driven off without much trouble on May 2, and Caballero failed to stop the Brazilians, although they suffered heavy casualties in a battle fought on the same day. On the 3rd the two forces met and under Rivas's command consolidated their position by building a small redoubt beside the river called Andai. A few messengers managed to get through to Alén, and Caballero's men tried floating cattle down to the garrison on rafts, but to all intents and purposes Humaitá was cut off, and there was nothing Caballero, López or the whole of the Paraguayan army could do to save it. This was, of course, exactly what López had expected and there was no reason to feel dissatisfied with events so far. The rest of the army had struggled through the Chaco safely and by May was digging in behind the Tebicuary, while Caxias was still wondering where the Paraguayans had gone.

But by then López's interest in the fate of Humaitá was waning. He had a new problem on his mind. In his new capital of San Fernando, four miles north of the Tebicuary, he had discovered a threat from within. Some of the leading figures in Paraguay, the men he had most trusted, the soldiers and civilians he had befriended and made important, were planning to destroy him. While he had been fighting heroically for his country, López believed, a monstrous conspiracy was being formed against him, and among its members were his brothers and the American minister, Charles Ames Washburn, who, while the Paraguayan army was struggling for survival, had been cowering in his Legation at Asuncion, waiting for his Brazilian friends to come and save him.

Chapter 23

Ever since the end of the Paraguayan War, the great conspiracy against López has remained a subject of controversy, and after a hundred years of argument the truth about whether it existed or not will never be fully established. In general, the Paraguayan witnesses maintained that there was a conspiracy: the foreigners insisted that there was not. Since most of the Paraguayans were the men who had investigated it and most of the foreigners were said to have been involved in it, neither group was unbiased, and the Paraguayans who were accused of complicity were unable to add their testimony since none of them survived the war.

The chief witnesses for the conspiracy theory include Resquín, Juan C. Centurión, Silvestre Aveiro, soldiers who were appointed to investigate the conspiracy and Father Fidel Maiz. In view of the latter's involvement in the alleged conspiracy against López at the time of the President's accession, his position as one of the most feared inquisitors was ironical. He had been freed after writing a fulsome and abject admission of guilt that appeared in the *Semanario* in December 1866, and since then had served López with grateful loyalty.

Although the accounts of these witnesses differ in detail, the general theme is the same. The conspiracy arose because of the hopelessness of Paraguay's position, which became increasingly obvious towards the end of 1867. Venancio and Benigno López were both involved, and Benigno was one of the men considered as a possible replacement for their brother. Another favoured candidate was Berges, and according to Centurión there was considerable rivalry between the two, with Berges favouring a constitutional government, and Benigno a continuation of the existing constitution but with himself as President. Aveiro maintained that the whole idea of picking a new president began in September 1867, when López was ill at Humaitá. He claimed that among the twelve members of the conspiracy's *comité directivo* were Benigno and Venancio López, Saturnino Bedoya, Berges, Washburn, Bliss and Leite-Pereira.

According to Centurión, the crucial moment was the passing of Humaitá. Bedoya, who was still being held at Humaitá, was until then quite serene, but as soon as the ironclads had forced their way past the batteries he became extremely agitated. He went to see Bishop Palacios but his speech was so incomprehensible that the Bishop could understand only that he was very afraid of what would happen if and when the enemy ships reached Asuncion. Palacios went straight to López, who listened quite calmly and expressed an interest in finding out more about what was happening in the capital. He was especially interested in what Benigno was doing. He ordered Bedoya to be arrested and then told Palacios and Barrios to put to him a series of questions. Bedoya realised that he was in serious trouble (the questions were put to him under oath) and, as Centurión phrased it, López saw that "by pulling on this thread he would be led to the ball."

López regarded the meeting in Asuncion with great suspicion and on March 16 he wrote to Sanchez for an explanation. How could he have been so docile towards Benigno and Venancio? To most people the fact that the meeting was called is perfectly understandable: the war had apparently reached a crisis in which Marshal López was unable to participate. It was logical that Sanchez and the others should have met to decide whether they should fight or not. López simply demanded to know why Sanchez had put such an absurd question to a meeting of sensible men.

Sanchez wrote a long and carefully worded reply on March 27. He referred to a letter written to him by López in January, which had referred to his equivocal behaviour at the time of the battle of Tuyuti and the complete dominion that Benigno seemed to exercise over him. In his second letter López said that Bedoya, with the agreement of Benigno, was preparing a revolution which would let the Allies into the country. Venancio was involved and Sanchez was criticised for allowing him to call the Asuncion meeting – a criminal abuse of his powers, in the Marshal's opinion.

Sanchez denied all these charges. He was not aware of doing anything wrong at the time of Tuyuti and denied knowing anything about a conspiracy. He pointed out that he owed everything to López and his father. Why would he turn against the family now, in the autumn of his life (he was about 80 at this stage)?

Resquín claimed that Washburn's role was to act as a link between the conspirators and the Allies. He said that the minister had made contact with Caxias during his visit to the Allied camp early in 1867. The head of the plot, in his opinion, was Benigno López. Towards the end of March 1868, a letter in his handwriting addressed to Caxias was found, together with a map outlining the Paraguayan defences.

This, briefly, was the case for the conspiracy. It was backed up by a certain amount of circumstantial evidence, some of which may simply have been coincidence, but the accounts of Resquín and the others do contain some inconsistencies. If Washburn had established contact with Caxias in early 1867, why did it take so long for anything positive to happen? Why did Barrios and Bruguez go to such lengths to complete the evacuation of Humaitá, when it would have been a comparatively simple matter to surrender the army, or at least inform Caxias of its vulnerability? And if there was a conspiracy involving such important and distinguished men, then why did they make such a mess of it? Why did they allow themselves to be whisked off, one by one, without doing anything to save themselves or their fellow plotters? Another reason to doubt the existence of the conspiracy is the fact that Washburn, Bliss, Masterman, von Versen and other foreigners who were said to be involved all strenuously denied the existence of any such plot, even when they were safely out of Paraguay. But even if one comes to the conclusion that there never was a conspiracy, one can certainly understand how López believed that there was. The plot was allegedly discovered shortly after the Allies had forced López to abandon Humaitá: this, López believed, was the beginning of the end. During his march through the Chaco he seems actually to have considered escaping through the jungle to Bolivia. He could not bring himself to accept responsibility for this latest reverse, any more than he had regarded the defeat of Estigarribia as the result of his own incompetent strategy.

In the past he had always found a scapegoat for catastrophe - Mesa was blamed for the defeat at the Riachuelo, Estigarribia and Robles were both traitors, and hundreds of others had been judged guilty of similar treachery because they had failed to achieve the impossible. Since the fall of Humaitá would be a more serious reverse than anything that had happened so far, López's search for scapegoats inevitably took him to the highest ranks of civilian and military life. The idea of a conspiracy, a huge plot involving everyone around him was a splendid solution to López's problems. It enabled him to blame everything on to other people and at the same time reinforce his conviction that he was a martyr, a lone patriot fighting on behalf of an unworthy and ungrateful country.

The key figures in this plot almost chose themselves. Benigno and Venancio López were obvious candidates. They had never been on good terms with their brother, and although the terrified Venancio did his best to keep out of trouble, Benigno talked to anyone. One evening in September, 1867, after he had been dining with Gould, and having too many drinks, he poured out his troubles to Silvestre Aveiro, and complained bitterly about the way he was treated by his brother Francisco. He spoke on similar lines to Cuberville – a friend and informant of López and Elisa Lynch - and seems to have discussed politics with all and sundry.

Another person who said too much was Washburn. He was a man who liked to talk, and was always keen to give his views on how other people should conduct their own affairs. This included López and the Paraguayans generally. The result was that at dinner parties and *soirées* Washburn plunged recklessly into conversations that were indiscreet to the point of folly. Masterman, who came to view Washburn with a rather jaundiced eye, summed the minister's actions up neatly: "Mr. Washburn did talk most imprudently. Amongst ourselves it was all very well to say what we thought of the war and the character of López, but he used in his blundering Spanish, to tell things to natives - to this very Don Benigno, to Berges, to many others, and especially to a smooth-spoken flattering Italian named Parodi, who 'Your Excellency-ed' him into the most perilous of confidences, and then betrayed all to Mrs. Lynch - which, perfectly right in themselves as mere personal opinion, became treason and conspiracy if the point of view were shifted a little.'

The following year, the United States House of Congress formed a special committee to examine the behaviour of its diplomatic representative in Paraguay, and during it Commander W.A. Kirkland, of the gunboat *Wasp* gave evidence about a letter he had written to Admiral C.A. Davis describing a conversation he had had with Mrs. Washburn. This letter read in part: 'Mr. Washburn told me that he had never heard of a revolution or conspiracy against the government. But on one occasion Mrs. Washburn, when her husband was not present, stated there was a plan to turn López out of power and to put in his place his two brothers Venancio and Benigno.' Kirkland then elaborated on this, and told the committee: "It was on the passage down the river, two or three days after we left the batteries. Mrs. Washburn said distinctly that there was no conspiracy, but that there was a plan. It was at the dinner table. Mr. Washburn had finished his dinner and had gone out for something, and shortly after came back. This remark struck me as rather singular, and I wrote of it to the admiral. I know that she made a distinction between the words 'conspiracy and 'plan.'

In his memoirs, Washburn admitted that during conversations at the Plaza Vieja or at Señora Bedoya's quinta the names of Benigno López, Saturnino Bedoya and José Berges were put forward at various times as possible replacements for López, but he always denied strenuously that these conversations had ever amounted to a conspiracy. All those taking part had ever done, he insisted was talk - and it is only natural that, considering the situation in the country at the time, they should have discussed the possibility of somebody else becoming president, as it was quite possible that López would be killed in battle or taken prisoner. In this context, Mrs. Washburn's otherwise pedantic insistence on the word 'plan,' which clearly implies it amounted to something less sinister than a 'conspiracy' becomes more understandable. By 1868, Washburn, Benigno López, Saturnino Bedoya, Berges, Bedoya himself and others had become fairly intimate. There is little reason to doubt that they indulged in wishful thinking, and discussed how pleasant life would be without Francisco López. Having reached that stage, it was a short step to agreeing that it was time somebody did something and they may have even talked about how and what should be done.

But as for doing something themselves, that was a different matter. They were not leaders - Aveiro claimed that the conspiracy failed because there was no strong man at its head - and probably all they did was to while away the hours with pipe dreams. They were not opposed to the idea of conspiring against López. They were merely unable to do so effectively, because they lacked a leader who was prepared to take the risk involved.

Unfortunately, López was told what they said by his spies, at least one of whom worked in the American Legation, and rapidly came to the conclusion that something far more serious was going on. He was suspicious of the meetings that had taken place at Asuncion just before the arrival of the Brazilian ironclads, and his doubts were apparently confirmed by Washburn's extraordinary refusal to go to Luque. Whichever way one looks at that incident, it could not be regarded as a sign of sympathy for the Paraguayan cause and with López there were never any shades of grey. If people were not for him they were against and if they were against they deserved to be punished. Having convinced himself that the conspiracy existed, he set out to destroy it.

Benigno was summoned from his ranch in the Villa Concepcion department and questioned in his turn.[74] His brother asked him: "Well, what are you people in the capital up to?"

Benigno replied: "Sir, since we had not heard much from you or the army since Humaitá was besieged, we thought the time had arrived to think of taking some action to save ourselves and our interests."

López turned to Caballero, who was present during the interview, and said: "You see, Caballero, how this lot are more like Negroes (Brazilians) than the Negroes themselves." After this, Benigno was kept under house arrest. Others were then questioned and more names added to the list of suspects. From this beginning, everything else snowballed. The citizens of Paraguay, who during the last three years had seen their husbands and sons sent off to be killed in the army, or thrown into prison, were already in such a state of nervous terror that they betrayed each other to the inquisitors without remorse, confessing to everything, implicating anyone they could think if. If the tribunals wished to be told that Washburn was a conspirator, then they would be told exactly that: when the inquisitors asked for further names they came tumbling out in a torrent. Those named were then arrested, and in their turn added others to the list. In this way the conspiracy, which originated in the gossip of a few civilians in Asuncion, came to involve hundreds of people, the majority of whom could not possibly have been involved in a conspiracy, even if it had existed. It took some time for this situation to develop, however, and for six weeks after the evacuation of the city, the residents of the Legation lived in a fool's paradise in which they imagined that the war was virtually over. The whole group was banking on this, and in the meantime managed to antagonise the Paraguayan authorities still further.

On March 3 Manlove and Watts went to see some cows that they kept near the Legation and on the way were stopped by the police who told them to go to the police station. Instead Manlove went to see Sanabria, got into an argument with him, and was only rescued from serious trouble by the arrival of Washburn. Watts was not so lucky. He went to the police station as instructed and did not return. This was an ominous indication of what could happen to the rest of them, if the Allied did not act quickly and when it became clear that the ironclads were not coming back, Washburn's guests became seriously alarmed. It was a crushing blow for them all when, six weeks after the evacuation, they heard that López had escaped from Humaitá and was marching through the Chaco with the bulk of his army. 'We had fancied our own deliverance was at hand and that the caged tiger was fast in leash,' lamented Washburn. 'Our indignation and contempt for the Brazilians was intense.'

For everybody, the American Legation had been a stepping stone on the road to safety: the failure of the Brazilian fleet meant that it came increasingly to represent safety itself and a pretty inadequate form of safety at that. The police forbade everybody except Washburn, his secretary, Meinke, and his Paraguayan servant, Basilio, to leave the building, and the strain of living in such a tense and uncertain atmosphere, in close proximity to so many people, soon began to tell on everybody. Things were not improved when the Legation was besieged by a horde of starving animals, for although the city had been evacuated of people, their pets remained. The dogs were not much of a problem. There were only a few of them and they died quickly. But the cats soon became a menace to the inhabitants.

The first glimpse of hope came on May 6 when Gaspar López, a clerk in the foreign office, came to the Legation with the news that the United States gunboat *Wasp* had arrived in the River Paraguay, The hope that this meant help was on the way was dampened when López went on to say that Caxias had refused to allow the ships to pass through the Allied blockade. To try and sort out this complication Washburn went down to San Fernando on May 12, and the following day had an interview with López in which he put forward a request for permission to leave the country on behalf of Dr. Carreras, who claimed that an uncle in Chile had left him a fortune which, under the terms of the will, had to be inherited within one year. López was not sympathetic. After an angry scene, Washburn left, and three days later returned to Asuncion. He had been unable to make direct contact with the *Wasp*, and Carreras's request had not even been considered. In fact, the trip had simply added to Washburn's worries. He noticed gloomily that his English friends kept well away from him, and Thompson in particular 'gave me to understand that the less he said the better it might be for him.'

Washburn did see Stewart, but even that meeting had unfortunate results. The Scot told him that the British government was about to intercede on behalf of its nationals living in Paraguay, and Washburn passed this information on to the engineers at the Legation. As a result, when Fernandez called to ask them to go back to work at the arsenal they refused. It then became apparent that the report was a false alarm, and the engineers found themselves in a worse position than ever. One of their number had already been arrested, which made the remainder more than ever determined to stay in the Legation for as long as possible. But they had only a limited amount of money, and as food was so expensive it dwindled rapidly. Many of the children fell ill and Masterman was kept busy attending them. The responsibility for these and all the other people in the Legation rested squarely upon Washburn's shoulders. They had sought refuge with him and he had granted it. This refuge now consisted of nothing more substantial than a vague concept called diplomatic immunity. On top of everything, Washburn's daughter was ill. Rodriquez, the Uruguayan, was also in poor health, and it was clear that by inviting so many people to stay with him Washburn had made a terrible mistake.

Two of the Calas girls and Watts had already gone. At any moment the police patrolling the dusty dirt roads outside might demand the surrender of the others and even Washburn's own person was not sacrosanct, as he was reminded at night when he could hear the police whispering beneath his windows. He knew that López hated him, and he remembered the dictator's treatment of other diplomats who had failed to please him: poor Laurent-Cochelet and his plain, provincial wife, after months of insults and open hostility, had been kept at Humaitá for days under continual bombardment by the Allied guns. Had López been hoping that they would be killed by the enemy? And if he could do such terrible things then, what would he do now, when he was that much more desperate? Washburn played billiards, with Masterman and Manlove, occasionally went riding and in the evenings he and his wife would invite their guests to play whist or chess, but these diversions were never sufficient. The terrifying future hung over the whole Legation group and like poor Dona Cordal, more than a year before, they waited fearfully for the last stroke of the tiger's paw.

Chapter 24

While the Allies were still considering how to take Humaitá and Washburn was becoming involved in the labyrinthine horrors of the conspiracy, 8,000 men of the Paraguayan army were struggling through the Chaco to Monte Lindo and relative safety. Thompson was sent to construct another battery at the mouth of the Tebicuary, where there was a small area of firm ground called Fortin Island. By this time not even López expected the battery to be able to stop the ironclads, but it was hoped that it would at least discourage them from passing too often. The Brazilians made no attempt to stop the army crossing back into Paraguay and Thompson was then put in command of Fortin.

This was the first fighting command he had held in the war, and the fact that it was in such a key position indicates the trust that López had in him, at a time when the purges of the conspiracy were reaching their peak. López's headquarters at San Fernando, four miles north of the Tebicuary, were situated on a patch of firm ground roughly thirty yards square, while the soldiers camped around it. The marshal, with his usual energy, set to work to improve the position, draining the swamps, building barracks for the men, putting up telegraph lines and workshops. By the middle of July the Tebicuary defences, though far from impregnable, were at least tenable, and there was little the men holding it could do but wait and dig more trenches. As they did so they could occasionally hear, drifting up river on the cold gusts of the south wind, a dull rumble like distant thunder or the throbbing of far away drums. It was the sound of the Allied guns bombarding the abandoned fortress of Humaitá.

At Humaitá there was a lull after the withdrawal of the main army. The Allies had established themselves at Andai, Humaitá was finally surrounded, and for the moment they were content. Alén was hardly content, but he was not in a position to do much more than wait for something to happen. Caballero had established a small fort called Cora, halfway between Timbo and Andai, but he had lost too many men to try another attack, and so he waited as well. In the meantime, the supplies at Humaitá began to run out, and the spectre of starvation loomed larger. On July 9 the Paraguayans failed in another attempt to seize two ironclads and this, if anything, made the fortress's position even worse, since it showed how desperate the Paraguayans were becoming.

If Humaitá could not be saved, then it should have been completely evacuated while there was still a chance of doing so. But when Alén asked for permission to cross into the Chaco and fight through Rivas's troops to Timbo, López curtly refused, and ordered that the defence continue. It was typical of his state of mind that he refused to admit that Humaitá was bound to fall, even though the year before he had made such sensible and logical preparations for its evacuation. This hopelessly unrealistic attitude filled Alén with despair. He could not fight on for much longer, and he could not retreat, for the idea of disobeying López's orders was not a practicable proposition to a Paraguayan. Caught between two equally impossible alternatives, he tried to solve his dilemma by committing suicide, but only managed to blow out an eye. The fate of Humaitá then devolved upon Colonel Martinez.

The Brazilians sensed that the Paraguayans were weakening and on 16 July Osorio attacked with 16,000 men. They were driven off with the loss of 2,000 men and two days later another attack on Cora broke down. Neither battle gained the Paraguayans anything, except time, and time was by then an enemy. Food had almost completely gone, and the men were eating the horses and hides of cattle which they had slaughtered days and weeks before - they cut it up into thin strips and boiled it, to make it a little more tender.

On July 21 three more ironclads passed Humaitá and on July 23 Martinez on his own initiative decided to retreat. Thirty canoes took the wounded across to the Chaco, and the next day, under the cover of celebrations for López's birthday, the rest of the garrison was ferried across, the military bands staying until the last, playing cheerful marches, melancholy *tristes*, and the inevitable *Palomita*, a repetitive but haunting song so popular during the war that it became almost a second national anthem.

The Allies noticed nothing during the night, and Martinez and his men were able to make themselves reasonably secure in the Chaco, where they could get some protection from the redoubt. But the most difficult part of the operation was still to come. Apart from the firm ground along the edge of the river, the whole of the point ahead of them was covered by marsh, the centre of which formed a lake called the Laguna Vera. As Rivas's fort at Andai blocked the road, the only possible way out was across this lake, on the far side of which Caballero's men were waiting. The Paraguayans managed to drag their 30 canoes to the edge without attracting attention, but as soon as they began ferrying the women and wounded men across they were spotted. Instantly the full weight of the Allied forces was concentrated on them. Rivas was reinforced until he had 10,000 men, 2,000 of whom lay hidden in the woods to the east of the lake firing at the canoes as they passed, while the others advanced on Martinez's men who had dug in at Isla Poi, the patch of land to the south of the lake. The Laguna Vera itself was connected to the River Paraguay, and when it became known that the Humaitá garrison was trying to break out, sixty small boats were sent into the lake to attack the canoes as they crossed. Eleven guns were moved into position, and the ironclads added the weight of their heavy guns to the bombardment.

Of the 2,500 men who had left Humaitá, nearly half attempted to cross the Laguna Vera in the canoes. Roughly 1,000 succeeded, among them Colonel Alén, who was taken, on a stretcher, with other wounded on one of the first trips, and two English surgeons, Skinner and Stevens. It was not long, however, before the last of the canoes was sunk. The survivors, Martinez, Gill and Ortiz among them, were hopelessly trapped. There was still no question of surrender, and when the Brazilians attacked Isla Poi on July 28 they were driven off with heavy losses, although ammunition was so low that Martinez used broken up muskets as grape shot for his five brass 3pr guns. This was a postponement rather than a victory, a paroxysm, the last spasm of a dying army. For days the ironclads poured shells into a huddle of men who had no shelter, who could not fight back, who could do nothing except lie in the mud, knowing there was nothing to wait for now but death. In a week 10,000 shells crashed among them, more than 40 an hour, sometimes two or three shells a minute, which churned up the ground and impartially crushed the bodies of the living and the dead. On August 2 the Brazilians sent in a messenger under a flag of truce to plead with Martinez to give in and end a slaughter which had become senseless. The flag was fired on and the bombardment resumed.

On August 4 Padre Ignacio Esmerata, a Brazilian chaplain, holding a crucifix and white flag before him, splashed through the mud and reeds towards the Paraguayan position. In the centre of the camp he found Martinez and this time he agreed to meet Rivas the next day. When they met Martinez reluctantly agreed to surrender. Even then he and his officers had to go from hole to hole persuading the men who had not eaten for four days that there really was no hope, that they had no bullets left to shoot, that there was no food to ease the clawing hunger inside them, that there was nothing remaining but death and that death like that was useless. Only then did the men file out from the torn trees and pile their empty muskets in a clearing, surrounded by saluting Brazilian soldiers. And only then could the Allies truly say that they had conquered Humaitá.

A few weeks later Burton visited the scene of Martinez's gallant stand and found 'fresh traces of the death-struggle still lay around, and everything spoke of the powerful and vehement nationality of Paraguay- the miserable remains of personal property told eloquently of the heart which the little Republic had thrown into the struggle. The poor rags, ponchos of door-rug, were rotting like those that wore them and amongst fragments of letters we picked up were instructions for loading heavy guns... there was a stand of broken sabres and bayonets, stirrups of wood and metal.... I felt something of the *hysteria passio* at the thought of so much wasted heroism. And this personal inspection of the site where the last struggle had lately ended impressed me highly with the Paraguayan strength of purpose, and with the probability of such men fighting to the last.'

The booty captured on the point was hardly impressive - five guns, 800 muskets, 99 officers and 1,200 men, 300 of them wounded. It was little better at Humaitá, which the Allies occupied on July 25, the first man to enter being, according to legend, a French pedlar (some said an Italian baker). The Allies captured 144 abandoned iron guns and 36 of brass, but of these only about 60 were serviceable. In the single-storey house behind the ruined church that had been López's home for so long they found several large packing cases containing furniture from Paris. Elsewhere they discovered 100 cases containing bottles of palm oil, and fifty sacks of maté. That was all.

When Burton visited it, Humaitá and the fort and redoubts that surrounded it were already crumbling into decay. The lines of trenches where the Paraguayan soldiers sheltered from the heavy guns of the ironclads were being levelled, or had fallen into disrepair. Standing at Cierva, where 1,600 men had defied Caxias' 6,000 until their ammunition was exhausted, he looked out across an empty wasteland. It was 'a desert; not a living being remained in this part of Paraguay; it was odorous of carnage ... and the enceinte showed only two long lines of graves.' At Timbo, where the Argentineans and Paraguayans had fought savagely in the tangled woods, the bodies of the dead lay where they had fallen, unburied and apparently forgotten, the Paraguayans 'distinguished by their fighting gear, regimental caps, cross-belts that carried their ammunition pouches, and a piece of half-tanned leather wrapped around the loins....' On the point where Martinez had surrendered, a scattering of wooden crosses showed where the Allied skirmishers had been buried. In Humaitá, beyond the piles of Whitworth shells collected by the frugal defenders, was the cemetery, graves made of red tile mosaics, some so small that they must have been the tombs of children. All was quiet now, and the pitiful inadequacy of the batteries that had inspired the awe of the Allies for so long was revealed. The 12-ton *Cristiano* was gone, taken to Brazil as a trophy of conquest and the brick casemate of the Londres battery had begun to collapse. The church of San Carlos Borromeo was 'a mere heap of picturesque ruins, with hardwood timber barely supported by cracked walls of brick.... one belfry, with the roof and facade, has been reduced to heaps; the south-eastern tower still rises above the ruins, but in a sadly shaky condition.'

Two years after Humaitá fell, R.B. Cunninghame Graham, a young Scot, passed the fortress on board a Brazilian gunboat, and fifty years later recalled: "The ruined church stood up against a back-ground of palm trees, some of which had been shattered by the long bombardment it had undergone, like a gaunt skeleton. Originally built of brick and painted white its red-tiled roof showed gaps where shells had fallen on it, and sagged dangerously. The tower, that seemed as if at any moment it might topple over, looked like the ghost of an abandoned lighthouse, its lamp extinguished, and its only function to guide derelicts towards their doom.

'A thin white mist enveloped but did not hide the ruined buildings of the deserted town. It hung upon the river like a veil of muslin, deadening the harsh cries of the water fowl, the chattering of the parrots, making the swishing of the wings of storks and cormorants as they flew overhead seem like a message from a world unknown and unsuspected. Nothing was stirring as the sun rose, as it rises in the tropics, without preamble, full-fledged, and ready to pour ruin on the world. As it fell on the ruined church and tower, the torn and shattered houses and the straggling groups of dark-leafed orange trees, it dispelled the air of mystery that the mist lent to them, showing them stark and miserable, and an example of what the might, the majesty and power of civilisation could accomplish with but the feeble means it had at its disposal but fifty years ago...

'We took our morning *maté*, all gazing curiously at the ruins of a place that but a scant two years before had undergone a fierce bombardment that had lasted months and was a household word in South America. No one said anything; even the Negro sailors ceased their chattering. As we forged past, fighting the current, as near the bank as it was safe to go, for the masts and funnels of several gunboats stuck up like artificial shoals, the commander, a lieutenant in the Brazilian navy, silently took off his cap and stood bareheaded till we had passed the church....'

In time the neglected barracks disappeared, the houses where López and his officers had lived, and planned and hoped were pulled down. The rusting guns were taken away by their new owners to become souvenirs of a battle that had happened long ago. The palisades and trenches were demolished and their traces worn away by the rain. The grass of the marshes spread over the graves of Cierva and the long-horned cattle of the *esteros* returned to graze where they had grazed long before the soldiers ever came. Only the church tower was left, the church tower that had been so frail when it was built that no one dared hang the bells that were meant to ring there. It remained a symbol of a tragedy that for a brief moment held the attention of a world that marvelled at the courage of the men who fought and died in its shadow. But even the memory of Humaitá crumbled in time and although there have been few chapters in the story of human courage that can match its last terrible months there have been even fewer whose fame has so quickly faded. Paraguay was far away, and unimportant. The United States was winning a new world in the west, and in Europe attention was soon diverted to the quarrel between Prussia and France. Within a few years the epic of Humaitá was forgotten by the world at large. And so the sublime, magnificent, wasted heroism of the Paraguayans failed to defeat their enemies, failed to hold their fortress and failed to save their country. And when they died, the memory of their courage died with them.

The surrender of Martinez did not mean the end of the story of Humaitá. López added a characteristic postscript. While the rest of the garrison remained in the swamps, Col. Alén and the few who had escaped with him cut their way through the jungle, crossed the Bermejo, came at last to Monte Lindo and then rejoined the army. López did not receive them as heroes. He regarded Alén as a traitor who had abandoned his post, fled from an impregnable fortress supplied with ample provisions, and ordered him to be arrested for desertion. He would have liked to do the same to Martinez, but the colonel was safe in an Allied prison camp. So López contented himself with arresting his wife, who was made to walk twelve miles to Asuncion where she was put on to a steamer and taken to the camp at San Fernando. She was charged with treason.

Chapter 25

By the time Juliana Martinez was arrested, so many people had been sent off to López's new prison camp at San Fernando that her fate attracted little attention. López believed that the conspirators planned to attempt their coup d'état on July 24, his birthday, and a mass of arrests took place before that date. It was almost impossible for Washburn and his group to discover what was happening because nobody would talk to them. They were 'surrounded by an appalling mystery, and were as ignorant of the cause of it as though we had been all the while a thousand miles away.' They knew that Benigno López had been taken down river in chains, and other prominent citizens had also vanished, among them Washburn's friend, Captain Simon Fidanza, who had sold his ship to the Government some years before. Manlove had also left the Legation after quarrelling with Washburn and was also believed to have been arrested. Every so often the minister received a discouraging letter from Kirkland of the *Wasp* saying that Caxias would still not let him pass through the blockade. The vulnerability of the group was brought home to them on June 16 when Leite-Pereira, the Portuguese consul, appeared at the Legation door to ask for asylum for himself and his wife. He had become suspect because it was known that he had helped Portuguese prisoners captured while serving in the Allied armies to buy goods and he had been told that his diplomatic immunity would no longer be respected.

His request put Washburn in a terrible dilemma. 'I was playing as it were with life and death,' he recalled. 'If I received Pereira into my house it might cause the death of Rodriquez and Carreras and others; if I sent him and his wife away they might be subjected to torture and execution.' Leite-Pereira told him that he would stay only until López demanded his surrender, and after consulting the two Uruguayans, Washburn agreed to let them come in, although Leite-Pereira's fate had itself shown that diplomatic immunity could no longer be regarded as a protection. It was not long before his fears were justified. On June 23 Benitez, who had succeeded Berges as foreign minister, politely inquired whether Leite-Pereira and his wife were in the Legation. Washburn replied that they were, and on June 27 Benitez wrote again, asking him to surrender them. This was exactly the ultimatum that Washburn had feared, but in an attempt to put off the inevitable he wrote back saying that he was not obliged to surrender them until Leite-Pereira was accused of a crime. He also maintained that if the Portuguese had done something wrong then he must have done it while he was a consul, and therefore would be covered by his diplomatic immunity. There was no reply to this for several days and Washburn was beginning to hope that López had had a change of heart and was not going to insist on Leite-Pereira being given up. But on July 11, with life in the Legation just returning to the state of nervous tension which passed for normal, a bombshell arrived from Benitez in the shape of a 40-page letter.

It demanded not only the surrender of Leite-Pereira, but also listed the minister's own offences, first in not going to Luque as requested in February, and also in taking in so many people as refugees. It ended with a curt demand that the asylum be ended immediately, and ordered all those not connected with the Legation to leave the building the next day. With Benitez's letter the hopes of the residents of the American Legation collapsed like a house of cards. It seemed obvious that Washburn could no longer protect them, and that sooner or later López would think of some excuse for arresting them all. Leite-Pereira blamed himself for the predicament in which the refugees were now placed, and volunteered to leave the Legation immediately. Washburn resignedly said that it was entirely up to him, but he refused to promise to remain in Paraguay until the end of the war, so the alternatives were not exactly equal: by staying the Portuguese would be safe - if that was the word - only until Washburn himself could arrange to leave, and after that would be once more at López's mercy. In López's case, mercy was not a quality that aged well, and Leite-Pereira decided to give himself up the next day, July 12.

"That night [Leite-Pereira and his wife] were the two most miserable beings that it has ever been my fortune to meet. They both seemed to realise that their separation was to be final," Washburn wrote. The English workmen also decided to go to the police station and tell Fernandez that they were willing to work wherever the President required them. The next day the refugees found the Legation surrounded by police and the English feared that they would be arrested as soon as they stepped outside. Washburn therefore went to see Fernandez who said that they were to go to the Asuncion railway station, where they would be told what was going to happen to them. The minister also wrote to Benitez that his guests had decided to leave the Legation anyway - a white lie designed to save face - and he supposed that there would be no objection to Mrs. Leite-Pereira, Rodriquez and Carreras staying. The English, with the exception of Masterman, whose official position as surgeon to the Legation had saved him, left the building at 3pm, when peasants arrived with carts to help them with their luggage. An hour afterwards, Leite-Pereira walked out of the Legation and was arrested at the corner of the Plaza Vieja, watched by his wife, a Paraguayan who had lived several years in Europe, and was almost frantic with despair.

Washburn's attempt to save the two Uruguayans failed almost immediately. On July 13, Benitez demanded their surrender saying there 'existed offences' on their part, and adding blandly: 'Now you know they are guilty [I trust] you will hasten to dismiss them.' This demand was much more painful for Washburn, who had come to admire Rodriguez greatly during his stay. Masterman recalled him as 'a young and handsome fellow, of remarkably pleasing manners and polished address. He had read much, spoke French well, and was learning English.' Carreras, who was now about 60 and in poor health, still believed that by remaining in the Legation he would escape, since López would never dare violate it, and anyway, the war would soon be over, but Rodriguez was more realistic. He persuaded Carreras, who was in an extremely nervous state, that they had to leave, and like Leite-Pereira they walked out of the building and were arrested on the same corner by the waiting police. It was, Washburn wrote, 'the saddest event of my whole life.'

Even their departure did not satisfy López. On the same day another letter arrived from Benitez, this time demanding the surrender of Masterman and Bliss. Washburn refused to accept this: the two men were both members of the Legation staff, and were consequently covered by the same diplomatic immunity as himself, he wrote. To surrender them would be to abdicate his functions as a minister, and he would ultimately have to give up his wife, his secretary and everyone else. Indignantly he demanded passports for everybody in the Legation. Benitez's reply to this, while not insisting on Bliss and Masterman's immediate surrender, said that both of them had charges to face, and that they were both involved in the conspiracy - the first that Washburn had heard of it. This was the most serious development so far, from Washburn's point of view. If those who had already been arrested had all been accused of complicity in this plot, then it was certain that Washburn himself must be under suspicion, since they had all been staying at his house. In addition, he had for long been on close terms with men like Berges, Benigno López and Bedoya all of whom had been arrested. Although he had shown considerable courage under the tremendous pressure, the minister began to exhibit signs of panic and strain.

Part of the problem was that Washburn's indiscreet dinner table conversations of the past had caught up with him. López's inquisitors were asking all the prisoners if Washburn was a member of the plot, and most of them were incriminating him as fast as their tongues would let them. Things were complicated by the fact that López had a spy conveniently installed inside the Legation. This was the mother of Basilio, the minister's Paraguayan servant, who was, according to Masterman, 'a dreadful old woman, scarcely more than four feet in height, a dark-brown shrivelled creature, with a most witch-like face.' Benitez thus had a considerable advantage in the long correspondence that began, and Washburn was soon tripping over himself in his attempts to avert suspicion.

To make the atmosphere in the Legion even worse, reports filtered in that the entire male population of Luque, the centre of the civil government since the evacuation of Asuncion, had been arrested. The English workmen at the station had heard a train come in one night, and although no lights were allowed, they could hear the clanking of chains and men groaning as they were driven along by the guards. The only officials remaining there were Benitez, Sanabria and Fernandez, the rumours said, and the arrested men included about eighty Italians, twenty Frenchman (including Narcisse Lasserre, whose gift of brandy had helped revive Masterman's flagging spirits during his imprisonment) and several of other nationalities. Chapperon, the Italian consul, told Washburn that they were all accused of plotting to kill Sanabria and Fernandez. The only foreigner left in Luque was José Solis, an agent of Mrs. Lynch. It seemed that the mass arrests had been arranged with admirable efficiency, Sanabria picking the victims up one by one so that there was no chance of them getting together and resisting. He was given enthusiastic assistance by Julian Aquino, the manager of the *Semanario*, who had glorified López in his newspaper for years, and helped Sanabria put fetters on the prisoners. But as soon as the last one was safely on board the train, Sanabria looked at him cheerfully and said 'you next' whereupon Aquino found himself fettered in his turn. The whole group was then shipped off to San Fernando. While he pondered on the implications of this, Washburn faced a bombardment of confessions, accusations and threats. Benitez enclosed statements from Carreras and Berges and even Fidanza, which accused Washburn of being the leader of the conspiracy, whose intention was to hand Paraguay over to the Allies, and for which Benigno had supplied the funds. Masterman, who was acutely aware that his own life probably depended on the way Washburn handled the situation, watched his actions with mounting alarm. In his replies, Washburn stressed his friendship for Paraguay, taking this to ridiculous limits: he claimed that 'he hoped to see the Allies defeated' and that he 'had strained every nerve to provoke a war between Brazil and the United States, in favour of Paraguay.'

Benitez wrote again on July 21 to say the revolt was due to start on July 24. He urged Washburn to hand over Bliss and Masterman at once, before they had a chance to escape, and that evening Mrs. Lynch called at the Legation. She expressed surprise at what was happening and told the minister that a conspiracy had been discovered in which Benigno and Venancio López played the chief parts. Washburn insisted that all those who had been in the Legation had been innocent. Mrs. Lynch said in surprise: "But they have confessed."

Washburn replied that that did not necessarily prove that they were guilty, but Mrs. Lynch said: 'Oh no, there has been no constraint put upon them. It has all been voluntary. The President would never use constraint or force them to confess against their will. He is very kind hearted.' She added that the discovery of the plot had greatly upset López, but Washburn refused to surrender his guests, and denied that he had any packages from Berges. This did not please Mrs. Lynch, and when the minister said that his wife would soon be going to Buenos Aires with their baby she said: 'If she can!' and stormed out.

One of Washburn's greatest fears was that the police would force their way into the Legation and search it. Although they would find no papers from Berges, there were plenty of other incriminating documents. Masterman had already prepared a statement about the treatment he had received which he hid in a large jar; Bliss had begun an account of the bombardment of the ironclads, but torn it up in case it was found; Washburn himself had written masses of documents including a 300-page manuscript on the history of Paraguay which could not be replaced and was extremely critical of López. Bliss, an expert linguist and historian, had helped him prepare some of it, and Rodriguez and Carreras had supplied other details. He hid his manuscript between the pages of an atlas, but he then realised that he had left his study door open, and since he did not trust his servants he removed it and finally put the sheets of paper beneath an oil-cover tablecloth. The President's birthday came and went without incident. There were the usual receptions and dances, but Washburn refused to leave the Legation and on the following day Benitez called at the Legation in person. He seemed very agitated to Washburn (who himself seemed very agitated to Masterman) and again demanded the Berges' papers. Washburn refused to admit that he had them. Benitez left saying: '*Sabemos todos* - we know all!'

Although the failure of the revolt to materialise seemed to take some urgency out of the correspondence, it still continued, with Benitez winning most of the points. He had earlier tricked Washburn into implying that he knew that the uprising would take place on the 24th, and when Washburn later attempted to defend the characters of Bliss and Masterman, the minister dryly observed: 'Your excellency spoke in the same high terms of Carreras, Rodriguez and the others confessed criminals before they were taken prisoners, and now they are liars and perjurers.' This was a reference to Washburn's hysterical claim that Carreras and the others were ingrates who had told lies to incriminate him, a ridiculous assertion, since it was obvious that they had all done so only because they were being tortured. Washburn by now was making so many mistakes that, according to Masterman, that 'the native prosecutors began at last to believe from his manner that the story they had themselves concocted was true, and that the *'papeles de Berges'* which had never existed were actually hidden in the iron safe. I frankly confess that had I not known him personally I should have thought so too.' Washburn's correspondence with Benitez was in fact so compromising that most of it was published in the *Semanario* early in August, to prove the existence of the conspiracy and Washburn's part in it. Thanks to Basilio's mother, the detail was excellent. 'One document', Masterman remembered, 'purporting to be the evidence of Don Benigno López, was quite a curiosity in a way. It described with wonderful minuteness a visit he had paid to Mr. Washburn, how they talked together, where they sat, of the interruption to their treasonable conferences by the entrance of 'Cati' (Mrs. Washburn's maid Kate) with a tray of glasses with brandy and water, of the gold he then paid to him, and the two clothes-basketfuls of paper money his slaves afterwards brought up for distribution amongst the conspirators, and so on. All except the payment of the money and part of the conversation was true without doubt...'

Outside the Legation, arrests were still continuing. Fernandez had been seized and his house was boarded up, with cloth nailed over the doors so that any attempt to open it would be noticed. He was accused of being involved with Benigno López in a plot to kill the President. The guards surrounding the headquarters at San Fernando had surprised a trumpeter from the army going to visit Benigno in his hut.[75] He was arrested and interrogated and claimed that Benigno plotted with Fernandez – who was his neighbour at Paraguarí – to stab López to death, a knife being considered more reliable than firearms. After the dead was done, Fernandez and Benigno planned to escape on horseback, presumably to the enemy lines. Sanabria, who had organised the arrests with such skill, had also been taken away to San Fernando. The English were all in the Cordilleras, and nobody knew what had happened to them. Basilio and the other servants learned from the soldiers that only twenty men were left in Luque. They had all signed enthusiastic declarations against the 'traitors' but their own arrests were apparently imminent.

A few months before, Washburn had been bored; now he was afraid of death and, for those who remained in the Legation, the chances of survival seemed non-existent. 'The days, the terrible days!' Washburn recalled. 'Bliss and Masterman regarded themselves as lost. The chances seemed to be at least twenty to one against them. These anxious days were a sort of eternity. The dread of another letter from Benitez was constantly haunting us... it was a relief when darkness closed upon us, for after that we never received any letters; but the nights were so long and sleepless it was a greater relief for the day to dawn...this was my experience for months; a brief sleep for a couple of hours was all the anxieties of the time would permit.'

It seemed that nobody in Paraguay could consider himself safe any longer, even those who, like Fernandez and Sanabria, had once been on good terms with López and, in August Washburn realised why Benitez had seemed nervous when he called at the Legation on July 25. The Minister was strolling near the river when he saw Benitez walking rapidly towards one of the steamers. Benitez saw Washburn, but turned away to avoid having to speak. Like so many others before him he had been summoned to San Fernando, and within a few days was lying in chains in the prison camp. The terrible lunges of the tiger's paw were coming closer and closer to Washburn and he was on the verge of complete despair when, a few days after Benitez's departure, he heard through the servants the news he had been awaiting for months: a *cañonero Americano* had been allowed through the blockade at last, and on August 29 the wonderful news was confirmed by Luis Caminos, the new foreign minister, who enclosed a letter from the commanding officer of the *Wasp*, Commander Kirkland.

The last Washburn had heard from Kirkland was that he had bean unable to get through the blockade, and was therefore going back to Montevideo to await further orders. Washburn had not expected him to return so soon, and naturally enough was delighted at his sudden reappearance, especially since Caminos politely asked him for a list of passports required. The *Wasp*, Washburn believed had arrived just in time, for he was sure that López was planning to have him killed in such a way that his death could be explained away as suicide. The passports arrived on September 8, but with them was a letter that crushed the hopes of Masterman and Bliss. Caminos said that they were criminals and must remain behind to be tried by the 'tribunal of the country'. According to Washburn the three men agreed, after some discussion that 'if I could get away and give the alarm to our squadron as to their situation it would be the best thing for me to do. They thought that probably before they would be killed, something would come to their relief.'

Masterman remembered the incident slightly differently, and according to his version Washburn 'suddenly forgot that "he had been staying in the country solely to guard those who had sought his protections and it is possible that the sudden arrival of the *Wasp* was too much for the minister's resolution. After the tension and uncertainty all he wanted to do was to get out of Paraguay as soon as possible, even if that meant abandoning Bliss and Masterman. Washburn was so anxious to wash his hands of them that he at first refused to accompany them into the streets, as Masterman requested, so that they might be arrested in his presence.

The two men spent their last few hours in the Legation preparing for the ordeal that faced them. Masterman made out a deed of gift to Washburn of all his baggage and scientific instruments, which the minister had agreed to protect for him, and wrote a series of letters to his mother and friends in England. He then packed a few items to take with him and hid some quinine and opium in the lining of his coat. In the afternoon of September 9, Mrs. Leite-Pereira, who had been in the Legation ever since her husband's arrest, left to go to her mother's house a few miles from the capital. Masterman, who had come to admire her very much, watched her go sadly. He never saw her again, nor did he discover what became of her. By the evening, the Legation was a mixture of gloom and relief. The two groups - those who were to go to the *Wasp* and those who were bound for prison - drew apart instinctively, recognising that the bond of common danger that had kept them together all these months had been cut. The contrast of their destinies was forcing them apart, turning them into strangers. Chapperon and Cuberville, the Italian and French consuls came to the Legation early the next morning. Washburn asked the Italian to guard all the personal property that had been left in his care and Cuberville added to Masterman's gloom by telling him that Libertad, the chancellor at the French consulate, had been denounced as a member of the conspiracy, and was expected to be arrested shortly. He confirmed that all the foreigners in Luque had been seized.

Since López had refused to allow the *Wasp* to sail up to Asuncion, Washburn had arranged to board her at Villeta, thirty-five miles away, and was to go there by steamer. It was decided that Mrs. Washburn should leave the Legation first - so that she would be spared the unpleasant sight of Bliss and Masterman being seized by the waiting police and at the appointed time she went to the door, accompanied by Meinke, the secretary, her child and her two English servants. Masterman went to the gate with her, and dodged back quickly as the police made a sudden grab for him. Then, when she had rounded the corner of the square and was out of sight, the others left the Legation for the last time.

They walked together at first, but Washburn was so anxious to rejoin his wife, and get to the safety of the steamer that it was as much as the two consuls and the rest of the party could do to keep up with him. He was a few paces ahead of them when they reached the end of the colonnade where the police were waiting, and there was no opportunity for formal farewells. As Masterman tried to approach him 'the police who had been closing around us, simultaneously drew their swords, rushed forward, and roughly separated us from the consuls. I raised my hat, and said loudly and cheerfully, "Goodbye, Mr. Washburn; don't forget us." He half turned his face, which was deathly pale, made a deprecative gesture with his hand, and hurried away.'

Bliss and Masterman, together with Baltazar, a Negro servant of Dr. Carreras, were marched brusquely down to the police station. After being kept waiting for some time, they were taken in turn inside the building, stripped and thoroughly searched. Masterman's quinine and opium were found, and the travelling bag containing spare clothes, sheet and mattress was taken from him. His clothes were returned, and when he had dressed he was made to sit down so that the fetters could be fitted. Then he was put into a windowless cell until 7pm when the door burst open and two men came in and replaced his fetters with irons that weighed more than 30 pounds.

Later that evening, the sergeant reappeared, and Masterman was taken outside, where saw Baltazar and Bliss with similar bars riveted to their ankles, sitting sidesaddle on two mules. Masterman was lifted on to another. The police sarcastically wished the three men a pleasant journey, and with jeers and shouts of *'Buenos noches'* ringing in their ears they set off. The sergeant escorting them was fortunately an old patient of Masterman's, and he eased the pain of the iron bars by tying them to the strap of one of the stirrups, so that the prisoners could support them with their hands, but it was still a wretched journey. First the prisoners found that they were not bound not for the railways station, but for Villeta itself; apart from the pain of the bars and the constant jolting of the mules, Masterman was filled with the 'inexpressible sadness' of seeing again the beautiful lanes and woods where he had sketched and ridden so often, and which now, like everything in Paraguay, told only of misery and catastrophe.

'The broad moon was shining brightly in the cloudless sky: every copse, every dell, where the ferns and tall arums grew, was visible with painful distinctness. The white *quintas*, shaded with trellised vines and climbing roses where I had passed so many happy hours and the familiar gardens and fields around them, called up scenes and reminiscences I would gladly have forgotten until better days. The houses were empty, many already falling to decay; their owners were dead, or prisoners like myself; the fences destroyed and the gardens trampled by straying cattle. Destruction and desolation, war, pestilence and famine had swept all trace of gladness from the land, leaving only bitter memories and vain regrets.'

The agonies of the journey and the desolation of the countryside were in sharp contrast to the beauty of an evening that was 'still and warm, the air fragrant with the perfume of the orange blossoms and the flowering orchids which hung in festoons from the wayside trees; and the fireflies were sparkling and flashing brilliantly amid their branches.'

But the most poignant moment came when the road took them near the river. There, miles away and far beneath them, Masterman 'saw distinctly the lights of the steamer that was carrying Mr. Washburn and his family down to the gunboat.'

Chapter 26

López's retreat to the Tebicuary had gained him several weeks in which to recover and prepare for the next Allied attack. But by then Paraguay had passed the point where time alone could provide a solution to its problems. Just what losses the country had suffered it is impossible to tell, since the population of Paraguay, even at the beginning of the war, is largely a matter of guesswork. By the middle of 1868, however, it had probably been reduced to around 300,000. Of these perhaps 50,000 were men of 15 and over. If one accepts a population of 600,000 for 1864, then half had already died. Of the males more than 80 per cent had been killed, or had died of starvation, wounds or sickness (or execution).

The terrible state of affairs that Gould had reported the year before had grown steadily worse, until the scale of suffering went beyond the merely horrific and entered a new dimension that is almost beyond comprehension. It was not possible that a nation could suffer such losses and still fight on. Resistance was no longer logical, for the whole race was disappearing, and an instinct of self-preservation should surely have made the Paraguayans rebel against their fate. But there was no rebellion. The morale of the army, weakened, beaten, exhausted, outnumbered as it was, was still high: the soldiers fought with the courage, the same joy even, that they had displayed three years before, although they must have known that their country was ruined.

The extent of the catastrophe is indicated by the responses to López's final mobilisation order in November 1867.[76] The order was to report on what manpower remained. The *partido* of Yutí reported that there remained 371 man, of whom 94 were youngsters of around 12 and

35 were over 70. Another 120 were aged over 60 and the majority of the remainder were either injured, sick or diseased. Villa Rica, once a prosperous, well-populated town was even more pathetic. Of the 563 men listed 238 were boys of 12 to 14, seven more boys were in a church band, five were listed as slaves or freedmen, 29 were wounded soldiers, 260 militiamen were over 50 and the remainder were listed as blind, deaf and dumb or insane. Reports from other towns and villages were similar. By the beginning of 1868 virtually all the able-bodied men in Paraguay had already been called up for service in the army: there were no reserves of manpower left.

Caxias believed that Paraguay had approximately 14,000 men under arms at this stage. Other Allied estimates ranged from 12,000 up to 20,000. Thompson, who was in a better position to know, estimated the total that had reached the Tebicuary as 8,000. This figure was later reinforced by the survivors of Martinez's army, the garrison of Timbo, and other troops who were brought down from the Matto Grosso, which was finally abandoned at the end of July, but even so this total could not have amounted to much more than 10.000 and probably half at least were men over 60 and boys under 15. The Allies, by contrast, were living a life of luxury. Their total strength was about 35,000 men of whom nearly 30,000 were Brazilian. The remainder were nearly all Argentineans, for the Uruguayans had almost vanished. Thompson claimed that the Paraguayan attack on Tuyuti in November 1867, had reduced their army to 20 men and a general, and Burton was unable to find a Uruguayan army at all when he visited the front the next year.

Between the Argentineans and Brazilians, rivalry was as bad as ever. The Argentineans resented their position as junior partners, and their army consisted to a considerable extent of foreigners. It was a motley collection, dressed in mixed uniforms, badly and irregularly paid. Burton found there was "no ardour for the cause and *esprit de corps* is unknown." This was mainly because of the unpopularity of the war. "All are agreed that in the case of war with the Empire the Confederation could turn out 50,000 men at arms."

Fresh revolts against the war had broken out in Argentina the previous year, and Hutchinson saw some troops from Tucuman and Salta being marched down to the river front at Rosario, mutiny against their officers. One group - known ironically as the *Voluntarios* - were so reluctant to fight for the cause that they were in chains, but the others seemed to be just as unenthusiastic: 'The manacled part of the *corps d'armée* was got safe on board the steamer; but when the soldiers were being brought by their officers they stopped just after the Customs House and two of them shot two of their officers through the brain. The whole group then dispersed, passing up through the principal Plaza and by the door of the *Gefatura,* escaping to the camp. No attempt was made by the rebels in power to capture them, for the Paraguayan war is becoming so unpopular that the sympathy of the people is with everyone who can draw out of it.'

Mitre, the man who had led Argentina into the war, was coming to the end of his term of office as president, and under the terms of the Argentinean Constitution could not run again. This was probably just as well. He had recently had to face an attempted impeachment for plunging the country into the war, and when the election came his nominee, Rufino Elisalde, was soundly beaten by Sarmiento, who had been Argentinean Ambassador to the United States since 1865. The Brazilians army had its own problems to contend with. Materially it was well supplied. But morale was generally low. Corruption existed everywhere in Brazil at that time, including the army, and the quality of the troops was not improving. As initial enthusiasm for the war died away, it became increasingly difficult to find volunteers. The emperor therefore announced that slaves who joined the army would be given their freedom. This produced a considerable response - 6,000 slaves from the royal estates alone joined up - and it also helped the cause of emancipation, with which Pedro was in wholehearted sympathy. But the slaves who went to the war were more interested in staying alive to enjoy their new freedom rather than in dying for a cause which they neither understood nor cared about.

Despite all efforts, it was becoming difficult to keep the army up to strength although between October 27, 1867 and February 10, 1868, more than 19,000 recruits were sent to the front. Battalions that were originally 700 strong were now down to 500 men, and the Paraguayans jeered that when the Allies received new 'volunteers' they sent back the chains by return. John Codman wrote: 'At the present time appearances are very discouraging. The Brazilians regret that they undertook the war but they see no honourable way of withdrawing without acknowledging a defeat. Even were they to accomplish the object of increasing their territory and could they succeed in trampling Paraguay utterly under foot they would be poorly compensated for all their loss of blood and treasure. The emperor still goes about, examining the dockyards, the ships and the machine shops, while there is an air of dejection upon his face painful to behold.'

Political differences among the Brazilian officers did not help matters. Some were influenced by the republicanism of their Spanish-speaking Allies, others by the military-style dictatorships found beyond the Empire - Paraguay itself was a leading example. Osorio and Caxias became the figureheads of the liberal and conservative wings respectively, and it was claimed of Caxias that he would not make a decisive move until his political friends were in office.

Despite declining morale, as the siege of Humaitá neared its climax, the Allies began to make tentative moves northwards, and their first major reconnaissance of the new line was made on June 8, when 3,000 men tried to cross the Yacaré, a small stream that flowed into the Tebicuary. They were driven back by the Paraguayans, but this was clearly the beginning rather than the end of the matter. At Fortin Island, Thompson was ready for anything that might happen. Although most of his time was spent in strengthening the defences there, he had a room at San Fernando, and occasionally visited López's headquarters there. He had 'from whisperings...gathered that something extraordinary was taking place and that many people were in irons', but it was not until the second week in July that López told him about the conspiracy. The President said the revolt was timed to take place on July 24, and would coincide with an attempt by the Brazilians to force their way past the Fortin batteries.

Four of them had already approached the position once, but went back down the river, and this and López's warning gave Thompson plenty of time to get ready. Although López was almost certainly wrong in believing in the conspiracy, his prediction about the ironclads was quite correct. They arrived in the area on July 23 and the next day the Bahia and the *Silvado,* the first with a monitor lashed to her port side, approached Fortin Island at full speed. After a few long shots, Thompson ordered his men to hold their fire so their shots should make the greatest possible impact.

When Burton saw the ironclads later he thought they looked 'like plum puddings from which the plums have been plucked out,' but even so they had done their job, and a weapon to which they had no real answer had once more outflanked the Paraguayan position. Although the ironclads repassed the batteries later that day and did not challenge them again, the comparative ease with which they had done so and the imminent fall of Humaitá made López consider a continuation of the retreat to an even stronger position.

For the time being, though, the conspiracy was occupying most of his attention. The atmosphere at the army headquarters was tense, nervous, and tinged with probably justified paranoia. The slightest incident was enough to arouse suspicion – and immediate denunciation. Centurión found himself in trouble again when he tried to defend a man called Captain Juan S. Silva, who had been captured by the Allies on 24 May and later joined the enemy forces. He was re-captured by the Paraguayans and López ordered that he be publicly humiliated and punished as a lesson to others. This was supervised by Bruguez and Barrios and after a final fifty lashes Silva was taken to Centurión, who was told to take a statement from him. The guards were still beating and abusing him and Centurión told them to stop, because the man was already in the hands of justice and it was not right to punish him unnecessarily. This was reported to the captain of the guard, who told Resquín. He in turn told López, adding that Centurión was obviously an accomplice and a traitor as well. López behaved much more sensibly. He told Resquín that Centurión was young and inexperienced. There was no need to punish him: "Just give him a good talking to, as only you know how."

Centurión knew nothing of all this when he was called to see Resquín. On his arrival his sword was taken away and Resquín demanded to know what he and Silva had talked about. Centurión said that they had discussed nothing of importance. Resquín called him a fool (*zonzo*) and said he was going to be shot immediately. Centurión protested that he had simply told the guards not to ill-treat a prisoner. Resquín retorted that since he had spoke in defence of a traitor he had become an accomplice and therefore deserved to be flogged. Then he told him that thanks to the clemency of Marshal López he was to be pardoned. Angry, humiliated and above all relieved Centurión went back to the wretched Silva and took down his confession. What happened to him afterwards he never discovered.

By the end of July, with the army securely installed at San Fernando (at least until the Allies caught up with them), López had convinced himself that the conspiracy was a reality. He called a meeting of Barrios, Resquín, Bruguez, Palacios and some others and announced that the conspirators had established communications with the enemy and had given them details of the Paraguayan plans. Resquín said that in the circumstances the traitors should be treated with contempt and tortured if they refused to tell the truth. López said that he did not think it right to use such methods in the modern age. Palacios, as anxious to please as ever, suggested that the conspirators should be executed. López turned on him sarcastically and said that he was just as interested in finding out the truth as the Bishop, but he did not intend to use the methods he was advocating.[77] In view of his ruthless behaviour to those who had displeased him in the past (and, as we shall see, in the future as well) this statement contains more than a hint of hypocrisy, but López was clearly intending to go by the book.

The consequence of this meeting was the formation of six two-man tribunals, whose task was to examine those accused or suspected of being involved in the conspiracy. Centurión was given the special task of helping the statements to be prepared (a tribute perhaps to his European education). Aveiro and Major Serrano were given a supervisory role and reported to López everything that the suspects confessed. If they were not sure about the veracity or completeness of the evidence, López gave them permission to use stronger measures – in other words, torture, just as Resquín had suggested earlier.

The steamers were bringing suspects down in scores and ultimately hundreds all during July and August, and Thompson himself had a nasty moment as a result of the action against the ironclads. During the battle a man had stuck his head out of a turret of one of the ships and shouted something, and although Thompson did not hear what was said, the telegraph clerk at the battery immediately informed López. The President told Thompson later that it was the traitor Recalde whom he had nearly captured at Yataity Cora, and began ranting against the treachery that surrounded him. He blamed Thompson for not stopping the ships.

An even more unpleasant incident came a few days later. Thompson had gone to headquarters, where he had a room next to that of General Bruguez, one of his closest friends. That evening he 'went into his room to see him and found that all his things were gone, and other things in their place. There was a boy in the room and I asked him for General Bruguez; he didn't know. I then asked him if he had moved... 'Yes.' 'Where?' 'I don't know.'

'I then imagined that something must be wrong with him and asked no further questions: I had asked too many already. Next day I dined with López: Barrios, Bruguez and the Bishop always used to dine with him, but Bruguez was not there. López's little boy asked where he was and they all told him with smiles, "He is gone...."' Months later Thompson learned that his friend had been bayoneted to death.

Barrios's smile faded rapidly on August 15 when he was arrested in his turn. He must have been worried about his position for months, in view of the fact that he was married to López's sister Innocencia: being part of the López clan was no longer an advantage. On the day of his arrest he returned to his house after a morning at headquarters and had a furious row with his wife during which he accused her of being involved in the conspiracy. He ordered her to stay in her room when he returned to headquarters and came back home again at about 1pm, without his sword: he had been placed under house arrest. He sat on a leather chair by the front door and called his aides together. He thanked them for their loyal service and said that from now on they were to report to General Resquín. Then he went indoors, took a razor from its bamboo sheath, went into the room where his wife was waiting and calmly cut his throat.

Innocencia rushed to the door, covered in blood and screaming for help. The sentry at the door had been ordered to let no one leave and, in true Paraguayan fashion, therefore refused to let her pass, but the noise attracted the attention of others, and Doctors Stewart and Skinner ran to the house to discover that Barrios's razor had missed the artery. They were able to save his life. He was imprisoned and went mad shortly afterwards.

The Bishop was thrown into prison soon after and Saturnino Bedoya, who had been under detention since the beginning of the year was tortured to death at about this time. López, according to

Thompson, was distressed at the news, and said that had he known he was dying he would have had him shot 'for the sake of appearances.'

Centurión hated being involved in the work of the tribunals (which were to become known as the *fiscales de sangre*) and was greatly relieved when Luis Caminos, who had been appointed minister of war in succession to Barrios, appointed him as his secretary. This meant that Centurión would leave San Fernando for the somewhat healthier atmosphere of Luque. The next day, one of the suspects from Asuncion admitted that he had received a letter from Barrios, written in the handwriting of his secretary, Captain Andres Maciel. Serrano, who seems to have developed something like a hatred for Centurión, claimed that this was proof of his complicity in the conspiracy and demanded that Aveiro arrest him. Aveiro refused, on the grounds that if he arrested everyone who was accused of treason the prison camps would soon be full of innocent people, but Serrano was not satisfied and went to López, demanding that Centurión be put in chains. López said that there had been no hint from the tribunals that he was involved and it would set a bad precedent to send people to prison on the merest hint of suspicion. Since numerous people had already been executed for that very reason, this remark can hardly be regarded as a statement of policy, but simply indicates that López rather liked Centurión. Even so, the incident deprived Centurión of the chance to escape to Luque. Caminos went off without him, and Centurión was left at San Fernando, not sure of what was going to happen to him and still fearing the worst.

These fears were well justified, because conditions in the prison at San Fernando camp were almost beyond belief: by the end of August López had contrived to concentrate in one small area nearly all the leading men (and women) of Paraguay, together with hundreds of others condemned to play supporting roles in the tragedy. Apart from the miserable conditions, the prisoners' days were made more hideous by frequent tortures, and executions that became almost a daily occurrence.

By this time the net had already closed around the French chemist Narcisse Lasserre and his family. Unlike many of the French settlers, the Lasserres had prospered in Paraguay. Apart from Narcisse and his wife Dorothée Duprat de Lasserre, the family also comprised Dorothée's parents and her brother Aristide. They were so comfortably off – far better, one suspects, than they would have been back home in France – that they never thought of leaving the country even when the war broke out. They simply got on with the business of making money, although Narcisse did warn his wife to be careful what she said when speaking to people outside the family.

By 1868, even the Lasserres were beginning to realise that things were becoming serious. Their friend, Laurent-Cochelet, had returned to France, and although Mme Lasserre took it for granted that his successor, de Cuberville, would at least turn out to be a good Frenchman, he proved to be a considerable disappointment. Many French exiles confided in him and he then passed on what they said to Mrs Lynch, who obtained the information by the simple expedient of getting him drunk. When Asuncion was evacuated the Lasserres objected at having to move, but eventually went to Luque, where they busied themselves working and distilling *caña*.

On 6 July a soldier came to the house and asked Narcisse to go with him to the police station, where the chief of police wanted to speak to him. The next day his mother-in-law went to the French consulate to see if the Consul, de Cuberville, knew what had become of him. De Cuberville, who had proved a sad disappointment to the diplomatic corps and the French residents alike, was surprised to hear that Lasserre had been arrested. "It was just what I had feared!" he exclaimed. The mother-in-law wanted to know what he was afraid of but de Cuberville would not, or could not answer, although he went with her to see Dorothée and assure her that there was no political motive in her husband's detention.

This was wishful thinking. Dorothée soon received two messages from her husband – written in orange juice – saying that he had been arrested, but had no idea why. De Cuberville admitted that he had been taken from Luque to Asuncion. She was with de Cuberville and the Italian consul, Chapperon, when they were summoned to the Foreign Ministry and told that everyone in the Narcisse household was to be arrested, by force if necessary.

She returned home in floods of tears and that night her father and two French carpenters who were sharing their house were arrested. At 2am on 19 July there was another knock on the door. This time her brother Aristide was taken away. Dorothée's state of mind was made worse when de Cuberville told her, with an air of theatrical mystery, that a great conspiracy against López had been discovered. Soon after this her faith in de Cuberville, whose drinking was growing worse, was further undermined when another French settler called Theophile Yanté told her: "He has betrayed us … he has spied on us …beware of him, he will leave us all to die here! He has sold us!"

Unknown to Dorothée, her family was probably taken to the camp at San Fernando at about this time. Among those who also suffered there was Alonzo Taylor. After leaving the American Legation, Taylor and other English workmen spent several days in the railway station before being taken up into the cordilleras east of the capital. Some were sent to the arsenal at Caacupé, while Taylor was sent to the soap works in Luque. At 10pm on July 21 he returned to his house, and shortly afterwards there was a knock at the door. Without opening it, he suspiciously asked who was there, and a man's voice said that he was to report to Asuncion. Knowing it was useless to resist, Taylor got his horse and accompanied his caller, a cavalry soldier, to the riverbank at the capital where he found a crowd of other men waiting.

He was immediately put in irons, and the next day they were taken on board the steamer *Salto de Guayra.* Mrs. Lynch came on board shortly after 11am with her eldest son Francisco (Panchito) and some officers, and the ship went down river to the mouth of the Tebicuary and from there he was marched to San Fernando.

Except for a brief period in the morning, when they were marched into the woods, the prisoners were kept tied up in an agonisingly simple device known as the *'cepo de lazo',* the rope stocks. In this, a hide rope was made fast to a stake in the ground. The first prisoner lay down on his back., and the rope was looped around both ankles. The second man lay two yards away and was tied in the same way with the same rope. The process was repeated until the rope was full. The loose end was then looped round another stake and the rope pulled tight by three soldiers until it was taut. 'We suffered terribly' Taylor wrote. 'My ankles were soon covered with sores and almost dislocated by the strain on them.'

The camp was divided into a series of smaller areas known as *guardias*, each about twenty yards square, containing about fifty men roped in this fashion. There was no protection of any kind from the sun and rain, and food consisted of the offal of the cattle killed to feed the troops. The sentries 'used to kick and thrash us as they pleased. They had orders to shoot or bayonet any who tried to escape. A request for a little water was often answered by a flogging.' Taylor had been given no reason for his arrest, and still hoped that he might be the victim of some mistake.

A few days after his arrival he saw Serrano, with whom he had been very friendly, walking through the camp. Serrano, although Taylor did not realise it yet, was one of the men appointed to investigate the conspiracy, so that attracting his attention was not a very good idea. However Taylor called out "Major Serrano, do you know Thompson?" Serrano came over and said politely, but firmly: "He has now power here." Taylor said that he only wanted to ask him for some food and clothes and after a pause Serrano ordered a sergeant to untie him. He took him to one side and said: "Do you know why you are here?" Taylor shook his head and replied: "No, I do not. I wish I did."

"There are several charges against you," Serrano said. "The first, that you are fully acquainted with the name of the proposed new president; the second, that you have received a sum of money from Captain Fidanza; and Tubo has confessed, and divulged that you are one of his accomplices." Tubo was an Italian who had arrived in Asuncion a few years before and opened a school to which Taylor had sent one of his sons. Tubo made this a pretext for occasionally borrowing money from him, and then tried to initiate him into a masonic lodge that he claimed to be forming. Taylor was suspicious, and after checking with John Watts, decided that the whole thing was a racket for extorting money from the gullible and refused to join. Taylor told Serrano that the charges were quite false, and that both he and Tubo knew it, but the major said that he would give him until the next day to confess, adding comfortingly: "If you make a clean breast of it, the president will be merciful and your life will be spared." Indignantly Taylor again insisted that he had nothing to confess and protested that his reputation in the country and among his own countrymen was so high that he need fear no accusation.

Serrano looked at his old friend, the man with whom he used to take *maté* nearly every day, and said: "Yes, you once had clean hands. But things have changed, and you have become as dirty as the rest." Then he gave orders for Taylor to be tied up again, and walked away. Any hopes that Taylor might have had that their old friendship would result in Serrano being merciful were dispelled the next day, when he was again asked to confess. He refused, and Serrano ordered the sergeant with him to put Taylor into the '*cepo Uruguayana*'.

Taylor had already heard of this particular horror. It was a torture said to have originated in the days of Simon Bolivar, the South American liberator, when it was called the '*cepo Boliviano*' but its name was changed by López after the defeat of Estigarribia. Now Taylor was about to experience it himself.

'I sat on the ground with my knees up, my legs were first tied tightly together, and then my hands behind me, with my palms outwards. A musket was then fastened under my knees; six more of them, tied together in a bundle, were then put on my shoulders, and they were looped together with hide ropes at one end; they then made a running loop on the other side, from the lower musket to the other; and two soldiers hauling on the end of it forced my face down to my knees, and secured it so.'

After that he was simply left. 'First the feet went to sleep, then a tingling commenced in the toes, gradually extending to the knees, and the same in the hands and arms, and increased until the agony was unbearable. My tongue swelled up and I thought that my jaws would have been displaced: I lost all feeling in one side of my face for a fortnight afterwards. The suffering was dreadful, I should certainly have confessed if I had anything to confess, and I have no doubt many would acknowledge or invent anything to escape bearing the horrible agony of this torment. I remained two hours as I have described, and I considered myself fortunate in escaping then; for many were put in the *Uruguayana* twice, and others six times, and with eight muskets on the nape of the neck.' At the end of two hours, Serrano had Taylor released and began questioning him again, but Taylor was so paralysed with the pain that he was unable to speak. Serrano, irritated by this display of weakness, complained that thanks to the clemency of López he had only been in the Uruguayana for a short while and if he did not immediately tell him the name of the new president he would repeat the torture with eight muskets - and Taylor would be made to wear three sets of irons as well. Taylor was still so exhausted that this threat made no impression on him and in disgust Serrano had him taken back to the compound.

The next day, July 25, he was questioned about the alleged mining of the railway bridge at Ibicuí, but Taylor knew nothing of this and the matter was dropped. The next day Serrano and Aveiro questioned him about Tubo. Taylor explained how he had become involved with the Italian and Aveiro said: `Do you know we have Tubo here?"

"No. How should I?" Taylor said.

'We will have you face to face," Serrano said, and Tubo was then brought in with Centurión. The investigation proved to be something of an anti-climax. Tubo claimed that Taylor had signed a paper agreeing to join the masons, but when Taylor indignantly denied this, Tubo hesitated and said: "I think he did."

Whatever his doubts about participating in the work of the tribunals, Centurión knew that his liberty and probably life depended on getting results. He said angrily: "Your thinking is no use: did or did not Alonzo Taylor sign the paper?"

At this Tubo became very embarrassed and was unable to answer. To Taylor's relief he was taken away, and he never saw him again. Tubo was later shot. Centurión then switched the subject to the more dangerous issue of the Legation. He wondered why so many of the English had refused to sign contracts and when Taylor hedged, the questioner became angry. Taylor said desperately: "I do not know, but I do know that we Englishmen are heartily sick of the war, and the reason we went to the American Legation was because, there being no English consul in Asuncion, we thought we might get protection there until we could leave for England. My other object in going there was in order that Mrs Taylor, who was near her confinement, might have the benefit of Mr. Masterman's assistance, as there was no other medical man in Asuncion. Besides, I knew Mr. Masterman." Centurión said: "Indeed! Then it is your opinion that the 'Niggers' (Brazilians) will take the town and that you may be able to serve them?"

Taylor refused to be tricked so easily and said: "No; I have always been faithful to His Excellency and we have all done our duty, but are sick of the war, and want to leave the country." Serrano sighed: "You were once a good servant, Alonzo, but for some months you behaved very badly." Then the interrogation ended, and Taylor was taken back to the *cepo de lazo.* His firmness, and perhaps memories of happier days, apparently convinced Serrano that he was telling the truth, and Taylor was not questioned again. Although this could be regarded as a tacit admission of innocence, he was not released. He slipped back into the monotonous routine of life in San Fernando, 'one unvarying round of privations, fresh prisoners, punishments and executions.'

There was no relief from torment: it simply varied in degree. The sun, rain and the thousands of insects that delighted in the wounds and bruises that covered the prisoners' bodies, were constant companions, like the continual hunger. To get food most of the prisoners bartered away their clothes with the guards, who would offer a few spikes of maize or some bread for a coat or shirt. The more elaborate tortures, such as the *cepo Uruguayana* were carried out in the privacy of the bushes surrounding the camp: the other prisoners could only hear the victims' screams. More routine beatings would be carried out where the victim lay, and Taylor once saw two Uruguayans flogged to death a short distance from him. There were women in the camp as well as men, some old and grey haired, others young and pretty, like Dolores Recalde, 'a tall and very beautiful girl' related to the traitor and Joséfa Requelme, a 'handsome woman with very fine eyes.' They were housed in small, A-shaped huts, and tortured there as well. This routine was unchanged until August 4, when 45 people, including three Italians, were taken away. There was a long pause and then 'a volley and a few straggling shots gave us food for meditation.'

These executions were the first to be carried out at San Fernando, but during the next four weeks something like seven hundred people were shot, usually after weeks of torture. The behaviour of the guards at San Fernando cannot be explained simply by saying that they were obeying orders; it is quite clear from the testimonies of the survivors that they enjoyed their work, and in their almost casual sadism one can perhaps see the reverse side of the stupendous courage that enabled the Paraguayan army to resist its enemies for so long. Both seemed to have stemmed from the same sources, the fatalism, disregard of suffering, and subservience to authority that López exploited so well: if the Guaraní soldiers were indifferent to their own fate, they were equally indifferent to that of others.

Taylor kept a record of the days by making dots on the lining of his hat with a stump of lead pencil. He also used it to keep a record of those who were shot, long marks for the important men, short marks for the others, but he later lost both pencil and lining. He estimated that he had seen 350 people marched off to be shot during the long weeks of August, but said that there were probably even more than that. Masterman claimed that the true figure was 700. One day near the end of the month Taylor saw Watts and another Englishman named Stark, who had been a merchant in Asuncion for years, taken from the compound next to him and marched away to be shot. He was convinced that within a few days, probably less, he would be executed in his turn.

Chapter 27

What saved Taylor was the approach of the Allied army. The Tebicuary was good enough as a temporary position, but it was not strong enough to resist the Allies for long, and once Humaitá had fallen Caballero was recalled from Timbo and Thompson sent off to the north to look for another position. He eventually found a site at the River Pikysyry, which drained the northern part of the Laguna Ypoa and entered the River Paraguay as a narrow but fast flowing stream. The marshy land for six miles to the south was a tangled maze of palms and forest. The front that the army would have to hold was about six miles long, further inland the widening river became quite impassable, and the position could not be outflanked. At the mouth of the River Pikysyry was a small area of firm land called Angostura, which would be suitable for the river battery. The River Paraguay was 600 yards wide at this point. The Pikysyry marked the boundary between the southern swamps and the gently rising uplands which formed the central and most densely populated part of Paraguay. These hills, called *lomas*, rose to a height of just over 2,000 feet near Cerro Leon, away to the east, but were not in any sense a military barrier. However, at the new line it would be much easier to supply the army and the health of the men could be expected to improve, with better food and a healthier climate.

The disadvantage of the Pikysyry was that it was only forty miles south of Asuncion. If the Paraguayans failed to stop the Allied advance there, the last natural barrier, the capital was doomed and the most fertile part of the country would fall into the hands of the enemy. Defeat would also mean that the Allies could drive the Paraguayans into the open, where their cavalry, artillery and overwhelming numbers would soon destroy what remained of the army. The Pikysyry was probably the strongest position so far held by the Paraguayans, but it was the place where they would have to stand and, as their motto said, conquer or die.

Despite this, López saw the advantages of the position at once and, with his customary promptness, began to make arrangements for the retreat. Thompson, now a lieutenant colonel, was sent off to Fortin Island to arrange for the artillery there to be sent north to Angostura. The Paraguayan camp became the scene of the same intense activity that had proceeded the evacuation of Humaitá earlier in the year. Since the ironclads had made no further attempt to pass the Fortin battery, the river to the north was open to the small Paraguayan steamers, and they were soon busily ferrying men, guns and supplies up to Angostura and the Pikysyry. Convoys of wagons and carts began to converge there until Angostura was crammed with supplies and stores of all kinds, protected from the rain by animal hides. Among the weapons that Thompson put into his battery was the Criollo, brought down from Asuncion to add weight to the group of guns that would once again try to stop the ironclads when they made their inevitable attack on the Paraguayan position. Thompson worked on the defences at Angostura throughout the month of August, generally in terrible conditions. The weather was bad, and the continual rain soon turned a naturally marshy position into a quagmire; the men slithered in the mud and their hands slipped on greasy ropes, while the heavy 8in guns seemed only to sink further into the sticky glue.

On August 26, the first Brazilians appeared at the Yacaré, the scene of the ambush of June 8. This time, however, they were backed by the whole Allied army, and the Paraguayan skirmishers fell back before them towards the Tebicuary. On the same day López left San Fernando and the great retreat began. The Allies were right behind the Paraguayans, and it was debatable whether the rearguard and handful of guns at Fortin could delay the ironclads and advancing troops long enough for the army to reach the Pikysyry - where the defences wee in any case still not completed. But once again López's timing had been excellent. The Allies approached the Tebicuary with caution, and treated the defences with a respect that they scarcely deserved. Only three

32prs had been left at Fortin, although dummies had been installed in place of the other guns, but on the 26th three ironclads reconnoitred this insubstantial obstacle and decided it could be reduced only by a prolonged bombardment. This lasted until the 28th but with little effect. The garrison then pushed their guns into the river and headed north. They had held up the Allies for three precious days and only retreated because the Brazilians had managed to cross the Tebicuary further to the east.

North of the river, the Allies trudged after the enemy steadily, following a road traced by white-wooden poles, topped by lightning conductors that carried the telegraph wires with which López had controlled his country. But in the flooded plains and marshes the advance bogged down. The frantic pace set by the Paraguayans cost them enormous masses of material, but the bulk of the army itself reached the Pikysyry safely. And despite the haste, López did not forget the prisoners. At the end of August those who had survived the bloodletting of the previous three weeks were formed up in a long column and driven north through some of the worst country in Paraguay.

The daily executions had reduced the number to roughly 260, of whom 14 were foreigners. Before starting, their fetters were taken off but they had to carry them as they marched and at night they were put in the *cepo de lazo* as usual. As the procession began, Taylor noticed a few familiar faces - Leite-Pereira, Washburn's friend Captain Fidanza and four Paraguayan women, Dolores Recalde, two elderly spinster sisters named Egusquiza, whose brother had been López's agent in Buenos Aires and Dona Juliana Martinez, wife of the defender of Humaitá. In the middle of the crowd were two closed bullock carts said to contain Innocencia and Rafaela López, the sisters of the President, who had themselves been arrested.

For some of the journey, Taylor walked alongside Juliana Martinez. Aged 24, she had once been one of the most beautiful women in Paraguay, but by then 'her body was covered with wounds, her face blackened and distorted and she had a raw place on the back of her neck the size of the palm of [a] hand....' This mark was caused by the *cepo Uruguayana:* she had so far endured it six times. Despite all that she had suffered, with a touching pathetic display of vanity her main concern was 'to know if a large black mark she had over one of her eyes would disappear, or if it would disfigure her for life.' In a week, the prisoners somehow covered a hundred miles, finally reaching Villeta, a few miles north of the Pikysyry, where López was establishing his new capital. They had been there several days when a group of new prisoners was brought in, and among them Taylor recognised Masterman.

Chapter 28

Masterman, Bliss and Baltazar reached the end of their journey from Asuncion early on the morning of September 11. The mules trudged up a low hill covered with rough grass and shrubs overlooking Villeta, and halted before a group of officers. The prisoners were untied and collapsed to the ground. Almost immediately an *alferez* (sergeant) began beating them with the flat of his sword until they stumbled to their feet again and they were driven to a compound made of hide ropes. Then they were at last allowed to sleep. This was when Taylor saw them. In the afternoon Masterman was woken by a blow from a stick, and told to walk to a grove of orange trees about half a mile away, a painful business since his legs were still weighed down by 30lbs of iron. He finally reached a group of huts and saw Bliss and Baltazar being marched off to one side. He was taken in to one of the huts where he was interrogated by José Falcon, who had become a minister under Carlos Antonio López, and was serving as a captain in the army. A priest took down everything that was said.

Falcon studied his prisoner for a few moments and then said: 'Ah! We have got you at last. Now, confess that Washburn is the chief of the conspirators and that you took refuge in the Legation for the purpose of plotting against the government.'

'I have no confession to make,' Masterman insisted.

'Confess, or I will see if we cannot make you,' Falcon threatened and when this made no impression he told the priest to take Masterman outside and put him in the *potro* (rack). A corporal and two soldiers came forward carrying ropes and several muskets and after a final demand for a confession, Masterman was forced to his knees, and, like Taylor before him, put in the *cepo Uruguayana.* Masterman still made no reply, and after some time he was untied. Then he was asked to confess, and as he still refused he was tied up again, this time with two muskets on the back of his neck. He tried to ease the pressure by putting his head forward, in the process cutting his mouth on the lower musket, but as the cords were tightened the pain became so intense that he fainted When he recovered he was lying on the grass, completely exhausted. By then he was at the end of his tether, and as the soldiers came forward again, he said wearily: 'I am guilty, I will confess.' He was immediately untied, and, as he gratefully drank some water, Masterman could hear Baltazar in one of the other huts pleading for mercy. Then there was the sound of heavy blows, and a series of loud shrieks: the servant's fingers were being crushed by a mallet.

This experience showed Masterman how the interrogators had managed to assemble such an overwhelming mass of evidence against Washburn from Berges, Carreras, Benigno López and the others. He repeated the same tissue of lies, consoling himself with the thought that however dishonourable it might seem, at least Washburn was safely on board the *Wasp* and out of López's clutches. Some of the other alleged 'conspirators' were already dead, including Rodriguez, Gomez, the former mayor of Asuncion, Saturnino Bedoya, and Barrios. Since the latter's descent into madness had unfortunately made his evidence unreliable he was shot. The remainder of the supposed conspirators had already made their own confessions, so Masterman could ease his conscience by telling himself that he was only repeating something which they had already admitted.

Even so, shame at breaking down made Masterman's confession a rather lame affair, and Falcon became increasingly impatient. He indicated what he wanted Masterman to say by asking leading questions, but refused to grant the priest's request that he be allowed to put the prisoner into the *Uruguayana* again. During the questioning several other officers came in, including Aveiro and Serrano, from whose conversation Masterman gathered that his best course of action was to abuse Washburn as much as possible, since he was the principal object of López's hatred.

In the evening another priest named Father Roman came in and asked Falcon for Masterman's confession. He read it through quickly and threw it contemptuously on the table. 'What wretched trash!' he said, and turned to Masterman. 'Look you, I will go for a short ride, and if on my return I do not find that you have confessed clearly that the great beast Washburn is the chief conspirator, that he was in treaty with Caxias and that he received money and letters from the enemy, and that you knew it, I will put you in the *Uruguayana* and keep you there until you die.'

When Roman was gone, the captain, a short, fat man, chewing unhappily on a cigar, took a deep breath. He put on his silver-rimmed glasses and said wearily: 'Come, Masterman, let us have the whole of the story. Tell us how the great beast intended to destroy us all.' The questioning had gone on for six hours and Masterman was completely exhausted. He watched, too tired to protest or object, as Falcon's pen scratched its way over the paper. The new confession went well for two pages, but then Falcon asked Masterman how much money Washburn had paid him. 'Nothing; he never offered me money, for I might have accepted it,' Masterman said.

The priest turned to Falcon impatiently and pleaded: 'Señor Capitan, put this *anariu,* this son of the fiend, in the *potro.* Crush him at once. He is misleading us with lies.' Masterman became afraid that he would again be tortured and that he might be forced to make a statement that would incriminate people such as Narcisse Lasserre, close friends who might still be alive. Thinking quickly, he made up a new story to the effect that he and Washburn had fallen out over politics and other matters. During the long months in the Legation, they had in fact had several arguments over such matters as English and American literature, accents and the benefits or otherwise of a republican form of government. For months before his arrest, Masterman had only gone to Washburn's apartment on business. Masterman magnified these disagreements into a bitter feud, and since Basilio's mother had already told the police that the two men were not on good terms, his story sounded convincing enough. Masterman claimed that Washburn had told him just enough to incriminate him, but not enough to upset the plot if he should tell the police. Falcon seemed to accept this, and allowed Masterman to sleep while the confession was being copied. Then he was told to sign it, and after being given some bread was taken off to a *guardia* where he was tied up in the *cepo de lazo.*

The first thing that Masterman saw the next morning was a corpse. It was the body of an Argentinean officer called Gaspar Campos, who had been captured at the battle of Tuyuti. He had died during the night and "lay on his back in a pool of rain water, staring blankly at the rising sun." Shortly afterwards the guards who came round to wake up the sleeping prisoners put the body on to a hide, dragged it off and threw it into the river. Masterman then studied the scene around him About forty prisoners lay in the *guardia* and for as far as he could see there were similar enclosures, each containing a similar number of inmates. In the one nearest he saw Venancio López, Captain Fidanza, and several officers of high rank. Dr. Carreras was in the same *guardia* as Masterman. After two months lying in the open without any shelter he was a pitiful sight. Masterman could scarcely recognise him as he sat on a rolled-up blanket, trying to frame questions without the guard noticing. He slowly unrolled the rags covering his hands, and showed Masterman his crushed and mutilated fingers. Then he 'sat motionless, with sunken eyes bent on the ground, and his scanty grey hair blowing unheeded over his face.'

Bliss, wrapped in a long white overcoat, lay behind Masterman, while in the farthest corner he could see Baltazar lying on the ground in such misery that he refused to eat. A few days later he died. The only other person Masterman knew in the *guardia* was Taylor who was with a group of Italians some distance away, looking ill and exhausted. The builder noticed him looking in his direction and raised his hands in a gesture of sympathy. The rest of the prisoners were strangers - some priests, some prisoners of war in 'the last stage of misery, most quite naked, covered with wounds, and the majority too feeble to walk,' and a group of felons, all naked, lying in a huddled heap on the ground. The kitchen was behind the *guardia*. In the morning the prisoners received some boiled meat and broth, and in the evening were given some scraps left by the soldiers. They were always hungry, and Masterman often saw Carreras, 'once the most influential man in Uruguay, an ex-prime minister, eagerly gnawing the gristle from a few well-picked bones contemptuously thrown him by a passer-by'.

Although Masterman had not eaten for three days, apart from the bread the night before, he found he was unable to eat anything. He could only beg for water, which was refused. In the afternoon he was taken to be interrogated, this time by Roman, who asked him the same sort of questions that Falcon had put the day before, and at 8pm sent him off to be questioned by Major Aveiro and Lieutenant Levalle, a Paraguayan who had been educated in England. They ordered him to write in Spanish a letter to his mother - he had already sent her one via Washburn - in which he admitted conspiring against López. One phrase puzzled Aveiro when Levalle read the letter out to him. This referred to 'H.E. the President and the Government of Paraguay.'

Aveiro said: 'But his Excellency is the Government - there is no other ruler here.' He was quite unable to see that a distinction could be drawn between the two. Bliss was then brought in to confirm Masterman's story about sending a letter to his mother, and Masterman told him quickly what he had already admitted, so that the American would be able to answer accordingly. After a few more questions, they were released, and from then on began to receive slightly better food. This was probably because Washburn had escaped, and had vowed to send help as soon as he cold. Even so, they still had to suffer the tortures of the weather and the tropical summer was beginning- the heat was intense, far worse than the rain, and thirst a continual agony. After a week the camp was moved and soon hundreds of prisoners were coming down the hillside to form up in a huge procession. From one of the huts nearby Masterman saw Benigno López crawl out, well dressed but heavily ironed. From another came Berges 'leaning feebly on a stake.... followed by his successor, Don Gumesindo Benitez, bareheaded and with naked fettered feet.'

When the crowd was finally assembled the order was given to march and they set off towards the east. On the way Masterman managed to get beside Carreras, who asked him eagerly if Washburn was safe. 'Yes, he is safe,' Masterman whispered, and asked the Uruguayan if there was any truth in the confession he had signed. He still had a lurking suspicion that there really had been a conspiracy. Carreras shook his head violently: "No, no," he said, "lies, all lies, from beginning to end."

"Why did you tell them?" asked Masterman - a faintly ridiculous question in view of what had happened to him, as he later realised. 'That terrible Father Maiz tortured me in the *Uruguayana* on three successive days, and then smashed my fingers with a mallet.' Carreras said. Maiz was the leading inquisitor into the conspiracy. A tall good-looking man of about 30, he had liberal views and considerable ability, but he was intent mainly on saving his own skin, and therefore carried out his new duties with great zeal.

The prisoners stayed at a new camp for four days, and soon after their arrival Bliss and Masterman were put apart from the rest and given slightly better treatment - the unseen influence of Washburn was probably again playing a part. Then they were suddenly ordered to move again. From the south came the rumbling thunder of guns, and every so often the sound of exploding shells. The Allies were approaching the Pikysyry, and López had decided to move the trophies of his treason plot to a safer place. Bliss and Masterman were taken away from the prisoners and after a while joined a small party made up of the most important of the political prisoners, including Leite-Pereira, Fidanza, Benigno, Venancio, Berges and Carreras. With painful slowness they staggered off through the trees: Carreras was so feeble that he collapsed to the ground with exhaustion every time the party halted, while Venancio 'a short stout man, with most martial whiskers and mustachios, in undress colonel's uniform, a cap glittering with gold embroidery on his head, and carrying a blue earthenware vessel in one hand and a bottle of rum in the other... walked with an angry impatient expression of face, frequently looking back at his brother who, heavily ironed, could move but slowly.'

Two hours later, as they came to the crest of a hill, the group met up with the main body of prisoners, an incredible spectacle that to Masterman seemed like something out of Dante's Inferno. At first they could see little because of the great clouds of dust: then they could make out 'a heaving tumultuous throng, swaying from side to side, and slowly creeping towards the hills in the distance. The red rays of the setting sun flashed now and then from whirling sword blades within it and more constantly from the line of bayonets without; small groups were detached in the rear, from which the horrible din, in the distance a confused roar, swelled loudest; heavy blows, dull thuds or quick incisive lashes resounded on all sides, with an incessant clanking of fetters, groans, shouts and curses...'

Although it was claimed that there were six hundred prisoners in the procession - among them Alonzo Taylor - Masterman thought there might have been twice that number. They came on ' in three vast herds, hemmed in by soldiers on foot and horseback, fully armed and with sticks in their hands, with which they thrashed those outside and those who fell from exhaustion whilst the officers with drawn swords rode amongst them dealing out blows right and left in wanton cruelty. . . .' As a complete contrast to this hideous scene, Mrs. Lynch came past shortly after in her carriage and pair, bowing and smiling graciously. The prisoners meekly took off their hats 'all well knowing that a word from her could send us to the scaffold, or worse.'

They marched in this fashion for perhaps six miles before being allowed to halt. Then they were tied down as usual in the *cepo de lazo* for the night. Although Masterman fully expected to move on again the next day, this turned out to be their last move. The systematic brutality continued much as before. The victims would be marched off behind an orange grove not far away, a sight that so sickened him that Masterman claimed 'I have not tasted one of the fruit since I left Paraguay.' On September 27, four days after Benigno López had been tortured in the *Uruguayana*, Carreras and Benitez were taken behind the orange grove, followed by two priests and a group of men with spades. After several hours came a volley of musketry and a thin cloud of smoke rising over the bushes. The shooting of these two men was was a signal for the start of a series of executions that soon began to rival those of San Fernando in scale and regularity. Sanabria was shot on the same day and on the next between forty and fifty men, mostly officers. The tortures became more prolonged, with Benigno and Berges being the most frequent victims.

September passed, and October. Masterman was periodically examined by Father Roman and occasionally by Father Maiz, but he was not tortured again. In November, de Libertad, the chancellor at the French consulate was arrested as he had feared but before anything worse could happen a French gunboat arrived to take him away.

By early December it must have seemed that there was nobody left to arrest, but there were still a few more suspects to arrive. Venancio López was given a better hut, and his place was taken by what Masterman considered 'most deplorable object I have ever seen in human shape:

two men came staggering along, bearing him in a hide suspended from a bamboo, nearly naked, and with his head resting on his knees; and I should have thought him dead but for the groan he uttered as they threw their burden on the ground. I saw his wild haggard face for a moment as they dragged him along to the hut, but did not recognise him, and no wonder; his huge joints showed that he had once been a tall, stout man, but he was now so emaciated that the sharp bony ridges seemed cutting through the skin, and he remained doubled up as when I first caught sight of him; yet, helpless cripple as he was, he wore double irons...' Shaken by this sight, Masterman waited until the officer in charge was taking his siesta then asked a sergeant who treated him with wary friendliness who the new arrival was. The sergeant glanced round cautiously pointed to the broken wreck and said: 'Colonel Alén They have so crushed him with the *Uruguayana* that he will never rise again.'

Chapter 29

Alén and the other prisoners had suffered and were suffering so horribly because López had won his race to the Pikysyry defences. The ironclads, which could have caused havoc during the retreat, did not approach Thompson's battery at Angostura until September 8, eleven days after Fortin Island was abandoned, and in the meantime he had managed to establish fifteen heavy guns, in two batteries 700 yards apart, facing the river.

Thompson was warned that the ironclads were approaching, and arranged an ambush by covering the guns in the lower battery with leaves and branches so that it could not be seen. One ship, the *Silvado* passed this battery without seeing it, whereupon the guns opened fire. The *Criollo* hit her at the waterline, and when the *Silvado* sailed back down half an hour later she was hit again on the port side. After this the ironclads stayed clear of the batteries although they would usually steam up from their base at Palmas, a few miles down river and engage the Paraguayans in relatively harmless long-range duels. On September 23, the first Allied troops reached the Surubi, a small stream six miles from the Pikysyry and began to cross. The Paraguayans dealt them a sharp reverse, but the next day the main army arrived and the Paraguayans fell back. The Allies set up their headquarter and main base at Palmas from where they made a series of careful reconnaissances of the Paraguayan line.

The frantic efforts of the proceeding weeks had transformed a strong natural position into a powerful series of earthworks. The main trench ran for 10,000 yards along the north bank of the River Pikysyry, but the river itself was the strongest feature. Its mouth was blocked by two dikes that had raised the water level by nearly five feet and spilled water over on to the swampy ground to the south which had already been inundated by the exceptionally high level of the River Paraguay that lasted throughout the summer of 1868 - 69. Along the whole trench and including the river batteries, the Paraguayans had positioned more than 100 guns.

The long retreat had cost the army large masses of stores, and the ammunition situation was critical. Some of the guns had only twenty or thirty rounds left and although the remaining supplies at Asuncion were brought down, few of the guns had more than 100 rounds. The infantry were given 24 packets containing ten rounds, which they carried in bandoliers of hide slung round their necks, so that they would have ammunition with them in case of a sudden march. The army consisted of around 10,000 troops, more than half of them boys aged from ten to 15, divided into five divisions, including the garrison of Angostura under Thompson, on the far right of the line.

Previous experience had shown that an attack on Paraguayans in well-built defences was a costly, and usually fruitless operation, and the prospect of challenging the trenches with a frontal attack appealed to Caxias so little that he gave it up almost immediately. Since he could not go through the Paraguayan trench he proposed to go around. On October 1, early in the morning, four ironclads forced their way passed the two Angostura batteries, taking the usual pounding from the guns, but all reaching the upper reaches in safety. Having accomplished this the ironclads began to pass up and down the river with increasing frequency.

By the 15th, there were ten above Angostura, and the Paraguayans' flank was already halfway turned. On the same day the second stage of the Allied plan began when General Argolo crossed from Palmas and began work on a new road through the Chaco. Once this was finished the Allies would be able to supply the ironclads without danger - and would also be able to march an army right round the Paraguayan position. Then the ironclads already above Angostura would ferry them back across the River Paraguay and attack the Pikysyry lines from the rear.

The Paraguayans always had a small force in the Chaco skirmishing with the enemy, but they were too few in number to stop Argolo, and his greatest problem was physical. The road, made of palm trunks laid crossways, had to cross many *esteros* and wide expanses of swamp, but on November 25 the engineers reached a place called Puerto del Chaco at the mouth of the River Aracuay, which flowed into the Paraguay a mile below Villeta. This became the main base for the enemy ironclads. Four camps protected the road itself, each manned by two battalions of infantry, and a redoubt at the northern end.

López refused at first to believe that the Allies meant to use this road to outflank him. He considered it was only a diversion, and that the main attack would come from the army south of the Pikysyry. At length, however, the scouts' reports on the movement of enemy troops along the road could not be ignored.

The first priority was to create a mobile reserve that could attack the Brazilians wherever they landed. Thompson was deprived of five of his six battalions, and the rest of the Pikysyry trench was similarly denuded. This reserve, under the command of Caballero, was to be kept at López's headquarters at Ita Yvaté until it became clear where the Allies were going to land. It was generally assumed, however, that the Brazilians would make directly for Villeta, which the ironclads had been bombarding for several weeks. This town, which lay about three miles north of Angostura, was a small village of white-washed and tiled houses built in a rough square whose river side had been left open. The Brazilians on the opposite bank could plainly see the slightly larger building tht had been López's home for several weeks, and the small church, its tower a short distance away, that had been turned into a hospital. Beyond it the hills began to rise in long grassy ridges crowned with clumps of trees, dotted here and there with palms and orange groves and abandoned *quintas.* The ridges rose steadily until, far away in the distance the soldiers could see the blue-purple peaks that marked the western spur of the Paraguayan cordillera.

Thirty five miles to the north-east, over the peaks of Lambaré, five sharp points rising into the sky, was Asuncion. Far to the east, buried somewhere among the blue ridges, was Cerro Leon, López's Champ de Mars, the parade ground where his army had marched and trained five years before. It would have been characteristic of the Allies to have contemplated this view for several weeks before acting, but the River Paraguay had other plans. Swollen by rains, it was rising to a phenomenal level: the naval base at Cerrito, two hundred miles downstream, was flooded out, the low lying banks all the way north were swamped and the plains beyond submerged, and the flood threatened to wash away all that Argolo's men had worked to achieve.

Leaving the Argentineans, the remnants of the Uruguayans and a brigade of 1,500 Brazilians to hold the Pikysyry line, Caxias therefore shifted the bulk of his army to the west bank of the Paraguay and marched them up the log road to Puerto del Chaco. On December 5, 8,000 men boarded the ironclads and were ferried back across the river. Instead of making for Villeta, the expected landing point, the squadron went four miles north to San Antonio, an old orange-loading port. This unopposed landing put the Brazilians between López and his capital, and threatened the Paraguayan army with encirclement. It was claimed that Luis Caminos, López's foreign secretary and minister of war, had been told to resist such landings with 2,000 men from Asuncion, but Caminos did not appear, and by December 6 the ironclads had ferried over 32,000 men. On the same day, Caxias began to move south. At this critical juncture, Washburn's replacement finally reached Paraguay. He was General Martin C. McMahon, who had been born in Canada of Irish parents and had served on the Union side in the Civil War. General McMahon finally reached Paraguay on December 3, more than five months after he had been nominated to succeed Washburn.

His first action was to demand the release of Bliss and Masterman. López however refused to give up his prisoners unconditionally. He explained that both were guilty of conspiring against him with Washburn, and the American officers, who had been greatly unimpressed with Washburn, were inclined to believe him. A demand for the prisoners' release was softened to a request and the Americans were already more than half convinced of the guilt of Bliss and Masterman when they first met them on December 5. Kirkland and Fleet Captain Francis M. Ramsay were sent to see the two prisoners, but since the interview was conducted in the presence of Maiz, Roman, Aveiro and Levalle, who could speak English, Masterman's replies were necessarily guarded. Ramsay became more and more perplexed as he read out the pages of lies that Masterman had signed.

'But is this really true?' he asked. Still afraid that something might go wrong, Masterman said: 'I beg you will ask me no questions.' The attitude of the two Americans, who were obviously on very good terms with the Paraguayans, was so hostile that he feared the whole visit might even be another attempt to get him to betray unwitting confidences about the conspiracy. He was so uncertain that as Ramsay and Kirkland left he said: 'I hoped I was going with you.' Ramsay replied coldly: 'Yes, you will go on board, of course.'

For five days Masterman heard no more. He was tied up in the *cepo de lazo* each night, and became convinced that he had been forgotten. Then, on December 10, exactly three months after his arrest, he was released. Maiz shook his hand and congratulated him and Aveiro, showing a rare generosity, gave him a glass of rum. Two hours later horses were brought and Bliss and Masterman began their long ride to Asuncion. At 11pm they boarded the *Wasp*, but as they saluted Kirkland, overjoyed and scarcely able to believe that they were safe at last, he called a master-at-arms and said: 'Take these men forward and put a sentry over them.' Masterman was thunderstruck. He protested, but Kirkland repeated the order. Slowly realising what might have happened, Masterman said: 'When you saw us last we were treated as criminals. I hope you do not consider that we are so?'

Kirkland said: 'I receive you as criminals and I shall treat you as criminals until you are proved to be innocent. Go forward.'

Convinced that López's version of the conspiracy was true, MacMahon, Davis and Kirkland had agreed to treat Bliss and Masterman as prisoners who would be put on trial in the United States. Sympathetic as they were to the Paraguayan cause they regarded the two men as traitors to the man and the nation that had shown them nothing but kindness and to whom they owed their loyalty, if nothing else. On December 13 the *Wasp* finally hauled up her anchor and sailed away. It was not quite the way Bliss and Masterman would have chosen to leave the country, but at least they had left it alive.

Chapter 30

December 1868 was a time of destiny. It was a month that saw McMahon arrive and Bliss and Masterman escape. It saw the great conspiracy, which had added so much fear and suffering to Paraguay's anguish throughout the year, come to a climax in which some of its victims would find an almost miraculous salvation, and others would confront the muskets of the firing squads. It was a month of joy for the few and for the majority of despair, misery, sorrow and death. It was a month of endings.

No man had a greater influence on the events of that month than Marshal Caxias, commander in chief of the Allied armies. Thanks to the landing at San Antonio, he had López firmly trapped. There were 32,000 Brazilians under his direct command and perhaps 8,000 more Allied troops south of the Pikysyry or in the Chaco. López had 10,000 men, strung along the six-mile Pikysyry trench. The trench itself could hold up the Argentineans and Thompson's battery at Angostura was still keeping the Allied supply ships at bay, but it was quite useless as a defence against an attack from the north. A further retreat, however, was out of the question. There was really nowhere left to retreat to by that stage, and Caxias's cavalry was in a position to cut off any attempt to do so. The only practical alternative was to fight. As soon as the Brazilians' landing was reported to López he ordered Caballero and the reserve of 5,000 men to go and meet them. Caballero took up his position south of the River Itóróró, a small, tumbling stream that cut its way through a sand stone cliff before plunging into the River Paraguay between San Antonio and Villeta. About half a mile up river was a small wooden bridge only three metres wide where the main road to Asuncion passed on its way south. It was the only crossing point for miles, and became the focal point of the battle that took place on December 6. Caxias's plan was for Argolo to attack the bridge itself, while Osorio's 3rd Corps moved out to the left and crossed the river higher up. Unfortunately, the troops got lost in the thick woods, and Argolo's lst Corps was left to do most of the fighting on its own.

The battle was a furious and merciless affair. Caballero had positioned his twelve field guns under the command of Major Moreno, directly behind the bridge, and although Argolo's men managed to force a hand-to-hand fight they were driven off. This happened three times before Caxias finally won the day by leading the reserves into action with a charge that cleared the bridge and captured six of the guns. Caballero reeled south having lost 1,200 men. The Brazilians, who had lost 3,000, advanced to the *guardia* of Ypané, where the ironclads ferried over reinforcements of cavalry and artillery.

On December 11 they advanced again towards the wooden line of the River Avay, another small stream that entered the Paraguay just north of Villeta. This had no advantages for the defence and Caballero had asked López for permission to retreat to a better position. López replied that if Caballero would not defend the position he would send a general who would. Stung by this insult, Caballero dug in to await the Brazilians. It was the middle of Paraguay's summer and the heat was blistering, but when the Brazilians approached the river it began to rain, and as they were about to cross Caballero swept into the attack with a force of 4,000 men and twelve guns.

The battle developed into one of the most vicious ever fought in South America. The tiny force under Caballero's command represented half of López's entire army and the soldiers fought knowing that the fate of their country depended entirely on stopping the Brazilians crossing the Avay. The Brazilian 3rd Corps, which had missed the fighting at the Itóróró, suffered heavily from the furious Paraguayan onslaught. Three infantry battalions were saved from annihilation only by the charge of the cavalry under General José Antonio Correa da Camara and Osorio was hit in the jaw by a bullet. Refusing to leave the field, he had himself carried about in a cart so that his men could see he was not dead.

One of the Paraguayans who took part in the battle was a twelve-year-old recruit named Miguel Faria, who had run away from home with the intention of joining the army and was drafted into the artillery. His battery was sent to the Avay, where the battle had already been going on for some time. The boy was puzzled at first by the appearance of the bridge, which from a distance seemed to be piled up with bundles of firewood. He asked his officer what they were, and was told grimly that he would find out soon enough. As the men drew closer Faria realised that the bundles were actually bodies, hanging over the sides of the bridge and held in position by others who had fallen across their feet. The battle lasted four hours, and the Brazilians lost a total of 4,000 men. The 26th, 28th, 42nd, 44th, 48th and 55th *Voluntarios da Patria* battalions were so depleted that they were disbanded. But the Paraguayan losses had been staggering.

They had fought on, as usual, long after there was any hope of victory or even of escape, and the battle only ended when the whole force was surrounded by the Brazilian cavalry and slaughtered. Caballero was pulled off his horse, and his poncho and silver spurs taken by enemy plunderers, but was so loosely guarded that he was able to escape and return to his own lines the next day. Major Moreno, the artillery leader, and Colonel Rivarola, who led the cavalry, were both wounded but managed to escape, as did the boy soldier, Miguel Faria. Just 200 men reached Ita Yvaté altogether. Behind them more than half the army lay dead, another 500 were wounded, and 700 were prisoners, among them Major Serrano, Alonzo Taylor's old friend and torturer. All the guns were captured.

That evening Thompson saw the Brazilians appear on the crest of the hills above Villeta, only four miles from Angostura and within striking distance of Ita Yvaté and the heart of López's defence. To meet this threat, Thompson suggested digging another trench from Angostura to Ita Yvaté, facing north, with its left flank resting on the northern Angostura battery. This would have enclosed the Paraguayan army in a rough rectangle and might have given the troops enough protection to hold the enemy at bay, but by then López had neither the men nor the time to complete it. Instead he began work on a small redoubt which was meant to be the first of a chain of defence works around Ita Yvaté. Even this was over-ambitious and as a final resort López ordered his men to dig a small ditch two feet wide by two feet deep running in a rough semi-circle round his headquarters, although the rear, towards Cerro Leon, was open.

To man it he scraped up a force of roughly 3,000 troops, including several men from the prison camp who were released and sent back to the army. His personal cavalry escort, which had not been involved in any fighting, was held as a reserve. The Pikysyry line was held by 1,500 troops, and as a result of López's efforts to build up a reserve force earlier in the month most of them were wounded, invalids or boys. Thompson, meanwhile, turned Angostura into a small redoubt in case the enemy should try to attack from the rear. For four days there was a pause in the fighting as Caxias reorganised his troops.

While he did so, several hundred people, were lying in the woods, listening to the sounds of shells and rifles and wondering if the Allied soldiers would reach them in time. For weeks the prisoners had been hearing the rumble of guns as the ironclads bombarded Angostura, and this was later joined by the sounds of artillery to the north, steadily coming closer, and the growing agitation of the prison guards told them that the Paraguayan forces were almost surrounded. Within days, it seemed, the Allies would break through and rescue them, and the prisoners most of whom had been held for months, concentrated on surviving for just a little longer. The main threat was of not starvation but execution. Throughout the month the shootings continued until it seemed as though López was hurrying to take his revenge on those whom he believed had betrayed him before he was himself destroyed.

Still, the Allies had to arrive in the end and after the crossing of the Avay the gunfire became louder than ever and it seemed that one more battle would crush López completely. Then, on December 17 Colonel Marcó, who had been chief of police under Carlos Antonio López, rode into the camp with a group of officers. When they reached the centre, Marcó ordered the prisoners to gather round him in a rough semi-circle, and began reading a series of names from a piece of paper. As each name was called out the emaciated ranks parted and a prisoner shuffled forward. By the time Marcó had finished reading nearly all of the important people who still survived were standing before him. Benigno López was the most prominent, a pathetic creature meekly waiting for the death that he had always known awaited him.

BENIGNO LOPEZ. (Executed by his brother, Dec. 27, 1868.)

Benigno Lopez, Solano's brother, was executed by his brother on 27 December, 1868.

Bishop Palacios, who had betrayed his trust as a priest and fawned before López in an unsuccessful attempt to retain his favour, was beside him, an abject, ignorant nonentity for whom it is difficult to grieve. Berges, perhaps the most able man in Paraguay, who had argued his country's case so brilliantly so many times, was sentenced with them. Two foreigners were called, Fidanza, Washburn's Italian friend, and Leite-Pereira, who had once sought Washburn's protection. Dean Bogado and another priest called Sosa had sold their souls to López and like Palacios were selected to die anyway. The hero of Humaitá, Colonel Alén, was called upon to pay for failing to achieve the impossible. Most pathetic of all were the women, the once beautiful Dolores Recalde, Luisa Egusquiza, whose sister had already died, and Juliana Martinez, who was so weak from constant torture that she had to be dragged forward by the soldiers.

When the line was complete Marcó ordered the condemned to turn and they marched off towards the trees, accompanied by three priests carrying chairs, whose duty would be to confess the victims before they were shot. As they trailed off into the wood, Taylor noticed that Juliana Martinez's greatest fear had come true. The huge black bruise that she had worried about on the retreat from San Fernando still marked her face, and would be with her until she died. He and the other prisoners waited tensely and then 'at the expiration of an hour a volley was heard, then a dropping shot, and all was over. The Guard came back, one old soldier wearing Captain Fidanza's *surtout*, and the officer the uniform coat of Leite-Pereira, with its gilt buttons.'

These executions, carried out at a moment when the whole structure of López's regime seemed to be crashing in ruins about him, were the climax of the long succession of reprisals resulting from the treason conspiracy. Although a few alleged participants still survived - Venancio López was the most prominent - by the end of 1868 López had killed almost everyone whom he considered in any way suspect. Documents captured a few days later recorded the following details:

Foreigners executed	107
Foreigners died in prison	113
Paraguayans executed	176
Paraguayans died in prison	88
Executed August 22 (nationality not given)	85
Died between San Fernando and Pikysyry	27
Total deaths to December 1868	596

This list does not include those who were shot during the month of December and probably Masterman is right in estimating that the final total included nearly all of the 700 or 800 people originally arrested in connection with the conspiracy.

For the prisoners who remained, the liberation of which they had almost despaired, was almost with them. On the morning of December 21, with the Allied shells already whistling overhead and crashing into the woods around the camp, the prisoners were tied up again almost as soon as they were released. Taylor believed this was because the guards hoped a few stray shells would kill them, and thus solve a rather embarrassing problem. But nobody was hurt, although the bombardment was almost incessant, and on December 25 López and Mrs. Lynch, accompanied by a group of officers, came galloping through the camp. The President hardly noticed the prisoners, but it seemed to Taylor that Mrs. Lynch drew his attention to them and López turned his horse and ordered them to stand in a row. He asked: 'Are you all prisoners?'

Von Truenfeld, the German telegrapher who had been brought into the camp a few days before, said they were. As he stepped forward López asked why he was a prisoner. Von Truenfeld replied, truthfully enough, that he did not know, and López told him that he was free. Stunned for a moment at this unexpected generosity, Taylor then approached and asked for the same mercy. He was so ragged and changed that López failed to recognise him, and when Taylor told him his name he seemed very surprised and said: 'What are you doing here? You are at liberty.'

In a similar fashion, ten other prisoners were granted their freedom, and López and his party then rode off again through the trees. Although the prisoners were free, there was nowhere for them to go. The sounds of battle all round promised ultimate rescue, but could also mean instant death. So they stayed where they were, accompanied by an officer but not guarded, until 5am on December 27 when the firing suddenly became intense, and a crowd of Brazilian horsemen burst out of the trees and charged towards them. Realising that they had bean mistaken for Paraguayan soldiers - and by this stage there was little way of telling the difference between soldiers and prisoners - Taylor and two Argentineans ran for safety and although Taylor was slightly injured in the shoulder by a bullet, they managed to reach the woods and hide there until the cavalry had gone. Several of the other prisoners were too weak to escape and were cut down and killed by the very men they had waited so long to see. Later in the afternoon, Brazilian infantry arrived, and this time Taylor and his companions were taken before Caxias himself who listened to their story and then allowed them to go free. Four days later Taylor was taken on board the British gunboat *HMS Cracker* which had recently arrived in Paraguay.

'Everybody on board did all they could for me; but it was some days before I could speak plainly, and could only lie huddled up on the deck,' he wrote. It was hardly surprising: in July he had weighed 178 pounds when he went on board the *Cracker* he was down to 98.

Chapter 31

The battle that resulted in Taylor being freed began on December 21. During the lull that followed the action of the 17th, both sides had prepared for it, and General MacMahon, who landed in Paraguay as soon as Bliss and Masterman were safely on board the *Wasp,* was there to see it take place. Although his acquaintance with López had begun rather inauspiciously, whatever ill feeling resulted from the Legation affair soon disappeared. The new minister, a soldier himself, could only admire the heroic way in which the Paraguayans fought for their country, and saw for himself the complete devotion which the soldiers, officers and men, felt for López.

In this emotional and dramatic atmosphere, he found it easy enough to dismiss Washburn's stories of tortures and atrocities as nonsense and become a frank partisan of the Paraguayan cause. He rapidly became an intimate friend of the President, and spent the first ten days after his arrival at his headquarters at Ita Yvaté. The headquarters itself, about half a mile inside the semi-circular trench, consisted of a group of one-storey buildings thatched with straw and arranged as the three sides of a square, enclosing an area of just over an acre.

Almost incredibly, considering what they had been through, the Paraguayan officers seemed bored. MacMahon watched them outside the headquarters, spinning coins to pass the time 'and so one evening, when López remarked at dinner to some of his principal officers "Caxias will attack me tomorrow at half past four o'clock" there was visible an expression of delight on the faces of all the officers present. He added: "He is landing his sailors and the crews of the transports at Las Palmas to make a diversion from below, but he will attack in force from the direction of Villeta." This conversation took place on the evening of December 20, and the attack took place the next day as López had forecast. The Brazilians at Villeta marched south in two columns, the largest of which, under Caxias, headed for the trench at Villeta, and in Thompson's caustic words 'sat down in front of the strongest portion of it.' At the same time Mena Barreto, with the cavalry and some infantry continued to the Pikysyry trench, charged down from the hill above and took it from the rear, killing about 700 and capturing 200 men and all the artillery. The survivors fled east to Ita Yvaté or crowded into Angostura, which still held despite being completely cut off. Throughout the morning the Brazilians 'kept up a pretty constant but badly directed fire"[78] on the Paraguayan positions at Ita Yvaté, and there was some skirmishing in the rear when the Brazilian cavalry raided the cattle pens. Then in the afternoon the firing increased and at 3pm 25,000 Brazilians prepared to attack an army of approximately 3,000 half- starved men and boys.

While the cavalry moved to threaten the Paraguayan right, the Brazilian infantry formed up under cover of some woods in a low valley fronting the left of the position, but the preparations took a long time, and as the infantry began their advance the artillery seemed to cease firing, just when it should have intensified the barrage. The Paraguayans were left undisturbed to pick off the slow moving infantry as they came forward, and after a hard fight the attack was driven back. A second attempt to break through on the right wing also failed, although the Allied artillery was moved forward. Even so, the battle was fiercely fought and López's headquarters, 'began to swarm with wounded, yet none withdrew from the lines except those whose wounds were such as to positively and immediately incapacitate them from further fighting. There were children of tender years who crawled back, dragging shattered limbs or with ghastly bullet wounds in their half-naked bodies. They neither wept nor groaned nor asked for surgical attention headquarters. When they felt the merciful hand of death heavy upon them they would lie down and die as silently as they had suffered.'[79]

While the Paraguayans were trying to reform, the Brazilian cavalry suddenly appeared on the far right, where the defending troops had been withdrawn to fight off the last attack. Two squadrons crossed the deserted trench and galloped to within a hundred yards of López's headquarters. 'A few officers and others rode madly against the column attacking it with the fury of desperation. There were a few shots from the carbines a little unimportant work with the sabre, when the Brazilians seemed suddenly to lose heart, turned sharply to the right and fled."[80] Within moments another 2,000 horsemen appeared from the same place and advanced into the heart of the Paraguayan position. This time it seemed as though nothing could stop them. López sent his personal staff to attack them when they were only eighty yards away, and for the first time in the war the Government Escort, led by 70-year-old Colonel Toledo, charged into battle. These 200 horsemen flung themselves at the head of the Brazilian column and began hacking away with their sabres. Within minutes Toledo was dead, and his body was brought back, slung across a horse, but despite their enormous superiority, the Brazilians failed to spread out. After a while, the charge stopped altogether, and then the column turned and retreated, under heavy fire from what remained of the Paraguayan artillery.

With this astonishing engagement the battle petered out. The Paraguayans still held their trench, and could claim, with justification to have won the battle. The cost, however, had been so great that it was clear that they could never fight another. By the end of the day López had fewer than 2,000 troops left. The Allies had lost 3,500 men and since landing at San Antonio the Brazilians had seen their army reduced from 32,000 men to 20,000. But their proportional superiority had grown even greater. The Paraguayans had also lost 14 guns, including the Whitworth 32pr captured at Tuyuti and were almost out of ammunition. Conditions for those who survived around López's headquarters were deplorable.

'There were no means of caring for the wounded in such numbers, nor could men be spared off the field, or to bury the dead. Many children, almost unnoticed, were lying around the corridors grievously wounded and silently waiting for death. Women were busy making lint by the light of lanterns from whatever materia1 could be collected for that purpose. Garments of all descriptions were torn into bandages. Groups of officers, many of them wounded, were sitting here and there discussing the events of the day. The President sat apart with a few of his chief officers similarly occupied. Random bullets splintered the woodwork of the buildings from time to time, and an unearthly peacock, perched on the ridge-pole, made the night hideous with his screams every time a shot came near enough to disturb his slumbers....'[81]

However hopeless the situation appeared, López was still determined to fight on and he sent a messenger to Angostura to tell Thompson to force his way through the Brazilians and rejoin the main army. This messenger was unable to get through the enemy lines until the next night, December 22, and while Thompson was preparing to evacuate his post another message arrived. In it López wrote: 'The situation has changed; I sustain myself well and the enemy can only attack me very weakly, being completely demoralised. You must therefore sustain yourselves at all hazards, if this order arrives in time. The chief drawback of the enemy is the immense number of wounded he has, which cannot be attended to, as the road he has opened through our trench barely permits him to convey his most distinguished wounded. The order of yesterday will therefore not be executed, unless in an extreme case, which I hope will not arrive, as I count soon upon taking your provisions.'[82] That López could write such a letter at this stage could be regarded as a tribute to his remarkable powers of self-deception. He was almost surrounded by an army that outnumbered him by more than ten to one and was still growing, he had only a handful of guns, no cavalry and was short of ammunition. But in fact López knew quite well that his position was hopeless and had already made plans, which indicate that he was a good deal more pessimistic than his message suggested. On December 23 while the women of the camp were burying the dead, López decided to send his sons to the safety of Pirebebuy, thirty miles to the north east, which he had named as his new capital. He put them in the care of his new friend MacMahon.

At the same time, conscious that his own death might be very close, he entrusted MacMahon with another document, which was in effect his will. It read: 'As the representative of a friendly nation, and to provide against all that may happen, allow me to entrust to your care the subjoined document, by which I transfer to Doña Elisa Lynch all my private effects of whatever description. I beg you will have the goodness to keep the document until it can be securely delivered to the aforesaid lady, or returned to me, in the unforeseen event of my having no personal communication with you.'[83]

Profoundly affected by this expression of confidence and friendship, MacMahon and his party set off, a procession of carriages and horsemen inching their way along roads already crowded with refugees heading east to the cordilleras and away from the pounding guns and flashing sabres of the Brazilian cavalry. On this journey MacMahon saw, for the first time, what the war had done to the people of Paraguay. He estimated that about 6,000 wounded soldiers and other refugees were on the road, some of them in ox-carts, mostly on foot. Behind them they could hear the guns firing, and every so often the deeper, reverberating roar of the ironclads. They crossed the River Ycaty, swollen by the recent rain, and on the other side passed still more 'weary wounded, whose painful faces were very sad.

'At each little stream we passed we found them pouring water on their undressed wounds, and here and there one who, knowing that his time was nigh at hand, was lying down quietly and silently for his last sleep, as if it were the most natural thing in the world for a Paraguayan to lie down and die unnoticed.' From the general horror, some incidents stood out: a mother carrying her dead child on a board on her head; a dying colonel lying in an ox-cart, who turned out to be the brother of a 10-year-old 'soldier' in MacMahon's party; another ten-year-old who had fought in the trenches leading a horse carrying his wounded father away from the battlefield; and everywhere around MacMahon could see 'the decaying symbols of a vanished prosperity, the bloom of flowers and the ripening harvests, which rather added to the air of desolation which hung upon these deserted homesteads.'

The day after leaving Ita Yvaté, after a journey that had taken them past scenes of harrowing, almost unbearable suffering, MacMahon and his party reached Paraguarí, at the foot of the Azcurra escarpment that separated them from Piribebuy. Physically and emotionally exhausted they rested there briefly and then, with what must have seemed to be an almost callous mockery of Paraguay's martyrdom 'a merry peal of bells broke forth from the steeple of the old church. It was Christmas Eve.'[84]

Chapter 32

For five days after the fighting of December 21 the Allies battered the Paraguayans with artillery fire and riflemen hidden in the woods shot at anyone who moved. While they did so, the Argentineans moved across the captured Pikysyry trench to reinforce them, and more field guns were brought up from the base at Palmas. López also tried to strengthen his shattered army, and sent to Cerro Leon, where several thousand men were in hospitals, asking for reinforcements. On the 23rd a battalion of 500 men arrived, and on Christmas Day - although it is doubtful if anyone felt like celebrating the birth of the Son of God in a land which God himself seemed to have abandoned - more troops marched in from Caapucu.

The sailors from the steamers and men from the prison camps were added to the force surrounding López's headquarters. All these reinforcements were organised into four battalions, one called the 40th although this elite unit had been eliminated so many times by then that it is doubtful whether any of its original members still remained alive. On the 24th, convinced that the Paraguayan army must have been completely destroyed, the Allies asked López to surrender. After consulting his officers, he prepared an answer that was taken by Colonel Aveiro and López's eldest son, Panchito. Characteristically enough, it was a refusal, although López did offer 'to treat for the termination of the war upon bases equally honourable for all the belligerents, but I am not disposed to listen to an intimation that I lay down my arms.'[85] He pointed out, quite rightly, that all his previous attempts to negotiate a settlement had 'met with no answer but the contempt and silence of the Allied governments and new and bloody battles on the part of their armed representatives, as you call yourselves. I then more clearly saw that the tendency of the war of the Allies was against the existence of the Republic of Paraguay, and though deploring the blood spilled in so many years of war, I could say nothing, and, placing the fate of my Fatherland and its generous sons in the hands of the God of Nations, I fought its enemies with loyalty and conscience, and I am disposed to continue fighting until that God and our arms decide the definite fate of the cause..."

This letter, and its offer of negotiations, was ignored - the time for talk had long since passed - and on December 25, forty-six heavy guns began what Thompson at Angostura thought was the fiercest bombardment of the war. López's house was struck and under a sky filled with smoke the Brazilians attacked. Although he had only six field guns left, López somehow contrived to drive them back. In the evening enemy cavalry moved round to the rear. The Paraguayan Dragoons, the only unit left intact, charged into them, were surrounded and wiped out. Despite this, the Brazilians withdrew, and the Paraguayan line still held. But by the end of the day López had less than 1,000 men left, and the Argentineans had finally arrived to help the Brazilians in the attack. The odds had risen to well over twenty to one.

All this time, Thompson had been doing his best to help the force at Ita Yvaté, although his own position at Angostura was almost as precarious, and the refugees who had come into the batteries after the taking of the Pikysyry trench put an extra strain on his food supplies without doing much to increase the fighting strength of the garrison. Even before the Allied advance on Ita Yvaté Thompson had tried to get extra supplies from López, foreseeing - though prudently not saying so - that the Allies would eventually cut him off from the main army. López had told him to see Resquín, but all he had managed to obtain was enough beef for three days and twelve sacks of Indian corn.

The regular garrison consisted of 53 officers and 684 men, of whom 320 were artillerymen. These had been joined by an equal number of troops from Pikysyry, most of them boys who had lost their weapons. In addition Thompson found himself responsible for 421 wounded officers and men and about 500 women. The total population of the garrison had thus risen from 700 to 2,400, most of them of no value at all from a military point of view. Even so, Thompson did what he could to improve the food situation and relieve the crushing pressure on the main force at Ita Yvaté. On the 22nd and 23rd he sent skirmishers along the Pikysyry trench to collect any weapons they could find and bring in the wounded, most of whom still lay where they had fallen during Mena Barreto's successful attack on the 21st. Then he sent 500 men to the Chaco on a plundering expedition. He knew from scouts that the Allies still had most of their supplies and reasoned that this would be guarded by a relatively small force.

But in this dreadful year of 1868 fortune never favoured Paraguay. Four prisoners were taken, who told Thompson that the Brazilians had evacuated the Chaco the night before. The haul consisted only of the personal trunk of the commander of the ironclad, *Brazil*, a few swords and odds and ends, 27 mules, three horses - and 120 cases of claret. This failure meant that the supply position remained acute, and on the night of December 26 Thompson sent another force to a large enclosure halfway to Villeta, which returned with 248 cattle. It was a great boost to the garrison's morale and apparently the position at Ita Yvaté was not quite as desperate as the garrison had thought. The two sections of the army could still communicate by semaphore, and on the same day López signalled to Thompson: 'Here we are getting on very well, and there is no fear. The enemy is in his last agony and desperate, and nothing troubles him so much as the impossibility of moving with great number of wounded he has.' The next day, with the Argentineans leading the attack, the Allies closed in on Ita Yvaté from all sides.

By the evening of December 27 the roaring of the guns on the hills around Ita Yvaté had died away. Occasionally Thompson and the anxious men at Angostura heard the sharp crack of a rifle, and through binoculars they could see men moving among the trees, but 'no one would ever have hinted at the possibility of López having been defeated, and we really knew nothing.' For the last week López had held off an army that outnumbered him by twenty to one and had survived two major onslaughts, on the 21st and the 25th. It was conceivable that he had done so again, and if so he might still reverse the course of events and relieve Angostura; in which case those who had expressed defeatist sentiments could expect the same sort of reward that had befallen Barrios, Bruguez, Robles and the hundreds of others who had incurred the President's displeasure. The one clue that he had not escaped was a tent which Thompson could see in front of López's house. There was no reason why the Paraguayans should have put it up, and the obvious conclusion was that the Allies had done so.

This theory was given weight the next day, December 28, when Allied troops began to form up on the hill above Angostura. In the afternoon a messenger came down to the Paraguayan position under flag of truce. Thompson told the messenger to take it to López's headquarters, but at that moment one of his men rushed up to say that a Brazilian ironclad was coming down river under a flag of truce. The Paraguayans told her to stop, but she still came on and Thompson sent Ortiz, who had led the cattle rustling party a few nights before, to see what she wanted. The ship still continued down river, and Thompson had a blank cartridge fired. When this failed to stop her he recalled Ortiz and fired a broadside from the 8 in guns into the ship, which at last made her turn round and sail back up the river.

Furious at this breach of truce, Thompson composed a letter of protest, signed by himself and Carrillo, which was taken to the Allied camp the next morning by a group of officers. The Allies apologised but at the same time they took the opportunity to tell the Paraguayans that López had bean defeated and his army destroyed. They offered to let Thompson examine López's house at Ita Yvaté, if he wished, and to add confirmation they sent a letter, written by one of the Englishmen captured at Ita Yvaté (probably Dr. Stewart) explaining what had happened. This was all convincing enough, but to make quite sure Thompson sent five officers to Ita Yvaté. They returned late the same day, having spoken to many of the Paraguayan wounded, and sadly told Thompson that the reports were all true. The Paraguayan army had been wiped out, and López had vanished.

Since the last hope of relief had gone, Thompson saw that further resistance was useless. Apart from the huge Allied superiority in men and weapons, the Paraguayan guns only had 90 rounds of ammunition each, not enough for two hours' firing if an attack were launched. Still, he was a foreigner, and the army he commanded was the only one left with which the Paraguayans could continue the war. Unwilling to make such an important decision himself he called together the chiefs, the officers and lastly the troops and explained the case to them, putting it to them 'whether it would not be better to capitulate and save their lives, which could then be of use to their country, rather than that we should all die there, killing certainly a large number of the enemy, but with the certainty of everyone perishing. With the exception of Lieutenant Fleitas, all were for capitulating...'

There remained only the formalities. Thompson and Carrillo jointly signed a letter announcing that the garrison had agreed to surrender, and leave Angostura 'provided we do so with all the honours of war, everyone keeping the rank he now holds, and his adjutants, assistants etc. guaranteeing that the troops will lay down their arms at a convenient place, without this condition extending to the chiefs and officers who will keep theirs. Your Excellencies will guarantee the liberty of everyone to go wherever he pleases.' Considering the relative positions of the two armies the Paraguayans were hardly in a position to make terms, but the Allies, now the war was safely won, were in a benevolent mood. Caxias, Gelly y Obes, the Argentinean commander, and Enrique Castro, in command of the diminutive Uruguayan contingent, agreed to the terms and at noon on December 30 the garrison of Angostura marched out and laid down their arms. Just before they did so a young lieutenant called José Maria Fanna took down the flag which had flown over Angostura so bravely, wrapped it round a cannon ball and threw it into the river rather than see it surrendered to the enemy.

Thompson himself was treated with great respect and courtesy, but he remained aloof and politely rejected Caxias's offer of a free passage to Buenos Aires or England. His attitude was conditioned partly by the terrible conditions at Ita Yvaté, where he found '700 of our wounded in López's house alone, their wounds not having been dressed. The ground was still covered with dead in different stages of decomposition.' Following Thompson's protests, Caxias allowed him to send for some medical students who had been at Angostura to come and treat the wounded, and Gelly y Obes lent him twenty-five men to assist them. By talking to the wounded, Thompson was able to learn what had happened during the last battle.

It had been a slaughter. The Allies had at last realised that the rear of the Paraguayan position was undefended, and the main attack came from that direction. The Paraguayan guns were all dismounted, although two or three of them kept firing, propped up on the ground, but there was no really organised defence. The Paraguayans fought on individually until they were killed or disarmed. López's personal papers and possessions were captured, the prisoners, including Taylor, were released, and other survivors gave themselves up. Dr. Stewart was one of them, and he remembered later seeing the victorious Brazilian troopers going through the woods around the house, bayoneting the wounded as they lay in the shade of the trees.

After two days at Ita Yvaté, doing what he could for the Paraguayan survivors, Thompson went to Villeta where the *Cracker* was anchored and then to Asuncion for two days before going down river to Buenos Aires. For him, as for Washburn, Masterman and Taylor the long ordeal of the Paraguayan war was over. Although h is story ended there, for the man he had served so well the war went on.

From the point of view of historical symmetry, López should have died on December 27, leading his men in a last charge against the oncoming tide. It seems, from the methodical way he drew up his will and sent his family off to Pirebebuy with MacMahon, that he did not expect to survive the battle. But on the last day he changed his mind (or perhaps was persuaded to do so) and with sixty men, including most of his staff officers - all that remained of the 10,000 men under his command at the start of the month - he retreated to the woods beyond Ita Yvaté and from there rode off towards Cerro Leon. With him were Resquín, Caballero and Elisa Lynch. She had preferred to wait beside him at Ita Yvaté rather than go on to Pirebebuy with the children, and although the safety of the British gunboat awaited her she followed him still, though even López scarcely knew where he was going, or why.

Caxias made no attempt to catch him, a decision that shocked the Allies almost as much as it mystified them. Mena Barreto begged for permission to chase him with the cavalry, only half of whom had actually taken part in the last day's fighting. That would have left 8,000 men to chase a group of less than 100, but Caxias refused, and when he later relented and decided that a pursuit might be worthwhile he chose to send the 54th Volunteers, a regiment of infantry who had already suffered severely in the fighting. They marched bravely to a plane called Potrero Marmore where a family of half-naked refugees told them that they had seen López mount a fresh horse two hours before, and gallop off towards the east. Realising the futility of chasing a man on horseback on foot, the 54th turned and marched wearily back to Ita Yvaté.

This apparent lack of concern over the fate of the President - and the Allies had maintained ever since the Triple Alliance was formed that their quarrel was with López rather than the Paraguayan nation - was so amazing that a variety of theories was put forward to explain it. Burton hinted darkly that Caxias, a well-known Conservative, was acting out of party political considerations. Thompson asked: 'Was it from imbecility, or from a wish to make more money out of the army contracts? Was it to have an excuse for still maintaining a Brazilian army in Paraguay, or was there an understanding between Caxias and López? Or was it done with the view of allowing López to reassemble the remainder of the Paraguayans in order to exterminate them in civilised warfare?'

Thompson himself believed in the latter theory. 'The Brazilians,' he wrote bitterly, 'have purposely allowed many of their prisoners to go and join him as they are determined not to leave a Paraguayan of any age or sex alive.... the Allies...while professing extreme humanity have, under the cloak of "civilised warfare" exterminated the Paraguayan nation and never once tried to get at López, the pretended aim of their warfare.'

This harsh accusation of genocide was no doubt unfair, but even if the Allies had no desire to wipe out the Paraguayan nation, their sheer incompetence was tending to bring this about. Caxias let López go because he did not think he could do any more harm. Besides, he was old and tired and wanted to go back to Brazil to enjoy the rewards that were certain to be his. On January 2 he entered Asuncion and announced that the war was over.

It was to last for fifteen more months.

Part 4:
To Cerro Cora

Chapter 33

The city that Marshal Caxias entered had been deserted for nearly a year, but the houses, mostly boarded up, had been untouched, and Asuncion seemed superficially exactly the same as on the day that its 20,000 inhabitants had left. It consisted mostly of single-storey buildings, dominated by the enormous, unfinished palace that Alonzo Taylor was building for López when the war broke out. It was the first building that the Allies saw as the ironclads rounded the bend and entered Asuncion Bay and consisted of a main body and two wings, with the centre capped by a large square tower. One of its four pinnacles had been destroyed by the bombardment of the ironclads, and never restored. Nearby was the wooden landing stage, at the nearer end of the town and to the right of it was the arsenal where 30 English craftsmen and 120 Paraguayan labourers had managed to cast more than 100 guns. Whytehead had been succeeded by another Englishman called Nesbitt, who in 1868 had turned down the offer of a passage to Buenos Aires on an English gunboat and was believed to be somewhere in the hills with López. The most important street in the city was the Calle de Asuncion, which ran along the river front past the palace towards the station, three quarters of a mile from the pier. The old cathedral, known as the church of the Encarnacion, was situated on this street not far from the palace. The body was built of pink, blue and white painted brick - the national colours of Paraguay, for even though abandoned Asuncion still demonstrated the intense patriotism and pride that had inspired the men it had taken the Allies four years to subdue.

Beyond the church was the Plaza de la Cathedral, the nucleus of the older part of the city, where festivals and presidential birthdays were celebrated with races, bullfights and dances to the pounding of the enormous Indian drum called La Gomba. The Government House, once Dr. Francia's palace, was on this square, the windows barred, and surrounded by barracks, and behind it was the prison where Masterman and so many others had been imprisoned. The new cathedral was on the opposite square. Carlos Antonio had built it in 1845, and his own palace, a two storey building, was next to it, joined by long walls to another large house that had once been the home of General Vicente Barrios.

Taylor's railway station lay at the end of the street, occupying the whole of one block. Its clock tower was the highest building in the city, but the station's zinc roofs had been stripped to provide metal for canister shot. At the far end of the city was the old customs house, an extraordinary building whose roof ran parallel with the ground. Since this happened to have a slope of ten degrees, it always seemed to Masterman that the whole thing was sliding into the river. Beyond that was Mrs. Lynch's original home, converted by the Brazilians into a military hospital. The Calle de la Cathedral, the second most important road in Asuncion, ran inland from the Plaza de la Cathedral. Some distance down it was the impressive, but unfinished palace of Benigno López, which the Argentineans promptly commandeered for their headquarters. It was built on one side of the Plaza del Mercado, and at another corner was a house owned by López himself. Osorio, recovering from the wound he had received, occupied this house before moving into the palace of Dr. Francia. The chapel of San Francisco was to the west of it. The scaffolding of bamboo and pale trunk still clung to the unfinished dome, as it had done for years. The Plaza Vieja, with the United States Legation bounding one side, was south of the market place. Soon after the landing, the Legation was taken over by one of the enterprising speculators who followed the victorious army and turned into the Gran Hotel del Cristo. Another large building nearby became the Brazilian military hospital.

With its curious mixture of styles, its half-finished buildings, its patriotic flagpoles and coats of arms, Asuncion was representative of Paraguay itself. Like the ambitions of the Lópezes, it was incomplete, and although even the unfinished palaces and churches were impressive enough they could not disguise the primitive conditions of the rest of the city. The streets, although well pavemented, were simply sand, deeply rutted by rain water and the single-storey houses where the middle class and the poor lived were often mean and dirty. Burton described the city as 'the true type and expression of Paraguay - of a people robbed and spoiled. The Presidential House would have paid the paving of half the town. Public conveniences are nowhere; the streets are wretched; the drainage has not been dreamed of and every third building, from the chapel to the theatre, is unfinished.'

Burton, however, spoke of Montevideo and Buenos Aires in equally disparaging terms, and for all its faults Asuncion did look like a city that was trying to better itself, and although it seemed that these hopes would never be achieved, the most remarkable thing about the city was that it was there at all, preserved like a fossil, untouched and undamaged, except by the Brazilian shell which had knocked the pinnacle from the President's palace. To the south, Paraguay had been laid waste and even the people had been moved, as the Allies advanced. But though the people had left the capital, not even the railway had been touched. Possibly, mused Burton, 'in their overwhelming national self-confidence, the Paraguayans expected, despite all disasters to come into their own again.'

Such a possibility was quite clearly absurd. At any rate, the Allies behaved as though it was. The Brazilians were interested in peace now, and a few weeks after the troops marched in to Asuncion, José Maria de Silva Paranhos, Minister of Foreign Affairs at Rio, arrived to organise the puppet government that would rule Paraguay now that López had been defeated. Unfortunately Paraguay was at this stage little more than a geographical expression for an area whose inhabitants had either died or disappeared and although most of the prominent exile families such as the Recaldes, the Decouds, the Machains and Felix Equsquiza had returned and there were several candidates for the role of nominal head of government Paranhos refused to do anything until the situation in the conquered country had clarified itself and there were some people for the government to govern.

The military leaders soon changed. Caxias, who fainted at a victory mass on January 5, resigned his command and left for Rio in March. He was retired a month later, with the title of Duke. Argolo and Osorio, both injured, went home, as did Ignacio, the Viconde de Inhauma.

Only Mena Barreto remained of the men who had led the Brazilians to López's capital, although Emilio Mitre, Bartolomeo's brother, was still in command of the Argentinean contingent. The Allied armies seemed content to sit in their billets at Asuncion and Luque, and wait. There was an inevitable reaction after the ferocious battles of December and no one was anxious to start the fighting again. The war had become a bore. The junior officers strutted around the capital bombastically proud of their victory, eager to quarrel with any who criticised. 'If any ridiculous assertion concerning López be received with the least reserve, they raise their voice and with open sneer, deprecate "any defence of the tyrant...." They all believe that such a campaign has never been fought; that such hardships have never been endured; that such battles have never been won....' Burton wrote.

While the army enjoyed its victory, the carpetbaggers moved in, fastening like leeches on the body of Paraguay as their fellow profiteers were doing to the ruins of the American Confederacy. Burton had seen some of them on the steamer as he came up the River Paraguay to Asuncion 'the veriest ruffians, riff-raff, ragamuffins that I had seen in South America, even at Montevideo. The feminine camp followers were clad in calico dressed, glowing shawls and satin bottines. The masculine, surly because not permitted to be in first class, slept on the quarterdeck.... expectorated to windward, and smelt rancidly of cabbage and garlic, of sausage and bad baccy.'

By April 1869 they were already well established and hotels were opening rapidly. The Hotel de La Minute offered good treatment for reasonable prices, better at any rate than the old Hotel de Francia. The Hotel de Paris was being prepared some distance away. Others, simply dirty huts, were assembled near the landing stage, calling themselves the Garibaldi, Au Petit Francais, Le Sapeur, and other names, which gave the sound, if not the appearance, of Parisian class and elegance. In between the landing stage and the arsenal booths and market stalls did a flourishing trade. Most of them were made from doors, window frames and other materials stolen from the empty houses of the abandoned city, for although the Brazilian authorities had made some attempt to stop looting and plundering, it was still going on, and the profiteers were profiting handsomely.

One Brazilian returned home after cleaning up 30,000 silver dollars in three days[86] and the general shortage of provisions offered excellent opportunities for those who were prepared to take advantage of them. Cabbages were selling for up to 10 dollars a dozen, and it cost 3s. to have shirt washed. The main trouble was that almost everything had to be shipped up the river from the Plate or Brazil, for Paraguay, once so fertile and productive, was almost a desert. The cotton fields near Luque, which had been attentively cultivated a few years before, had been allowed to run wild, and were black with neglect. Yerba maté, which had once provided half the Republic's exports, had become so scarce that it cost two dollars a pound, and tobacco was nearly as expensive. In the euphoria of victory, and the money-making that resulted, the fate of López and the final conclusion of the war tended to be forgotten. Despite all their boasting and fine words, Burton was astounded to discover that 'the Allies knew nothing about the plans or position of Marshal-President López. He might have been at his provisional capital Pirebebuy, the "light skin", east of the Piraju terminus of the railway; or at Cerro Leon, south east of the Ypacaray Lake, whilst others placed his actual camp at Azcurra, further to the north east. All these are places on the Cuchilla or ridge communicating with the main ridge, and between ten to fifty miles distance. Of the geographical features only the names were known. Some declared that the Paraguayan position could be surrounded, which is not probable; others that Azcurra is a tableland, upon which cavalry attacking from the river could not operate. None could explain what there was to prevent the enemy retiring into the mountain fastness.'

While López's whereabouts and movements were a complete mystery to the Allies, the President himself was kept well informed of the Allied activities by a number of spies who had survived the debacle at Ita Yvaté and were skilfully playing on the complacency of the conquerors. Colonel Wisner von Morgenstern, who had been such a great companion of López and Elisa Lynch, ran a small bar in Asuncion, where an attractive young lady rumoured to be his daughter (an interesting rumour, since another one accused him of being a homosexual) deftly extracted secrets from the Allies officers who were granted her favours. The Paraguayan Legion, roughly 420 exiles who had fought with the Argentinean forces during the war, was also regarded with some suspicion.

Its leaders, Colonel Iturburu and Colonel Baes, whose niece was married to Dr. Stewart, were believed to be in sympathy with López, and it was hinted that some of the men and their officers were itching for the opportunity to escape and join him. South of the capital the ridges and woods where the war had reached its bloody climax had somehow been abandoned by the victor to the vanquished. The dead Paraguayans still lay around Villeta and Ita Yvate but their living compatriots prowled among them, picking up arms and ammunition, undeterred by the ironclads, which patrolled the river to the west. In April, as if unaware that the war was over, the Paraguayans suddenly attacked the Allied outposts beyond Asuncion. A train, carrying two guns and carriages crammed with men, steamed down the line towards Luque where the soldiers did considerable damage, killed forty men, and then retreated at leisure, stopping on the way to pick up two of the wounded who had fallen from the train. The cavalry from Rio Grande do Sul, outraged at this impudence, charged the train with lances, and suffered accordingly. A few weeks later Paraguayan guerrillas attacked a Brazilian cavalry patrol and drove off all their horses.

Marshal Guilherme Xavier de Souza, who had succeeded Caxias as commander in chief, should have done something about the situation. But he was not really interested in the war for he was only a stand-in commander, waiting until he could hand over the whole dreary business to Prince Luis Gaston d'Orleans, Comte d'Eu, the 27-year-old husband of Pedro II's eldest daughter Isabel, who on March 22 had been appointed commander in chief of the Allied armies in Paraguay. The Comte had married Isabel in October 1864, and ever since the war started had been pestering his father-in-law for permission to go and fight. He was a French Bourbon, the grandson of Louis Philippe, the last king of France, but he had made his home in Brazil and when his wife came to the throne he would be her consort. He was anxious to prove his loyalty to his adopted country for he was unpopular and considered arrogant. Pedro II reluctantly overlooked his youth and inexperience and granted his wish. In the middle of April, the Comte d'Eu arrived in Asuncion to face a situation that a few months before had seemed impossible.

The Paraguayans had gone down to defeat at the end of 1868 with a heroism that has scarcely, if ever been equalled. Since then, inspired by the driving will of President López, they had made a recovery that was, if anything, even more remarkable. After fleeing from Ita Yvaté, López had made his way to Cerro Leon, where he found Luis Caminos and 1,500 men of the Asuncion garrison. These formed the nucleus of a new army which was made up of men from the hospitals at Cerro Leon, who had escaped from Allied prisoner of war camps, and others who had been released by the Allies on the assumption that the war was over. They also included survivors of the battle of Ita Yvaté, including Centurión. They owed their escape primarily to the energetic heroism of Major Patricio Escobar, who led the survivors across the estero of Ypecuá, which was more than three feet deep in places and extended for miles. Centurión and the others entered it around midday and kept walking through the night, reaching the other side at dawn. Escobar, despite being wounded in the face and both hands, ordered boats to be made of hides and wood and carried 400 wounded across and then commandeered carts that were being used to evacuate Carapeguá. They were sent to hospitals that were being constructed at Pirebebuy. Other soldiers, many of them wounded, continued to reach Azcurra in groups of 25 or 30 men, throughout January 1869.

By April it was estimated that the army had reached a total of 6,000 men, and by July may have exceeded 10,000. This remarkable revival took place in the hills north of the Azcurra escarpment, around the new capital of Piribebuy, and was due largely to the remarkable will power of López and the patriotism of the Paraguayans themselves. López continued the work of Escobar by sending parties across the Ypecuá Lake to scavenge for weapons and was even able to construct some artillery pieces. When MacMahon got to Pirebebuy on December 26 he found a small town, which normally had a population of three to four thousand people. It consisted basically of four streets intersecting at right angles, enclosing a green plaza about a quarter of a mile across.

The Vice President, Sanchez, had a house there and the rest of the cabinet and some troops were also in residence. By then the population was three times its usual size, thanks to the influx of refugees, and for most of them there was no shelter at all. Soon cholera struck the town and 'for some weeks it seemed as if the three scourges from which men pray to be delivered - war, pestilence and famine had combined to destroy this unhappy people.' Much of the remaining population of the country, reduced by more than half, was living in the cordilleras, including many women who had been organised into labour battalions the previous year. Many of the English who had been working in Asuncion were sent there when the city was evacuated and put to work in a new arsenal established at Caacupe. Other weapons and ammunition were plundered from the battlefields around the Pikysyry, the women made cartridges, and as the Paraguayans grew stronger they began raiding the Brazilians and capturing still more supplies. McMahon who had successfully reached Pirebebuy in December watched this with amazement.

He told the House of Representatives later in the year: 'On my first arrival the population had all been transferred from that portion of the country which was given up to the Allies to the interior, and then there was great distress among the people - great scarcity of food. But an order was issued for planting in all directions and in a very little while the whole country seemed to be producing and at the time I left there was a very promising harvest of maize, mandioca, and vegetables of various kinds such as they could get.'

What made this recovery all the more incredible was that none of the Paraguayans seems to have any illusions about their chances of winning the war. The memoirs of Centurión and others make it clear that they knew there was no chance even of avoiding defeat. What motivated them was a stubborn determination never to surrender. They might die – but they would never be defeated. Centurión wrote: "They marched with their spirits high and their courage serene, resolved to realise the supreme self-sacrifice of dying for the ideals of their country."

MacMahon did not remain in Paraguay to see the tragedy develop. On March 5, Elihu B. Washburne[87] the minister's brother and close friend of the new President, General U.S. Grant, became Secretary of State. It was understood this would only be a temporary post and that after a few days he would resign and go to Paris as American Ambassador to France. He resigned, as promised, on March 16 but in the meantime had issued orders recalling MacMahon from his post in Paraguay, an action taken mainly to please his brother Charles, whose conduct in Paraguay had been bitterly criticised. A few weeks later MacMahon left the country and returned to the United States. Captain Ramsay, who had begrudgingly liberated Bliss and Masterman, visited López at this time - to ask MacMahon for permission to marry his sister - and he, too, came back with glowing accounts of the transformation that the President had achieved. He was convinced that the Paraguayans could hold out indefinitely.

On July 7, the Comte d'Eu and his chief officers including Osorio, who had recovered from his wounds and returned to the front, discussed the situation at a council of war held at Piraju, just south of the escarpment. As a result of this meeting the Brazilians - and by this stage of the war all active operations were conducted by Imperial troops alone - decided to try to outflank the long Azcurra position, while a small detachment remained at Piraju to convince López that the main attack would come by way of the steep and more easily defended Azcurra pass itself. On August 1, the main army of 20,000 men under the command of the Comte d'Eu and Osorio, set off on their march round the Paraguayan left flank.

On August 11 they were within sight of Piribebuy, having met little more than token opposition. In the town itself, swollen to a population of more than 10,000, were 1,800 Paraguayan troops under the command of Colonel Pablo Caballero (not to be confused with the more famous Bernardino). At dawn the Brazilians opened fire with nearly fifty rifled canon, smashing the white walled houses, but not subduing the defenders. Major Hilario Amarilla, in charge of the town's fourteen small guns, fired until his ammunition was exhausted and then loaded them with stones, broken weapons and finally coconuts. Then even this supply rank out and the Brazilians found a vulnerable point in the defences at the south-east corner of the town.

Advancing behind the protection of wagons piled high with alfalfa grass, the infantry, under Mena Barreto, forced their way over the last defences and poured into the centre of the town. As they did so, at about 11 am, Mena Barreto fell mortally wounded, with two musket balls in his stomach, and what should have been a mopping-up operation developed into a savage massacre as the Brazilians avenged their fallen leader. One of the first to die was a sergeant known as Master Fermin, an instructor in the Boys' Battalion, a unit of children formed to take the place of men. He was being carried across the plaza when the Brazilians broke in and as he lay on his stretcher in the church, unable to move, the enraged infantry cut his throat. Even so, the last embers of defiance were not completely extinguished. From the ruins of their town and the battered trenches a group of Paraguayan women suddenly arose and began hurling stones, bottles and anything else they could find at the enemy. While these were being subdued the Brazilians found a column of refugees and supply carts trying to escape along the road to Caacupe in the north, and tore into them furiously, slaughtering anyone they could. Behind them, a cloud of dense smoke suddenly erupted from the main hospital where 300 Paraguayan wounded were trapped.

When the fighting was over and the last Paraguayan soldiers had been killed, the women and children were assembled in the square and forced to watch until the hospital was completely destroyed. Then the victors cut the throats of the handful of wounded who still remained alive. Caballero, who had been captured was then brought out and stretched between two cannon wheels. While his wife looked on he was beheaded on the orders of the Conde d'Eu. The Brazilian troops then looted the town thoroughly, capturing Paraguay's state archives and the treasury, and in one house came across Elisa Lynch's piano: while the killing went on outside, an officer sat down to play his favourite tunes, and somewhere else in the house found the second volume of Don Quixote.[88] The first was nowhere to be seen. Others, more practical perhaps, discovered some silver coins in the courtyard and in the cellars a few bottles of champagne which they used to celebrate their victory.

The day after the battle, the Comte d'Eu moved north, hoping to take Caacupe and trap López, but the Marshal saw the danger and evacuated the whole Azcurra ridge, retreating north to Campo Grande. In the opinion of Centurión, the order to retreat, given at 5pm on 13 August, marked the real beginning of what was to become Paraguay's martyrdom. López left 1,200 wounded at Caacupe under the care of Dr. Domingo Parodi (the Italian physician in whom Washburn had so unwisely confided), who had by now been made a sergeant major in the medical service. These were found by the Brazilians on August 15, together with the last, uncompleted edition of *La Estrella*, the Paraguayan army's newspaper, and 70 foreigners, many of them English engineers.

The Paraguayan retreat by this stage was virtually a rout, and the Brazilians pushed on rapidly, hoping to destroy the last remnants of

López's army in the open before he could find a new position to hold. Osorio, who had not fully recovered retired from his injuries, found the pace too hot and retired from the fray at Caacupe, being succeeded as commander of the 1st Corps by General J.L. Mena Barreto, a brother of the man who had fallen at Pirebebuy.

He had his chance for revenge at dawn on August 16 when the Paraguayan rearguard, 900 men under Bernardino Caballero, was found at Campo Grande, guarding the escape of the rest of the army. Despite being hopelessly outnumbered, Caballero fought on with his usual courage – and luck: he was captured, but managed to escape. His troops included the youngsters of the Boys' Battalion, whose ages ranged from 11 to 14, and who wore false beards to fool the Brazilians into thinking that they were men. Their age helped to account for the inaccuracy of the Paraguayan fire (their muskets were too heavy for them to lift and hold steady) and one Brazilian officer wrote after seeing their bodies lying scattered across the field: "There is no pleasure in fighting so many children."[89]

One of the few prisoners taken was Colonel Florentin Oviedo. The Brazilians asked him how many troops Caballero had commanded, Oviedo replied: "I don't know, sir. But if you want to find out the truth, go the battlefields and count the number of Paraguayan bodies, then add to that the number of prisoners you have taken and you will have the total."

Chapter 34

As though recognising that the Brazilian advance had removed the last threat of a Lopizta revival, the Allies established their puppet government in Asuncion, a triumvirate composed of Cirilo Antonio Rivarola, a former soldier who had been imprisoned by López and released by the Allies in May, and two former exiles, Carlos Loizaga and José Diaz de Bedoya. They immediately issued a statement decreeing that López was no longer to be considered Paraguayan and should be outlawed from the country.

In the cordilleras the object of this optimistic statement was still eluding his pursuers, although only just. He retreated from Caraguatay only hours before the Brazilians entered it and enemy cavalry patrols rapidly spread out far and wide to clear up the last outposts of resistance. As early as May 17 a column of renegade Paraguayans, led by a Uruguayan officer called Coronado, had captured Ibicuí, where López had his iron foundry. The Paraguayan commander, Captain Julian Insfran, was executed and only the protests of his Paraguayan soldiers prevented Coronado from killing the other prisoners. On 18 August a column of Brazilians neared the River Manduvira, where the last ships of the Paraguayan navy had taken refuge. But the Parguayans heard that they were coming and set the ships on fire. The troopers, under General Camara, arrived too late to save them and several Brazilians were killed when one of the magazines exploded in a final flourish of defiance. The ships were the *Rio Apa, Anhambay, Salto, Guaira, Ypora, Paraná*, and *Pirabebe*, all of which had done gallant and effective service during the war.

When the war turned against them in 1869, the Paraguayans dragged their fleet up a tiny river to this place, Vapor Cué, the place of the steam. When the Brazilian army broke through they sent a regiment of cavalry to capture the ships, but the Paraguayans managed to scuttle them before they arrived. Some of them were raised in the 1930s and the site is now a national monument.

At Caraguatay, however, the Allied pursuit slackened. The army was hindered by supply problems and remained in the town for several weeks. López also halted, at San Estanislao, sixty miles to the north, which he reached on August 25. There he unearthed another conspiracy and stayed for nearly three weeks while it was investigated. A man and a woman had been arrested, and although the man escaped the woman said under torture that they were both spies and had arranged with a young ensign called Aquino to assassinate López. Aquino was arrested and admitted with some pride that he was indeed conspiring to kill the President. When López asked him why he explained: "I wanted to kill you for various reasons. We have already lost our country and if we have followed you this far you must understand that it is only to follow you in person. And there is no doubt that every day you become more and more of a tyrant." López said that unfortunately he had never had the opportunity to carry out his wish. Aquino shrugged and replied that one day someone would have better luck. In the end about eighty people were seized, including Colonel Mongelós and Major Riveros, commander and deputy commander of the Government Escort, who were shot for not discovering the plot.

The retreat continued on September 12 and then halted again at Igatimy for six days while further enquiries were made. As a result another 60 people were shot, including Aquino. This time suspicion focused on Venancio López, who had been brought all the way as a prisoner. Hilario Marcó, the former police chief who had handled the executions of December 21 with such exemplary efficiency, was supposed to be guarding him, but the two men were old friends from before the war and during the march Venancio was given more and more liberty. On 15 October, during celebrations to mark the anniversary of López's accession to the presidency, a woman from Asuncion innocently told the President that she had seen his younger brother a few days before. López listened politely and then called Marcó and demanded to know why Venancio had been allowed out in public when he should have been in prison. Marcó could not provide a satisfactory answer and was arrested. Venancio was interrogated by Luis Caminos, Resquín and Sanchez and admitted that there had been a plot. He and Marcó had planned to poison López and then escape in two canoes hidden on the River Curuguatay.

Marcó was duly tortured and shot (as was his wife) but not before he had named more conspirators, including Dona Juana López, the President's mother. His sisters, Rafaela and Innocencia were also implicated.

For Centurión, the main concern was not the conspiracy but his own health. He was confined to his bed with fever and was covered with boils, which were only made bearable by means of a special unction prepared by his batman. He forgot his miseries one day when he heard a voice cry out his name and say that the Marshal wanted to see him. Centurión dressed and went to headquarters where López and Mrs Lynch were waiting for him. The latter smiled at him reassuringly and then a servant came in carrying a tray bearing three glasses of cognac. López and Mrs Lynch took one each and López told Centurión to take the other. When he had done so, López raised his glass in salute and said: "To the health of *Colonel* Centurión!" Centurión was later to recall this sudden and unexpected promotion as one of the highlights of his career. At one stroke all the doubts and uncertainties that he had suffered for so long had been removed. He could now regard himself as one of the élite, the inner circle: he was a success.

After this the retreat continued, and López marched steadily north into the brooding forests and shadowy mists of legend. If the last few years had been a steadily worsening nightmare, the next months became a surrealist fantasy in which the army marched not to escape but simply in search of a suitable place to die. Every step carried them away from the hills and orange groves and white-walled *quintas* that represented home and into the thickening green fastness that stretched away from Paraguay into the Matto Grosso and endlessly on to the rain forests of the Amazon.

At first there were several thousand people, many of them women, divided into the *residentas,* the families who were regarded as loyal to López, and the *destinadas,* who were suspected in some way. Among the latter was Dorothée de Lasserre.

The Frenchwoman had been arrested in January 1869, shortly after de Cuberville had brought her the unwelcome news that López had escaped from Lomas Valentinas and had made his way to the cordillera. He advised Dorothée and her mother to hide somewhere for a few days, but Dorothée believed in obeying the law and at 2pm on January 2 soldiers came to her home and took her to the command post in Luque. She and her mother were forced to join a column of prisoners and refugees making their way inland towards the Azcurra escarpment and López. At first they were reasonably placed – they had horses, for one thing – but these were later taken from them and they had to proceed on foot in pouring rain, along a road that was littered with the bodies of dead animals and people.

The *destinadas* took a different route from the main army, reaching Pirebebuy on 11 January. Mme Lasserre was then told that she was to go to a place called Yhú, further north. How do we get there, she asked? You walk, was the answer. She pointed out that the government had taken her own horses and left her with nothing and eventually she managed to secure not only horses but a cart as well. She and her mother reached Yhú on 21 March and stayed there five months. They were given some land to farm and some seed to sow, but they still went hungry and Dorothée's misery was compounded when her servant finally left her (she could not endure life without potatoes).

In September they set off again, and during the march Dorothée became friendly with Mrs Leite-Pereira, the widow of the Portuguese ambassador, who had been shot in December 1868. They reached Igatimi late in the month and then, on 23 October resumed their march, a column of more than 2,000 wretched, starving, miserable people. It was, Mme Lasserre recalled, pouring with rain, they had no food and no yerba maté. Then Mrs Leite-Pereira's horse died and Dorothée pointed out that in France it was quite acceptable to eat horses. The animal was duly cut up and cooked and although Dorothée's mother and Mrs Leite-Pereira refused to eat the meat, Dorothée closed her eyes and tucked in, as did many others. By nightfall only the skin and hooves remained.

The hunger returned during the next few days, however, and Dorothée began to have fantasies about being rescued by the Brazilians, who brought with them wagons of food and salt, white horses for the young and coaches for the old. But the fantasies, like the Brazilians, refused to materialise. Instead of meat and salt the dwindling column lived off sour oranges, snakes and dogs.

López and the main column, including what was left of the army, reached Igatimi on 30 October. Despite his other preoccupations he had established a workshop there for the repair of damaged weapons – another example of his extraordinary willpower and foresight – and the army stayed there while its equipment was overhauled. López also decided to clear up the conspiracy mystery once and for all by putting his mother on trial. A group of senior officers, including Centurión, was assembled and López asked what they thought he should do. Sanchez, the vice president, said that whatever López decided would be well done and most of the others said it would be worthy for a son to pardon his own mother of a crime. Aveiro said she should be made to answer the charges brought against her. Then Father Maiz quoted the Bible in support of clemency and asked Centurión what he felt. Centurión, terrified of saying the wrong thing, despite his recent promotion, nevertheless agreed with Maiz. López then surprised them all by saying that he sided with Aveiro. He owed it to the memory of those who had died so heroically to press the charges. The retreat resumed, this time with López's mother quite definitely under arrest.

As the weeks, passed the column dwindled. There was no food, and the weather grew hotter. In their tens and later their hundreds, the marchers collapsed beside the road to be found later by the Brazilians, while around them lay more mementoes of calamity; broken carts, rusting guns, dead and dying animals. By the end of the year the condition of the army was worse than ever and López seems to have been approaching complete despair. Even the smallest incidents were enough to enrage him, as an officer called Major Bernal found out when he inadvertently allowed the *polenta* to be burnt. López had him arrested and shouted at him: "Even the *polenta* turns out badly, which shows what a shameless person you are!" Knowing what was likely to happen, Bernal suddenly jumped on a horse and escaped. A few days later Centurión found himself in trouble. Two criminals, one of them a priest, managed to escape from the headquarters because the half-starving guard fell asleep in the middle of the night. Resquín made sure that Centurión was blamed and he was hauled off to López who was furious and shouted out that Centurión was to be taken away and shot. At this point, the terrified young man saw a shape by the door. Although he could not recognise her he knew that it must be Mrs Lynch, who said to López, softly, as a supplicant: " Señor, let him go…" And so he was released.

Others were not so lucky. On 11 December Centurión asked Aveiro what he should do with the women prisoners. Aveiro sent him to López, who took a piece of paper and wrote down some names. They included the sisters of the late General Barrios and Pancha Garmendia. The note said that they were to be executed. The sentence was carried out on 11 December and they were probably lanced to death because the soldiers were short of ammunition.

Somewhere along the way in these last months, the gathering legend says, seven high-wheeled carts left the straggling column and turned into the woods. They contained the Paraguayan national treasure, several million pounds worth of gold, silver and jewels. It was impossible to haul this immense amount of plunder any further, and it could not be left for the Brazilians. One cart was pushed into a river and swallowed up in the mud. The others were driven on further into a huge swamp, and there the contents were removed and buried. Another story says that the soldiers who buried the treasure were shot immediately afterwards and their bodies hurled on top of the money boxes, so that they would not be able to reveal the location of the haul. A secondary motive, according to Alexander K. MacDonald, a settler who arrived in Paraguay twenty years later, was that their ghosts would scare off the curious, and the peasants he knew and who told him the stories of the war and its aftermath believed this legend so firmly that they still made a long detour rather than go anywhere near the spot where the treasure was reputed to be buried. The last person to know the precise location was possibly Elisa Lynch. Years after the war was over she returned to Paraguay, but was not allowed to stay. Furious, she is said to have torn up the map that could have led her to the spot. Since then there have been several attempts to find the treasure, but no one has succeeded: if it existed then, it exists today.

Miguel Faria, the twelve-year-old who had been so puzzled by the corpses on the bridge over the Avay, took part in this retreat and years later described his experiences to MacDonald. 'If a man fell from exhaustion he was flogged,' he said. 'If this treatment did not have the desired effect the poor beggar was thrust through and left to die like a dog. Passing the low trackless *esteros* they hopped from tussock to tussock to avoid the potholes of water. Men marched on until they dropped. Some would be seen apparently sitting down with the rifle still over their shoulders, and a glance at their eyes showed that they were stone dead; others lay back against tussocks as though merely resting for a moment, so highly strung with fear of being put to the sword by their own officers they remained erect to the last gasp.' The roads by which the army marched were, like all the roads in Paraguay, little more than tracks through the jungle.

MacDonald knew these *picadas* well. In the north they were less marshy than those which the army had found in the Chaco and on the retreat to the Pikysyry, but the denseness of the forest provided its own hazards: 'Masses of foliage ferns and luxuriant creepers made a perfect screen on either side. Huge tree ferns peeped out here and there and detours were rendered necessary now and then to avoid the many trunks of fallen trees. The larger branches, linked together, overhead, by vines innumerable formed a natural archway, impenetrable to the scorching rays of tropic sunshine. A rough wooden cross by the roadside indicated the last resting place of some poor beggar...'

There were many 'poor beggars' who found their last resting place along the road that López's army took. Starvation was a continual threat, far more real than the pursuing Brazilians and most of the time Faria lived on palm nuts, the starch from the pith of the palm trees, and oranges that looked inviting but tasted as bitter as lemons. He never ate horse or dog meat, because there was none. He was once given some mule flesh and on another occasion some of the soldiers caught a donkey, but the meal that he remembered best consisted of two cats. MacDonald recorded: 'He scalded them with hot water, scraped their hair off and gave them a bit of a boil - in their skins. He says that cat's flesh is delicious.'

As an artilleryman, Faria probably suffered more than the infantry. The bullocks had been eaten or had died and it was left to the famished gunners themselves to haul the guns through the forest. Long lines of men pulled on slippery ropes all day long through mud and across rivers, encouraged by a mounted officer who 'would gallop up one side and down the other, slapping every man on the back with the flat of his sword.'

When the retreat began López had intended to shepherd every Paraguayan who remained alive away from the Allies and into the northern woods, leaving the enemy nothing but empty fields and deserted villages. But despite all his efforts the long column dwindled every day. Some died, and others were killed and others simply waited until the army had passed on and then singly, in families or in small groups, left López to his dreams and went back to their homes and the mercy of the conquerors. The pathetic sight of these refugees coming into Asuncion almost daily carrying with them all that they possessed soon became a commonplace, a nuisance. Many of them were left to starve, and MacMahon maintained: 'I was told by a foreign resident of Asuncion that they were brought in laden with packs and various things, paraded around the streets, sometimes two or three days, to be exhibited almost entirely naked and no provision being made for clothing them, or providing for their comfort or necessity; that they were treated with insult and abuse and turned loose upon the streets, subjected to the caprices of the brutalised soldiers of Brazil. He said that formerly he thought it a piece of barbarity on the part of López to drive this population back within his own lines but now, since his residence in Asuncion, he was satisfied that López acted wisely and humanely in so doing, as it preserved them from the brutal indifference of the Allied authorities and the more brutal lusts of their soldiery.'

The Allies were certainly indifferent to the fate of the people they claimed to be liberating from a monstrous dictatorship and this was partly due to impatience. The new president of Argentina, Domingo Faustino Sarmiento, wrote to his ambassador in Washington: 'The war is finished although that brute still has twenty pieces of artillery and two thousand dogs which will have to die beneath the hooves of our horses. These people do not even move one to compassion. A pack of wolves.'[90]

By the end of the year López had reached a place called Arroyo Guazú and there he finally put his mother in trial. It lasted for nine days, but came to no conclusion. She was again imprisoned. Shortly afterwards, two of the English engineers were released. One was called Hunter and Centurión names the other as Nervit, possibly a misspelling of Nesbitt, the man who had succeeded Mr Whytehead in charge of the Asuncion arsenal. Their release had tragic consequences. While trying to make their way back to Asuncion they were attacked, robbed and murdered. It is possible that a fellow victim was a son of Alonzo Taylor.

The rain continued to pour down throughout most of January 1870. The main army reached Zanja Pypucú on the seventeenth and waited for the wagons to catch them up. Centurión took the opportunity to eat a delicious fruit called *araticú*, which he devoured with relish: he had never tasted anything so rich and delicious, he recalled. That night he collapsed with stomach pains and dysentery. The fruit was poisonous.

For Dorothée Duprat de Lasserre and her mother, the long march was almost over. The guards no longer urged the survivors forward, perhaps because there was nowhere left for them to go (they were right by the old border with Brazil) and they seemed content to sit and wait, although it was hard to tell whether they were waiting for orders, food or for the Brazilians to arrive.

For Dorothée and her mother the first priority was food. A mule was killed and Dorothée persuaded her mother to taste some soup she had made with the bones. On 28 November some Indians came to the camp with food, which the prisoners exchanged for clothes. On 2 December there was a sensation when it transpired that three well-known families had disappeared. They had, it seemed, escaped, perhaps with the help of the Indians. A few nights later 200 hundred girls escaped from the camp and Dorothée reasoned that the Brazilians must be very close. She wanted to try to follow them, but her mother was too tired, hungry and exhausted to join her. Dorothée could do what she like, she said, but she was staying in the camp.

By this time the guards were too exhausted and famished to make any real attempt to keep the prisoners confined and one night Dorothée, with Mrs Leite-Pereira and a woman called Joana left the camp, with a friendly Indian to guide them. But after a few hours he said he could not find the Brazilians and advised them to return to camp. An attempt to escape a few days later also ended in disappointment.

On 24 December a woman called Josefa Rojas came to tell them that the Brazilians had arrived and were waiting for them. Dorothée thought it was probably a trap set by López, but others confirmed the story. Dorothée told her mother that it was time for them to go. The old woman was still fearful but at last she agreed and together with other prisoners they left the security that the camp had come to represent and walked along the path that was supposed to lead them to the Brazilians. Soon they saw soldiers ahead, coming towards them, and realised from their uniforms that they were indeed Brazilians, who welcomed them and took them back to their camp. They were given meat, salt and flour, luxuries that they had not enjoyed for months.

Throughout her ordeal, Dorothée had been sustained by the thought that one day her family would be reunited. She suddenly realised that it was Christmas Eve – what a gift that would be, to be once again with Narcisse, her brother and her father. But the liberators could not bring her the one present that she really desired. Instead, they told her that her brother had been shot at San Fernando on 8 August and her husband and father on 22 August. The blow was so great, that Dorothée said she could still feel it as she sat at her desk, writing her memoirs a year later.

For the main army, the long retreat was also nearing an end. On February 8, 1870, the Paraguayans reached the river Aquidaban-Niqui, a tributary of the River Aquidaban, thirty miles from the present day Brazilian border. There the army found a circus of gigantic rocks, a natural amphitheatre in the foothills of the Amambay Mountains. It was known as Cerro Cora and has been called 'one of the most wildly beautiful scenic attractions in Paraguay'.[91] Centurión recalled it as a large open space, with woods to the west and, to the south, some mountains that rose sharply out of the forest. It was there that the remnants of the exodus camped, López establishing his headquarters in the centre where some shrubs afforded a little shade. The wagons and carts were grouped together nearby.

For the survivors, the last few months had been the worst of the whole retreat. By the end of the march, Centurión recalled, the soldiers received only one meal a day and one cow had to serve 500 people. They found that the hide, if put in a stewpot over a fire for a few hours, softened and became quite palatable. But because the soldiers seldom had time to do this, they tried to turn the hide into a paste, which was so hard that no stomach could digest it. They added to this a sort of bread made from roots and fruits gathered from the woods, providing "a food which, instead of improving the health of the troops, contributed marvellously to its annihilation because of the various illnesses that it caused."[92]

Not all of the survivors even reached Cerro Cora. The army may still have totalled 5,000 men in December 1969, but by March it had broken into smaller groups, some still trying to hold positions that López regarded as strategically important, others scattered here and there, moving north, but as separate units, because it was easier to survive and forage for food in small groups than as a united, cohesive army.

Venancio López was one of those who did not reach Cerro Cora. Early in February, López sent Caballero and a party off to look for food and near the Chiriguelo he found Escobar preparing a report to López about the death of his brother. Caballero read it and suggested that it might be better to omit some of the details. On 13 February an adjutant came to Cerro Cora to present the official report - and then told López what had happened. Venancio, who was hopelessly compromised by his involvement in plots against his brother, had collapsed by the roadside, unable or unwilling to walk any further. An officer beat him with his sword in an effort to make him rise. Escobar was told and hurried to the scene, only to find Venancio dead of the wounds he had received. Of the officer who had inflicted them there was no sign – realising what he had done he had fled immediately afterwards. Escobar buried the body by the road and continued the retreat.

By the time the army reached Cerro Cora fewer than 500 men remained. The last muster sheet showed a total of 470 men, all suffering terribly from starvation and the ordeal of the march. The whole group, including women and children, numbered about 1,000 people. None of them had any hope of winning the war, or even of surviving it, and one cannot help wondering – not for the first time – what compelled the Paraguayans to carry on fighting when defeat was inevitable. To Centurión the answer lay in the intense patriotism that they all felt and a stubborn refusal to surrender, least of all to the inevitable. Recalling the scene decades later, Centurión wrote that Cerro Cora was a holy shrine. In reaching it at all, the Paraguayans had secured a moral triumph that lifted them above their enemies. And he insisted that they had not been beaten – just exterminated.

López recognised better than anyone that Cerro Cora represented the end of the retreat. All they could do now was wait and, as if in response to a cue, on 12 February General Camarra left the port of Concepcion on the River Paraguay, with a fresh army. His mission was to corner López and end the war.

For three weeks they went through the routine of camp life, gathering fruit from the woods around, hunting game and fishing. For López and Elisa Lynch these last days were a period of false calm, a stillness that preceded a final storm. They would rise some time after nine, and take a leisurely breakfast. López would attend to the affairs of state that now were meaningless, and then they would walk together in the forests, looking back on the seventeen years that had spent together. Elisa, who could not think of life without him, wanted him to try even now to escape into the Chaco and then to Bolivia. But López, who could not think of life without Paraguay, refused. It seems clear that he knew exactly what lay in store for him. He had already transferred some of his property to Elisa, presumably because he knew that he would not survive the war and wanted to make sure that she was provided for. There was nothing else to do after that but wait for the Brazilians to arrive.

To the south, the Brazilians searched for the trail. Finally scouts and deserters told General Camara where López had taken refuge. A traitor called Colonel Silvestre Carmona told Camarra that he knew a secret route that would enable them to approach the Paraguayan camp unseen.

At Cerro Cora the atmosphere was one of expectancy. There remained only the last formalities. On February 27 López and Mrs. Lynch invited the officers to dine with. Among those present, one can assume, would have been Resquín, Caminos, Aveiro, Angel Moreno the artilleryman, Juan Centurión, perhaps Sanchez and Maiz as well. It was a starlit night and, in their light and those of the campfires that surrounded them, López climbed on to a rock and spoke. He said how upset he had been to hear rumours that he was planning to flee through the Chaco to Bolivia. It was a lie. He made it clear that he intended to stay with those who had followed him so loyally and courageously.

"If you have followed me until this moment, it is because you knew that I, your leader, would fall with the last of you, on the final battlefield. Remember that the victor is the one who dies for a noble cause, not the one who remains alive on the scene of the fight. The generation that will come out of this disaster will have in its mind the memory of this defeat and in its blood, like venom, a hatred for the victor. But there will be other generations that will do us justice by applauding the greatness of our sacrifice. I will be more derided than you. I will be placed outside the laws of God and man, I will be buried beneath the weight of mountains of ignominy. But my day will come, too, and I will rise from the abyss of slander and grow in the eyes of posterity until I take my rightful place in history."[93]

He spoke about the obligations of patriotism and even managed to make a few jokes about the enemy and then, as his audience relaxed and laughed, thinking of the good times and forgetting the bad, with a flourish typical of him, he announced that a medal was to be awarded to all those who had reached Cerro Cora with him. It bore the inscription: *Vencio penurias y fatigas. Campaña de Amambay.* (He overcame penury and fatigue: the Amambay Campaign). It was by his own dominant personality and such imaginative gestures that López had enabled

Paraguay to survive for so long and Centurión recalled that the soldiers' hearts were lifted by the speech and the medal and they all vowed never to desert the man who had promised to stay with them.

On March 1 the camp rose early and saluted the flag flapping in the hot northern breeze. López called a conference of his senior officers, including Aveiro and Centurión and asked if they wished to seek refuge in the hills or stand and fight where they were. Aveiro spoke for the majority when he said that to abandon the field now would only mean postponing for a few days the fate that they all expected. López said: "Very well, we'll fight until we are all dead."

Most of the soldiers were at the Aquidaban under Colonel Moreno. He commanded a hundred troopers and four guns in the centre, another hundred infantry on the left, while Colonel Juan de la Cruz Avail with eighty lancers was on the rights. In the woods beyond were ninety men of the vanguard. At 6am one of these men came running back through the trees, shouting that the Brazilians had attacked and had already overrun the vanguard.

Moreno immediately sent warning to López, and drew up his men to meet the attack. At the same time another report came in to say that the enemy were advancing through the wood of Chiriguelo on the other side of the camp. López sent an officer called Solis to find out what was happening there, but he was killed before he could return, and López sent Centurión in his place. Accompanied by an adjutant called Riveros, Centurión galloped towards the River Aquidaban. When they reached it they found that the enemy had already crossed and killed most of the defenders, They raced back to the camp and told López, who calmly gave the order: "To arms, everyone."[94]

Five minutes later Centurión saw a column of enemy cavalry moving slowly towards the camp. He was mounted on a good horse and decided that the Paraguayans only chance lay in a hand to hand battle: most of his men were armed only with sabres and lances, while the Brazilians had carbines. Followed by about 100 men, Centurión charged into the attack, but the Brazilians simply withdrew and began firing. An officer told Centurión that his horse had been wounded. He looked down and said that the horse did not seem to feel the wound. At that moment he was struck on the side of the face by a bullet that knocked out all his teeth and tore open a wound that ran from the upper left of his face to the lower right: the same bullet then killed his horse. Covered in blood, his face horribly disfigured, Centurión staggered to his feet, not knowing where he was going or what was happening. Then he heard a woman's voice calling him. He crawled into her hut and watched as the Brazilians ran past, chasing three Paraguayan soldiers who were bayoneted to death.

Under the weight of the Brazilians' two-pronged attack the defenders were overwhelmed, and in the centre of the camp pandemonium ensued. López tried to persuade Mrs. Lynch to escape in her carriage with their three youngest children. At length she gave in and was pushed inside. As the carriage rumbled slowly away, with fifteen-year-old Panchito acting as escort, the Brazilian cavalry charged into the clearing.

It had taken only fifteen minutes to overwhelm the handful of soldiers and as the cavalry swept into the panic-stricken refugees, hacking and chopping with their sabres, until they noticed López himself, a stout, black-bearded man dressed in a blue uniform, mounted on a white horse. The troops had been offered a prize of £100 for killing him, and a great shout of triumph went up: "*E o López!* It's López! *E o López!*" They swarmed around him exultantly, slashing and stabbing, while the handful of Paraguayans still capable of fighting tried to defend him. Then a corporal named José Francisco Lacerda and known as Chico Diablo, managed to stab López in the stomach with his lance. Another soldier cut the Marshal's head open with his sabre. Two Paraguayan officers arrived, a Captain Francisco Arguello and a Lieutenant Chamorro. "Kill these devils of *macacos*!" shouted López, and the two men managed to fight off the enemy before themselves being killed.

Then Aveiro appeared with a horse, which López managed to mount. Aveiro led him away from the fighting to the edge of the Aquidaban-Niqui, but by then López was so weakened by his wounds and loss of blood that he fell from the horse and Aveiro was unable to raise him. Two more Paraguayan officers arrived and with the assistance of one of them, named Ignacio Ibarra, Aveiro helped López struggle across the stream. The bank on the other side was so steep, however, that López could not climb it. He sent the two officers off to see if there was another way. López was left alone and held on to the roots of a palm tree with one hand, his body half covered by water.

The Brazilians had lost him in the woods and while he lay there a Paraguayan subaltern named Victoriano Silva appeared and offered to help. López, conscious that he was dying, sent him away, and gave him his riding whip as a last memento. A few seconds later the Brazilians found him. Silva saw the troopers ride up and open fire, but General Camara was nearby and he galloped up to the scene furiously and told them to stop. He shouted across the river to López: "Mariscal rindase, que le garante la vida!" (Marshall, give yourself up, your life will be spared!) Somehow the dying President crawled up to his knees.

In a gesture of magnificent defiance he drew his sword and hurled it at the enemy shouting as he did so his dying words: "Muero con mi patria!" (I die with my country!)" A cavalryman from Rio Grande, named Joao Soares, splashed his way across the river and finished him off with a shot in the back from his Spencer carbine.

The killing however had not quite finished. While the Brazilian cavalry were hunting for López, others were chasing the coach containing Elisa Lynch and her children. After a short pursuit they finally overhauled it and an officer called on the occupants to surrender. Wheeling round, Panchito López kicked his horse and shouted: "A Paraguayan officer does not surrender!" While his mother screamed at him to stop, he charged into the cavalrymen and was impaled on the lance of a Brazilian trooper. Elisa ran from the coach and took him in her arms, but he was already dead. After a few minutes the Brazilians escorted the grieving mother back to the coach, where her other children were waiting, and laid Panchito's body on the back of the coach. Then Mrs. Lynch was taken back to the clearing where she had last seen her lover. Camara was waiting and told her: "The Marshal refused to surrender. He is dead." Unwilling to show her emotion, Mrs. Lynch said: "Take me to the place."

She was led to the river's edge. Before her lay the body of her lover, the man whom she had followed with unswerving devotion for seventeen years: it had been slung across two poles, carried back across the river and them dumped in the mud for the entertainment of the troops. Somebody had taken the President's watch which was inscribed with the Paraguayan motto 'Paz y Justicia' and a ring with the more appropriate slogan Vencer o Morir (Conquer or Die), the slogan which López's soldiers had adopted with such tragic literalness. Souvenir hunters had stripped his body, and some had pulled hair from his head as a token of their victory. One officer, according to one version, sat down beside the fallen Paraguayan and sliced off an ear, holding it triumphantly aloft with the cry: 'I promised to take it home!'

But by the time Mrs. Lynch arrived, the souvenir hunters had gone and López's body lay alone. All around the Brazilian soldiers were celebrating his death, which they recognised as meaning the end of the war. Mrs. Lynch looked at the dancing, singing, almost hysterical soldiers and, turning to Major Floriano Vieira Peixota, later a president of Brazil, said: "And is this the civilisation you have brought us with your guns?"

After the failure of the Paraguayan invasion of Uruguay, the war switched to Paraguay itself, and ranged from Humaitá in the south to Cerro Cora in the far north. The shaded areas show the disputed border lands annexed by Brazil and Argentina after their victory.

Chapter 35

When the exultant soldiers had gone, with the assistance of her friend Isidora Diaz, Elisa Lynch dug a grave for her lover on the banks of the river where he fell, and buried him beside Panchito, their son. Many of López's closest supporters died with him during the fifteen minutes of savage fighting that had ended the war, among them Luis Caminos and Sanchez, who was well into his eighties.

Centurión survived. After the Brazilians had gone he left the hut where he had taken refuge and hid in some shrubs where he was later found by the Brazilians and made prisoner. Resquín, Aveiro, Maiz, José Falcón, Moreno and others were captured on March 1, and Caballero, who was still away on his hunting expedition when the battle took place, surrendered soon afterwards. Patricio Escobar also missed the fighting at Cerro Cora, and surrendered a few days later. After their capture, according to Maiz, the prisoners were ordered to sign a paper drawn up by José Falcon, which thanked the Comte d'Eu for freeing them from the tyrant. Then the remaining soldiers were forced to begin their journey south by marching across his grave. In Rosario and Concepcion, ports on the River Paraguay which the Brazilians had already occupied, the news of the end of the war was received with understandable enthusiasm by the Brazilian troops, and many of the Paraguayan civilians seem to have shared their joy, although their motives were no doubt a good deal different. For the soldiers who had been with López at his death, there was no happiness. As they trailed behind the victors, the Brazilian Lieutenant Dianisio Cerqueira noticed tears streaming down their faces as, almost for the first time, they realised that the war had done to the country they loved, and how useless their devotion and heroism had ultimately proved to be.[95] It was as though the President's death had suddenly broken a spell and enabled them to see clearly for the first time. Many of the women, who had been dragged along in the army's wake, turned on Elisa Lynch as soon as López was dead, and she had to ask for protection from the Brazilians who had killed him.

She was treated with the greatest courtesy and Major Ernesto Augusto da Cunha Mattos, who had been taken prisoner at the second battle of Tuyuti and freed after the victory at Ita Yvaté, enabling him to return to the army in time to take part in the last campaign, offered to protect her.[96] He remembered that while he was a prisoner Mrs. Lynch had tried to alleviate his sufferings by offering him sweets and rum.

The hatred was waiting for her in Asuncion, where 90 women signed a petition that was forwarded to Rio demanding that she be forced to surrender the money that she had extorted over the years. Paranhos replied that the assumption that Mrs. Lynch had great wealth was not borne out by the inventory made of her possessions when she was captured...."The personal effects of the inventory are not of great value and certainly represent much less than what Mrs. Lynch must legitimately have acquired in Paraguay."

Exactly what she had acquired is a mystery. She had been given, or had bought, extensive estates in the Chaco and in eastern Paraguay, but these were confiscated after the war. Washburn claimed that the money she had left at the American Legation was later buried near San Fernando, and she also sent a considerable amount of money out of the country, mainly in 1868, when several large cases were sent to France on the warship *Decidée*. More money was sent abroad through Dr. Stewart and through MacMahon as well. Mrs. Lynch claimed that she had asked Stewart to send money to his brother in Scotland, under his own name, but on the understanding that she would be able to claim it if necessary. Whatever she managed to salt away she looked up as insurance rather than a primary objective. Elisa Lynch was an intimidating woman, who probably earned the hatred so many felt for her, but she had loved López, and she loved Paraguay in her fashion, and it was only when the war was clearly lost that she began to prepare for the day when she might be forced to return to Europe. That day had come.

She left Asuncion and Paraguay and returned to Paris where she bought a house on the Rue de Rivoli. She was 36, too old to resume the career that she had abandoned to go to Paraguay, and too full of memories to settle down. Too much had happened in the intervening years and from then on Elisa Lynch was a wanderer.

In 1871 she crossed paths with Dr. Stewart again, when she brought a legal action to get the money she had given him restored to her. She won the case, but Stewart – by now posing as a bitter enemy of López and one of his chief victims – declared himself bankrupt and she never received the money. In 1873 - 74 Cunninghame Graham saw her several times in London, where she had a house near Hyde Park Gate. He wrote: "She was then apparently about 40 years of age. Of middle height, well made, beginning to put on a little flesh, with her abundant fair hair just flecked with grey. In her well made Parisian clothes she looked more French than English, and had no touch of that untidiness that so often marks the Irishwoman. She was still distinguished looking. Her face was oval and her lips a little full, her eyes were large and grey if I remember rightly her appearance did not seem that of one who had looked death so often in the face, lived for so long in the circumstances so strange and terrifying, buried her lover and her son with her own hands, and lived to tell the tale."

She made one attempt to return to Paraguay, in 1875, but when the women of the capital heard that she had arrived they sent a petition to the President urging him to send her away and he agreed. After only a few hours Elisa Lynch reboarded the steamer and left her adopted country for ever. On the return journey, her youngest son Leopoldo died. Later in life she went on a three-year pilgrimage to Jerusalem, and then in 1886 she died in Paris and was buried in Pere Lachaise Cemetery. Cunninghame Graham says she died in poverty, but since he hated both her and López that was probably wishful thinking. Later her ashes were returned to Asuncion.

Elisa's tomb in La Recoleta

Washburn died three years later, in 1889. His activities in Paraguay had been so extraordinary that on March 19, 1869, the House of Representatives decided to investigate the whole business, including the actions of the United States naval authorities in the area. The hearings began on March 30, with Washburn as the first witness and concluded in November. Out of the 314 page report that resulted nobody emerged unscathed. The majority censured the naval men and maintained that the arrest of Bliss and Masterman was an insult to the flag. The minority blamed Washburn, saying that his acceptance of their arrests could not be justified by any consideration of personal safety and that he should not have accepted his passports without first insisting that Bliss and Masterman be granted theirs as well. On the other hand it referred to both men as being 'adventurers and of doubtful reputation' and questioned the wisdom of granting them custody in the first place.

The two men in question, who loathed each other intensely (Bliss reminded Masterman of Uriah Heap), gave evidence on Washburn's behalf, and then Masterman returned to England where he wrote his memoirs. Bliss returned to the United States where he died in 1885. Washburn completed the history of Paraguay he had begun in Asuncion and which included his version of the events that had taken place. He wrote a few books and articles, invented a machine called a typograph, but was never offered another diplomatic post.

Colonel Thompson returned safely to England and he too wrote a book about his war experiences. But within a few years the lure of the country he had served so well proved too strong and he returned to Paraguay and took up a position on the railways he had helped to build. He died in 1875, aged only 37. Valpy and Burrell, who were freed in the cordilleras, also survived. Valpy also briefly returned to Paraguay some years later and in 1888 was involved in negotiations to reduce interest payments on a Paraguayan debt with the Baring bank. Taylor went to Buenos Aires, where he slowly recovered from the ill treatment he had received during the last months of the war. The luckiest of all the English survivors was probably Dr. Skinner. He had escaped from Humaitá with Colonel Alén and marched all the way to Cerro Cora on the last retreat. On June 20, 1870, safe in Buenos Aires, he wrote to Washburn: 'I was taken prisoner on March 1, 1870, when López was killed and was with him ten minutes before his death and very thin and weak I was. The Brazilians set me free as the Comte d'Eu ascertained that I was one of the monster's victims and not one of his accomplices.

'Thank God, now that the war is over and all the dreadful atrocities of the unparalleled brute López cannot fail to be brought to light your veracity and honour must be thoroughly established and all your conduct vindicated. I was very much grieved at hearing them doubted in some papers and attempts made to gloss over, or rather to deny the fact of his being the very worst devil that ever polluted the earth. Who but he ever flogged his own mother and sisters and killed his brothers, one after a mock trial and the other by starvation and flogging with a doubled lasso, a lance thrust finishing the scene of torture when the victim could no longer stand? Who else exterminated a whole people by starvation, whilst he and his bastards passed a life of comfort, feasting, nay drinking choice wines *ad libitum* surrounded by every comfort attainable in a retreat from a pursuing army? More still, at the time of his death he had stores sufficient to have saved numbers, amongst them several cart loads of salt, which his victims and followers had not tasted for months. I myself felt the want of it more than any of the privations, much more so than short rations....'

Despite his hatred for López, Skinner was another survivor who later returned to Paraguay. In December 1871 he was made Director of the Military Hospital, with the rank of colonel, but the following year died after accidentally falling from his horse.

Dr. Fox, who had been arrested with Masterman and Dr. Rhind in 1866, also lived. He was allowed to leave on a British gunboat in 1868, seriously ill, but Rhind died in Paraguay a year after his release. As we have seen, Dr. Stewart returned to Scotland, but soon after his legal brush with Mrs. Lynch, went back to Paraguay where he had large estates and settled in a villa outside Asuncion. He became head of the Paraguayan medical services and died in 1916, at the age of 86.

Of the Paraguayans, Resquín, Maiz, Aveiro, Caballero and the other leading López supporters had to be protected from the vengeance of the provisional government, but were later released. Maiz went through the ordeal of a mock execution and was taken to Rio de Janeiro, but by the end of the year, he confessed in his memoirs, he was homesick for Paraguay - even though it was little more than a desert - and returned soon after. He wrote his memoirs in 1919, and died in the 1920s. Resquín and Centurión also wrote their accounts of what happened. Miguel Faria, the boy-soldier who had first seen action at the Avay, wandered through the northern forests for months with some companions: they were afraid to give themselves up to the Brazilians in case they were shot. He finally returned to his hometown to find it almost deserted, the streets patrolled by jaguars, settled down and became a relatively prosperous farmer.

Dona Juana López and her two daughters, Innocencia and Rafaela, were allowed to return to Asuncion. According to Brazilians reports the two daughters took rapid consolation from the misery they had endured in the arms of some of the leading Brazilian soldiers, Innocencia doing her bit towards the re-population of her country by producing a daughter, the father of whom was said to be General Camara.[97] Rafaela married again after the war, her husband being a Brazilian called Milciades Augusto Aceredo Pedra. The three women lived in one of the family villas just outside Asuncion, and were eventually allowed to bring López's body back from Cerro Cora and give it a decent burial, although his mother is said to have been the only one to shed tears at his death.

For Caballero the war was not so much an end as a beginning. In 1874 he founded the Republican (Colorado) Party, and dominated the government of the country for thirty years. He was president himself from 1882 to 1886, while his close colleague General Patricio Escobar was president from then until 1890. One of their chief supporters was Centurión, who went to England after being released from captivity and there met a beautiful Cuban woman. They married and went to Cuba, where Centurión practised law before they returned to Paraguay in 1878. He entered politics, became attorney general and later a senator. He died in 1903. José Falcón, who had worked with him as a *tribunal de sangre,* returned to the post of director of the National Archive, to which he had been appointed in 1854, and died in 1883.

The other principals in the story had chequered careers. In April 1870 Urquiza, the great *caudillo* of Entre Rios, whose support had been sought in vain by both sides, was shot in the face and killed by followers of Ricardo Luis Jordan, another *gaucho* politician, two months after signing a treaty with Sarmiento designed to cement the unity of Argentina. Sarmiento himself retired as president of Argentina in 1874. In 1887 his health began to deteriorate and he went abroad in search of a better climate - to Asuncion. He was challenged to a duel for writing an article critical of Dr. Francia, but President Escobar refused to allow it to take place (Sarmiento was 76 at the time) and the following year he died peacefully in the Paraguayan capital. Mitre, who had led Argentina into the war, never succeeded in regaining his position as ruler of the country, although he was probably its most popular citizen. He failed in an attempt to become president in 1874 and then made an unsuccessful attempt to start a revolution. In 1891 he considered running for the presidency again, but withdrew, and died in 1906.

Dom Pedro II, whose determination to crush López had resulted in the war dragging on so long, and with such disastrous consequences, was in part at least one if its victims. Although personally popular, the monarchy that he represented came to be looked upon as an anachronism. In 1889 a revolution led by military men who had picked up many of their ideas in the Plate forced him to abdicate, and he died in exile in Paris two years later, a few miles from where Elisa Lynch had died three years earlier. The new Republic's first president was Manoel Deodora da Fonseca, who had been wounded at the Itóróró. Caxias died in 1880. The Comte d'Eu, who brought the war to its conclusion, was exiled at the same time as his father-in-law and died in France in 1922.

Of the victorious Allies, Brazil suffered most from the war. About 100,000 Brazilian soldiers and sailors died, and the financial cost amounted to 300 million dollars. The strain put upon the Empire's social and economic structure was so great that the war contributed to its eventual collapse less than twenty years later. The acquisition of the disputed border territories was not much of a consolation. Uruguay came out of it all fairly well. Montevideo, like Buenos Aires, was one of the major supply ports for the Allied war effort, and business flourished: by 1866 customs revenues were 81 per cent higher than they were in 1862.[98] The Colorado party could feel particularly pleased with themselves since, despite the unfortunate demise of Flores, they retained power for the next ninety years. The cost in lives and money was as negligible as the Republic's contribution to the Allied cause.

Argentina did best of all. Her contribution to the war effort declined rapidly after 1866, and during the next four years more lives were lost in civil war than on the Paraguayan front. Trade, on the other hand, was stimulated; everything used in the war went through Argentinean territory, and the ports in particular benefited. There was certainly no hold up in the economic transformation that had begun during Mitre's presidency and accelerated under Sarmiento. Between 1868 and 1874 280,000 immigrants poured into the country, 70,000 of them in 1874 alone,[99] and by 1895 more than a quarter of Argentina's population of nearly four million were foreign born.[100] In 1874 there were 826 miles of railways; by 1890 there were 5,848, double that amount ten years later and more than 20,000 miles by 1912.[101] Trade rose from 72 million pesos in 1868 to 102 million in 1874.[102] Much of this prosperity was due to the opening up of the pampas and the experience gained in the war in Paraguay proved useful when it came to expanding south and west and exterminating most of the Indian tribes who lived there. The war, for Argentina, was the beginning of a golden age.

Chapter 36

For Paraguay, the war meant complete devastation, the end of its brief period as a leader in the race to material prosperity, the end of its few days of life, the end of hope. In almost every sense except a geographical one, Paraguay died with López and was buried with him at the Aquidaban-Niqui. In 1871 the Allied occupation authorities carried out a census which revealed a population of 221,079. Of these, 106,254 were women, 86,079 were children, and just 28,746 were men. By men the census takers referred to males over the age of 15. The number of true adult males was probably 14,000 - about half the number who watch the average English Premier Division football match on a Saturday afternoon.

If one accepts a population of 500,000 for the year 1864, then more than half died during the war, while the male population alone was reduced by nearly ninety per cent. Moreover, the mortality rate was highest among those sections of the community whose value to the nation was greatest. The cream of the economic, social and political elite was virtually exterminated, making the task of recovery all the more difficult. As an example: on September 17, 1864, a list of the 78 most prominent citizens of Asuncion was published in the *Semanario.* By the end of the war, according to Washburn only 'three or four' were still definitely alive. Of the remainder nine died in the army, 19 of natural causes (which in Paraguay included disease, starvation and other direct consequences of the war), 11 died in prison, 20 were executed, 2 were captured by the Allies, 1 deserted, and 3 survived. The fates of the remainder were unknown, but it is probably that most of them perished.

The foreigners, who had played such an important role in developing Paraguay during the pre-war years, vanished almost completely. Of the 54 foreigners who had signed the subscription list to López in late 1867 only two, Bliss and José Solis, escaped death. Of a hundred French citizens in Paraguay only two left alive. The Spaniards and others suffered similarly. Only the British, whose technical skills made them indispensable, survived the wholesale slaughter, and the majority of them left Paraguay for ever as soon as they were able. In view of these figures, it was understandable that contemporary judgements on the Paraguayan tragedy sounded like obituaries. Masterman wrote: 'The Paraguayan nation exists no longer - there is a gap in the family of nations; but the story of their sufferings and their heroism should not perish with them.' This, of course, is just what did happen, within a few years. In his pompous and surprisingly unfeeling manner Masterman went on to say of the Paraguayans: 'I can but feel that their destruction sooner or later would be a necessity... they were not capable of true civilisation; they would have remained children to the end of their days.' He looked forward to the time when German and Anglo-Saxon immigration would fill the void left by the extermination of the Guaranís: 'It is well that it should be so; still I feel like one who sees some old wood, once a mere waste of encumbered ground, and which could only be entered by stealth, being at length converted into the home of a busy industry, and covered with houses and streets. He admits that the change is a vast improvement; yet he remembers with sad regret the picturesque beauties of the useless rotting old trees and the bright wild flowers which grew beneath them.' The *Manchester Guardian,* on April 14, 1870, commented on the war: 'It has destroyed a remarkable system of Government. It has overturned the only South American State wherein the native Indian race showed any present likelihood of obtaining or recovering such strength and organisation as to fit it for the task of government. No other race in South America has been able to boast of so much internal peace.'

This was a more valid, and certainly more sympathetic opinion, seeing as it did the real tragedy lying in the extinction of the promise of the future rather than the reality of the present, and C.T. Hazewell writing in *Harper's Magazine* in January 1871 took a similar view: 'The numbers considered, no contest has made a profounder impression on the minds of competent observers than the Paraguayan war, which was brought to a close in 1870 after being waged for five years or more with almost incredible ferocity. The fierce vindictiveness that marked its course partook rather of the character of a civil war than a contest among nations. This was owing, it appears, to the peculiar position that Paraguay held In South America, and which must, in time, had her power been allowed to increase, have converted her into a conquering power of the first class. She was the Prussia of South America, and all her resources in men and money were at the unlimited command of her chief, who was a dictator in even more than the Roman sense of the word. Had the Paraguayans been somewhat more numerous, though even only by a few thousands, it is highly probable that López would have made Paraguay the first of the South American countries. The country might have become to modern South America what the Incan dominion was in times anterior to the Spanish conquest - an all extending because an all embracing nation....'

The Paraguayan survivors contemplated the misery around them with a stunned incomprehension. Cunninghame Graham spoke to many of them and wrote: 'Often in those years now so far away that they seem like the history of a dream by someone else, talking to Paraguayans who had been taken prisoner and by a miracle escaped an ignominious death, they spoke about it with reluctance, and as if ashamed; not that they had the least illusions about López, whom they cursed, and hoped that he was suffering all the tortures of the damned, but that their love of country and the ideal not quite unnatural that in some way, in spite of all his tyranny, López had stood for it against the enemy.'

It was almost unbearable to have to admit that the suffering they had endured had not only been in vain but had actually contributed to their appalling fate. They could only look back on the past of a few years before with hopeless regret, knowing it would never return. Manuel Frutos, a survivor, told the Chilean historian Alberto de Herera: 'We were rich, sir, we swam in wealth, we were happy. My native town of Ititimi then had 24 schools; now it has but one. There was not a citizen who did not possess a house, tools to work, and extensive plantings. We did not know hunger. We were a well-fed race, healthy and strong. We were happy and joyous, despite what is called our tyranny...but the war came and we lost all. We fought desperately because we loved our land insanely.[103]"

The provisional government, which was installed in August 1869, announced a grandiose programme of reforms, which sounded well enough but had almost no practical effect: there was by then almost nothing left to reform. What was needed was massive aid for the refugees, who were still streaming into Asuncion from the hills, but the government's resources were quite insufficient for this task, and the charitable organisations that exist to cope with such tragedies in the modern world had no counter-part in the 1870s.

The Allies did little. They were too busy squabbling over the remains of Paraguay to worry about the condition of the remains themselves. The Argentineans, who had already taken the disputed Misiones province, insisted on the terms of the Triple Alliance Treaty, which recognised the whole of the Chaco as belonging to them, and in November 1869 occupied Villa Occidentale, just across the River Paraguay from Asuncion. Despite their other problems, the triumvirate under Rivarola refused to accept this, and was able to secure Brazilian backing. The haggling went on until 1876, with the Argentineans finally agreeing that the land north of the River Pilcomayo (which included Villa Occidentale) should be subject to arbitration. In 1878 President Rutherford B. Hayes of the United States awarded this to Paraguay: despite this the Republic had been forced to cede 62,000 square kilometres of land to Brazil and 94,000 to Argentina. It was only after the signing of the peace treaty in 1876, which ended the Allied occupation, that Paraguay could make any real attempt at recovery, and the absence of a strong male population meant that foreigners rapidly gained control over much of the country's economy. E.R. and H.S. Service, whose 1954 study of Tobati, a town north of Caacupe, provides a valuable insight into the consequences of the war, wrote: 'The catastrophe visited on Paraguay defies description... industry and foreign trade were at a standstill, and the small pre-war commercial class virtually disappeared. Petty merchants and peddlers, who were mostly 'Turcos' and Italians, followed in the wake of the foreign troops and established themselves in the fashion of the carpetbaggers of the North American Civil War period. Meanwhile the small class of aristocratic landowners, the native *latifundistas* and *haciendados,* had fled Paraguay carrying such portable valuables as they could manage. In the confusion of the occupation government records including title to land were lost, destroyed or removed from Paraguay. The important landowners never returned to establish themselves in their native land, except for a few isolated cases. Even today the relative absence of a native middle and upper classes is a striking feature of the social and political aspects of Paraguay's national culture.'

The population of the country rose slowly. The immigration that Masterman predicted never really materialised. While millions of Europeans were pouring into the United States, Brazil and Argentina, only a handful made their way up the Paraná to Paraguay. According to E. Bourgade de la Dardye, a hundred settlers arrived in 1886, 563 in 1887, 1,064 in 1888, and 1,914 in 1889. The total number of immigrants was around 40,000,many of them groups who went to Paraguay in search of religious or political freedom and did not play a large part in the general life of the Republic. The best known group was the Mennonites, who established colonies in the Chaco. Another colony was established by a group of Australian communists, but the enterprise failed. Other colonies included 5,000 Japanese.

By 1950 the total population had reached about 1,600,000 but the gap between Paraguay and its two great neighbours had grown wider. Argentina, with 1,800,000 in 1865, now has a population of more than 20,000,000 and Brazil has grown from 10,000,000 to nearly 100,000,000. Asuncion which Carlos Antonio López had planned as his showplace, remained a small town rather than a city, and the Services found it to be 'one of the smallest and... certainly the least modernised of the South American capitals. It has no public water system, nor is there any public sewage disposal; both private homes and public buildings must have their own wells and cesspools.'

The balance of the sexes, the most obvious and best known result of the war, was corrected in time (the Brazilian occupation forces helped) but even after the Second World War the Services noted that women were still very prominent in economic activities. They found that there was a considerable amount of sexual freedom and that virginity, though desirable, was not regarded as an essential in a prospective bride and that illegitimacy was common. In Tobati itself, they found that after the age of 18 the proportion of men to women decreased - 265 men to

425 women, although this was mainly a feature of town life and was not really characteristic of the country as a whole.

The governments who had to cope with the aftermath of the war found that a shortage of hard cash was their main problem. Although Uruguay, in a generous gesture, renounced its share of the war indemnity, there was no money in the national treasury and little chance of earning any. Desperate and sometimes disastrous measures were taken - as when the railway line was sold in 1876 to a speculator for one million paper pesos, which was not even the value of the Asuncion railway station. As a last resort, Caballero decided to sell off government lands to private bidders. Because of the chaos and losses caused by the war, it was almost impossible to establish ownership of land, and huge areas had become state property in the absence of any other claimants. The sales themselves were badly organised. The Land Acts did not limit the amount of land that could be held by a single buyer, and there was no compulsion upon the buyer to develop the land he acquired. It was an ideal situation for speculators. Government employees found that they could buy land on loans from the National Bank and then sell it at a handsome profit to others, mainly foreigners. Two years after the Acts came into force (in 1885) land in eastern Paraguay was selling at ten times the sale price, the profit inevitably going to the speculators. By the time the sales eventually came to a stop 90,000 square miles of public land in the Chaco had been sold off and 36,000 square miles of eastern Paraguay, including 7,200 square miles of yerba mate plantations, which were still regarded as the best in South America. One Argentinean named Carlos Casado deftly acquired a stretch of land as large as the states of Connecticut, Massachusetts and New Hampshire combined. All in all, more than half of Paraguay had been sold to foreign investors for less than five million dollars. Paraguay's economic subjection to foreign, mainly Argentine interests, dates from that period. Today about seventy five per cent of the country's industry is Argentine-owned, and the Services concluded: 'From an economic and political point of view Paraguay is notable as an archetypal example of the consequences of being a small backward under-developed nation striving to maintain itself as an independent entity, when in fact it enjoys only semi-colonial status at best.' Apart from everything else, the war wiped out all the progress that had been made in Paraguay under

Carlos Antonio López and his son, and other circumstances tended to make it impossible for the Republic ever to regain its prosperity and affluence. It had no minerals, the basis of the industrial societies that were shaping the world in the late nineteenth century.

This meant it had no real industry, which in turn meant that it had to import most of the manufactured goods it required. Because of the vast distance separating Paraguay from the industrial nations, these goods inevitably cost more than they did elsewhere. At the same time, the agriculture on which its prosperity was based had been destroyed and its previous customers found other suppliers, or learned to do without Paraguayan products. The country's geographical position again tended to make its products expensive in foreign markets.

One result was the development of a sort of economic apathy among many people in Paraguay - a feeling that no matter what they did, no real improvement could be expected. It was widely felt (and according to the Services still is) that anyone who bettered his lot own his success to cheating or luck. Indeed, one of the great national occupations since the war has consisted of hunting for the treasure that was buried by many families in 1869 and never recovered. It became for thousands the one chance of material happiness - the Paraguayan equivalent of winning the Lottery. Without such luck, the majority expected the future to be exactly the same as the immediate past. The Services wrote: '[The Paraguayan's] experience and that of his ancestors is that consistent application to his work could be expected to maintain him in the status in which he was born, but with no chance of enhancing it. A rich man whose family was not ' always wealthy' must have gained his position as a result of luck or influence. We never discovered any sentiment among the peasants that hard work and intelligent management or enterprise could achieve other than a small ephemeral reward.'

Today Paraguay has a population of about 2.4 million, of whom 500,000 live abroad, for political or economic reasons. Its per capita income is £84 a year, lower than any other country in the Western Hemisphere with the exception of Bolivia and Haiti. It suffers widely from poverty, malnutrition and disease, all of which were conspicuously absent in 1864. It was not until the present century that the number of children at school reached the figure that had existed in 1862. Today 90 per cent of the population is still illiterate.

It cannot be said that Paraguay has even gained its freedom as a result of the war, despite the noble claims of the Allies to be fighting on behalf of the Paraguayan people against the tyranny of the dictator López. The war removed good and bad alike, and replaced them with a system that seemed in some ways simply to echo the very abuses that Paraguay had always escaped, and which were characteristic of its neighbours. Between 1810 and 1870 the Republic had three presidents; between 1870 and 1932 it had 29, only a handful of whom finished their four year term. Democracy has never taken root; anarchy, until recent times, has been commonplace. It is difficult to maintain that what has happened to Paraguay since López's death is in any way better than what occurred before the beginning of the war in which he died. Once Paraguay could claim to be the only stable country in Spanish-speaking America, the only state where crime was not a major problem. After 1870 neither claim could be made. In the 1930s Paraguay even fought another war, this time against Bolivia, the other great loser of South American history, for control of the Chaco.

Despite Bolivia's apparent advantages, including a larger, better trained army, the Paraguayans, led by Jose Felix Estigarribia, a general who was a member of the same family as the man who surrendered at Uruguayana, defeated them and established their claim to the disputed region. It was believed to contain vast amounts of oil, but did not and Paraguay lost 25,000 men conquering a region that has always proved economically useless.

For López himself, who had led Paraguay to perhaps the greatest disaster any nation has ever suffered, fate reserved a strange and most ironic fate. Although it has always been an accepted convention for military commanders to vow rhetorically to give their life for their people, López's last words were a statement of simple fact. He had, as he claimed, died with his country. Almost immediately, many of the people who had followed him with such tragic devotion turned against him. Adolfo Aponte, who was Minister of Justice in 1919, wrote at that time: 'All the survivors of the war of any education were Anti-Lopiztas, even Father Maiz. A veteran of the war said to me...."we all felt relieved at the death of López and as if we had awakened from a frightful dream, for we were more frightened of him than the enemy." Cunninghame Graham met one such survivor, a man called Izquierdo who was then making a dubious living as a lawyer. He had taken part in one of the attacks on the Allied ironclads and although wounded managed to reach the Chaco. Cunninghame Graham said that his character was bad and his appearance unprepossessing. But even so he had risked his life to serve his president. Now 'he had no words too strong to show his hatred and contempt of López.'

According to Cunninghame Graham, Izquierdo would indignantly express his contempt for López, saying: "Call him a *Carai Guazu* (Great Chief)! He should have been called *Chancho Guazu* (Great Pig), a pot bellied coward, eating and drinking of the best he and his concubine Madame Lynch, may the great God of Heaven have pardoned neither of them, whilst we who fought as we thought for the independence of our country were half starved, beaten and treated worse than dogs. I spit on his shadow!'

Other Paraguayans whom the Scottish writer met shared this opinion. But then, as memories of the war began to fade that view gradually mellowed: in the early 1900s a writer called Juan O'Leary wrote a biography of López which hailed him as a hero and a patriot: a strange quirk, considering that O'Leary's mother and other members of his family had been among López's victims and he had himself been brought up to hate him as a monster. This opinion of López gained popularity in Paraguay and in the 1920s a statue was erected beside the River Aquidaban at the spot where he died. In the early 1930s Cunninghame Graham, horrified at the cult that was growing around a man he still considered to be among the greatest villains the world has ever seen, wrote his hysterical and impassioned biography, designed to stop this insidious development before it became established. But three years later the Pantheon that López had begun in Asuncion was completed on the orders of President Rafael Franco and the dictator's bones were laid to rest there, with all honours. He is today generally regarded as Paraguay's greatest national hero.

In view of the disastrous consequences of his rule this may seem remarkable, but it is perhaps explicable. Francisco Solano López, during his lifetime, *was* Paraguay in a greater sense even than Napoleon was France or Hitler was Germany. Any consideration of the man, therefore inevitably becomes a consideration of the country as well, and to condemn the one is to condemn the other. The fact that Paraguay's tragedy was largely his fault has been obscured by the almost unbelievably heroic way in which that tragedy occurred: because of López his people were able to stage an exhibition of defiant patriotism that has never been equalled. The Paraguayans of today, as intensely patriotic as ever, take a pride in the desperate courage of their forefathers, and by a simple extension tend to take a pride in the man who led them. To an outsider it might see strange to glorify a man who destroyed his country, but it is not unknown in other lands: Louis XIV and Napoleon, Charles XII and Philip II all ultimately did more harm than good to their respective countries, and yet all are national heroes today.

To probe deeper into the character of López is to enter probably the most controversial subject in South American history. The tragic consequences of his rule make it difficult to be dispassionate, and López has tended to be regarded either as a monster, or as a hero virtually without blemish. It must certainly be admitted that he does not conform to the conventional prototype of a hero. His ambitions were for his country, but only because he was its ruler. Personally he was completely selfish and saw nothing wrong, for example, in living in comparative luxury on the retreat to Cerro Cora, while his followers starved to death all round him. If López sympathised with their sufferings at all it was only because they fought less well when they were starving than when they were well fed. His chief concern when they died was that he could not replace them, and it is doubtful if he wept over the casualty lists for any humanitarian considerations.

Although Elisa Lynch claimed after the war that her lover had been blamed for atrocities committed in his name by other people the known facts indicate otherwise. Thompson and other reliable witnesses have testified to the ruthless way in which López punished those who incurred his displeasure and although he does not seem to have been so sadistic that he actually watched his victims tortured or killed, he knew when it was taking place. He was always willing to use extreme measures in the cause of discipline - the decimation of the 10th Battalion after Curuzu is a case in point. At Ita Yvaté, Thompson relates, a soldier was overheard uttering defeatist (and quite realistic) sentiments. He was taken in to López and the facts explained. Without looking up, he said: 'Take him outside and kill him.' The soldier was taken away and his head split open with a sabre. It is impossible to believe that the more illustrious victims of the war - Barrios, Benigno López Berges and so on - died without his knowledge - nobody would have risked making such an important decision without his approval.

One of the most frequent criticisms of López in his own lifetime was that he was a coward. He certainly had a morbid terror of gunfire, which occasionally led him to panic, and he took care never to come within rifle range of the enemy unless it was absolutely impossible to avoid doing so: the first time, it happened, according to Thompson, was at Ita Yvaté. Even so, although he made no effort to inspire his men by personal example, they do not seem to have resented it. Their loyalty remained unshaken, and despite his critics López showed no fear when he was surrounded at Humaitá nor when the Allies were threatening to overwhelm him at Ita Yvaté. He remained unshaken by the most disastrous reverses. This may not have been obvious courage but it was still courage of a kind.

He was said to be shamelessly debauched. Yet he remained emotionally, if perhaps not physically, faithful to Elisa Lynch from the moment he met her, and would undoubtedly have married her had she been free. López cannot be looked upon as the innocent leader of a nation assailed by three greedy and powerful neighbours. Paraguay had grounds for concern over the fate of the Blanco regime in Uruguay, and was quite right to be suspicious of Brazil and Argentina: but these justifiable suspicions did not start the war. The spark that set light to the whole powder keg was provided by López himself. As a diplomat and statesman he was a disastrous failure, and the responsibility for Paraguay embarking upon a war against such enormous odds is almost entirely his.

His strategy was initially just as bad. He committed Paraguay to two offensives that militarily could not possibly have succeeded, and he dissipated his initial manpower superiority in the most reckless and wasteful fashion. Yet he was continually seeking peace. He made repeated attempts to negotiate a settlement, but the Allies, inspired by the Emperor of Brazil, refused a compromise. Their adherence to the terms of the Triple Alliance was responsible to a large extent for the continuation of the war, and their claims to have no quarrel with the Paraguayan people were proved to be quite hypocritical. The Brazilians and Argentineans regarded the war as a way of increasing their territories at Paraguay's expense, and although in both cases the war began as a war of self-defence, it soon developed into one of conquest for which the continued existence of López provided a convenient excuse. When López was dead both the Brazilians and the Argentineans treated the prostrate republic as a pawn in their own private power struggle. They did nothing to help the people they claimed to have liberated and the fact that Paraguay was able to survive at all was mainly due to the jealousy that existed between them.

As a general, López developed remarkably. After the first battle of Tuyuti he repeatedly anticipated Allied moves, prepared for them, and thwarted them. His recovery after that battle was a tribute to his tenacity and stubborn courage: his escape from Humaitá was a brilliant feat of arms, and the way in which he rebuilt his army after the disastrous battles of December 1868, was a triumph of will power and organisational ability. He showed throughout the war a far greater grasp of the advantages of modern developments - the telegraph, rifled artillery and so on - than any of the Allied generals. Considering the means at his disposal he was an innovator of great originality, and had the odds been a little more equal there is little doubt that he would have been able to defeat the Allied invasion.

Despite all that can be said in favour of López, however, there remains something terrifying about him. Underneath his courteous and calm exterior was a different man, given to fits of blind and savage rage, who could order men to be flogged unmercifully until they told him the lies that he wanted to hear. After the occupation of Humaitá and the discovery of the alleged conspiracy, the darker side of his personality, which had always been just visible, suddenly came to the surface with terrible results.

A full-scale psychological study of López might answer many of the questions that his personality raises not least the problem of his mental state. Insanity would have explained much that happened in Paraguay in the last two years of the war, but the evidence of eyewitnesses indicates that López was never insane, even though mentally he may have bean abnormal. MacMahon and other apologists were impressed by his undoubted good qualities - and MacMahon knew López at the blackest period of his life, when his defects were most in evidence. Thompson, Washburn and Masterman, who all regarded López as a monster, never looked upon him as a madman, and Washburn went out of his way to stress López's sanity.

From a more detached point of view than was possible for men such as Washburn, one tends to agree that López was not mad. Instead he seems to have had a Jekyll and Hyde personality, in which the Hyde character became increasingly prominent as the tide of war turned against Paraguay. In his Jekyll state López was logical, calm, far-sighted and determined, always one jump ahead of his enemies, keeping them continually off-balance with a succession of well-planned and audacious moves that were often worthier of more success than they actually achieved. When Hyde took over, he could behave with a complete disregard of the facts and stubbornly pursue courses that he should have known were doomed. He would sublimate his disappointments and despair with acts of sadism that were often almost casual.

Although he always remained outwardly calm and courteous, the way in which his ambitions were shattered had a profound and disastrous effect upon López's personality. He had bouts of church going, and began to drink heavily, but on a different level he began to turn to fantasy to supply the glories that reality denied him. There was certainly something glorious about his end, as he died sword in hand with a noble phrase on his lips, and his whole career was so spectacular that one can to some extent understand the strange metamorphosis that turned him from monster to hero. As a symbol of his nation one can perhaps understand this, but on a more personal level the first reaction is horror. One thinks of López not at Cerro Cora but at Humaitá, having two prisoner flogged until they told him it was not Marco Paz who had died but Mitre, or sending poor Juliana Martinez off to her death. These were acts of such horrifying and irrational brutality that one can see why men like Thompson and Washburn were in such fear of López and hated him so much. Madness might have excused such acts: but López was sane. Equally important in the long run was his selfishness and indifference to other people. López manipulated people without considering them as individuals: he accepted the faithful devotion of his followers as if it was his right, rather than a privilege and saw his countrymen basically as extras playing supporting roles in the drama of his own life.

Harsh though the Allied peace terms were, the time ultimately came when López should have accepted them and gone into exile: this would at least have ended the war and thus saved a few thousand lives, and he knew before long he would ultimately be beaten, and that continued resistance would not make the peace that would one day be forced upon Paraguay any less harsh. In the words of Thompson, he ultimately preferred to sacrifice the last man, woman and child of a brave and devoted and suffering people simply to keep himself in power a little while longer.

The Guaranís of Paraguay were like children. They followed López blindly and foolishly, completely and without question. For five years they followed him and died for him without complaint, and López took their love and allowed them to perish, the victims of his distorted ambitions and their own devotion. Paraguay was too small to maintain his dreams, but he refused to reduce them or sacrifice his own hopes for the benefit of a nation that gave him everything.

Paraguay was destroyed so completely that the war, and Paraguay itself, is almost unknown outside South America, and more sympathy and sense of loss is felt by the world as a whole for the extinction of the Dodo than for the slaughter of the nation that followed López to destruction. The Guaraní soldiers fought as no other nation as ever fought for what they believed to be the freedom of their country, they died for it and their reward was to lie forgotten in the marshes where they fell.

Bibliography

Acosta, Juan F. Perez, *Carlos Antonio Lopez,* Asuncion, 1948

Alcala, Guido Rodriguez de, *Residentas, Destinadas y Traidoras,* Asuncion

Archibald, E. H. H., *The wooden fighting ship in the Royal Navy,*

Atkinson, William C., *A history of Spain and Portugal,*

Baillie, Alexander F., *A Paraguayan Treasure,*

Barrett, William E., *Woman on Horseback,* Doubleday, 1952

Baxter, J. P., *The Introduction of the Ironclad Warship*

Bethell, Leslie, *The Paraguayan War (1864-1870),* University of London Institute of Latin American Studies, 1996

Beverina, Juan, *La Guerra del Paraguay,* Buenos Aires 1921

Bourgade de la Dardye, E.,*Paraguay,* George Philip and Son, Liverpool, 1892

Box, Pelham Horton, *The Origins of the Paraguayan War,*Russell and Russell, New York 1967

Bray, Arturo, *Hombres y Epocas del Paraguay,* El lector, Asuncion, 1957

Brodsky, Alyn, *Madame Lynch and Friend,*Cassell, London, 1975

Bunkley, A. W., *The Life of Sarmiento*

Burton, Sir Richard, *Letters from the Battlefields of Paraguay,* London, 1870

Carcano, Ramon J., *Guerra del Paraguay (2 volumes)* Buenos Aires, 1941

Carcano, Ramon José, *Guerra del Paraguay: origenes y causas,* Buenos Aires, 1939

Carcano, Ramon José, *Guerra del Paraguay (two volumes),* Buenos Aires, 1941

Cardozo, Efraim, *Hace 100 anos (12 volumes),* Asuncio, 1967

Cardozo, Efraím, *Paraguay Independiente,* Carlos Schauman, Asuncion, 1988

Cawthorne, Nigel, *The Empress of South America,* William Heinemann, 2003

Centurión, Juan C., *Memorias o Reminiscencias Historicas Sobre la Guerra del Paraguay (4 volumes),* El Lector, Asuncion

Chaves, Maria Concepcion L. de, *Madame Lynch y Solano Lopez,* Buenos Aires, 1976

Chiavenato, Julio José, *Genocido Americano,*Carlos Schauman, Asuncion, 1984

Codman, John, *Ten months in Brazil,* London, 1867

Committee on Foreign Affairs, *Report on the memorial of Porter C. Bliss and George F. Masterman in relation to their imprisonment in Paraguay,* Washington, DC 1870

Cunninghame-Graham, Robert, *Portrait of a Dictator,* London, 1933

Dombrowski, Katharina von, *Land of Women,* Little, Brown and Co., Boston, 1932

Enright, Anne, *The Pleasure of Elisz Lynch,* Jonathan Cape, 2002

Farcau, Bruce W., *The Chaco War 1932-1935,* Praeger, Westport, Connecticut, 1996

Ferns, H. S.,*Argentina,*

Garmendia, José I., *Recuerdos de la Guerra del Paraguay,* Buenos Aires, 1889

Gimlette, John, *At the Tomb of the Inflatable Pig,* Hutchinson, 2003

Godoi, Juan Silvano, *Ultimas operaciones del General José Eduvigis Diaz,*Buenos Aires, 1897

Godoi, Juan Silvano, *Monografias Históricas,* Buenos Aires, 1893

Godoi, Juan Silvano, *Ultimas Operaciones de Guerra del General Eduvigas Diaz,* Buenos Aires, 1897

Godoi, Juan Silvano, *Monografias Históricos,* Buenos Aires, 1893

Herring, Hubert, *A History of Latin America,* New York, 1968

Humphreys, R. A., *Modern Latin America,*

Hutchinson, Thomas Joseph, *The Paraná: with incidents of the Paraguayan War and South American Recollections, from 1861-1868,* London, 1868

Jeffery, William H., *Mitre and Argentina,*

Jourdan, E. C., *Historia das Campnhas do Uruguay, Matto Grosso e Paraguay,* Rio de Janeiro 1893

Kennedy. Cdr. A. J., *La Plata, Brazil and Paraguay during the present war,* 1869

Kleinpenning, Jan M. G., *Rural Paraguay, 1870-1932,* Centre for Latin American Redsearch and Documentation, Amsterdam, 1992

Koebel, W. H. , *Paraguay,* London, 1916

Kolinski, Charles J., *Historical Dictionary of Paraguay,* The Scarecrow press, Metuchen, NJ, 1973

Kolinski, Charles J. , *Independence or death! The story of the Paraguayan War,* Gainesville, FLA, 1965

Kolinski, Charles K., *The death of Francisco Solano Lopez,* The Historian, November 1963

Lasserre, Mme Duprat de, *Sufferings of a French Lady in Paraguay,* Buenos Aires, 1870

Lewis, Paul H., *Political Parties and Generations in Paraguay's Liberal Era 1869-1940,* University of North Carolina Press

Lewis, Paul H., *Political Parties and Generations in Paraguay's Liberal Era,* U. of North Carolina Press, 1993

Lynch, Elisa Alicia, *Exposición y Protesta,* Buenos Aires, 1875

MacDonald, Alexander, *Picturesque Paraguay,* Charles H. Kelly, London, 1911

Maiz, Fidel, *Etapas de ma vida,* Asuncion, 1919

Marchant, Anyda, *Viscount Maua and the Empire of Brazil,*

Marshall, A., *Brazil,*

Masterman, George Frederick, *Seven Eventful Years in Paraguay,* London, 1869

McLynn, Frank, *From the Sierras to the Pampas,* Century, London, 1991

McMahon, Martin T., *The War in Paraguayand Paraguay and her Enemies: Harper's Magazine, XL.,* New York, 1870

Medina, Anastasio Rolon, *El Lustro Terrible,* La Humanidad, Asuncion, 1964

Meyer, Gordon, *The River and the People,* Methuen, 1965

O'Leary, Juan E., *El Mariscal Solano Lopez,* Montevideo, 1930

O'Leary, Juan E., *Historia de la Guerra de la Triple Alianza,* Carlos Schauman, Asuncion, 1992

Page, Thomas Jefferson, *La Plata, the Argentine Confederation and Paraguay,* New York, 1859

Pendle, George, *The Lands and Peoples of Paraguay and Uruguay,* New York, 1959

Pereyra, Carlos, *Francisco Solano Lopez y la Guerra del Paraguay,* Buenos Aires, 1953

Phelps, Gilbert, *Tragedy of Paraguay,* Charles Knight and Co. 1975

Plá, Josefina, *The British in Paraguay 1850-1870,* The Richmond Publishing Co. Ltd. 1976

Preston, A. and Major J., *Send a Gunboat!,*

Ray, G. Whitfield, *Through Five Republics on Horseback,* Toronto, 1907

Rebaudi, Dr A., *Guerra del Paraguay,* Buenos Aires, 1917

Rebaudi, Dr. A., *Guerra del Paraguay*

Un episodio "Vencer o Morir!", Tucuman, 1918

Rees, Sian, *The Shadows of Elisa Lynch,* Hodder Headline, 2003

Resquín, F. I., *Datos historicos de la Guerra del Paraguay con la Triple Alianza,* Asuncion, 1895

Robertson W. S., *A history of the Spanish American Republics,*

Robertson, W. S., *Rise of the Spanish Republics,*

Service, E. R. and H. S., *Tobati: a Paraguayan Town,*

Shelby, Graham, *Madame Lynch: el fuego de una vida,* Editorial Sudamericana, 1990

Thompson, George, *The war in Paraguay,* London, 1869

Warren, Harris Gaylord, *Rebirth of the Paraguayan Republic: the first Colorado Era, 1878-1904,* University of Pittsburgh Press, 1985

Warren, Harris Gaylord, *Paraguay and the Triple Alliance: the Postwar Decade 1869-1878,* University of Texas, Austin. 1978

Warren, Harris Gaylord, *Paraguay: an informal history,* University of Oklahoma Press, 1949

Washburn, Charles A., *The History of Paraguay, with notes of personal observations and reminiscences of diplomacy under difficulties (2 volumes),* AMS edition published 1973

White, E. L., *El Supremo,*

Whitfield Ray, G., *Through Five Republics on Horseback,* Toronto, 1907

Wilgus, A. C (editor), *South American Dictators,*

Williams, John Hoyt, *The Rise and Fall of the Paraguayan Republic 1800-1870,* University of Texas Press, 1979

Williams, Mary K., *Dom Pedro the Magnanimous,*

Woodham Smith, Cecil, *The Great Hunger,* Signet 1964

Young, Henry Lyon, *Elisa Lynch, Regent of Paraguay,* Anthony Blond, London, 1966

Endnotes

[1] Masterman
[2] Washburn
[3] Raine
[4] Washburn
[5] Services
[6] Raine
[7] Cunninghame-Graham
[8] Washburn
[9] Hemming
[10] Box
[11] Ferns
[12] Thompson
[13] Kolinski
[14] Burton
[15] Thompson
[16] Washburn
[17] Box
[18] Burton
[19] Raine
[20] Centurión
[21] Raine
[22] Masterman
[23] This was Benigno López
[24] Pelham Box
[25] Barrett
[26] Herring
[27] Herring
[28] Humphreys
[29] Humphreys
[30] Pendle
[31] Herring

[32] Herring
[33] Pelham Box
[34] Washburn
[35] Beale
[36] Pelham Box
[37] Burton
[38] Thompson
[39] Kolinski
[40] Thompson
[41] Kolinski
[42] Kolinski
[43] Burton
[44] Pelham Box
[45] Hutchinson
[46] The full text of the treaty is printed in both Masterman and Kolinski's works
[47] Hutchinson
[48] Kolinski
[49] Washburn
[50] Masterman
[51] Hutchinson
[52] Masterman
[53] Hutchinson
[54] Thompson
[55] Thompson
[56] Thompson
[57] Ephraim Cardoso
[58] Kolinski
[59] Hutchinson
[60] Thompson
[61] Kolinski
[62] Kolinski
[63] Medina
[64] Washburn
[65] Josefina Plá
[66] Cunninghame-Graham
[67] Peterson
[68] Josefina Plá
[69] Medina
[70] Burton
[71] Washburn
[72] Centurión
[73] Centurión
[74] Centurión
[75] Centurión
[76] John Hoyt Williams

[77] Centurión
[78] McMahon
[79] McMahon
[80] McMahon
[81] McMahon
[82] Thompson
[83] McMahon
[84] McMahon
[85] Thompson
[86] Burton
[87] For some reason he spelled his name with a final 'e'.
[88] Kolinski
[89] Kolinski
[90] Meyer
[91] Kolinski
[92] Centurión
[93] Medina
[94] Centurión
[95] Kolinski
[96] Kolinski
[97] Kolinski
[98] Hutchinson
[99] Herring
[100] Ferns
[101] Ferns
[102] Herring
[103] Raine